Post Keynesian Macroeconomic Theory

To Louise

Post Keynesian Macroeconomic Theory

A Foundation for Successful Economic Policies for the Twenty-first Century

Paul Davidson

Holly Chair of Excellence in Political Economy
University of Tennessee

Edward Elgar

Published by
Edward Elgar Publishing Limited
Gower House
Croft Road
Aldershot
Hants GU11 3HR
England

Edward Elgar Publishing Company
Old Post Road
Brookfield
Vermont 05036
USA

British Library Cataloguing in Publication Data
Davidson, Paul
   Post Keynesian Macroeconomic Theory:
   Foundation for Successful Economic
   Policies for the Twenty-first Century
   I. Title
   339

Library of Congress Cataloguing in Publication Data
Davidson, Paul.
   Post Keynesian macroeconomic theory: a foundation for successful
economic policies for the twenty-first century/by Paul Davidson.
      p.   cm.
   Includes bibliographical references and index.
   1. Keynesian economics.   2. Macroeconomics.   3. Economics–
–History—20th century.   4. Keynes, John Maynard, 1883–1946.
I. Title.
HB99.7.D393   1994
339.3—dc20   93–38374
                                                                   CIP

ISBN 1 85278 835 6
     1 85278 836 4 (paperback)

Printed in Great Britain at the University Press, Cambridge

Contents

Figures

Tables

Introduction

When the Old Keynesian analysis developed in the United States in the 1940s and 1950s failed to provide good policy guidelines for the stagflation period of the 1970s, it became fashionable among younger economists to declare that Keynesian economics was dead.[1] Hi-tech forms of classical economics were resurrected as the analytical framework used to justify the elimination of governmental responsibility for maintaining full employment.

This classical counter-revolution in economic theory provided the rationale for the decontrolling of financial, utility, and product markets that became the economic hallmark of the last years of the Carter presidency in the United States. It also conferred intellectual prestige on the siren song 'Get The Government Off The Backs Of The People' that became the triumphant march to power of the Reagan Administration in the United States and the Thatcher Government in the United Kingdom. The economic facts of the 1980s overwhelmed the Panglossian *laissez-faire* philosophy that produced the Reagan and Thatcher politico-economic revolutions. Monetarism and New Classical theories failed to explain the unfolding economic events.

A New Keynesian analytical framework was created as a counterpoint to the instantaneous solutions predicted by New Classical theory. Those who professed to be New Keynesians had never read Keynes. They still believed in the conclusions of the classical analysis, at least in the long run. They claimed that Keynes's

> *General Theory* is an obscure book . . . [it] is an outdated book. The rigor with which we develop economic theories and the data and statistical techniques with which we test our theories were unknown half a century ago. We are in a much better position than Keynes was to figure out how the economy works. . . . Few macroeconomists take such a dim view of classical economics [as Keynes did]. . . . Classical economics is right in the long run. Moreover, economists today are more interested in the long-run equilibrium. The long run is not so far away. . . . [There is] widespread acceptance of classical economics.[2]

It is paradoxical that, having adopted a Keynesian appellation for themselves, these economists describe Keynes's 1936 analysis as enigmatic and antiquated. Even more astonishing is their belief that the eighteenth and

1

early nineteenth century classical theory is relevant to the modern world while Keynes's twentieth century analysis is not.

Despite the bravado claim that their 'rigour' and 'statistical techniques' permit New Keynesians to be in 'a better position than Keynes to figure out how the economy works', the record of recent years does not support the idea that today's mainstream economists have any idea of how a monetary, entrepreneurial economy operates. For example, in March 1990, as a recession was already under way, *The Wall Street Journal* reported that '60 per cent of macroeconomic forecasters don't expect a recession in the next three years'. In November 1990, four months after the recession began, *The New York Times* reported that the National Bureau of Economic Research's forecasting model, a preeminent mainstream model reflecting the best statistical techniques of modern macroeconometrics, was predicting real economic growth of 4 per cent and that there was less than a 5 per cent probability of a recession *beginning* by February 1991. Not until the summer of 1991, when the recession bottomed out, were mainstream economists willing to admit that the economy was in recession. Even then most predicted the recession would be short and followed by a brisk recovery. By the summer of 1993, as this is being written, the promised swift rejuvenation has still not appeared. An anaemic improvement is all that has occurred so far despite over twenty reductions in the interest rate engineered by the Federal Reserve System during the 36 months since the recession began. After three years we are still waiting to experience long run bliss.

The New Keynesian economists have not lived up to their claim of having bettered Keynes in figuring out how the economy works. The theoretical framework used by New Keynesians and other mainstream economists has not helped society to understand economic circumstances and trends. Despite the advances in economic data collection and statistical techniques of analysis used by central banks, governments, and many private sector enterprises, economic performance has been exceedingly poor compared to the magnificent record of the early post-war decades when Keynes's policies were still in vogue. Surely this evidence suggests that mainstream macroeconomics has gone off the track.

The purpose of this volume is to encourage students of economics to return to the path of Keynes's revolutionary analysis of a money-using entrepreneurial economy. Once economists become more familiar with this theory that is applicable to the enterprise economy in which we live, then they may be able to understand the causes of real world economic problems and to design policies to resolve them.

Knoxville, Tennessee

NOTES

1. Robert E. Lucas, 'The Death of Keynesian Economics', *Issues and Ideas*, 1980.
2. N.G. Mankiw, 'The Reincarnation of Keynesian Economics', *European Economic Review*, **36**, 1992, pp. 560–61.

1. The background for Keynes's revolution

On New Year's Day in 1935 the English economist, John Maynard Keynes, wrote a letter to George Bernard Shaw. In this letter he stated:

> To understand my new state of mind, however, you have to know that I believe myself to be writing a book on economic theory which will largely revolutionize not I suppose at once but in the course of the next ten years the way the world thinks about economic problems. When my new theory has been duly assimilated and mixed with politics and feelings and passions, I cannot predict what the final upshot will be in its effect on actions and affairs, but there will be a great change and in particular the Ricardian Foundations of Marxism will be knocked away.
>
> I can't expect you or anyone else to believe this at the present stage, but for myself I don't merely hope what I say. In my own mind I am quite sure.[1]

A little over a year later, Keynes published a book that, for several decades, did revolutionize the way most economists and politicians thought about developing economic policies to deal with unemployment. That book was entitled *The General Theory of Employment, Interest, and Money*.

Keynes's book produced innovative thinking in policy discussions. Yet, orthodox economists failed to adopt the logically consistent innovative theoretical analysis laid down by Keynes. Instead, what developed in mainstream professional writings and popular economics textbooks was a modernized version of the pre-Keynesian classical system where Keynes's policy suggestions for solving the unemployment problem were grafted on to the axiomatic foundations of classical microeconomic theory. In the first three decades following World War II, the resulting Neoclassical Synthesis Keynesianism[2] (or what in the 1990s is sometimes referred to as Old Keynesianism) conquered mainstream academic discussions as completely as the Holy Inquisition conquered Spain (to paraphrase one of Keynes's more colourful expressions).

Keynes began work on his revolutionary book in 1932. Unlike the United States, Great Britain had been suffering from a great recession since the end of World War I. Between 1922 and 1936 the unemployment rate in Britain fell below 10 per cent in only one year. In 1927 it was 9.7 per cent.

In the United States, the roaring 20s had been a period of unbridled prosperity. In 1929, only 3.2 per cent of American workers were unemployed. The stock market climbed to unprecedented highs and everybody seemed to be getting rich. It is no wonder that English economists were more concerned about the problem of chronic and persistent unemployment when the Great Depression of the 1930s began than were American economists.

Just a few days before the stock market crash of October 24, 1929, one of the most eminent American economists of the time, Professor Irving Fisher of Yale University, told an audience that the stock market had reached a high plateau from which it could only go up. Then, suddenly, the bottom fell out. It is said that Professor Fisher lost between $8 million and $10 million in the stock market crash. The Great Depression had hit America.

From 1929 to 1933 the American economy went downhill. It seemed as if the system was enmeshed in a catastrophe from which it could not escape. Unemployment went from 3.2 per cent in 1929 to 24.9 per cent by 1933. One out of every four workers in the United States was unemployed by the time Roosevelt was elected president. A measure of the standard of living of Americans, the real gross national product per capita, fell by 52 per cent between 1929 and 1933. By 1933, the average American family was living on less than half of what it had earned in 1929. The American capitalist dream appeared to be shattered.

The economic experts of those times, including Professor Irving Fisher, argued that the high levels of unemployment being experienced in the United States in the early 1930s could not persist. The economy would soon right itself as long as the government did not interfere with the workings of the market-place. The prevailing orthodox classical theory provided the rationale for the '*laissez-faire*' or 'no government intervention' philosophy that dominated economic discussions before Keynes's *General Theory* was published.

It is claimed that, in 1751, the Marquis d'Argenson was the first writer to use the phrase '*laissez-faire*' in his argument for removing the visible hand of government from economic affairs. He said that 'To govern better one must govern less'. Although the phrase *laissez-faire* does not appear in the writings of the founding fathers of classical theory such as Adam Smith or David Ricardo, the idea is there. The pursuit of self-interest, unfettered by government interference is at the heart of the philosophy of classical economics.

In his 1776 classic, *The Wealth of Nations*, Adam Smith wrote:

> It is not from the benevolence of the butcher, the brewer, or the baker that we expect our dinner, but from regard to their own self-interest. We address ourselves, not to their humanity but to their self love, and never talk to them of our necessities, but of their advantage. . . . Every individual is continually

exerting himself to find out the most advantageous employment for whatever capital he can command. It is his own advantage, indeed and not that of society which he has in view. . . . He intends only his own gain, and he is in this, as in many other cases, led by an invisible hand to promote an end which was no part of his intention. By pursuing his own interest he frequently promotes that of the society more effectually than when he really intends to promote it.[3]

Classical theory argued that if the government intervened in economic matters during any 'temporary' period of unemployment, then the economic situation would deteriorate and the economy would take a longer time to right itself. If the government did not interfere with the invisible hand of the market processes operating during this transient period of unemployment, then only the weak and inefficient would be weeded out, leaving a stronger, more powerful economy to carry on. In true Social Darwinian fashion, what was being asserted was that the Great Depression was merely a symptom of Nature's providing for the 'survival of the fittest'. When the economic system righted itself, it would regenerate full employment and prosperity for all.

In the very first paragraph of his book, *The General Theory*, Keynes challenged this orthodox dogma when he wrote:

> I have called this book the *General Theory of Employment, Interest and Money*. . . . The object of such a title is to contrast the character of my arguments and conclusions with those of the classical theory of the subject . . . which dominates economic thought, both practical and theoretical of the governing and academic classes of this generation, as it has for a hundred years past. . . . The characteristics of the special case assumed by the classical theory happen not to be those of the economic society in which we actually live, with the result that its teaching is misleading and disastrous if we attempt to apply it to the facts of experience.[4]

Keynes explicitly tailored the exposition of his book to change the minds of his 'fellow economists' while hoping 'it will be intelligible to others'. Keynes's purpose was to persuade 'economists to reexamine critically certain of their basic assumptions'. Keynes believed that the fatal flaw of the classical system lay in the special axioms that were necessary to demonstrate the self-correcting tendency of an unfettered competitive economic system.

For several years before publication, Keynes circulated drafts of his work to world-famous professional colleagues in England. He took extraordinary time and effort to elicit comments from, and respond to, these economists as well as to his students in Cambridge. As a result of this ongoing dialogue, Keynes was fully aware of the arguments that his fellow economists would marshall to defend the classical orthodoxy. If he was to convince his professional colleagues of the errors of their ways, Keynes had to develop persuasive arguments to rebut the many comments he received.

The English experience of stagnating high levels of unemployment since World War I had convinced Keynes that the capitalist system was unlikely to survive unless proper policy actions were taken immediately. What was needed to galvanize professional support for his policy suggestions was something other than a tedious and contentious professional formalization of his model. Rightly or wrongly, in 1936, Keynes felt that

> It is a great fault of symbolic pseudo-mathematical methods of formalising a system of economic analysis . . . that they expressly assume strict independence between the factors involved and lose all their cogency and authority if this hypothesis is disallowed; whereas, in ordinary discourse, where we are not blindly manipulating but know all the time what we are doing and what the words mean, we can keep 'at the back of our heads' the necessary reserves and qualifications and the adjustments which we shall have to make later on, in a way in which we cannot keep complicated partial differentials 'at the back' of several pages of algebra which assume that they all vanish. Too large a proportion of recent 'mathematical' economics are mere concoctions, as imprecise as the initial assumptions they rest on, which allow the author to lose sight of the complexities and interdependencies of the real world in a maze of pretentious and unhelpful symbols.[5]

Keynes, a master expositor and essayist, developed his general theoretical analysis as an essay in persuasion just at the time that the economics profession was becoming more imbued with the belief in the necessity of presenting economic arguments in terms of formal mathematical models. Today's generation of economists, trained to think solely in terms of mathematical formulizations, have great difficulties in comprehending the analytical basis of Keynes's *General Theory* essay.

In an early draft of the Introduction to his *General Theory*, Keynes explained why he chose to de-emphasize formalisms when he wrote:

> In economics you cannot *convict* your opponent of error, you can only *convince* him of it. And, even if you are right, you cannot convince him . . . if his head is already so filled with contrary notions that he cannot catch the clues to your thought which you are trying to throw to him.[6]

Keynes believed that the classical formal analysis could never provide a meaningful explanation of unemployment or how it would be cured in the real world. He categorized the classical proposal for curing unemployment as an *'ignoratio elenchi'*.[7] Classical theorists, Keynes claimed, were engaged in offering a proof irrelevant to the proposition in question. Keynes compared classical economists to Euclidean geometers in a non-Euclidean world

> who, discovering that in experience straight lines apparently parallel often meet, rebuke the lines for not keeping straight – as the only remedy for the unfortunate collisions which are occurring. Yet in truth, there is no remedy except to throw over the axiom of parallels and to work out a non-Euclidean geometry. Something similar is today required in economics. We need to throw over . . . postulate[s] of the classical doctrine and to work out the behaviour of a system in which involuntary unemployment in the strict sense is possible.[8]

To explain the existence of involuntary unemployment in the real world, Keynes developed the economic theory analogue to non-Euclidean geometry where fundamental classical axioms were overthrown. If one accepts these classical axioms, then the only logical basis for unemployment involves some supply condition that causes wages and prices to be less than perfectly flexible.

During the depression, classical theorists argued that unemployment would end when the market would self-correct this supply imperfection. In the long run market forces would cause wages and prices to fall sufficiently to restore full employment. Keynes, on the other hand, argued 'We must not regard the conditions of supply . . . as the fundamental sources of our troubles. . . . [I]t is in the conditions of demand which our diagnosis must search and probe for an explanation.[9]

In 1936, the rigorous axiomatic foundations of classical demand theory had not been specified.[10] It is not surprising, therefore, that Keynes did not identify all the specific classical axioms that his analysis had thrown out. At the time (and even today) many readers are not clear as to what were the specific classical axioms Keynes rejected in developing his 'non-Euclidean' general economic theory, and why he had rejected them.

Many of the cleverest young economists who were entering the economics profession in the United States and England during the Great Depression (e.g., Paul Samuelson, James Tobin, J.R. Hicks, James Meade) recognized that the unemployment problem of the economic system seemed too deep and long to be sloughed off as merely a temporary aberration or friction that a self-adjusting market could cure. Common sense told them that the invisible hand might not be able to resurrect a prosperous economy in their lifetime. They were too impatient to wait for the long-run revival that was promised by classical theory.

Yet these young economists of the 1930s had been trained in the classical economics tradition. They, therefore, did not find Keynes's essay in persuasion an easy one to comprehend. As classically trained economists, these 'young Turks' were unwilling to dispense with any of the implicit fundamental axioms required by the classical theory of demand. For those disciplined to believe in the beneficence of the invisible hand, all classical axioms are, by definition, universal truths. It is a herculean task to question what one has been trained to believe in as self-evident verities. This younger generation were unwilling, or unable, to free their formal models of these classical restrictive axioms underlying demand conditions. Their minds were so filled with 'Euclidean' notions that they could not catch the 'non-Euclidean' analytical insights that Keynes was throwing to them.

Instead, this younger generation of professional economists tried to translate Keynes's conclusions into formalizations of the evolving axiomatic [neo]classical theory that was coming into vogue during this period as a result of the work of Hicks, Meade, Samuelson, and others. Unable to decipher Keynes's 'non-Euclidean' message, they tried to develop his insights through the classical theory that they had been brought up on by introducing *ad hoc* supply constraints (e.g., the fixed money wages and fixprice models) on the workings of the 'invisible hand'.

Today, most economists are even more rigorously trained in the mathematical formalisms of classical axiomatic value theory than earlier generations. Most are, therefore, still wedded to the axioms of classical analysis and are unwilling to contemplate the throwing over of some of their cherished classical universal truths. Accordingly, mainstream macroeconomic models are still founded on the special classical axioms. The resulting policy implications are, as Keynes noted, 'misleading and dangerous' if applied to the real world in which we live.

Until mainstream classical economists are willing at least to contemplate more general economic theories that are free of the restrictive demand axioms of classical theory, it is unlikely that the applicable general theory of unemployment in a monetary economy will be the basis of widespread public discussions. Mainstream economists do not have the relevant theoretical tools to develop proper policies for resolving the major economic problems of the day.

Beginning in the 1980s a New Keynesian macroeconomic school of thought developed. Like the earlier generation of Old Keynesians, the New Keynesians still profess allegiance to the axioms of classical demand theory as the bedrock microfoundations of macroeconomics. The New Keynesians' advance over the Old Keynesian model is the development of sophisticated *ad hoc* constraints on the conditions of aggregate supply (in terms of fixed nominal values, coordination failures and/or asymmetric information upon which supply decisions are made). These constraints are justified by claiming that, at least in the short run, nominal fixities exist in the real world.[11] If prices were only perfectly flexible and existing information freely available to all, then the logic of the New Keynesians would force them to admit that full employment is the inevitable outcome of an unfettered market system. In the long run with sufficient price flexibility assured by a free market mechanism, though we may all be dead, New and Old Keynesians can agree with their classical brethren that full employment and economic prosperity are inevitable.

These Old and New Keynesian explanations of the existence of unemployment are the modern-day logical equivalent of rebuking the apparent parallel lines 'for not keeping straight'. In truth, these Old and New Keynesian models accept that the classical system is the general theory, while Keynesian unemployment is a special case that occurs in the short run because of some unfortunate market (supply) imperfection. More than a half-century after Keynes's *General Theory*, these mainstream Keynesians still fail to see that Keynes was attacking the beliefs in the 'universal truths' that formed the very foundation of classical demand analysis.

Keynes's squabble with the classical theory was not over whether temporary wage and price stickiness is the cause of unemployment. In attempting to differentiate his product from classical analysis, Keynes noted

> For Classical Theory has been so accustomed to rest the supposedly self adjusting character of the economic system on the assumed fluidity of money-wages; and, when there is rigidity, to lay on this rigidity the blame for maladjustment.... My difference from this theory is primarily a difference of analysis.[12]

Any supply failure that produces a wage and/or price inflexibility – whether ephemeral or not – is not the essence of Keynes's analysis of unemployment. Keynes always insisted that it is the conditions underlying demand, and not supply, that are the fundamental cause of unemployment in a monetary economy.

Keynes's theoretical analysis was immediately shunted onto a wrong track by the writings of Hicks, Samuelson, Meade and others who claimed to have the analytical key to explain Keynes's general system. The result was that Keynes's revolution was aborted almost as soon as it was conceived. More than a half-century later, Keynes's 'non-Euclidean' revolutionary approach remains undiscovered in the modern mainstream economics literature. There is, therefore, an analytical void that needs to be filled if Keynes's revolution in economic thought is to be understood and revived. Hopefully, this volume will fill the theoretical (and resultant policy) gap that mainstream economists have failed to close.

In the 1970s, Neoclassical Synthesis Keynesianism was declared dead by a younger generation of technically trained classical scholars who called themselves New Classical economists. They emphasized the beauty of an intellectually precise, highly mathematical system that would demonstrate with hi-tech precision that the economic system could always achieve a full employment equilibrium as long as mechanisms consistent with the classical axioms are the fundamental analytical building blocks.

One of the founders of the New Classical school, Robert Lucas, agreed that the axioms required made New Classical analysis 'artificial, abstract, patently unreal'.[13] Lucas insisted that these postulates were necessary. They embodied the *only* scientific method of doing economics. These axioms permit the development of logical conclusions that are independent of political and economic institutions. The resulting immutable economic 'laws', it is alleged, are the social science equivalent of the unchanging scientific principles established by the 'hard' sciences.[14] Lucas's designation of what is the only scientific approach to economics means that Keynes's rejection of some classical axioms can be dismissed as 'unscientific' and not worthy of serious study. No wonder Keynes's analytical system is ignored in mainstream textbooks.[15]

In contrast to this rigid mindset methodology of mainstream economic theory, the goals of this volume are:

1. to explain the classical axioms that must be 'thrown over' to obtain a logically consistent Post Keynesian macroeconomic theory analogue to non-Euclidean geometry. The classical postulates that Keynes's analytical framework rejected are (a) the axiom of the neutrality of money; (b) the gross substitution axiom; and (c) the ergodic axiom;

2. to describe what most mainstream Keynesian economists believe is Keynes's formal model. These mainstream 'Keynesian' models depart from Keynes's explicit analytical arguments. They are not logically representations of what Keynes believed was his general analytical system. These models could be correctly named Non-Market Clearing Classical Models or NMCCM. They are modern-day variants of the kinds of classical (Euclidean) models that, in Keynes's time, were used by classical economists to explain unemployment as a temporary phenomenon. They typify the same mode of thinking that Keynes condemned as 'misleading' in the 1930s;

3. to develop the Post Keynesian analysis that has been evolved from Keynes's original logical framework;

4. to demonstrate that the analytical differences between the Keynes–Post Keynesian approach and the mainstream Keynesian and classical systems lead to significantly different long-term policy implications for dealing with the relevant economic problems facing modern money-using, entrepreneurial economies; and

5. to complete the task that Keynes hoped to do more than a half century ago, namely to convince the reader that the Keynes–Post Keynesian analytical framework is the general case applicable to the facts of experience.

This task is undertaken with some hope that, in current turbulent times, economists' minds are again open to the possibility of a fresh, non-classical axiomatic analysis to apply to the real world's economic problems as we approach the twenty-first century. This belief in the possible receptivity of mainstream economics to Keynes's 'difference in analysis' is suggested in the following quote from Alan Blinder, co-author of one of the most popular 'New Keynesian' textbooks. Blinder has recently recognized that New Classical economics

> is no longer an attractive intellectual fad in large part because it is not a theory about the world we actually live in. That approach was essentially a mathematical construct that really doesn't apply to the real world. In contrast, Keynesian economics was never intended to be an abstract theory, but a model for practical policy to solve a real world problem. Keynesian macroeconomics was theoretically messy, it wasn't neat mathematically, it didn't have all the strings tied, it had a lot of loose ends and still does. The whole thrust of the intellectual revolution led by Robert E. Lucas, Jr, of the University of Chicago and others was to tie up all the theoretical strings in nice, neat mathematical bows. Everything had to be precise. There was some masquerading among some people, not necessarily by Lucas, that this theorizing had something to do with the real economy.[16]

NOTES

1. *The Collected Writings of John Maynard Keynes*, 13, edited by D. Moggridge. London, Macmillan, 1973, p. 492.
2. Joan Robinson designated this synthesis 'Bastard Keynesianism' to warn readers that the resulting analytical system was a perversion of Keynes's own analytical framework.
3. A. Smith, *An Inquiry Into The Wealth of Nations*, Modern Library, New York, 1937, p. 14.
4. J.M. Keynes, *The General Theory of Employment, Interest and Money*, Harcourt Brace, New York, 1936, p. 3.
5. J.M. Keynes, *The General Theory of Employment, Interest and Money*, Harcourt Brace, New York, 1936, p. 297.
6. Quoted by Austin Robinson in his inaugural Keynes lecture before the British Academy on April 22, 1971.
7. J.M. Keynes, *The General Theory*, p. 259.
8. J.M. Keynes, *The General Theory of Employment, Interest and Money*, Harcourt Brace, New York, 1936, pp. 16–17.
9. 'Poverty In The Midst of Plenty: Is The Economic System Self-Adjusting?' in *The Collected Writings of John Maynard Keynes*, 13, edited by D. Moggridge, London, Macmillan, 1973, p. 486.

10. Economists began working on this task during the late 1930s as they developed a logically consistent neoclassical axiomatic value theory that evolved ultimately into the Arrow–Debreu model of the 1950s and later into the rational expectations–New Classical model of the 1970s.

11. For example, see the 'Symposium on Keynesian Economics Today' in the *Journal of Economic Perspectives*, **7**, 1993.

12. Keynes, *The General Theory of Employment, Interest and Money*, Harcourt Brace, New York, p. 257.

13. R.E. Lucas, *Studies in Business Cycle Theory*. MIT Press, Cambridge, Mass., 1981, p. 271. Lucas has argued that 'Progress in economic thinking means getting better and better abstract, analogue models, not better verbal observations about the real world' (Ibid., p. 276).

14. For example, see R.E. Lucas and T.J. Sargent, *Rational Expectations of Econometric Practices*, University of Minnesota Press, Minnesota, 1981, pp. xi–xii.

15. As we will explain in the following chapters, Lucas's claim to having the only 'scientific' methodology is based on the conflating of the axiom of ergodicity with scientific methodology. (See, for example, P.A. Samuelson, 'Classical and Neoclassical Theory', in *Monetary Theory*, edited by R.W. Clower, London, Penguin, 1969, p. 12, where it is specifically claimed that ergodicity is necessary for science.) This claim, however, is not correct. Modern physics as well as other 'hard sciences' have, in recent years, recognized that some processes that they deal with are nonergodic.

The question of economics as a nonergodic science is discussed in later chapters of this volume. Also, see P. Davidson, 'Rational Expectations: A Fallacious Foundation for Studying Crucial Decision-Making Processes', *Journal of Post Keynesian Economics*, **5**, 1982–83, and P. Davidson, 'A Technical Definition of Uncertainty and The Long Run Non-Neutrality of Money', *Cambridge Journal of Economics*, **12**, 1988.

16. A. Blinder, 'A Keynesian Restoration is Here', *Challenge*, **35**, September–October 1992, p. 18.

2. The essential difference between the general theory and the classical system

The nineteenth century economic proposition known as Say's Law is the foundation of the classical argument that a free market system inevitably generates full employment. This classical law evolved from the writings of a French economist, Jean Baptiste Say, who in 1803 claimed that 'products always exchange for products'. In 1808, the English economist, James Mill, translated Say's French language dictum as 'supply creates its own demand'. Mill's phraseology has since been established in economics as Say's Law. It was this economic law that Keynes railed against in his *General Theory*.

A simplified explanation of Say's Law is as follows:

The sole explanation of why people produce, that is supply things to the market, is to earn income. Engaging in income-earning productive activities is presumed to be disagreeable. People will work only if they can earn sufficient income to buy the products of others that can provide them with sufficient pleasure to compensate for the unpleasantness of the income-earning activity. If people are rational utility maximizers, then all income earned in the market by the selling of goods and services is spent to buy (demand) things produced by others. Say's Law implies that a recession or depression will never occur. The very act of production generates enough income, and demand, to purchase everything produced. Businessmen seeking profits are always able to find sufficient demand for any output produced by workers.

Under Say's Law, goods always exchange for goods. Money is only a 'veil' behind which the real economy operates unhampered by financial considerations. Money is neutral, i.e. money is merely used as an intermediary in the exchange of goods for goods. No inherent obstacle in the economic system exists to prevent output and employment from being at the maximum flow possible given the size of the population and the technology available to producers. Money is merely a lubricant that oils the wheels of production and exchange.

If Say's Law prevails, then the economy can always be fully employed. Any change in the quantity of money by itself cannot induce a change in production. An increase in the money supply, for example, can only be spent on the same quantity of goods produced by an already fully employed economy. Increasing the money supply therefore only creates too much money chasing too few goods. The result is an increase in the market prices of all goods. Thus, if one initially puts the rabbit called the 'neutral money axiom' into the classical theorist's hat, then it should not be a surprise when a logically consistent economist-conjurer pulls from his classical chapeau the conclusion that inflation is 'always and everywhere a monetary phenomenon' caused by 'too much money chasing too few goods'.

Say's Law and the underlying belief in the neutrality of money became a fundamental tenet of nineteenth century classical theory. By the early twentieth century, this neutrality of money became one of the basic axioms of *the* prevailing orthodoxy in economics textbooks. An axiom is defined as 'a statement universally accepted as true ... a statement that needs no proof because its truth is obvious'. Accordingly, for those who are trained in classical economic theory, the neutrality of money is an article of faith, requiring no proof or justification. For example, Blanchard has written that all models that are relevant for the study of macroeconomics 'impose the long-run neutrality of money as a maintained assumption. This is very much a matter of faith, based on theoretical considerations rather than on empirical evidence'.[1]

A religious person who accepts the existence of a Divine Being as a fundamental truth would reject any 'scientific' evidence that purports to demonstrate that there is no God. Similarly, a true believer in the axiomatic foundations of classical theory will deny that money can be shown to be ultimately non-neutral in the long run.[2] To presume the long-run neutrality of money is to reject, without proof, the possibility that changes in the quantity of money can affect either the number of workers employed by entrepreneurs or the total volume of goods and services produced by firms in the long run. Any empirical data that purport to demonstrate that changes in the quantity of money *per se* can affect the real economy must be summarily rejected by classical theorists if they are to remain logically within their long-run analytical framework.

Yet Keynes, and a modern group of Post Keynesian economists following Keynes's analytical lead, have developed a logical system that rejects the neutrality of money as a necessary initial axiom in either the short run or the long run. The resulting analytical system provides a more general theory of the economy since it requires fewer initial axioms. Once the neutrality of money is rejected as an axiomatic building block, then Say's Law is not applicable as the organizing principle for studying a market system where money is used as a means of settling contractual obligations.

Keynes explicitly threw out the classical neutrality of money assumption in 1933, when he described the principles that were guiding him in developing his *General Theory*. Keynes drew a distinction between classical theory and the theoretical framework that he was developing in the following manner:

> An economy which uses money but uses it merely as a *neutral* link between transactions in real things and real assets and does not allow it to enter into motives or decisions, might be called – for want of a better name – a *real-exchange economy*. The theory which I desiderate would deal, in contradistinction to this, with an economy in which money plays a part of its own and affects motives and decisions and is, in short, one of the operative factors in the situation, so that the course of events cannot be predicted either in the long period or in the short, without a knowledge of the behavior of money between the first state and the last. And it is this which we ought to mean when we speak of *a monetary economy*. . . .
>
> Booms and depressions are peculiar to an economy in which . . . *money is not neutral*. I believe that the next task is to work out in some detail such a monetary theory of production. That is the task on which I am now occupying myself in some confidence that I am not wasting my time.[3]

Here, in Keynes's own words, is the claim that a theory of production for a *money-using* economy rejects a 'universal truth', the neutrality of money. Yet this neutrality axiom had been the foundation of classical economic theory for 125 years, ever since Mill introduced Say's Law into English economics. No wonder Keynes's 'General Theory' was considered heretical by most of his professional colleagues who were wedded to the classical analysis. Keynes was delivering a mortal blow to the very foundation of classical faith – the neutrality of money. No wonder Keynes's original analysis and the further elaboration and evolution of Keynes's system by Post Keynesian economists in recent decades has been snubbed by the majority of economists who are ideologically bonded to either the old or new classical tradition. The Keynes–Post Keynesian axiomatic logic is heresy.

To accept Keynes's logic and its Post Keynesian development threatens the Panglossian conclusion that, in the long run, an unfettered market economy will always assure full employment for all those who want to work. The more general (i.e., less restrictive) axiomatic foundation of Keynes's analysis permits the possibility that an entrepreneurial system might be flawed. Consequently, there can be a permanent role for government to correct this imperfection. The Keynes–Post Keynesian logic is as antithetical to the classical philosophy as the views on the origin of human life as asserted by the 'scientific theory of evolution' are to the 'scientific creationism' Biblical view of some Fundamentalist Protestant religions.

REVISING KEYNES'S REVOLUTION

Keynes argued that 'Say's Law ... is not the true law relating the aggregate demand and supply functions'[4] for an economy possessing real world characteristics. Keynes's analysis indicated that the 'system is not self-adjusting, and, without purposive direction, it is incapable of translating our actual poverty into potential plenty'.[5] His message is just as relevant today as it was in the 1930s.

In the aforecited 1935 writing, Keynes expressly indicated that he rejected the neutrality of money axiom in his analysis. Keynes's logic also required him to throw over two other classical axioms: (1) *the gross substitution axiom* that asserts that everything is a substitute for everything else and (2) *the axiom of an ergodic economic environment*, the presumption that future economic events can be reliably predicted by studying the economy's past market price data.

There are five essential characteristics of the real world which Keynes believed could be properly captured by overthrowing these three axioms. These features are

1. Money matters in both the long and short run. Money affects real decision making and employment and output outcomes.[6] In contrast, classical analysis presumes money to be neutral and therefore economic outcomes are determined entirely by real forces.
2. The economic system is moving through calendar time from an irrevocable past to an uncertain and statistically unpredictable future. Past and present market data do not necessarily provide correct signals regarding future outcomes. This means, in the language of statisticians, that economic data are not necessarily generated by a stochastic ergodic process.[7] Hicks has stated this condition as: 'People know that they just don't know'.[8]
3. Contracts denominated in money terms are a ubiquitous human institution in an entrepreneurial economy. The civil law of contracts evolved to help humans efficiently organize time-consuming production and exchange processes in a world of nonergodic uncertainty.[9] In any money-using entrepreneurial economy, entrepreneurs' decisions regarding production and hiring depend on expectations of receiving contractual sales revenues (cash inflows) in excess of the contractual money costs of production (cash outflows). Since the money-wage contract is the most ubiquitous of these efficiency-oriented contracts, modern economies can be characterized as money-wage contract-based systems.[10]

In money-using entrepreneurial systems, *liquidity* is defined as being able to meet contractual obligations as they come due. Since production and exchange in an entrepreneurial system is organized on a money-contract basis, liquidity implies having access to money to meet purchase and/or debt contractual payments as they come due. When the future is uncertain and hence cash flows over time cannot be reliably predicted, it is quite sensible to demand and hold money and other liquid assets (readily resalable for money) to protect oneself from being unable to meet unforeseeable net cash outflow commitments. In a classical system, where goods essentially exchange for goods, there is no rational need to hold money for liquidity purposes.

4.   Money possesses two essential elasticity properties that differentiate it from the products of industry. These properties describe why (a) money does not grow on trees (money's elasticity of production is zero), and (b) why producible goods are not good liquid stores of value (the elasticity of substitution between liquid assets such as money and producible goods is zero). If money has these peculiar elasticity properties, then '[u]nemployment develops, that is to say, because people want the moon; – men cannot be employed when the object of desire (i.e., money) is something which cannot be produced and the demand for which cannot be readily choked off'[11] when the price of money rises relative to the price of producibles.

5.   Unemployment, rather than full employment, is a normal outcome in any entrepreneurial, market-oriented, money-contract-using system operating in a *laissez-faire* environment.

In a classical system, on the other hand, money is just another producible commodity, like peanuts. Consequently whether people spend their money income on other producibles or on the peanut money, all income is spent on the products of industry. Supply creates its own demand. Full employment is the inevitable outcome of a market economy as long as the only things that provide utility are producibles.

KEYNES'S AGGREGATE SUPPLY AND DEMAND ANALYSIS

Before Keynes, classical economists admitted that temporary unemployment could develop if supply imperfections (perhaps due to the existence of labour unions or monopolies) prevented prices from responding instantaneously to changes in the composition of demand.[12] If the market is free to adjust, then competitive market forces will, at least in the long run, force a change in relative market prices that reflect the difference in the compo-

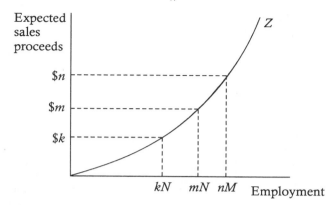

Figure 2.1   The aggregate supply curve

sition of demand and, therefore, clear all markets simultaneously. The long-run policy implication of this view is that the government should stand aside and permit the free market to right itself. Government interference only postpones the restoration of full employment. The historical record of unemployment throughout the 1920s in Great Britain convinced Keynes that this classical view was in error. Even if supply conditions are perfect, one cannot rely on supply to create its own demand.

Keynes's task was to explain why the determinants of aggregate demand were not identical with the determinants of aggregate supply as the classical analysis presumed. Keynes's aggregate supply function represents the relationship between entrepreneurs' expected sales revenues tomorrow and the amount of today's labour hiring that the entrepreneurs require to produce sufficient output to meet tomorrow's expected demand. In Figure 2.1, the aggregate supply curve (Z) emanates from the origin to indicate that if entrepreneurs expect zero sales revenue tomorrow they will hire zero workers today. If, on the other hand, they expect to sell $k worth of goods in the future they will hire kN workers today. Alternatively, if they expect a greater profit-maximizing sales revenue of $m tomorrow (where $m > k$), they will hire mN workers today, while if $n sales are expected then nN workers will be hired (where $n > m > k$). Accordingly, the aggregate supply curve is drawn (in Figure 2.1) as upward sloping to represent the common-sense notion that if entrepreneurs expect to sell more, they will hire more workers.

The aggregate demand function (D) represents the desired expenditures of all buyers at any level of aggregate employment. In Figure 2.2, D is drawn as upward sloping, but different than the aggregate supply function (Z). The positive slope of D represents the notion that if employment is larger,

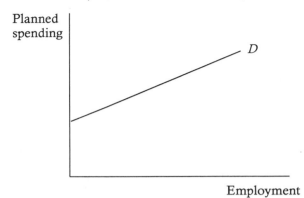

Figure 2.2   The aggregate demand function

more income is earned, and therefore the demand (spending) on goods and services will be larger.

A SIMPLE ILLUSTRATION OF KEYNES'S GENERAL CASE

The curves in Figure 2.3 are drawn to illustrate why a less than full employment equilibrium situation can persist. For descriptive simplicity assume that the production of the economy can be represented as an aggregation of what happens on a single tomato farm. On Monday morning, our representative entrepreneur, Farmer Brown, has to decide on the number of workers to hire to harvest sufficient tomatoes to maximize profits at next Saturday's market. Assume (as in Figure 2.3) that Farmer Brown expects his profit maximizing sales next Saturday to be z_1 dollars (say \$1 000) worth of tomatoes. According to this supply schedule he has calculated that hiring n_1 workers to produce q_1 tomatoes will bring in revenues of z_1 (where $z_1 = p_1 q_1$, and p_1 is the price at which Farmer Brown expects to be able to sell q_1 tomatoes). The resulting n_1 workers hired by Farmer Brown toil all week and receive their week's pay on Friday night from their employer.[13]

On Saturday morning, Farmer Brown takes his harvested tomatoes to market. At 8 a.m. the market opens and consumers (mainly, but not only, the employees of Farmer Brown and the other entrepreneurs in the system) come to market with the income (wages) they received the night before. Farmer Brown expects to sell the last tomato he has brought to market to the last customer expected to arrive a few seconds before closing time (5

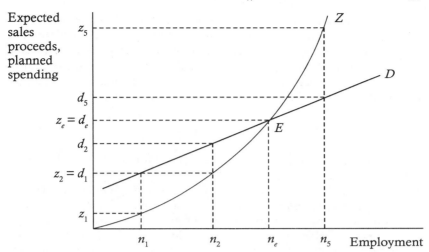

Figure 2.3 Why a less than full employment equilibrium situation can persist

p.m.). If his expectations regarding demand are met, then he correctly guessed the size of the market when he made his hiring decision last Monday morning.

From Figure 2.3, we can see that if, in the aggregate, all entrepreneurs hire the equivalent of n_1 workers, then the planned spending of buyers that make up the level of aggregate demand will be equal to $d_1 (= p_1q_1')$. As drawn in Figure 2.3, planned spending exceeds the amount entrepreneurs expected to sell $(d_1 > z_1)$. Several hours before the market closes (say 3 p.m.) Farmer Brown (representing all entrepreneurs in the system) finds he has sold his last tomato. For the rest of the market day disappointed buyers arrive at Farmer Brown's counter trying to purchase tomatoes, but his shelves are bare.[14]

On the following Monday morning Farmer Brown must again choose the number of workers to hire based on this Monday's expectations of sales for the following Saturday. Assume that Farmer Brown kept a record of how much money last Saturday's disappointed buyers said they would have spent had he still had tomatoes for sale. Brown may adopt the d_1 potential expenditures of last Saturday as the best estimate of next Saturday's sales proceeds (z_2), i.e. $z_2 (= p_2q_2)$. According to Figure 2.3, Farmer Brown will therefore hire n_2 workers in the expectation of earning z_2 revenue. Again, the workers labour in the fields and are paid on Friday evening.

Farmer Brown arrives at Saturday's market with q_2 tomatoes that he expects to sell at a price of p_2. The market doors open at 8 a.m. and buyers keep arriving at Farmer Brown's counter during the market day. From Figure 2.3, we see that Farmer Brown has underestimated demand that this Saturday will be $d_2 (= p_2 q_2')$. (The presumed unforeseen increase in demand is the result of more workers being hired and therefore swelling the number of tomato buyers.) As drawn in Figure 2.3, Farmer Brown's underestimate of market demand is less than it was last Saturday, i.e.,

$$(d_2 - z_2) < (d_1 - z_1).$$

Consequently, this Saturday Farmer Brown will not run out of tomatoes to sell until later in the day, say 4:15 p.m.

How many workers will representative Farmer Brown hire on the following Monday, and on each Monday after that? If this hypothesized process of adjusting expectations of next week's sales proceeds in the light of the past week's revenues plus evidence of disappointed buyers continues, then Farmer Brown's hiring decisions will tend to follow the dotted line in Figure 2.3 until Farmer Brown expects sales proceeds equal to z_e, when he hires n_e workers. Since $d_e = z_e$, on that Saturday Farmer Brown will sell his last tomato just as the clock strikes 5 p.m. and the market closes. There are no frustrated buyers. Farmer Brown (and all the other entrepreneurs) are just realizing their expectations of sales and there should be no further incentive to change employment plans.

Consequently, as long as the aggregate demand curves remain as drawn in Figure 2.3, then once entrepreneurs have hired the equilibrium level of employment (n_e), their expectations of sales are just being fulfilled by buyers' demands and there is no reason for them to alter their hiring plans.

This intersection of the aggregate supply and demand functions, point E in Figure 2.3, is designated *the effective demand* by Keynes.[15] The point of effective demand[16] can occur at any level of employment – even one where all workers who wish to work at the going real wage will not be employed.

A SIMPLE ILLUSTRATION OF SAY'S LAW

The main difference between the classical Say's Law analysis and Keynes's *General Theory* depends on the shape and position of the aggregate demand function *vis-à-vis* the aggregate supply function. Say's Law specifies that all expenditure (aggregate demand) on the products of industry is always exactly equal to the total costs of aggregate production including rents and gross profits (aggregate supply). This implies that the aggregate demand curve must be coincident to the aggregate supply curve, as drawn in Figure 2.4. The aggregate demand curve is merely superimposed on top of the

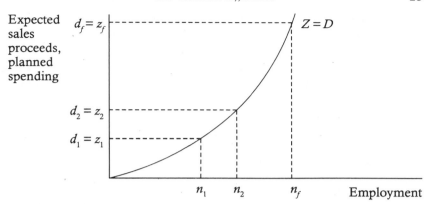

Figure 2.4   Aggregate supply and demand in a Say's Law world

aggregate supply curve, and, in Figure 2.4, whatever is supplied will be demanded.

Using our Farmer Brown example to illustrate Figure 2.4; if Farmer Brown expects sales revenue of $\$z_1$, then he will hire n_1 workers. On market day, as Figure 2.4 indicates, buyers will spend exactly $\$d_1 (= z_1)$. Entrepreneurial expectations will be exactly met. Alternatively, if Farmer Brown expects z_2 sales revenue, then he will hire n_2 workers. Again sales expectations will be exactly met. In a Say's Law regime, 'effective demand, instead of having a unique equilibrium value, is an infinite range of values all equally admissible; and the amount of employment is indeterminate except in so far as . . . [the full employment level of n_f (in Figure 2.4)] sets an upper limit'.[17] In a Say's Law world, there is no inherent obstacle to prevent the economy from achieving full employment – as long as entrepreneurs are willing to hire all the workers who want to work.

KEYNES'S TAXONOMIC ATTACK ON SAY'S LAW

In his biography of Keynes, Harrod highlighted the essential nature of the Keynesian Revolution. Harrod wrote 'classification in economics, as in biology, is crucial to the scientific structure'.[18] Harrod noted:

> The real defect with the classical system was that it deflected attention from what most needed attention. It was Keynes' extraordinarily powerful intuitive sense of what was important that convinced him that the old classification was inadequate. It was his highly developed logical capacity that enabled him to construct a new classification of his own.[19]

Keynes's taxonomic attack on the classical system can be algebraically demonstrated.

Let Z represent aggregate supply (or entrepreneurial expectations of sales receipts) in monetary terms, D aggregate demand (or planned expenditures) in money units, w the money-wage rate, and N the number of workers. The aggregate demand function is

$$D = f_d(w, N).\qquad(2.1)$$

The aggregate supply function is

$$Z = f_z(w, N).\qquad(2.2)$$

Say's Law asserts that

$$f_d(w, N) = f_z(w, N)\qquad(2.3)$$

'for *all* values of N, i.e., for all values of output and employment'.[20] In other words, in an economy subject to Say's Law, the total costs of aggregate production incurred by firms (for any given degree of competition or monopoly) at any level of employment are always recouped by the sale of that output. The aggregate demand and aggregate supply curves coincide (Figure 2.4). There is never a lack of effective demand to prevent entrepreneurs from hiring all who are willing and able to work at the going wage.

To challenge the applicability of Say's Law, Keynes had to develop a model where the aggregate demand and aggregate supply functions, $f_d(w, N)$ and $f_z(w, N)$, are not coincident (Figure 2.3).

Keynes accepted the 'age-old' normal (Marshallian) supply conditions based on the marginal cost function plus any monopoly mark-up[21] as a micro-basis for the aggregate supply function of equation (2.2). The existence of monopolistic power in the product and/or the labour markets is not a necessary condition for the existence of a barrier to full employment. A purely competitive market system with perfectly flexible wages and prices could still suffer from unemployment due to a lack of effective demand.

Keynes's heretical explanation of unemployment required explaining why aggregate demand does not coincide with aggregate supply, independent of the degree of competition in the market-place, i.e., why supply does not create its own demand, whether or not competitive conditions prevail.

Keynes developed an expanded taxonomy for the components on the aggregate demand relationship to differentiate his general case from the classical special case. In the classical system, there is only a single category of spending. All demand expenditure is a function of (and is equal to) income earned (supply). Keynes split aggregate demand into two categories, D_1 and D_2, i.e.,

$$D = D_1 + D_2. \tag{2.4}$$

Keynes's D_1 demand category represented *all* expenditures which 'depend on the level of aggregate income and, therefore, on the level of employment N',[22] i.e.

$$D_1 = f_1(w, N); \tag{2.5}$$

D_2, therefore, represented *all* expenditures *not* related to income and employment, i.e.

$$D_2 \neq f(w, N). \tag{2.6}$$

These two categories make up an exhaustive list of all possible classes of spending.

Keynes's task was to show that special postulates were required by the classical theory to demonstrate that the aggregate demand function consists solely of expenditures *equal* to current income, and if these axioms are dropped, then $f_1(w, N)$ is never equal to $f_z(w, N)$ *for all levels of* N, while D_2 spending ≥ 0.

The microfoundations of the classical economics case assure that all income is spent on the products of industry.[23] In the simplest classical case, all current expenditures are related to current income and are therefore classified under D_1 which is immediately spent. The marginal propensity to spend out of current income is unity and any additional supply creates its own additional demand. (In an intertemporal setting with gross substitutability over time agents plan to spend lifetime income on the products of industry over their life cycle, i.e. the long-run marginal propensity to spend is unity.) Consequently, in either the short run or the long run, $f_d(w, N) = f_z(w, N)$ for all values of N and Figure 2.4 is relevant.

Keynes's second expenditure category, D_2, is not related to current income and employment by being equal to 'planned' savings (which can be defined as $f_z(w, N) - f_1(w, N)$. To demonstrate why D_2 is not equal to planned savings, Keynes assumed the existence of an uncertain future that cannot be either foreknown or statistically predicted by analysing past and current market price signals. In such a nonergodic environment, future profits, the basis for current D_2 investment spending, can neither be reliably forecast from existing market information, nor endogenously determined from today's 'planned' savings function $(f_z(w, N) - f_1(w, N))$.[24] Rather investment expenditures depend on the exogenous (and therefore by definition, sensible but not rational) expectations of entrepreneurs, or what Keynes called 'animal spirits'. Thus, in either the short run or the long run, D_2 expenditures cannot be a function of current income and employment and equation (2.6) applies.

Explicit recognition of the possibility of two different classes of current demand for producible goods and services based on fewer axioms than required by the classical taxonomy makes Keynes's analysis the more general case. Classical theory where Say's Law prevails and where income-generating supply activities $(f_z(w, N))$ create their own identical demand so that all markets clear becomes 'a special case'[25] where

$$D_2 = 0 \tag{2.7}$$

and

$$D_1 = f_1(w, N) = f_z(w, N) = Z \tag{2.8}$$

for all values of w *and* N.

The next logical task for Keynes was to demonstrate that 'the characteristics of the special case assumed by classical theory happen not to be those of the economic society in which we actually live'.[26] In other words, Keynes had to demonstrate that even if $D_2 = 0$, the D_1 function would not be coincident with his macroanalogue of the age-old supply function.[27] To accomplish this, Keynes had to reject the special classical axiom of ubiquitous gross substitution as applicable to any economy that organizes on a money contractual basis in the face of an uncertain future. Under these more general conditions, some portion of a utility-maximizing agent's income might be withheld from the purchase of producible goods, i.e. the marginal propensity to spend out of current income on the products of industry is less than unity.

In an uncertain world, as we have already noted, liquidity provides utility by protecting the holder from fear of not being able to meet future contractual commitments. As long as producible goods are not gross substitutes for holding nonproducible liquid assets (including money) for liquidity purposes, then no change in relative prices can induce income earners to buy producibles with that portion of income they wish to use to purchase additional security from holding liquid assets. Or as Hahn put it: 'there are in this economy resting places for savings other than reproducible assets' and the existence of 'any non-reproducible asset allows for a choice between employment-inducing and non employment-inducing demand'.[28]

In an uncertain (nonergodic) world, where money and all other liquid assets possess certain essential properties,[29] agents can obtain utility (by being free of fear of possible insolvency or even bankruptcy) only by holding a portion of their income in the form of nonproducible money or other liquid assets. As long as the gross substitutability between nonproducible liquid assets (including money) and producible goods is approximately zero[30] then money is not neutral, even with perfectly flexible prices. Thus, the general case underlying the principle of effective demand is:

$$D_1 = f_1(w, N) \neq f_z(w, N) \qquad (2.9)$$

while the propensity to save $(f_z(w, N) - f_d(w, N))$ is equal to the amount out of current income that utility-maximizing agents plan to use to increase their holdings of nonproducible liquid assets.

By proclaiming a 'fundamental psychological law' associated with 'the detailed facts of experience' where the marginal propensity to consume is always less than unity, Keynes finessed the possibility that equation (2.8) was applicable to the real world. If the marginal propensity to consume is always less than unity, then $f_1(w, N)$ would never coincide with $f_z(w, N)$, even if $D_2 = 0$, and the special classical case is not applicable to 'the economic society in which we actually live'.[31]

In sum, Keynes's principle of effective demand demonstrates that, in a nonergodic world, it is the existence of nonproducible assets that are held for liquidity purposes and for which the products of industry are not gross substitutes that is the fundamental cause of involuntary unemployment. The lack of perfect price flexibility is not a necessary condition for demonstrating the existence of unemployment.

CAN FLEXIBLE WAGES ASSURE FULL EMPLOYMENT?

Pre-Keynesian classical economists claimed that unemployment occurred because wages were too high to sustain full employment. If money wages and prices were perfectly flexible and immediately declined if there was a drop in demand, then full employment would be restored. Unemployment could therefore be attributed to the 'fact' that workers (and unions) fixed the wage too high and then refused to cut wages in the face of unemployment. Keynes rejected this view.[32]

Keynes's principle of effective demand is not merely a novel way of demonstrating that wage inflexibilities are the necessary cause of unemployment. In Keynes's analysis, unemployment can develop even if wages are perfectly flexible. Changes in the money-wage rate induced by some

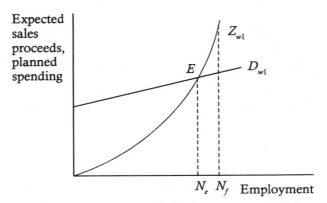

*Figure 2.5   The general theory of aggregate supply and demand in wage
units*

exogenous change in demand will not automatically restore full
employment.

At this stage in our overview of Keynes's system, it is not practical to
delve into the details of Keynes's answer to the classical 'too high' wage
problem. It is sufficient to note that if both aggregate demand and aggregate
supply money proceeds are deflated by the money wage, then Keynes's
effective demand analysis is presented in terms of his wage unit. Equations
(2.1) and (2.2) would be written as:

$$Z_w = f_a(N) \qquad\qquad (2.1w)$$

and

$$D_w = f_b(N) \qquad\qquad (2.2w)$$

where the subscript w indicates measured in wage units. Equations (2.1w)
and (2.2w) are drawn in Figure 2.5 for a given money wage, w_1. The point of
effective demand in Figure 2.5 is point E, and the equilibrium level of
employment is N_e where

$$D_w = f_b(N) = f_a(N) = Z_w. \qquad\qquad (2.3w)$$

What is the effect of a change in the money wage on this underemployment
point of effective demand? By construction, any change in the money wage,
say from w_1 to w_2, where $w_1 > w_2$, will not cause any change in the position
or shape of the aggregate supply function in wage units. Consequently, if a
change in the money wage is to increase the employment point of effective

demand and move the economy toward full employment equilibrium (N_f) in Figure 2.5, then the aggregate demand curve in wage units must be induced to shift upwards as a direct effect of the hypothesized decline in the money wage. As Keynes put it 'the precise question at issue is whether the reduction in money-wages will or will not be accompanied by . . . an aggregate demand . . . which is somewhat greater measured in wage units'.[33] Accordingly, Keynes's 'difference of analysis'[34] involves tracing how a change in the money wage affects D_1 and/or D_2 when both are measured in wage units relative to the unchanged aggregate supply function when the latter is also measured in terms of wage units. In other words, Keynes's parametrization of the money wage forces the analyst to evaluate how any change in the money wage works through the D_1 and D_2 components of aggregate demand if one is to claim that a too high wage causes unemployment and a change in the wage (i.e., flexible wages) *per se* will cure the unemployment problem. (This evaluation is carried out in Chapter 11 *infra*).

Harrod's argument regarding the importance of Keynes's new classification scheme is right on the mark. The classical taxonomy deflected attention away from the necessity of studying the components of aggregate demand to explain involuntary unemployment, whether money wages (and prices) were flexible or not. The absence of flexible wages and/or prices *per se* is not a necessary condition for underemployment equilibrium. Nor is the existence of perfectly flexible wages and/or prices a sufficient condition for guaranteeing full employment.

CONCLUSION

This chapter has explained how Keynes developed a more general theory than the classical one based on Say's Law. The revolutionary aspect of Keynes's approach involved eliminating three restrictive classical axioms that underlay the classical vision of the aggregate demand function. The chapters that follow will systematically, and in greater detail, develop Keynes's argument and indicate how it differs not only from the pre-Keynesian classical theory, but also from the New Classical, and Old and New Keynesian analyses that have dominated mainstream economics since Keynes's death.

NOTES

1. O.J. Blanchard, 'Why Does Money Affect Output? A Survey', in *Handbook of Monetary Economics*, II, edited by B.M. Friedman and F.H. Hahn, Elsevier, New York, 1990, p. 828.

2. This is not to deny that some members of the 'New Keynesian' school and even some Old Classical school Monetarists accept the notion that money may be non-neutral in the short run, because of some 'temporary' supply-side failure of the free market. Nevertheless all members of the mainstream orthodoxy of economics have faith in the long-run neutrality of money.

3. J.M. Keynes, 'A Monetary Theory of Production', in *The Collected Writings of John Maynard Keynes*, 13, p. 409 (some italics added).

4. Ibid., p. 26.

5. J.M. Keynes, 'Poverty In The Midst of Plenty: IS The System Self-Adjusting?', op. cit., p. 491.

6. Despite Friedman's use of the motto 'money matters', he remains faithful to the neutrality axiom. Friedman does not permit money to affect the long-run real outcome of his system. In describing his logical framework, Friedman states:

   that changes in the quantity of money as such *in the long run* have a negligible effect on real income so that nonmonetary forces are 'all that matter' for changes in real income over decades and money 'does not matter'. . . . I regard the description of our position as 'money is all that matters for changes in *nominal income* and for *short-run* changes in real income' as an exaggeration but one that gives the right flavor to our conclusions (M. Friedman, 'A Theoretical Framework For Monetary Analysis', in *Milton Friedman's Monetary Framework: A Debate With His Critics*, ed. by R.J. Gordon, University of Chicago Press, Chicago, 1974).

7. P. Davidson, 'Is Probability Theory Relevant for Uncertainty? A Post Keynesian Perspective', *Journal of Economic Perspectives*, 5, 1991. In order for the historical date to provide a statistical base for drawing reliable inferences about future outcomes, the data must be generated by an ergodic stochastic process. Such inferences are labelled 'rational expectations' by New Classical economists.

   Samuelson has elevated the presumption of an ergodic economic system to a necessary condition for making economics a science. (See P.A. Samuelson, 'What Classical and Neoclassical Theory Really Was' in *Monetary Theory*, edited by R.W. Clower, Penguin, London, 1969, pp. 184–5.) Hicks, on the other hand, argued that 'the usefulness of "statistical" or "stochastic" methods in economics is a good deal less than is conventionally supposed. We have no business to turn to them automatically; we should always ask ourselves before we apply them whether they are appropriate to the problem at hand. Very often they are not'. (See J.R. Hicks, *Causality in Economics*, Basic Books, New York, 1979, p. 121.)

8. J.R. Hicks, *Causality in Economics*, Basic Books, New York, 1979, p. vii.

9. P. Davidson, 'The Dual Nature of the Keynesian Revolution', *Journal of Post Keynesian Economics*, **2**, 1980.

10. With the legal abolition of slavery, only forward labour contracts enforceable in terms of money are permitted in modern economies.

11. J.M. Keynes, *The General Theory*, p. 235.

12. The classical axioms did not permit aggregate demand to be deficient.

13. The payroll will probably be financed by a working capital loan from Farmer Brown's banker.

14. Out of the z_1 sales revenue received, Farmer Brown pays off his working capital loan from the banker that financed his payroll. Whatever remains is his gross profit.

15. J.M. Keynes, *The General Theory*, pp. 25, 55.

16. The reader can see that a similar process of movement towards the point of effective demand can be described even if Farmer Brown started with over optimistic sales proceeds expectations of z_5 and hence hired n_5 workers. At the end of the first Saturday, in this case, Farmer Brown would find himself holding an unwanted inventory of unsold, but perishable tomatoes when the market doors closed at 5 p.m. Accordingly he would reduce his hiring level, but sales would then fall off further until the point of effective demand was reached.

17. J.M. Keynes, *The General Theory*, p. 26.
18. R.F. Harrod, *The Life of John Maynard Keynes*, Macmillan, London, 1951, p. 464.
19. Ibid., p. 463.
20. J.M. Keynes, *The General Theory of Employment, Interest and Money*, Harcourt Brace, New York, 1936, p. 26.
21. Keynes specifically indicated (1936, p. 245) that any degree of competition was compatible with his generalized aggregate supply function.
22. Ibid., p. 28.
23. Classical microfoundations assume that the earning of income always involves disutility, while the products of industry are the *only* scarce things which generate utility. It therefore follows that if future outcomes are knowable (i.e., ergodic), then utility maximizers will bear the irksomeness of engaging in income-producing activities only to the point where the marginal disutility of earning income equals the expected marginal utility of the products of industry that the agents 'know' they want to buy. All utility-maximizing agents are, on their budget constraint line, allocating *all* their income on purchasing producible goods and services. Given the classical postulates any demand to hold a nonproducible money or other nonproducible assets solely for liquidity purposes would be irrational. Even if people demanded nonproducible money, as long as producible goods are gross substitutes for money, then a change in relative prices could always induce utility maximizers to stop holding money and purchase the products of industry instead. Money is a neutral veil.
24. J.M. Keynes, *The General Theory*, p. 210.
25. J.M. Keynes, *The General Theory*, p. 3.
26. J.M. Keynes, *The General Theory*, p. 3.
27. Even if D_2 were to be defined in some way as related to aggregate income, i.e.

$$D_2 = f_2(w, N) \qquad (2.7')$$

so long as

$$f_1(w, N) + f_2(w, N) \neq f_z(w, N) \qquad (2.8'')$$

for all values of w and N, then Say's Law is not applicable. Hence, even if D_2 is defined as related to employment, classical theory is still a special case where $f_1(w, N) + f_2(w, N) = f_z(w, N)$ for all values of N.
28. R.F. Hahn, 'Keynesian Economics and General Equilibrium Theory: Reflections on Some Current Debates', in *The Microfoundations of Macroeconomics*, ed. by G.C. Harcourt, Macmillan, London, 1977, pp. 31, 39.
29. The two essential properties are (1) the elasticity of production for money and all other liquid assets is zero or negligible, and (2) the elasticity of substitution between money and all liquid assets *vis-à-vis* producible goods is zero or negligible (Keynes, 1936, p. 241). A zero elasticity of production is technical jargon for what every four year old knows is the truth about money, namely that *money does not grow on trees*. Consequently, money cannot be harvested by the use of otherwise unemployed labour in the private sector to the point where the marginal utility of picking an additional unit of money off the money tree equals the marginal disutility of reaching to harvest the leaf. (This common-sense notion that money does not grow on trees is forcibly knocked out of the heads of students who take any sophisticated university economics course on general equilibrium systems. Students are taught that money is merely another commodity like peanuts – which if it does not grow on trees does grow on the roots of bushes!
   A zero elasticity of substitution means that the products of industry are *not gross substitutes for nonproducible money and other assets held for liquidity purposes* no matter how much or how quickly relative prices change.
30. See J.M. Keynes, *The General Theory*, Chapter 17; and P. Davidson, 'Reviving Keynes's Revolution', *Journal of Post Keynesian Economics*, **6**, 1983–84.

31.   J.M. Keynes, *The General Theory*, p. 3.
32.   J.M. Keynes, *The General Theory*, p. 257.
33.   J.M. Keynes, *The General Theory*, pp. 259–60.
34.   J.M. Keynes, *The General Theory*, p. 257.

3. Expenditures related to income: Keynes's D_1 category

It is Keynes's taxonomy that fundamentally distinguishes his analysis from classical theory. All successful classification schemes require the taxonomist to define each category in terms of those necessary and sufficient common properties possessed, and/or common functions provided by any item for it to be a member of a specific class.

For example, even though a whale looks like a fish, swims like a fish, and will die (like a fish) if it is out of water for too long, a whale is not a fish. The taxonomy of biologists classifies all whales as mammals despite their obvious similarities to fish. Biologists have agreed that the necessary and sufficient characteristics for a species to be labelled a mammal are that the species bears its young alive *and* suckles the young. A creature's physical appearance, its habitat, or its swimming propensity are neither necessary nor sufficient for the biologists' classification.[1] No matter that the uninstructed layperson perceives a whale to be more similar to a fish than to his/her own mammalian self. Nor does it make any difference to the lifestyle of the whale who, oblivious to the biologists' taxonomy, continues to look, swim and die like a fish.

In the physical sciences, taxonomists often invent words to define specific categories. Thus certain things that share common properties are 'quarks', even though the average layperson has not the slightest idea what a quark is or what it feels, smells, tastes, looks, or sounds like. The word 'quark' does not appear in everyday conversation. Physicists are free to define a 'quark' any way they see fit.

Unfortunately, economists do not have the linguistic freedom of physicists. To communicate with policy makers and intelligent laypeople regarding economic matters, economists tend to use words adopted from nonstandardized, everyday speech to designate rigorous economic categories. All too often the result is that defenders of some economic position are using economic terms to mean one thing, while their antagonists use the same word to connotate something different. This ambiguity in economic language often perpetuates semantic confusions rather than shedding light on economic problems.

33

KEYNES'S D_1 CONCEPT AND THE CLASSICAL MICROTHEORY OF CONSUMPTION

Keynes's taxonomy was developed specifically to demonstrate that Say's Law is a special case and is not applicable to the facts of experience. Say's Law requires that *current* spending is equal to output *currently* produced by *today's* employed workers. Keynes's D_1 and D_2 categories also had to be defined in terms of *current* spending and *current* output if Keynes's general case analysis was to be comparable with the special case classical system. Thus D_1 is all current spending related to current output and D_2 is all expenditure *not* related to current output.

Had Keynes limited his nomenclature to D_1 and D_2 and these definitions, he would have obtained the clarity and precision similar to the physicist's use of the word 'quark'. The cost of this exactness, however, would have been that no policy maker, intelligent layperson, or even most professional colleagues of his time, would have been able to associate D_1 (or D_2) with any common-sense spending terminology.

To give a real world meaning to the D_1 spending category, Keynes used the vernacular word 'consumption' to characterize it. Substituting a C for D_1 Keynes developed 'the propensity to consume'[2] as today's purchase of currently produced goods by households. This substitution of the colloquial term consumption for D_1 misled others to associate D_1 spending with other things that in other contexts bear the name of consumption but are not necessarily identical to Keynes's D_1 category notion.

It was a simple matter for others to argue that the 'theory of consumption' (as opposed to the theory of D_1 spending) in *The General Theory* must be logically compatible with the classical microfoundations of consumption behaviour of utility-maximizing households. Classical microtheory relates consumption with the household receiving utility by the using up of economic producible goods and services. In classical theory consumption does not necessarily occur when a good is bought. Classical consumption occurs when a good is used up to obtain its utility. Saving can then be defined as that portion of any durable good that although bought today is inventoried to be used (and yield utility) in a future period. This difference in definition between classical theory's notion of consumption and Keynes's D_1 concept does not create any logical differences as long as one is classifying newly produced nondurables. They are used up in the period they are purchased. A durable good, on the other hand, takes time to wear out. It yields its utility over a number of time periods. Keynes's taxonomy means that today's produced consumer durable is classified as entirely 'consumption' in the current period. In classical microtheory terms, on the other hand, today's purchase of a newly produced durable is primarily a form of saving, i.e., the storing up of utility for release in future periods.

The purchase of a consumer durable *today* is a validation of the entrepreneurial expectation of sales that induced the firm to hire workers and create jobs currently. This is true whether the durable is called consumption or savings. That is the logic behind Keynes's classification of all purchases of new consumer durables as D_1 spending. For those who relate the term consumption to the harvesting of utility (the classical utility consumption), the current purchase of a consumer durable is savings *out of current income*. The durable will only be 'consumed' in the future as it yields its embodied utility. Is it any wonder that Professor Friedman, and other classical economists, believe 'saving' is just as likely to create jobs today as consumption.

Once economists associate consumption with the time period in which households absorb the utility embodied in producibles, then it becomes a logically simple matter to associate the relevant income concept for explaining consumption with the future time periods over which households obtain utility from the products of industry. This semantic switch from relating D_1 with current income to associating consumption with the time sequence of obtaining utility has produced a barren semantic debate among economists involving what is the proper time-period income for consumption decisions. Had Keynes insisted that his demand categories be defined strictly in relation to current income and output, then these semantic obfuscations that gave birth to the permanent income hypothesis and the life-cycle hypothesis could have been avoided.

As early as 1937, while Keynes was still refining his taxonomic approach (e.g., by adding the finance motive to his demand for money analysis), Hicks published his IS–LM representation of what he believed was Keynes's central argument. Thirty years later, Hicks would call this IS–LM analytical system (which is discussed in Chapter 7 *infra*) 'a potted version'[3] of Keynes's theory. Hicks's truncated view gave a further impetus to a retrograde movement of modification and alteration of Keynes's new taxonomy.

In the 1940s, Dillard, Hansen, Samuelson, Modigliani, Klein, and Tobin were among others who followed Hicks's lead and attempted to provide a simplified formalization that captured what each of these authors perceived as the essence of Keynes's *General Theory* in terms of a classical vulgarization of Keynes's taxonomic analysis. These widely publicized glosses accelerated the metastatic process which transformed Keynes's revolutionary anti-classical framework into what Samuelson labelled 'neoclassical synthesis Keynesianism'. Once Keynes's lexicon was shunted aside, it was easy for Neoclassical Synthesis (Old) Keynesians, and more recently the New Keynesians, to reintroduce into models they call

'Keynesian' the axioms of the classical model that Keynes had jettisoned. As early as 1962 Joan Robinson was warning that the evolving mainstream Keynesian analysis was 'Bastard Keynesianism'.[4] Unfortunately, this reproach went unheeded by mainstream economists.

The mainstream Keynesian theory that evolved was so inconsistent with Keynes's analytical framework that by the winter of 1981–82, John Hicks, a founding father of the Neoclassical Synthesis Keynesianism, renounced this perverse approach for trying to capture the essence of Keynes's ideas. Hicks wrote 'As time has gone on, I have myself become dissatisfied with it [the IS–LM apparatus]'.[5] Nevertheless, variants of Hicks's IS–LM analysis continue to be perpetuated in economics textbooks as the basic model for macroeconomic analysis. Thus to communicate with those already familiar with this approach as well as to highlight its deficiencies, it will be necessary to develop and use the IS–LM framework and compare its implications with those of Keynes's original analysis.

MODEL BUILDING

As an aid in explaining what 'causes' the events that we observe in the real world, investigators build models as simplifications of reality. The model builders hope to capture the essential elements that 'cause' events, while trying to eliminate peripheral details that might otherwise distract attention. Mathematical models attempt to represent symbolically the essential relations among the various variables that the model builder believes are essential to the understanding of what is going on about us.[6]

The simplest mathematical model consists of a single relation expressed as an equation. The more complicated the model, the more equational relationships are encompassed within the model. Each equation has one variable on the left-hand side (LHS) of the equal sign. This LHS variable is called the dependent variable. On the right-hand side (RHS) of the equal sign one or more variables may be listed. Each of the RHS variables is called an independent variable.

An exogenous variable is any variable whose value is given from outside the model. A variable is said to be exogenous in any model if, and only if, any time it appears in the model it is always an independent variable. An endogenous variable is a variable whose value will be determined (explained) by the model. Any variable that appears in at least one equation of the model as a dependent variable is always endogenous even if it appears in other equations of the model as an independent variable.

In a one-equation model there is only one endogenous (dependent) variable, although there can be one or more exogenous variables. In a one-equation model, therefore, the model builder can explain the magnitude of one bit of information (the endogenous variable) only if information about the magnitudes of all the exogenous variables is obtained from outside the model. Since the values of the exogenous variables are always given from outside the model, the investigator does not have to explain how the information regarding the values of the exogenous variables was obtained.

For example, in the one-equation model

$$z = 2x + 3y \qquad (3.1)$$

there are three variables: one endogenous variable, z, and two exogenous variables, x and y. In order for the model to explain what the value of z will be, two bits of information, the values of x and y, must be obtained from the outside. Accordingly, if I tell you that $x = 3$ and $y = 4$, then the model 'explains' that $z = 18$. If you ask me 'why does $x = 3$ and $y = 4$?', by the rules of model building I am permitted to respond: 'I don't have to tell you since, by accepting equation (3.1), you have agreed that x and y are exogenous in this model'.

Model building then consists of trying to build more complicated multi-equation models, where independent variables in the first equation become dependent (and therefore endogenous) variables in either the second, third, fourth, etc. equations – without introducing too many new exogenous variables in the later equations. Using this methodology, more powerful models can be built. By more powerful one means that the investigator moves the exogenous variables of earlier equations to the endogenous category in subsequent equations without significantly expanding the remaining number of exogenous variables. These models are more powerful because fewer bits of information are required from the outside to explain more within the model.

THE KEYNESIAN MODEL AND THE MULTIPLIER

Keynes's simple two-equation Keynesian model involved an aggregate supply function

$$Z = f_z(N) \qquad (3.2)$$

and an aggregate demand function

$$D = D_1 \, [= f_1(N)] + D_2. \qquad (3.3)$$

If we impose the equilibrium condition on these two equations that $D = Z$, then $[f_1(N) + D_2] - f_z(N) = 0$. The equilibrium values of Z (and D) can be expressed entirely in terms of the exogenous variable D_2:

$$Z - f_1(N) = D_2. \tag{3.4}$$

Instead of using this two-equation Keynes model, early Keynesians started with the one-equation model:

$$Y = C + I + G + F \tag{3.5}$$

where Y is aggregate supply or gross national product (GNP), C is consumption expenditures, I is gross investment expenditures, G is government expenditures, and F is the net sales in the foreign sector.

Initially, the purpose of the model is to explain how unemployment can exist in the simplest type of economy in the absence of government interference. We begin with a closed economy ($F = 0$) where there is no government spending ($G = 0$). Equation (3.5) reduces to

$$Y = C + I \tag{3.6}$$

where the value of current output (Y) is equal to the aggregate current income flow earned during the accounting period.[7]

In this one-equation model, there are two exogenous variables, C and I, and one endogenous variable Y. Thus, if one wants to explain (predict?) the magnitude of Y in the next period, one must obtain the next period's value of C and I from outside the model. For example, if next period $C = 1\,000$ and $I = 200$, then the next period's output will be $1\,200$.

The problem with this simple one-equation model is that a large amount of information (the values of C and I) has to be obtained from outside the model, for so little to be 'explained' within the model. Mainstream Keynesians expanded the system to a two-equation model:

$$Y = C + I \tag{3.6}$$

$$C = f(Y). \tag{3.7}$$

Equation (3.7) represents the propensity to consume. In this two equation system, there are two endogenous variables (Y and C) and one exogenous variable (I). Given the magnitude of I from outside, the model will determine the values for C and Y. To give some concreteness to this argument, suppose we assume that the specific function of the propensity to consume is

$$C = a_1 + b_1 Y \qquad (3.8)$$

where a and b are parameters or constants in the system (similar to the numbers 2 and 3 in equation (3.1)).

In the *General Theory*, Keynes argued that there are many other factors besides current income that could affect the spending of households on current output. These other factors (e.g., changes in consumer preferences, interest rates, taxes) are of secondary importance for understanding the relationship between D_1 spending and any level of current employment. In other words, although changes in these 'other' factors could alter the volume of D_1 spending at any level of employment, and therefore alter the values of the a's and b's of equation (3.8), as a first approximation, fluctuations in other factors could be swept away under the *ceteris paribus* assumption. 'We are left therefore, with the conclusion that in a given situation the propensity to consume may be considered a fairly stable function'[8] relating household consumption to current income. The term 'stable' in this context means that the magnitudes associated with the a and b parameters of equation (3.8) can be considered to be unchanged during the period of time that the 'given situation' lasts. Any change in these 'other factors' will alter the parameter values in equation (3.8).

Keynes claimed there was a 'fundamental psychological law, upon which we are entitled to depend with great confidence both *a priori* from our knowledge of human nature and from the detailed facts of experience ... that men are disposed, as a rule and on the average, to increase their consumption as their income increases, but not as much as the increase in their income'.[9] Keynes's psychological law means that the magnitude of the b parameter of equation (3.8) must be greater than zero but less than one, i.e., $0 < b_1 < 1$. The parameter b_1 is called the marginal propensity to consume. It measures the change in consumption associated with a change in income. If, for example, the marginal propensity to consume (b_1) is equal to 0.8, then if income increases by say \$100, this fundamental law indicates that consumption spending will rise by only \$80. In this arithmetical example, substituting (3.8) into (3.6) and solving for Y yields:

$$Y = [1/(1 - b_1)] (a_1 + I). \qquad (3.9)$$

The term in the square brackets in equation (3.9) is called the *multiplier*. Assuming b_1 is equal to 0.8, then the multiplier would have a value of 5. Further assume that a_1 is equal to \$400. If the value of the exogenous variable (*I*) in this model is $1 000, then the model determines that GNP is equal to $7 000. Alternatively, if the exogenous value of *I* is $1 500, then GNP is $9 500.

INTERPRETING THE MULTIPLIER MODEL AS A CONTROLLED EXPERIMENT

How do most economists interpret these mathematical manipulations using the multiplier and different values of the exogenous investment variable? Since economists try to portray themselves as 'scientists', their models are depicted as the symbolic equivalent of the controlled experiment in the 'hard sciences'. In a controlled experimental environment, the investigator chooses two like populations of subjects – one is designated the control group, the other the experimental group. The investigator designs the experiment so that the values of all possible variables are initially the same for the two groups. Then the value of only one variable for the experimental group is altered and any significant differences that occur between the two groups are recorded.

For example, suppose a scientist wishes to investigate whether the absence of Vitamin C in the diet will 'cause' the disease known as scurvy. Rats whose genetic make-up is as similar as possible are obtained. The rats are randomly sorted into two cages, an experimental cage and a control cage. The rats are fed identical diets except that the food of the experimental group will have all the vitamin C removed. The investigator records how many animals in each group develop scurvy over a period of time.

This experiment is designed to disprove the null hypothesis that the absence of vitamin C does *not* cause scurvy to develop. Given certain conventionally acceptable rules regarding statistical significance, if a significantly large number of rats in the experimental group develop scurvy compared to the control group, the investigator can reject the null hypothesis and, in the absence of any further evidence, the investigator can tentatively accept the alternative hypothesis that a lack of vitamin C is associated with the disease scurvy. This leads to the conclusion that taking vitamin C in one's diet will prevent the onset of scurvy.

In a similar manner, economists interpret multiplier data as follows: Suppose we have two economies, A and B. Both A and B are characterized by the same equations (3.6) and (3.8). Assume both economies have a marginal propensity to consume of 0.8. The control economy A is exposed to exogenous spending of $1 000, while the experimental economy B receives $1 500 worth of exogenous spending. The resulting GNP is $7 000 for economy A and $9 500 for economy B.

If these results are from a controlled experiment environment, then the economist can accept the argument that the GNP in B is $2 500 larger than in A because exogenous investment spending in B is $500 higher than in A.[10]

Of course, no real world controlled experiment was done to generate our arithmetic results. Only a conceptual one was undertaken. Consequently, using the two-equation multiplier model to predict the future level of aggregate income resulting from a change in exogenous spending can be quite misleading. A more cautious but accurate statement would be:

> If an economy experiences more exogenous spending, say an additional $500, next period than it would in other circumstances, and if equations (3.6) and (3.8) correctly characterize the economy's structure *in the next period* and the marginal propensity to consume is equal to 0.8, then the resulting GNP will be a multiple of 5 times the $500 greater exogenous spending than GNP would be if this additional exogenous spending did not take place.

Unfortunately such cautious but accurate statements are unlikely to please real world politicians and entrepreneurs who have to make decisions today and who do not want such waffling conditional forecasts regarding future outcomes.

WHY IS THE MULTIPLIER GREATER THAN UNITY?

Table 3.1 provides a simple economic illustration of why the multiplier is greater than unity. Assume a closed economy where $b_1 = 0.8$. Assume initially an additional $500 of exogenous spending on goods produced at Mr. Brown's factory. The first line (first round) of Table 3.1 shows that this initial spending creates $500 of additional spending for Mr. Brown and his workers. On the second round (line 2 of Table 3.1) Brown and his employees, having earned an extra $500, will endogenously spend an additional $400 on the products of Ms. Smith's factory. Ms. Smith and her workers having earned an additional $400 of income will spend, on the third round, an additional $320 on the products of Mr. Jones's factory. This will induce a fourth round increase in consumption of $256. This process of inducing additional consumption will continue over an infinite number of additional rounds, while the additional consumption spending stimulated in each round declines.

Table 3.1 illustrates the result of this conceptual 'rounds' experiment. It shows that an additional exogenous increase in investment expenditures of $500 induces, at the limit, an additional $2 000 in consumption spending. The resulting aggregate income increase is $2 500.

Table 3.1   A hypothetical conceptual 'rounds' experiment

Round	Additional exogenous investment spending	Additional endogenous consumption spending	Additional income
1	500		500
2		400	400
3		320	320
4		256	256
.	. . .	. . .	. . .
.	. . .	. . .	. . .
.	. . .	. . .	. . .
	$500	$2 000	$2 500

ALTERNATIVE CONSUMPTION HYPOTHESIS

As suggested earlier, the developers of the neoclassical synthesis (Old) Keynesian approach failed to comprehend the importance of Keynes's taxonomic division of aggregate demand into two exhaustive categories, one related to current income and the other not related to current income. As a consequence, a semantic dispute filled the mainstream economic literature. The question became what should be the proper consumption and income concept to be used in Keynes's propensity to consume relationship? This digression diverted attention from the taxonomic foundation of Keynes's revolution. The discussion degenerated into a dispute over the relevant income concept necessary to provide an empirical consumption function that exhibited the greatest statistical stability over a long period of calendar time.

In 1937 the Swedish economist Bertril Ohlin criticized Keynes for treating current income as the primary determinant of current consumption expenditures. Ohlin wrote:

> On what does this total sum of planned consumption depend? First of all on the consumer's expectations. Not his expected income during the first coming period only, but on what he expects to earn over a long period in the future. . . . This fact every American is willing to testify today; most of them expect growing incomes and base their consumption plans thereon . . . they actually correlate consumption plans and income expectations for many future periods.[11]

Years later similar criticisms by Friedman and Modigliani provided them with the lever to promote their own views under the labels of the permanent income hypothesis and the life-cycle hypothesis of consumption respectively. These hypotheses attempted to formalize Ohlin's criticism in a mathematical model of classical utility consumption over a long-term horizon.

The Permanent Income Hypothesis

Using the classical microtheory of utility consumption concept, Friedman developed the *permanent income theory of consumption*. In Friedman's lexicon today's income is divided into two components: transitory (or windfall) income and permanent income. Transitory income is associated with one-shot, non-repeatable changes in current income, e.g., winning the state lottery, or receiving a one-time bonus at work. Permanent income was defined in terms of long-term income flows that a forward-looking consumer can expect to receive each future period throughout his or her life. Friedman argued that any change in permanent income will affect consumption, while changes in transitory income will have little or no effect on consumption. Technically this implies that the marginal propensity to consume out of permanent income is less than, but close to, one. The marginal propensity to consume out of temporary income is approximately zero as all transitory income increments are saved. Friedman developed empirical evidence that, he claims, supports his permanent income hypothesis while these 'facts' are incompatible with Keynes's measured current income theory of consumption.[12]

In developing his analysis, Friedman uses the terms consumption and savings in a way that not only differs from Keynes's taxonomy, but would also appear strange to the ordinary layperson not educated in the lexicon of classical economics. Friedman designates consumption as 'the value of services consumed [utility]' during the period. Friedman's measure of consumption in any year is equal to the depreciation (or wearing out) of existing durables each year plus the year's purchase of all nondurables and services.[13] Savings are measured as anything that is purchased today that is not consumed today. To a layperson it might be a shock to discover that the purchase of a new gas-guzzling sports car is, in Friedman's taxonomy, primarily a form of private savings. Only that portion of the utility value of the sports car that depreciates during the current accounting period is classified as consumption. So unless the consumer totally wrecks his new car driving out of the showroom most of the purchase price will be recorded as savings in Friedman's scheme.

Friedman prides himself on *not* defining as consumption the purchase of currently produced durables such as ostentatious sports cars, mink coats, yachts, etc. Indeed, Professor Friedman boasts that his taxonomy is superior to others because 'much that one classified as consumption is reclassified as savings'.[14] When transitory (windfall) income is received, Friedman suggests 'Is not the windfall likely to be used for the purchase of durable goods?'.[15] If so, then by definition Friedman has validated his hypothesis that transitory incomes will (almost) always be 'saved' and not consumed. If a household suddenly received a large one-time windfall, how many additional nondurables could the household purchase *in the current accounting period*?

The average layperson would be surprised to learn that if he or she won a million dollar lottery and spent the receipts on newly produced yachts, fast cars, jewellery, mink coats, etc. these purchases are *not* classified as conspicuous consumption by mainstream economists but are instead judicious private savings. Such uncommon use of common language can be highly misleading. It encourages the uninitiated to believe that saving *per se* creates jobs just as much as consumption, even though the layperson associates savings with not spending income on the products of industry. Moreover saving is even better for society for it creates utility for the future.[16] Of course purchases of yachts and jewellery create jobs today in these durable goods-producing industries. These purchases are consumption in Keynes's lexicon. They are primarily savings in Friedman's.

The Life-cycle Hypothesis

Modigliani's life-cycle theory of consumption is based on the notion that people's earnings are bunched in fewer years than the life span during which they consume goods. Households attempt to finance consumption purchases during their early family formation years by borrowing, that is, by buying more than they earn in an accounting period. In their peak earning years, households earn more than they spend in each year as they pay off their earlier borrowings and save for retirement. During the retirement years, households earn less than they spend, i.e., they dissave.

Figures 3.1a and b reproduce the typical textbook illustration of consumption versus income and savings pattern over a life cycle of a typical consumer. In the first 20 years of life, the consumer is a normally a dependent in his or her parent's household. Accordingly, his or her consumption and income earnings pattern start only when he or she forms his or her own household. Figure 3.1a indicates that the typical income pattern will be that the household will start at a low level when the consumer is approximately 20 years old. Income of the average worker tends to rise with age and experience until it peaks somewhere between the age of 50 and 60 years. After retirement, income drops fairly sharply.

This typical worker's consumption pattern is much smoother over his

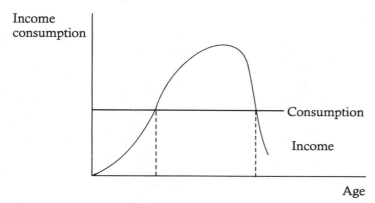

Figure 3.1a   Consumption versus income over the life cycle

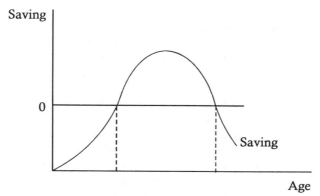

Figure 3.1b   Savings pattern over the life cycle

life span. (In the textbook illustration adopted here, consumption per year is presumed constant.) In the early years, the worker tends to borrow (dissave) to spend more than his or her income. During the middle to peak income years, the worker, according to the life-cycle hypothesis, tends to consume less than he or she earns each year, using the resulting saving first to pay off the debt that financed earlier years' consumption and then to put away financial provision for the retirement years. The life-cycle hypothesis presumes that during the retirement years the consumer dissaves, i.e., spends more than his or her income as he or she exhausts his or her wealth to maintain consumption. If the utility-maximizing worker has correctly foreseen the duration of his or her life span then he or she should be spending his or her last dime of savings close to his or her last minute of life.

Clearly, the life-cycle hypothesis is closely related to the permanent income hypothesis where both presume a lifetime marginal propensity to consume out of lifetime (permanent) income of unity.

One implication of the life-cycle hypothesis is that the young and old cohorts of the population will have low saving rates (i.e., a high average and marginal propensity to consume) out of current income while middle-aged people should exhibit high saving rates. The facts are not consistent with this implication of cohort consumption propensity. Investigators at the University of Wisconsin's Institute for the Study of Poverty, for example, studied a sample of 9 494 households. These investigators estimated the average propensity to consume for these households. Consumption expenditures were measured as out-of-pocket expenditures on food, housing, clothing, transportation, other nondurable goods and services plus the value of consumption flows (depreciation) of major consumer durables for each household. Income was measured after federal and state taxes plus the estimated rental value of owner-occupied housing, durables, and vehicles.

The results were compared by age groups and by the position of different age groups in the income distribution. For any level of income, the investigators found that average propensity to consume *decreased* with age. The investigators concluded that 'this study refutes a central prediction of the "textbook" version of the life cycle hypothesis – that the elderly dissave out of accumulated wealth to finance the continuation of preretirement consumption levels for retirement. In fact, our results show that the elderly spend less than the nonelderly at the same level of income and that the very oldest of the elderly have the lowest average propensity to consume . . . the expectation created by the life cycle hypothesis about the relationship between savings and age that underlies much theorizing . . . and important policy judgments does not appear to accord with the facts. It seems rather late for this discovery'.[17]

The moral associated with these alternative consumption hypotheses is that when Keynes's logical precise D_1 classification was converted into everyday language, the analysis relating current employment and aggregate demand was open to the abuse of individuals redefining vernacular words to fit their own purposes. In the ensuing discussion of which income concept was relevant for 'explaining' consumers' spending plans (as opposed to 'explaining' what spending was directly related to employment and aggregate income flows), professional attention was diverted from Keynes's analytical system. Little was gained but most of Keynes's revolution was lost.

NOTES

1. These latter characteristics, however, may be relevant in distinguishing between land and water animals. This suggests that the relevant properties for a specific taxonomy may be related to the problem under investigation.
2. J.M. Keynes, *The General Theory*, p. 96.
3. The term 'a potted version' is what Hicks used to describe his famous 1937 article 'Mr. Keynes and the Classics'. See J.R. Hicks, *Critical Essays in Monetary Theory*, Oxford University Press, Oxford, 1967, p. vii.
4. J. Robinson, review of 'Money, Trade and Economic Growth', *Economic Journal*, **72**, 1962, p. 691.
5. J.R. Hicks, 'IS–LM: An Explanation', *Journal of Post Keynesian Economics*, **3**, Winter 1980–81, p. 139.
6. Humankind cannot conceive of events being merely chaotic or random affairs. For the investigative mind both chaos and random events can be explained by well-defined models relating cause and effects.
7. The National Income and Product Accounts (NIPA), a double-entry bookkeeping system, records the market value of output as equal to the gross national income each accounting period.
8. J.M. Keynes, *The General Theory*, p. 95.
9. J.M. Keynes, *The General Theory*, p. 96. Although Keynes did not specify what detailed facts of experience he was relying on, Engel's curves relating incomes and specific categories of expenditures were readily available and would have supported this claimed 'law'.
10. If the marginal propensity to consume is 2/3, then the multiplier would be 3, and a $500 increase in exogenous spending results in an increase in GNP of only $1 500.
11. B. Ohlin, 'Some Notes of the Stockholm Theory of Savings and Investment I', *The Economic Journal*, **47**, 1937, pp. 62–3.
12. Milton Friedman, *The Theory of Permanent Income*, Princeton University Press, Princeton, 1957.
13. See M. Friedman, op. cit., p. 11. By definition, all nondurable goods and services must yield their utility during the current period.
14. M. Friedman, *Theory of Permanent Income*, p. 28.
15. Ibid., p. 28.
16. This may help explain the preponderance of mainstream support for policies that promote savings at the expense of consumption.
17. S. Danziger, J. Van der Haag, E. Smolensky, and M.K. Taussig, 'The Life Cycle Hypothesis and the Consumption Behavior of the Elderly', *Journal of Post Keynesian Economics*, **5**, 1982–83, pp. 224–6. This landmark study has never been refuted by any other empirical evidence. Despite these facts, mainstream textbooks continue to treat the life-cycle hypothesis and the related permanent income hypothesis as if they were applicable to the facts of experience.

4. Investment spending

Keynes's expenditure category D_2 was linked to the 'amount which it [the community] is expected to devote for new investment'.[1] In everyday speech, the term investment connotes different kinds of purchases in different contexts.

For the individual, investment denotes the purchase of something today that is expected to enhance one's cash inflows in the future. For the ordinary person the term investment is applied equally to the purchase of equity or debt securities (i.e., stocks and bonds) on an organized exchange market or to the purchase of a real durable good to be used in further production and exchange processes. Yet in macroeconomic textbooks the term investment is always associated with the latter concept and never with the former.

To avoid semantic problems in the following discussion, precise definitions of a number of key concepts underlining Keynes's analysis must be developed.

INVESTMENT, MARKETS, AND LIQUIDITY CONCEPTS

Investment

In everyday speech, investment purchases fall into two broad classes of asset purchases. These are the purchases of:

1. *Financial assets or securities* such as equities, bonds and other debt instruments. These securities may be newly issued or, if they are traded on an organized exchange, they may be purchased secondhand from other holders. The secondhand securities may have been issued many years earlier than the current period.
2. *Real assets or capital goods* such as plant and equipment. These capital goods are durable commodities that can be used in the production of ⁔s and services that are expected to be sold at a future date. These ⁔ may be either newly produced or purchased second hand. The ⁔roduced some time before the current period.

48

The purchase of financial assets is never an investment in Keynes's lexicon. From the standpoint of the community any transaction involving financial assets is an *asset transfer* between the buyer and the seller. The buyer has exchanged the asset money for the financial asset. The seller has transferred the possession of the asset for money.

If the financial asset is a new issue, it creates a new entry on the liability side of the seller's balance sheet to offset the asset improvement in the buyer's balance sheet. If a secondhand asset is involved, the seller is disinvesting assets by an amount equal to the buyer's investment. For the economy as a whole, the investment and disinvestment cancel.

Similarly, if secondhand capital goods can be resold, this resale is an *asset transfer* between buyer and seller. No community investment is involved. Only the purchase of newly produced real capital goods is an investment expenditure in Keynes's macroeconomic analysis.

Markets and Liquidity

In a market system, all purchases are made on either a spot market or a forward market. A *spot market* is any market where buyers and sellers contract for immediate payment and delivery at the moment of contract. A *forward* market is any market where the buyer and seller enter into a contractual agreement today for payment and delivery at specific dates in the future. A *contract* is a legal agreement between the parties to perform specific actions at a specified time. The contract is enforceable by the State under the civil law of contracts. In an entrepreneurial system, contracts are used to organize efficient production and exchange transactions.

Liquidity means the ability to meet all contractual obligations when they are due. *Money* is, by definition, the thing that legally discharges all contractual obligations. Money is, therefore, the liquid asset *par excellence*. Other assets may possess some lesser degree of liquidity depending on how well organized and orderly the market is for the resaleability of the asset for money.[2]

Liquid assets are financial assets that are traded in well-organized, orderly spot markets. A well-organized market is one where it is not costly to bring buyers and sellers together. A well-organized market requires a standardized product with low carrying costs. An orderly market means that changes in market prices can be expected to be small and appropriate given the news of the day. An orderly market requires an institution known as a 'market maker'. A *market maker* is defined as someone who publicly announces a willingness to act as a residual buyer or seller to assure orderliness if an abrupt disruptive change occurs on either the demand or supply side of the market. The market maker, following the preannounced rules of that market, guarantees that the next market price will not differ chaotically from the last transaction price despite the disruption.

To operate, the market maker requires a buffer stock of the asset being traded plus a significant stock of money (and/or immediate access to obtain additional money when required). When demand or supply tends towards unruly changes that threaten large swings in market prices, the market maker steps in to buy in a declining market, or sell in an advancing market to limit the otherwise too rapid market price movements.

A credible market-making institution is necessary if the public is going to consider a market orderly.[3] The existence of a market-making institution allows holders of the asset to sleep peacefully at night 'knowing' that the opening spot price tomorrow will not differ significantly from the closing price today.

Fully liquid assets are any assets that can be immediately converted into (resold for) money in a spot market where a market maker *'guarantees'* a fixed and unchanging net spot money price. A holder of a fully liquid asset can always sell out his or her position in that asset to obtain immediate access to a guaranteed quantity of cash as long as the market maker maintains his or her pledge.

Money is the basic fully liquid asset of the system because the spot price of money in terms of itself is certain and unchanging (no capital gain or loss in nominal terms is possible) as long as society honours and obeys the civil law of contracts.

Liquid assets are durables traded in well-organized, orderly markets where the market maker assures that the next price will not differ significantly from the last transaction price.

Illiquid assets are durables whose spot (resale) market is poorly organized, disorderly, thin or even notional because there is no market maker to organize the market.

Only liquid or fully liquid assets are held as a *store of value for liquidity purposes*. Illiquid assets may have value. The holder of an illiquid asset cannot expect to convert this value immediately into money if a sudden need for liquidity occurs.[4] Holders of illiquid assets are typically entrepreneurs who believe that they can use a specific real asset to produce a future flow of outputs that will be sold at a series of expected future dates for money at market prices that are more than the money cost of producing the flow of output.[5] This expected dated stream of future net money income flows (or quasi-rents) is the sole reason for demanding illiquid assets such as plant and equipment capital.

The boundaries between fully liquid, liquid, and illiquid assets are not watertight or even unchanging over time. The degree of liquidity associated with any asset depends on the degree of organization and orderliness of the relevant spot market at each moment of time. Depending on social practices and institutions, the degree of liquidity of any asset can change from time to time if the operating rules of the market maker change. Differences in degree of liquidity among assets are reflected in differences in the transaction costs and the stickiness of the money spot price over time. The smaller the transactions costs and/or the greater the stickiness, *ceteris paribus*, the greater the degree of liquidity of any asset. These factors depend, in large part, on the ability of a market maker maintaining orderliness.

Capital goods. 'It is by reason of the existence of durable equipment that the economic future is linked to the present ... therefore ... the expectations of the future should affect the present through the demand price for durable equipment'.[6] Plant and equipment are the main forms of fixed capital that are desired primarily for their use in the production process, i.e., for the dated net money income stream they are expected to yield over their useful lives. Real capital goods are illiquid since the spot markets for reselling these assets are thin, poorly organized, disorderly and discontinuous, if they exist at all.[7]

For any given short-period expectations of future sales, there is also an entrepreneurial demand for a minimum stock of raw material, semi-finished, and finished products that entrepreneurs consider necessary either to avoid the possibility of interrupting the production process or to iron out normal seasonal patterns. These inventories are called working capital or goods-in-process.

If, at any point of time, this stock of working capital exceeds the quantity that would normally be held to implement an efficient short-period production plan and if there is a *continuous, well-organized resale spot market* for specific working capital goods (e.g., the crude oil market), then the working capital surplus excess can be considered *liquid capital*. In the aggregate, stocks of liquid capital will exist only when there is a surfeit of working capital. (To ease the exposition the possibility of liquid capital will be ignored at this point. A further discussion will be found infra).

Working capital demand is normally directly related to entrepreneurial short-term production plans. The demand for fixed capital is primarily associated with long-term expectations of future net money income streams stretching far into the future. Unless it is specified otherwise in what follows, the demand for capital or investment can be considered synonymous with the demand for fixed capital.

CAPITAL, SAVINGS AND LIQUIDITY

Durability is a characteristic possessed by capital goods and by money and other financial assets (e.g., stocks, bonds). This quality of *durability* makes capital goods a primary form of wealth and a capitalized source of dated future income. Classical economic theorists, therefore, conceive of the demand for capital as primarily the demand for a store of value in the sense of embodying a stream of future utility.

Pre-Keynesian writers and today's classically-trained mainstream economists believe that the act of savings (i.e., the decision to abstain from consumption out of current income) is a demand to store value in durable, producible capital goods. This conflating of savings with the demand for producible capital goods underlies the Say's Law fallacy that today's increased desire to save on the part of households is the same thing as an increased desire to buy real *producible* capital goods today.

For Keynes, an act of savings does 'not necessitate' the purchase of any producible durables today or 'a week hence or a year hence or to consume any specific thing at any specified time'.[8] Today's desire to save is a desire to transfer command of unspecified resources to the indefinite and uncertain future.[9] Savers have to engage the two-step decision process illustrated in Figure 4.1.

In the first step, *the time preference decision*, each income-receiving household and firm chooses how to allocate current income between how much will be spent on D_1 (consumption) and how much will *not* be spent on currently produced goods and services, i.e., how much will be saved or non-consumption.[10] The second step, *the liquidity preference decision*,

Figure 4.1   Decisions about the use of current income

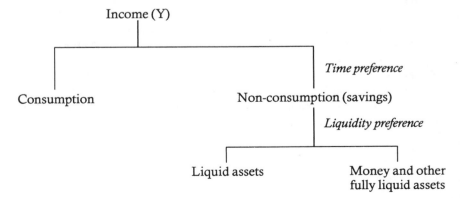

requires the saver to decide how to allocate this unspent income among alternative time machines (liquid stores of value) that can transport generalized purchasing power from today to the indefinite future.

In a monetary economy, all claims on resources are exercised through the use of money contracts. Only money can be used to settle contractual commitments for the purchase of goods and services today and at any future date. Saving involves not exercising currently earned claims (today's income). To move today's saving without committing these claims to the purchase of any specific resources at any specific future date requires storing these claims in assets that can be readily converted (liquidated) into money at any future date at the option of the holder. Only fully liquid and liquid assets can play this time-machine role. Illiquid assets, by definition, cannot provide liquidity at a currently unknown future date when the holder may want to exercise a claim on resources in excess of expected income on that date.

Keynes's concept of savings implies that in a monetary economy the saver's demand for a liquidity time machine does not require the use of current resources to satisfy this liquidity demand. Liquid assets, unlike the products of industry, are not produced by labour in the private sector.[11] The decision to save, therefore, will not create *per se* demand for illiquid real capital. This conclusion of Keynes is in stark contrast to the classical belief that any increase in households' demand for savings out of current income is equivalent to an expansion in demand for additional investment in newly produced real capital goods.

When 'Keynesians' ignored Keynes's taxonomy, it became impossible to dislodge this classical fallacy from their minds. The classical sophism that the decision to save meant a decision to buy producible durables was quickly resurrected in the economic growth literature.[12]

The Keynes–Post Keynesian perspective is that an entrepreneurial market economy where the future is uncertain is essentially different from a classical world. The former involves the use of a nonproducible money and the development of financial markets with intermediaries who 'make' the market by operating as residual buyers and sellers. This assures that:

1. readily reproducible capital goods are illiquid assets that will be demanded primarily as a factor of production rather than as a liquid store of value;
2. money is demanded both as a means of contractual settlement (i.e., exchange) and as a liquid store of value, i.e., a vehicle for transferring generalized purchasing power over time; while
3. titles to capital goods and debt contracts – securities – are demanded primarily as liquid stores of value, rather than to gain control of the

underlying real capital. Accordingly, there is a separation of ownership from control of real capital.[13]

ATTRIBUTES OF DURABLE ASSETS

It is the durability of all assets – money, capital goods, and securities – which links the uncertain economic future with the present. In the obscure and oft-neglected Chapters 16 and 17 of *The General Theory*, Keynes wrestled with the problem of trying to extricate himself from the short-period framework of the rest of his book. The essence of these chapters involves the problem of financing the demand for additional investments as the real wealth of the community accumulates.[14]

Keynes noted three attributes which all durable assets possess in different degrees and which affect their desirability: (1) q, the expected quasi-rents or money value of the output, net of the running expenses, which can be obtained by assisting some process of production or supplying services to a consumer; (2) c, the carrying costs (including wastage) of the asset over the period; and (3) l, the liquidity premium which arises from the power of disposal of the asset during the period.[15]

In a monetary economy the power of disposal over an asset involves the ease of reselling the asset for money in a well-organized, orderly spot market. The degree of liquidity cannot be discussed independently of the financial institutions that make the spot market for particular durables. For any asset that is simultaneously the means of contractual settlement as well as a store of value, the power of disposal must, by definition, be the greatest.

Kaldor prefers to treat Keynes's liquidity premium due to the power of disposal as a marginal risk premium, r, measure of the degree of illiquidity. The risk premium r represents a deduction from the net yield $(q - c)$ of the asset where 'the *uncertainty* of future value (or return) in terms of money, or on account of their imperfect marketability, carries a risk premium for which this yield must compensate'.[16] For Kaldor r represents the potential cost to the holder if he or she attempts to convert his or her store of value into money at some unspecific and unknown date when he or she may have to exercise command of resources in excess of his or her future cash income at that future time.[17] Explicit in the Kaldor formulation is the fact of a 'convenience yield' to the holding of money for which $r = 0$. For our immediate purpose it is a matter of indifference whether the Keynes l concept or Kaldor's r is used, since they are essentially mirror images of each other.

A fourth possible attribute of durables is a, the expected appreciation (or depreciation) in the money price of the asset at the end of the period compared with the current market price.[18] This quality of expected appreciation (or depreciation) is relevant only if there is a well-organized, continuous and orderly market for the durable.[19] For all illiquid assets, $a = 0$ and $l = 0$.

Keynes tended to measure the attributes of q, c, l, and a in a unit equal to a percentage (per period) of the initial cost of the asset to normalize for differing life expectancies of the various assets and differing initial costs. In most of what follows it will be more useful to conceive of these attributes in units of absolute dollar sums per period over the lives of the various assets. This latter unit of measure can be directly converted into the demand price of the asset (in the mind of the holder) by a present value calculation.

Investors are, by definition, not primarily interested in titles to real capital goods as a liquid store of value; their object is to acquire the services of real capital as inputs for the production process. To obtain the services of capital goods investors must acquire the physical presence of the capital stock; but what is relevant to the profit-maximizing firm's calculations is the *marginal unit supply price of the service* of the capital factor. Investors do not necessarily want title to the stock of capital. (Similarly, firms do not care whether they own their labour force (slaves) or allow others to hold title to the factor called labour. What is relevant is the marginal supply price of labour services.)

Savers are interested in protecting and possibly increasing the value of their liquid asset holdings. Savers want an *undated* source of liquidity available at any time in the future. Even if a well-organized spot resale market for plant and equipment existed, the market value of these capital goods would be less than the spot price of the associated debt and equity securities. If a saver possessed a physical capital instrument and intended to convert his or her store of value (e.g., a sausage machine) into future consumption goods in an earlier time pattern than the stream of anticipated earnings over the life of the sausage machine he or she would, at some point of time, have to find a sausage machine buyer. In selling, he or she would almost certainly disrupt the machine's physical (and value) productivity yield and incur delivery costs to dismantle and transport the equipment to the buyer. Moreover, since real capital assets are normally large indivisible physical units, the saver may be required to search out a buyer of the whole unit in a future period, even if he or she desires only to increase consumption in that period by some amount smaller than the expected value of the whole physical asset. The smaller the unit of asset, *ceteris paribus*, the greater its saleability is likely to be. Thus, as Makower and Marschak have shown, sales of large units 'not only increase the dispersion of future yields, but also reduce their actuarial values'.[20]

Accordingly, the problem of finding a buyer for a machine is likely to be complex and costly. It is here that financial titles are clearly superior to real physical goods as liquid stores of value. Financial assets can be bought and sold without any physical disruption to the asset usage. Values of fractionalized titles to physical goods are worth more than the indivisible physical goods themselves.

Since savers are interested in titles to real capital as a liquid store of value, while entrepreneurs desire the flow of productive services from capital goods, savers' liquidity preference decisions and entrepreneurs' investment decisions will look towards different price levels. Capital investment decisions depend on the market demand price relative to the minimum flow supply of capital goods. Liquidity decisions depend on the price of securities relative to their expected future price and the fear of being illiquid. The sole direct relationship between these decisions consists of the interest rate as the price for giving up a degree of liquidity relative to holding money, and the discount rate mechanism used in arriving at an estimate of the present value of the future stream of quasi-rents expected from the use of any real capital goods in the production and exchange processes.

The analysis in the rest of this chapter concentrates on the investment decision for *it* is the one that determines the rate of capital accumulation. The liquid store of value-holding decision will be discussed in detail in later chapters. At this stage it will be assumed that all increments in household wealth are stored only in money or other liquid financial assets and that the Monetary Authority provides an endogenous money supply at an exogenous interest rate so that a shortage of finance is never a constraint on the rate of investment.

THE DEMAND AND SUPPLY OF CAPITAL GOODS

The demand for fixed capital can be viewed, as a first approximation, as solely due to the desire of entrepreneurs to use capital to obtain the expected quasi-rents over their useful lives.[21] The demand price for fixed capital goods can therefore be associated solely with the sum of the discounted values of $(q - c)$.

If, at any point of time, the demand price for plant and equipment exceeds the minimum short-period flow-supply price necessary to encourage capital goods producers to exert the effort necessary to produce units in the current period, then there is an incentive for entrepreneurs to order new capital goods. If, on the other hand, the demand price is less than the minimum flow-supply price, there will be no current production of that asset.

This simple mechanism of comparing the demand price with the flow-supply price of capital goods[22] has been neglected in the economic literature in favour of a comparison of the expected rate of return on capital relative to the rate of interest. This latter view has not only been unproductive but it has encouraged many economists to search for a factor (such as the marginal physical productivity of capital expressed as an annual percentage) that is the *real* determinant of the *real* rate of return on capital goods. Although Keynes used the concept of the marginal efficiency of capital (defined as equal to a rate of discount[23]), Keynes always viewed the production of investment goods in a monetary economy as depending on the comparison of the demand price with the flow-supply price (or replacement costs). Keynes dismissed the notion that a marginal physical productivity of capital concept determined either the interest rate or the earnings of plant and equipment.[24]

Changes in the demand price relative to the flow-supply price of capital is the mechanism determining the rate of investment. This Keynesian demand price–supply price mechanism deserves elaboration.

If firms require the services of capital goods as inputs in the production process, then they must acquire the physical capital goods.[25] Each firm's demand for the flow of capital services leads to a *demand for a stock of capital goods*. 'If $Q_r [= (q - c)_r]$ is the prospective yield from an asset at time r and d_r is the present value of £1 deferred r years *at the current rate of interest*, $\Sigma Q_r d_r$, is the demand price of the investment'.[26] The demand price schedule for each unit of capital for each firm is therefore calculated in terms of an estimated present value:

$$PV = [Q_1 d_1] + [Q_2 d_2] + \ldots + [Q_n d_n] \qquad (4.1)$$

where PV is the estimated present value, Q_1 is the expected net quasi-rent in the first year, Q_n is the net quasi-rent in the nth year, $d_1 = [1/(1 + i)]$, $d_2 = [1/(1 + i)^2]$, $d_n = [1/(1 + i)^n]$, and i is the current rate of interest.[27]

Plotting these estimated demand prices on the ordinate axis and the quantity of capital (K) on the abscissa yields the stock demand curve for capital for a given firm.[28] The aggregate demand for a stock of capital goods at a point of time is derived from the summation of the demand curves of all firms. This stock demand curve for capital includes the Wicksteedian reservation demand of holders of existing capital at each moment of time. The capital stock demand curve in Figure 4.2 is D_k. It relates the maximum quantity of the capital good desired to be held by firms at alternative market prices, given quasi-rent expectations, the discount rate, and the number of firms in the economy:

$$D_k = f_1 (p_k, i, \phi, E) \qquad (4.2)$$

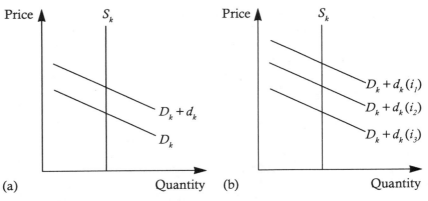

Figure 4.2   Demand and supply of capital

where D_k is the stock demand quantity for capital, p_k is the market price of capital goods, i is the rate of discount (related to the rate of interest), ϕ is a set of expectations about the growth in demand and the consequent future stream of quasi-rents which can be expected to be earned by each unit of capital, and E represents the number of entrepreneurial investors who can obtain finance for their demand for capital goods, where

$$f'_{1pk} < 0, \ f'_{1i} < 0, \ f'_{1\phi} > 0, \ f'_{1E} > 0.$$

As long as entrepreneurs prefer investment projects associated with expected quasi-rents that have higher present values per dollar of finance to those projects that have lower present values per dollar of finance committed,[29] the D_k will be downward sloping.[30]

Writing the stock demand for capital as equation (4.2) may suggest an undue precision to the reader unless he or she is made aware of the complexities and interdependencies underlying the symbols. Essentially,

> the demand-price of capital goods . . . depends on two things – on the estimated net prospective yield from fixed capital (estimated by the opinion of the market after such allowances as they choose to make for the uncertainty of anticipation, etc.) measured in money, and on the rate of interest at which this future yield is capitalised.[31]

Changes in any one of the independent variables can affect the others. For example, changes in the market rate of interest may affect the demand for capital not only by altering the rate of discount used in capitalizing the expected yield, but also by creating new expectations about (a) future sales (affecting ϕ) and (b) future interest rates (affecting E).[32] Variables on the right side of the stock demand equation (and in many of the other equations presented here) are independent only in the sense that any value of one is compatible, under the appropriate circumstances, with any value of the other and therefore the values of any of the independent variables cannot be inferred from one another.

At any point of time, the existing stock of capital is whatever has been inherited from the past. The stock supply schedule for capital goods (S_k) can be drawn as vertical in Figure 4.2a, i.e.

$$S_k = K_k \tag{4.3}$$

where S_k is the stock supply of capital and K_k is a predetermined constant. Barring production or depreciation of capital goods (e.g., in a pure exchange economy), the resulting spot market price will be whatever is necessary to allocate the stock without remainder among demanders.

For a production economy, flow considerations must be added to the stock analysis of capital. A stock is a *quantity* measured *at an instant of time*, while a flow can be viewed as the rate at which the stock quantity changes *per unit of time*. The flow demand for capital is attributable to the actual using up (or depreciation) of the existing capital stock per unit of time. For simplicity assume that depreciation is a (small) fraction, n, of the existing stock of capital per unit of time. Hence, the flow demand for capital is

$$d_k = nS_k = nK_k \tag{4.4}$$

where d_k is flow demand (depreciation) and $0 < n < 1$.

Combining equations (4.2) and (4.4) yields the total market demand for capital as

$$D_k + d_k = f_1(p_k, i, \phi, E) + nK_k. \tag{4.5}$$

Given the rate of depreciation n, the market demand curve, $D_k + d_k$, is parallel and to the right of the stock demand curve in Figure 4.2a. The horizontal difference between the two curves represents depreciation during the period.

The flow supply schedule of capital goods indicates the output quantities that will be offered on the market by the capital-goods industry at alternative expected market prices, i.e.

$$s_k = f_2(p_k) = I_g \tag{4.6}$$

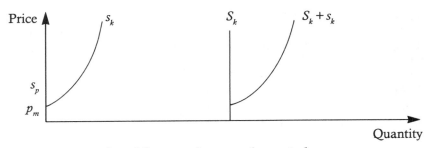

Figure 4.3   Stock and flow-supply curves for capital

where s_k denotes the flow supply of capital and I_g represents gross investment. The shape and position short-period flow-supply schedule of the representative firm (and therefore of the industry) will depend on the industry's marginal cost structure and the average degree of monopoly of capital-goods producers. The flow-supply curve of capital, s_k, is drawn as upward sloping in Figure 4.3 to reflect short-run rising marginal costs in the investment-goods industry, i.e. $f'_{2pk} > 0$.

The minimum flow-supply price, p_m, in Figure 4.3 represents the shut-down price for the industry. If the market price falls below this minimum flow price, that is, if buyers are not expected to accept offer contracts at a price of p_m or greater, no production will occur. Capital-goods producers find that given their expectations and objectives shutting down involves smaller losses than attempting to produce to contract.[33]

The market-supply schedule can be obtained by laterally summating the stock and flow schedules (Figure 4.3), i.e. by combining equations (4.3) and (4.6) to obtain

$$S_k + s_k = K_k + f_2(p_k). \tag{4.7}$$

The horizontal difference between the stock supply schedule and the market-supply curve in Figure 4.3 represents alternative gross output of the investment-goods industry at alternative market prices in a given period of time.

The market-demand function $(D_k + d_k)$ and the market-supply function $(S_k + s_k)$ are combined in Figure 4.4. If, at the beginning of the short period, the demand price (i.e., the spot price) for the existing stock of capital (p_s in Figure 4.4) exceeds the minimum flow-supply price, p_m, investors have long-term expectations of profit opportunities which are sufficiently great to encourage them to place some orders for newly producible capital goods.[34]

In the real world, the market for plant and equipment is typically

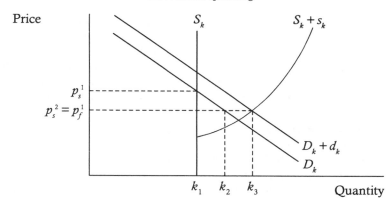

Figure 4.4   The market demand and supply of capital

organized on a 'custom building' or 'to contract' basis. Because of the specific nature of certain aspects of *fixed capital* (e.g., site location and industrial specification characteristics) contracts for orders are often placed on an individual basis before actual production and delivery. Orders for future delivery of capital goods will be a leading indicator of the flow of output that will be forthcoming from the capital goods industry.[35]

The flow of output in the capital-goods industry occurs at the point where the demand price for the period equals flow-supply price.[36] In each period, capital-goods producers tend to be in short-period equilibrium as

$$(D_k + d_k) - (S_k + s_k) = 0. \tag{4.8}$$

In any particular short period, positive or negative net investment will be occurring if $s_k - d_k \neq 0$. This difference between flow supply and flow demand (i.e., excess flow demand) represents a current addition to or depletion of existing stocks.[37] In Figure 4.4 for example, at the short-period flow price of p_f^1, the gross output of the capital-goods industry will be $k_3 - k_1$, while depreciation equals $k_3 - k_2$. The value of net investment $(p_n I_n)$ is equal to the difference between the flow-supply and demand quantities multiplied by the market price, i.e.

$$p_k I_n = p_k (s_k - d_s). \tag{4.9}$$

In Figure 4.4, while net investment output equals $k_2 - k_1$, capital growth during the period will be $(k_2 - k_1)/k_1$.

It is the expectations of investors about future quasi-rents relative to the current rate of discount and their ability to obtain finance – to execute this demand – that determines the position of the stock-demand curve and, given the rate of depreciation, the market-demand curve in Figure 4.2a. Any increase in the stock demand for capital goods will, *ceteris paribus,* increase the spot market price proportionately. The rightward shift of the D_k will also increase demand at each flow-supply price. The flow of output of capital goods will be higher as the producers of investment goods respond to the market.

A lower rate of discount, with any given set of expectations about the prospective money yield of capital, will entail a rightward shift in the stock demand for capital schedule. Given entrepreneurial expectations and the rate of depreciation, there is a different demand for capital schedule for every possible rate of discount (see Figure 4.2b). Given expectations of entrepreneurial investors, the existing stock of capital and its rate of depreciation, the market price for the capital stock depends on the current rate of interest.[38] As Keynes observed: 'A fall in the rate of interest stimulates the production of capital goods not because it decreases their costs of production but because it increases their demand price'.[39]

As long as the spot demand price for capital exceeds the minimum flow-supply price of capital goods, p_m, new gross investment will be undertaken. The rate of capital accumulation will thereby depend on the rate of capital depreciation and the elasticity of supply in the capital goods industries. It is the effect of a change in the rate of interest on the discounting process, and therefore on the demand for capital schedule, that links the money rate of interest to the level of investment output. Accordingly, the money rate of interest rules the roost – the activity in the capital goods sector – in the short run by limiting the demand for capital.[40]

THE THIRD EQUATION OF MAINSTREAM MACROECONOMIC MODELS

Keynes's complex spot-forward analysis of investment is not easily related to the two-equation model developed in Chapter 3. In 1969, Tobin[41] developed a q-theory of investment that is related to, but not the same as, this spot-forward price analysis.[42] Tobin developed a q-ratio as an index of investment demand. Tobin's q is the ratio of the spot price of titles to capital divided by the flow-supply price. (As Tobin puts it, $q = $ [market value of installed capital]/[replacement costs of installed capital].) Mainstream textbooks have great difficulty in trying to integrate Tobin's q-ratio into the basic macromodel. Two of the best selling textbooks[43] do not even mention Tobin's q-theory of investment. In any case, Tobin's q-ratio is not

the same as Keynes's ratio of the spot price for the hire purchase of capital
goods divided by the forward (flow-supply) price.

Instead, in attempting to synthesize classical microfoundations with
Keynesian macroeconomics, macrotheorists added a third equation to their
(Chapter 3) model.[44] This third equation, called the marginal efficiency of
investment, is

$$I = f(i). \tag{4.10}$$

It represents investment expenditure (I) as being inversely related to an
exogenously determined market rate of interest (i).

This marginal efficiency of investment simplification is obtained by
using a variant of the present value formulation of equation (4.1) where

$$SP = [Q_1/(1+r)] + [Q_2/(1+r)^2] + \ldots + [Q_n/(1+r)^n] \tag{4.11}$$

where SP is the supply price (cost of production of the capital good or flow-
supply price), and r is the calculated internal rate of return that makes the
stream of expected quasi-rents (ΣQ) equal to the cost of production (SP).

In this third-equation approach, each entrepreneur is asked to evaluate,
by using equation (4.11), the expected rate of return for all possible
investment projects. The projects are then arrayed starting from the
highest expected rate of return to the lowest expected rate of return. For
example, a typical entrepreneur might develop Table 4.1 as an array of
possible investments to be developed next to the local University campus.

Table 4.1 Hypothetical investment projects

Investment project	Supply price ($ hundred thousands)	Expected rate of return
Tavern	9.0	40.0%
Pizza Parlour	8.0	31.0%
Movie Theatre	8.5	18.0%
Laundromat	9.0	12.0%
Bookstore	9.5	5.0%

A statistical *ogive*, i.e., a cumulative frequency distribution curve, can be
constructed from this array. In Figure 4.5a, an ogive cumulates the total
costs of investment projects listed in Table 4.1 in terms of those projects
expected to earn a rate of return of x per cent or more. Since there are no

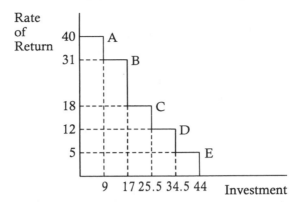

Figure 4.5a   The marginal efficiency of investment

projects on Table 4.1 that are expected to earn 41 per cent or more, the ogive in Figure 4.5a is coincident with the *y*-axis for all values that equal or exceed 41 per cent.

In Figure 4.5a, point A, with coordinates (40%,$9) indicates that a total of $900 000 invested (in a tavern) can be expected to yield 40 per cent or more. Point B, with coordinates (31%,$17) indicates that (two) investment projects with a total cost of $1.7 million can be expected to yield 31 per cent or more. Points C, D, and E can be similarly obtained by cumulating investments on Table 4.1. Connecting these points produces a step-like ogive that represents, at any given expected rate of return, the total investment expenditures that our entrepreneur can expect to yield that rate or more. This ogive is designated the marginal efficiency of investment. At each step it represents the rate of return that a marginal investment is expected to yield.

If all the entrepreneurs in the economy can conceive of projects that are expected to yield all possible rates of return between 40 per cent and some large negative return, then the aggregate marginal efficiency of the investment curve can be drawn as the downward-sloping curve *I* in Figure 4.5b. For algebraic simplicity this aggregate ogive is presumed to be a straight line described by the equation:

$$I = a_2 - b_2 i \qquad (4.12)$$

where $-b_2$ represents the slope and a_2 represents the *x*-intercept of our aggregate marginal efficiency of investment, or demand for investment, schedule.

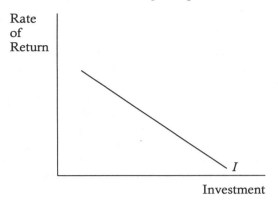

Figure 4.5b   The aggregate ogive

The resulting three-equation macromodel is:

$$Y = C + I \tag{4.13}$$

$$C = a_1 + b_1 Y \tag{4.14}$$

$$I = a_2 - b_2 i. \tag{4.12}$$

There are three endogenous variables (Y, C, and I) and one exogenous variable (i). Solving these equations simultaneously, we obtain:

$$Y = [1/(1 - b_1)][a_1 + a_2 - b_2 i]. \tag{4.13}$$

Once the parameter values of the a's and b's in equation (4.13) are identified, then for any exogenously given value of the market rate of interest, this three-equation model can be solved to produce the value of gross output (via equation (4.13)) and investment (via equation (4.12)). Given the endogenously determined value of Y, the model can then explain the magnitude of C through equation (4.14).

Hidden behind the a_2 and b_2 parameters in equation (4.12) is a mechanism that will cause a change in the value of these parameters if either expectations of future quasi-rents or the costs of producing investment goods change. If expected quasi-rent increase or if the flow-supply price of investment goods declines, then the expected rate of return for the projects listed in Table 4.1 will increase. The resulting rise in the a_2 and/or b_2 parameters involves shifting the ogive in Figure 4.5b to the right. More investment spending will be undertaken for any given market rate of interest.

This third equation of mainstream macroeconomic models tends to conceal more than it illuminates. By presenting the analysis of investment spending in this simple single equation form rather than Keynes's spot-forward-pricing system, mainstream models implicitly imply more stability (and rationality) to investment spending over time than exists in the real world. Keynes's analysis, on the other hand, explicitly lists all the independent variables underlying the stock and flow demands and supplies of plant and equipment. The Keynes approach focuses attention on the many factors that can produce instability in any marginal efficiency of investment described by equation (4.12). These considerations do not surface in the conventional mainstream three-equation model.

APPENDIX: SPOT AND FORWARD MARKETS

Time is a device that prevents everything from happening at once. Production takes time. A spot market, by its very definition of requiring immediate delivery, must deal solely with determining today's price of the inherited stock of any durable. The forward market, by requiring delivery at a future date, permits today's stock to be changed by short-period production and depreciation considerations.

The existence of a well-organized, freely competitive forward market will permit the entrepreneur to operate as if he is a price taker in the traditional competitive market-place. He can observe the forward price and compare it to his short-period flow-supply schedule to determine his short-period production decision. If the forward price

> shows a profit on his costs of production, then he [the entrepreneur] can go full steam ahead, selling his product forward and running no risk. If, on the other hand, this price does not cover his costs (even after allowing for what he loses by temporarily laying up his plant), then it cannot pay him to produce at all.[45]

The upper limit for the forward price of any producible durable is the Marshallian short-run flow-supply price. In the real world, most newly produced capital goods are typically sold on forward contracts rather than spot from shelf-inventory. The forward market for most capital goods is neither freely competitive nor well organized, nor are forward prices always public information. Consequently, although the output of capital goods producers is typically sold by forward contracts, the price may be agreed upon by negotiation, or by sealed bids, or by publicly announced prices as available to all buyers with or without any quantity restrictions. Nevertheless, entrepreneurs who operate in forward markets can avoid

major short-period production commitments until they have firm contractual orders.

There are two possible situations where the forward price is not equal to
the short-run flow-supply price of capital. These are (1) when the specified
future date of delivery is so close to the present date that technology
prevents any flow supply from being produced, or (2) when there is such a
redundancy in the existing stock there is no incentive for entrepreneurs to
produce any new capital goods during the period (i.e., gross investment is
zero). The first situation can be eliminated by treating the delivery date as
'immediate' and therefore an extension of a spot market analysis, while the
second will be treated in the analysis of contango *infra*.

BACKWARDATION AND CONTANGO[46]

If, at the beginning of a period, the stock demand or spot price for the
existing stock of capital, p_s in Figure 4.6, exceeds the short-period
equilibrium (flow-supply) price or forward price, p_f in Figure 4.6, then, in
the language of the market there is *backwardation*. In periods where there
is no existing surplus of capital, backwardation is normal. In a period where
backwardation occurs, the flow of output during the period will exceed (or
just equal) the quantity used up in the production process and net
investment will be positive (or zero). Thus, backwardation is associated
with accumulation and a growing economy (or, at the limit, with a
stationary economy).

On the other hand, if the spot price is below the forward price, there is a
contango in the market. Market participants, on average, believe that the

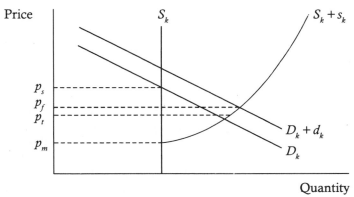

Figure 4.6   The spot price and the forward price

Post Keynesian macroeconomic theory

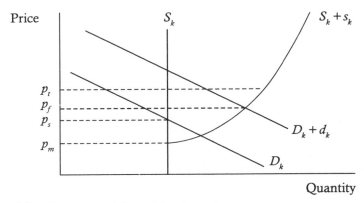

Figure 4.7   Contango with positive gross investment

inherited stock of capital is redundant when the forward price exceeds the spot price. A contango is the invisible hand of the market place signalling for a running down of existing stocks during the period. Two possible cases in the capital goods industry are compatible with a contango market.

In the first case, the market expects the existing stock to be redundant only to the extent that normal wearing-out will remove the surplus before the period is over. Net investment will be negative while gross investment is positive. The period ends with the economy possessing a smaller total stock of producible durables than it began with. Figure 4.7 illustrates this case.

In Figure 4.7, the spot price, p_s, is less than the short-period equilibrium flow-supply or forward price, p_f. The forward price is less than the long-run supply price, (p_t), and greater than the minimum flow-supply price, p_m.

In the second case, the inherited stock is expected to be so redundant that even at the end of the period, a surfeit of capital is expected. In this case, gross investment will be zero and net disinvestment will be equal to the rate of depreciation. Figure 4.8 illustrates this second contango situation where the existing stock is so redundant that it is expected to remain superfluous in future periods.

Today's spot price is far less than the minimum flow-supply price $(p_s < p_m)$. The combined stock plus flow-demand curve does not intersect the combined stock plus flow-supply curve and therefore a short-period equilibrium flow price cannot be defined. In this multiperiod redundancy case, the current marginal efficiency of investment is negative, even if the plant and equipment under discussion are still physically productive, i.e., fixed capital has a positive marginal physical productivity. This multiperiod redundancy situation dramatically illustrates that it is the scarcity of

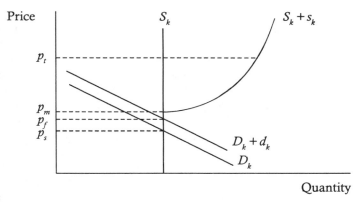

Figure 4.8   Contango with zero gross investment

capital and not its physical productivity that is relevant to determining how valuable real capital is and when there is an incentive to continue to accumulate 'physically productive' equipment.[47]

In this multiperiod contango case the forward price (which can never exceed the short-period equilibrium flow price) must be less than the minimum flow-supply price, p_m, or some producers of capital goods would be willing to enter into forward contracts. In this redundancy environment, the forward price (for delivery at the end of this period), while being below the minimum flow-supply price, p_m, will depend solely on the *expected* spot price at the end of the period when delivery will be required. In this multiperiod redundancy environment, forward prices merely reflect speculation about the value of the remaining surfeit of capital at the end of the period.

The *stationary state* is an economy where the newly produced plant and equipment exactly equal the amount of fixed capital that is wearing out in the period. The economy is neither growing nor declining. In the stationary state, the spot price will equal the forward price that will equal the long-run supply price.[48]

KEYNES, KEYNESIANS, AND THE STATIONARY STATE

If the expected stream of quasi-rents diminishes with any increase in capital stock while the values of q, c, and a for money are all zero, then it is the liquidity premium of money (i.e., the rate of interest) which 'rules the roost', in the sense that it limits long-run economic growth by constraining the demand for capital goods. The logic of the stationary state unfolds if expected future quasi-rents and the long-run supply price of capital goods are unchanged over time. The positive constraint on the yield on money (since $l > c$) limits the potential for interest rate declines no matter how much the supply of money increases. As the existing stock of capital increases, the consequent fall in the spot and forward prices of capital relative to its presumed unchanging long-run supply price tends to reduce the flow of new capital goods produced until only replacement demand remains. In other words, as fixed capital becomes less scarce, its prospective yield in terms of a future income stream falls relative to its flow-supply price, even if capital goods have not become less productive in the physical sense. Unless the expected future net money income stream can be increased relative to money flow-supply price, the accumulation of capital will cease.[49]

If the economy is to avoid the stationary state, then the ultimate source of continuing capital accumulation resides in investors believing in the continuous growth of profit opportunities (animal spirits). Capital goods will continue to be scarce. These profit expectations depend on the expected discount net nominal *value* productivity of capital exceeding its flow-supply price. There is no natural law of diminishing value productivity as long as either the demand for new consumer goods (or fashions) can be continually stimulated, and/or the income elasticity of demand for all existing goods equals unity,[50] and/or the populations of buyers (including governments, foreigners, etc.) and their exercised total purchasing power per period grows at least as rapidly as potential output, or technical change reduces costs of production, or some combination of these factors.

It is this view that underlies the notion that in a Golden Age there is a positive relationship between entrepreneurial animal spirits, the growth of effective demand, and profits. There is no necessary reason to expect a decline in the rate of return on capital over time as the wealth of nations grow. Nor is there any *a priori* reason to believe in the inevitability of the stationary state as long as profit expectations are enlarged over time.

Keynes, on the other hand, often assumed that if population growth was controlled, then long-term entrepreneurial expectations would remain unchanged. If this was the case, then as the stock of physical assets increased over time, excess flow demand of real capital will decline until the forward price falls below the supply price. At that point, 'it no longer pays to produce them (additional capital goods) *unless the rate of interest falls pari passu*'.[51] If the rate of interest is at its practical minimum, then a *laissez-faire* economic system has reached a true stationary state. Any further increase in the stock of capital goods will induce a contango in the market and yield an aggregate negative marginal efficiency of capital.

The imminence and inevitability of the stationary state in *The General Theory* are a result of the static framework on which it is based. Keynes clearly recognized that changes in technique, tastes, population, and institutions can still lead to progress.[52] Yet from the orthodoxy of the time he reflected the fear of a fundamental tendency for a decline in the prospective yield of capital goods relative to their flow-supply price, i.e. a fall in the rate of profit with accumulation.

RANDOM WALKS AND EFFICIENT MARKETS[53]

If both spot and forward markets exist for any good, then today's forward price is the market's best estimate for the price that can be expected in the future spot market that will occur on the date associated with delivery. If the spot price on that future delivery date is expected to be higher than the current forward price, then a profit could be expected by placing an order for future delivery at today's forward contract price. Upon delivery, one can expect to be able to resell the product at the higher spot price expected for that date. Consequently, today's forward price would be bid up until it equalled what the market expected to be tomorrow's spot price. A similar arbitrage situation could force today's forward price down if today's forward price exceeded the market's expectation of tomorrow's spot price.

Observations of statistical series of forward prices for commodities have shown that these series exhibit a random walk pattern. Working has developed the economic meaning of such random walks as follows:

> Pure random walk in a futures price is the price behavior that would result from perfect functioning of a futures market, the perfect futures market being defined as one in which the market price would constitute at all times the best estimate that could be made, from currently available information, of what the [spot] price would be at the delivery date of the futures contracts . . . the observation that the behavior of futures prices correspond closely to random walk thus led to the economic concept that futures prices are *reliably* anticipatory; that is, that they represent close approximations to the best current appraisals of prospects for the future.[54]

This efficient function of the market can be illustrated with the help of Figure 4.4. The relevant spot and forward (or flow-supply) prices in the current period, t_1, are p_s^1; and p_f^1 respectively. With these prices, the stock of capital at the beginning of the t_2 period will be k_2, and therefore the stock supply schedule at time t_2, can be represented by a vertical line at k_2.

If there is no change in entrepreneurial long-period expectations, then the stock demand schedule (the D_k curve) at the beginning of the t_2 period will be unchanged, and therefore the spot price at the beginning of t_2, p_s^2, will be equal to the forward price in t^1, namely p_f^1.

At any point of time, the forward price represents the market participants' best estimate as to what the market expects the future spot price to be. In a world of uncertainty, however, this best estimate is not necessarily a statistically reliable predictor of what the spot price will be on that future date.

For producible durables in periods of backwardation, the link between the forward (current flow-supply) price and the expected future spot price is based on a belief in the stickiness of flow-supply prices. This ultimately depends on the expectation of stickiness in the money-wage rate.[55] If next period's money-wage rate is expected to increase (relative to productivity), then the current and expected future spot price will increase. This change in expectations will manifest itself in an increase in current demand for capital bringing forth an increase in output and a higher forward price. The difference between the forward price before the change in expectations and after the change will depend on the short-period elasticity of flow supply.

In sum, changes in expectations about the future purchasing power of money in terms of producible durables, e.g., anticipation of increases in the flow-supply prices of reproducible goods in future periods will immediately affect the current spot price of durables and the current demand for contracts for forward delivery of durables and thereby affect the flow-supply price of durables.[56]

Classical economists assume that the future can be reliably predicted on the basis of current and past market prices. *If this belief is correct*, then the market participants form 'rational expectations' about the future by analysing recent market data. The market prices in time periods t_1 and t_2 as embodied in Figure 4.4 will then describe the actual path of the economy over time. Today's market prices are therefore efficient in the sense that today's forward market price is not only the best estimate of tomorrow's spot price *but* that, in the long run, market participants who use the current market price signals to form rational expectations about the future will not make persistent errors in their estimates. In a world of rational expectations, then, the future is merely the statistical reflection of the past.

If the economic world is uncertain rather than reliably statistically predictable, then there is no necessity that today's market expectation of a future spot price will reign in the market when tomorrow becomes today. In a world of uncertainty, today's markets cannot be relied upon to forecast the future accurately. Free markets need not be efficient markets.

REDUNDANT CAPITAL: A PROBLEM IN ABSORPTION AND SPECULATION

In any case of redundancy, the spot price today must fall sufficiently below the flow-supply price that is expected to exist in that future period when the redundancy will be worked off to compensate a buyer in the spot market for 'the carrying charges through the period[s] that is [are] expected to elapse before the redundant stocks are completely absorbed'.[57]

These carrying costs include (1) expected deterioration in quality or quantity; (2) warehouse and insurance charges; (3) interest charges; (4) any expected change in the money value of the goods due to expected changes in factors underlying the flow-supply schedule over the period in which the redundancy is being eliminated; and (5) the costs of transactions and brokerage fees if it is expected that the commodity may have to be sold before the surfeit is eliminated.

If average market opinion expects it to take n periods to work off the redundant stock, and if the total carrying cost per period is reckoned as x per cent of the expected short-period flow-supply price that will prevail when the capital goods industry recovers, then the current spot price must be nx below the expected flow-supply price in the nth period, i.e.

$$p_{t1}^s = (-nx)p_{tn}^f \qquad (4.15)$$

where p_{t1}^s is the current spot price and p_{tn}^f is the expected flow-supply price after the redundancy is eliminated. Today's spot price (or notional spot price for durables where organized spot markets do not exist) declines sufficiently below the flow-supply price to make it worthwhile for the buyer (holder) of capital goods to hold either the surplus until a future time when it can be profitably used, or use the plant and equipment currently and still earn a reasonable profit on the depressed spot price.

For example, if the airline industry has too many jet planes for the current travel market, some operators may find they are unable to meet all their contractual commitments regarding the financing of their current stock of planes. This liquidity problem will force some existing operators to attempt to sell off some planes at 'distressed' spot prices. To the extent that there exists a secondhand market in planes, the spot price will decline sufficiently so that potential buyers can start up 'cut-rate' airlines and earn a profitable rate of return on the depressed spot price in their special market niche. Once the redundancy has worn off, however, these cut-rate airlines will often find it impossible to earn a profit when they have to replace their depreciating stock with new aircraft purchased at normal flow-supply prices.

If *n* or *x* is so large that the product of *n* times *x* in equation (4.15) exceeds 100 per cent for any capital good, it would be abandoned by its owners. This redundant plant or piece of equipment becomes a 'free' good until the redundancy has been reduced sufficiently so that $nx < 100$ per cent. Once the one-shot capital loss due to the redundancy has been established in the notional or spot market valuation of capital goods, as long as $nx < 100$ per cent, then these goods can be held and ultimately used with the expectation of earning a normal profit on the *current* spot market valuation.

This scarcity theory of the demand for capital goods is compatible with both positive and negative expected rates of return on fixed capital goods even when such goods are still physically productive. 'A correct theory' of capital, according to Keynes, 'must be reversible so as to be able to cover the case of the marginal efficiency of capital corresponding either to a positive or a negative rate of interest; and it is, I think, only the scarcity theory outlined above which is capable of this'.[58]

Whenever there is a contango in the capital goods market, then previous investment decisions were, according to current expectations, grossly over-optimistic. Any attempt to employ labour with the entire current stock of capital to produce commodities for forward delivery at a date that is most physically efficient is expected to be uneconomical, i.e., is expected to earn a negative rate of return. In this situation, as in the real world, it is economical to leave some of the existing capacity of plant and equipment idle. In classical theory, on the other hand, the existence of idle capacity is always uneconomic.

It is through the spot price mechanism that the economic system, which abhors the existence of redundant capital, generates powerful forces to discourage any new production until the existing surplus is absorbed. Thus, as Keynes noted, 'the efforts to get rid of surplus stocks aggravate the slump, and the success of these efforts retards the recovery'.[59] Miscalculations, which are almost inevitable in a world of uncertainty and free markets, leave their imprint on the employment and production history of the economy. Obviously, miscalculations aggravated by speculative excesses can readily alter the output path of the economy.

NOTES

1.   J.M. Keynes, *The General Theory*, p. 29.
2.   Cf. J.R. Hicks, *Critical Essays in Monetary Theory*, Oxford University Press, Oxford, 1967, p. 36.
3.   In an organized spot market, whenever the market maker finds he or she is unable to carry out his or her function of maintaining orderliness, trading is often suspended to permit the market maker to reorganize his or her resources sufficiently so that order can be restored when the market is reopened.

4. Technically this is true for all fixed capital illiquid assets. Working capital illiquid assets may yield up their entire quasi-rents at a single future date.
5. For durable purchases by consumers (i.e., non-entrepreneurs), the holders of such assets are to receive a stream of future services at a lower expected present value (in terms of monetary costs and convenience) than attempts to purchase the services directly in the future.
6. J.M. Keynes, *The General Theory*, p. 146.
7. Producible capital goods lack the necessary elasticity properties which are required for liquidity, and therefore, by definition, for continuous well-organized spot markets (cf. Keynes, *The General Theory*, p. 249 n. 2). In a growing economy, *average opinion* will never expect producible capital goods to be a good store of value, for the expected future spot price (net of carrying costs) must always be less than the current spot price (a condition known as 'backwardation') if the existing stock of capital is growing over time. (See *infra* for a discussion of backwardation.)
8. J.M. Keynes, *The General Theory*, p. 210.
9. Neoclassical Keynesians often recognize that money and other liquid financial assets are the short-run time machines – i.e. vehicles for storing purchasing power. Nevertheless, they typically assume that in the long run real capital goods are an excellent substitute for money and financial assets for storing value. This time-machine function will be discussed in greater detail in the following chapter.
10. Classical theory presumes that the time preference decision is the only one that utility-maximizing savers make regarding the use of their current earned income claims.
11. See the essential elasticity properties of money and liquid assets in Chapter 6 *infra*.
12. For example, see J. Tobin, 'Money and Economic Growth', *Econometrica*, **33**, 1965.
13. Since A.A. Berle and G.C. Means's landmark study (*The Modern Corporation and Private Property*, Commerce Clearing House, New York, 1932), applied economists have recognized this separation of ownership from control as an important problem for developed capitalist economies. Since classical theory does not make the distinction between time preference and liquidity preference, it is not surprising that mainstream economic theorists have provided little guidance on this problem.
14. For similar views on these chapters, see J. Robinson, 'Own Rates of Interest', *The Economic Journal*, **71**, 1961, and R. Turvey, 'Does the Rate of Interest Rule the Roost?', in *The Theory of Interest Rates*, ed. F.H. Hahn and F.P.R. Brechling, Macmillan, London, 1965.
15. According to Keynes, a non monetary economy is one where there is no asset whose l is always greater than c. See Keynes, *The General Theory*, p. 239.
16. N. Kaldor, 'Keynes's Theory of the Own Rate of Interest', in *Essays on Economic Stability and Growth*, ed. N. Kaldor, Duckworth, London, 1960, p. 60. Italics added.
17. For assets where no spot markets exist $l=0$ or r is infinitely large. For these illiquid assets, ownership is irrevocable 'and indissoluble, like marriage, except by reason of death or other grave cause'.
18. J.M. Keynes, *The General Theory*, pp. 225–6.
19. The value of a depends on the resale future spot price minus the current spot price. Which future date spot price is relevant? If the cost of buying and selling the asset is negligible, then the holder will focus on the immediate future price. If there are significant transactions costs in buying and selling, then the expected appreciation must more than offset these transactions costs before one becomes bullish about the asset.
20. H. Makower and J. Marschak, 'Assets, Prices, and Monetary Theory', *Economics*, **5**, 1938, p. 279.
21. For the moment we are ignoring the possibility of expectations of price inflation (or deflation) which might increase the holding of some capital goods, since then $a>c$. Inflationary expectations can induce the accumulation of liquid capital goods for inventory speculation reasons, and even accelerate the rate of installation of new capacity by increasing expectations of future $(q-c)$ so that expectations of inflation could be viewed as an increase in the demand price of capital goods. This aspect will be dealt with later in this chapter.

22. Or as Keynes put it 'Over against the prospective yield of the investment we have the *supply price* of the capital asset, meaning by this . . . the price which would just induce a manufacturer to newly produce an additional unit of such assets'. See J.M. Keynes, *The General Theory*, p. 135.

23. J.M. Keynes, *The General Theory*, p. 135.

24. See J.M. Keynes, *The General Theory*, Chapter 16. For a further discussion of Keynes's repudiation of the marginal physical productivity of capital theory see the appendix to Chapter 8.

25. Even if there were extensive markets for hiring capital goods, this would merely push the investment purchasing decision to the firms that would rent capital goods to other firms, e.g., a 'Hertz Rent-A-Capital Good' firm.

26. Ibid., p. 137.

27. Actually, *i* represents the average subjective rate of discount used by entrepreneurs in evaluating any expected future income stream. For each entrepreneur the rate of discount used may differ (even if they are in the same industry) but the actual rate used will always exceed the market rate of interest on borrowing by a premium which is the minimum the entrepreneur feels is necessary to overcome the disutility of having to take on additional commitments and face the prospect of potential surprise. In essence this subjective premium which the entrepreneur wants before he will enter into a contract for the purchase and use of capital goods is a measure of 'the doubts in his own mind as to the probability of actually earning the prospective yield for which he hopes'. (See Keynes, *The General Theory*, p. 144.) In what follows we will use the terms of the rate of discount and the rate of interest interchangeably.

28. This assumes that the stock of capital can be aggregated along the abscissa by homogeneous physical units – an obviously unrealistic assumption. Keynes suggested that 'for each type of capital we can build up a schedule' (ibid., p. 136). Instead, for expositional simplicity the analysis that follows is based on a concept of a representative capital good.

29. Cf. J. Robinson, *Essays in Economic Growth*, p. 45.

30. If two or more units are equally profitable, the D_k curve will be horizontal across those units.

31. J.M. Keynes, *A Treatise on Money*, I, p. 202.

32. If current changes in financial conditions are considered temporary rather than permanent these expectations will affect the timing of investment projects, as well as affecting, via the organization of the financial markets, the willingness of banks to make loans and underwriters to float new issues. (See P. Davidson, *Money and The Real World*, Macmillan, London, 1972, Chs. 10, 13.)

33. The supply responses in the capital goods industry for any given expected market price may differ depending on whether the entrepreneurs are profit maximizers or not, and whether they produce to market or to contract. For simplicity of exposition, the supply response of capital-goods producers will be discussed in terms of profit-maximizing entrepreneurs producing to contract.

34. This can be true even if there is no current overutilization of capacity. In other words, net investment can be conceived as having two important – but independent – origins: (i) *a stock adjustment process* if the current equipment is being overutilized and the current level of demand is projected over the future life of the net investment; and (ii) *an expected growth in demand* or 'animal spirits' which induces net investment even when there is no current overutilization.

35. Since delivery occurs at some future point of time (the end of the period) after an offer contract is accepted by the buyer, there is a time dimension–units problem in placing the stock and flow demand and supply curves on the same 'timeless' quadrant as in Fig. 4.4. (This same time dimension–units problem exists in all Marshallian short-period diagrams but is traditionally ignored in a Marshallian timeless analysis. (See P. Davidson, 'Market Disequilibrium Adjustment: Marshall Revisited', *Economic Inquiry*, 1974.) Since delivery will take place at the end of the period, the present value or demand price for all units of capital goods which must be ordered must be less than the

demand price for a similar unit which can be obtained immediately by an amount equal to the current period's net yield. Thus, the stock demand, D_k, of Figure 4.4 should be drawn with a discontinuity at the point where it intersects the stock supply curve, S_k, as there must be some foregone expected net yield for the current period if delivery is obtained at the end of the period. Thus p_s is the spot price at the beginning of the current period, and p_f is Marshallian short-period flow-supply price or offer price for delivery of currently produced capital goods at the end of the current period. Since nothing fundamental will be changed by ignoring the time units problem, for reasons of expositional simplicity in most of what follows, diagrams with continuous demand curves will be utilized. (For the discontinuous demand case analysis, see P. Davidson, *Money and the Real World*, 2nd edition, Macmillan, London, 1978, pp. 77–8.

36. J.M. Keynes, *The General Theory*, p. 137.

37. The stock of capital can be changing each period even though it is fixed at each instant of time. A procedure which relates stock supply functions to excess flow demands and a time variable is 'mandatory if one wishes to conduct a systematic inquiry into problems of capital accumulation'. (See D.W. Bushaw and R.W. Clower, *Introduction to Mathematical Economics*, Homewood, Irwin, 1957, p. 22.

38. This approach highlights Keynes's insistence that knowledge of the prospective yield of capital is *not sufficient* to determine the rate of interest. Rather, the rate of interest is an exogenous variable in determining the demand for capital. (See Keynes, *The General Theory*, p. 137.) The rate of discount will be related to the rate of interest; if the latter changes, *ceteris paribus*, the former will change. Thus the rate of interest can be used as a proxy for the rate of discount as a variable which explains investment.

39. J.M. Keynes, *Treatise on Money*, I, p. 211.

40. With imperfections in loan markets, the lack of finance may also be an important element affecting activity, i.e., 'availability' may become as important as interest charges. (See P. Davidson, *Money and the Real World*, Chs. 9 and 13.)

41. J. Tobin, 'A General Equilibrium Approach to Monetary Theory', *Journal of Money, Credit, and Banking*, 1969.

42. The spot-forward analysis developed in this chapter has its origin in Keynes's *Treatise on Money*, 2, 1930 and was elaborated by P. Davidson in 'Money, Portfolio Balance, Capital Accumulation, and Economic Growth', *Econometrica*, 1968.

43. W.J. Baumol and A.S. Blinder, *Economics*, Harcourt, New York, 1985 and A.B. Abel and B.S. Bernanke, *Macroeconomics*, Addison-Wesley, Reading, 1992.

44. This permitted an integration of the marginal physical productivity of capital theory to be synthesized into Keynesian economics. (For example, see N.G. Mankiw, *Macroeconomics*, Worth, New York, 1992, p. 442.).

45. Keynes, *A Treatise on Money*, II, pp. 142–3. Even if the entrepreneur did not accept a forward contract, he could use the current forward price as the best estimate of the spot price that would prevail (and therefore what he could expect to get) on the delivery date.

46. The following analysis has its roots in Keynes's *Treatise On Money*, 1930. It was developed by P. Davidson in 'Money, Portfolio Balance, Capital Accumulation, and Economic Growth', *Econometrica*, 1968, and P. Davidson, *Money and The Real World*, Macmillan, London, 1972.

47. Compare Keynes, *The General Theory*, pp. 213–15.

48. In fact, the spot price will exceed the forward price by an amount just sufficient to cover the expected net yield earned from the present date to the delivery date. Thus, even in the stationary state, there will be a backwardation equal to the difference in the net yield that is expected to be earned by having immediate delivery as compared to delivery at the end of the period for a small marginal increment in the stock of capital.

49. Cf. Keynes, *The General Theory*, p. 165.

50. A unit income elasticity of demand for all goods and services is implicit in Say's Law.

51. Keynes, *The General Theory*, p. 228.

52. Keynes, *The General Theory*, pp. 220–21.

53. This section is derived in large measure from Chapter 24 of Keynes's *Treatise on Money* and Kaldor's 1939 article 'Speculation and Economic Growth'. The theory of the

demand for liquid capital is developed *infra*. Speculative demand will be discussed in later chapters.

54. H. Working, 'New Concepts Concerning Futures Markets and Prices', *American Economic Review*, **52**, 1962, pp. 446–7. Working continued: 'Conceiving the fluctuations of futures prices to be mainly appropriate responses to valid changes in expectations produces a great change in thought regarding them, as compared with regarding the price movements as mainly lacking economic justification'.

A futures price is a forward price on a futures market. This market is so well organized that one party to any transaction does not necessarily know the other party. In less-organized forward markets, buyers and sellers normally know each other.

55. Stickiness means the belief that changes in the variables between today and the next period are expected to be very small and continuous. Change in money wages in line with productivity changes implies no change in Marshallian flow-supply prices (for any given degree of monopoly) and hence is a sufficient but not a necessary condition for stickiness. Expectations of such sticky money wages are important to the efficient operation of markets in a monetary economy in a world of uncertainty, e.g. Kaldor, 'Speculation and Economic Growth', p. 35.

56. This mechanism for describing the effects of expected inflation differs from the one utilized by modern monetary neoclassicists who, following Fisher, claim that anticipated inflation creates a difference between the 'real' and the 'monetary' rates of interest. Keynes, however, was adamant in his belief that Fisher's mechanism of a difference between real and monetary rates of inflation was hopelessly misleading in analysing cases of expected inflation. See Keynes, *The General Theory*, pp. 142–3.

57. J.M. Keynes, *A Treatise on Money*, II, p. 136.

58. J.M. Keynes, *The General Theory*, pp. 214–15.

59. Keynes, *A Treatise on Money*, II, p. 145.

5. Government and the level of output

A nation's government can affect output and employment through its fiscal policy, i.e. through decisions regarding tax receipts and government expenditures. Fiscal policy that is concerned solely with the effects of government taxes and spending on current employment rates is called *functional finance*. The hope of those who favour functional finance is that the government will decide on its level of spending and taxation, running deficits or surpluses, 'to keep the total rate of spending in the country on goods and services, neither greater nor less than the rate which . . . would buy all the goods it is possible to produce'.[1] Government fiscal policy is conceived as the balancing wheel, exogenously increasing aggregate demand whenever private sector spending falls short of a full employment level of effective demand and reducing demand if aggregate demand exceeds the full employment level.

THE BALANCED BUDGET THEOREM: A SIMPLE MODEL

Functional finance opens several alternative routes for achieving full employment. There are three ways that fiscal policy can affect the level of effective demand. These are (1) a change in tax receipts with no change in government spending; (2) a change in government spending with no change in tax receipts; and (3) simultaneous changes in taxes and spending.

The principles involved can be illustrated by expanding the simple three model of mainstream macroeconomics. Equation (5.1) expands the output identity to include goods and services produced for purchase by the government (G):

$$Y = C + I + G, \tag{5.1}$$

assuming all taxes are paid by consumers. A simple consumption function can be written as:

$$C = a_3 + b_3 (Y - T) \tag{5.2}$$

where T is tax receipts, and b_3 is the marginal propensity to consume out of after-tax income. In the simplest case total tax receipts are exogenously fixed in absolute amounts and independent of the income and employment level of the economy. (Taxes that are not related to economic activity are not common but poll taxes, head taxes, and even some property taxes are possible examples.) If we assume that investment (I) and government expenditures are exogenous, then substituting (5.2) into (5.1) yields:

$$Y = [1/(1 - b_3)][a_3 - b_3 T + I + G]. \qquad (5.3)$$

If there is an exogenous increase in government spending $(\varDelta G)$, then the change in output is given by

$$\varDelta Y = [1/1 - b_3] \varDelta G. \qquad (5.4)$$

A change in government spending has the same multiplier effect as an exogenous change in investment.[2]

If there is an exogenous change in tax receipts with no change in government spending, then the change in output is obtained from (5.3) as:

$$\varDelta Y = [(-b_3/(1 - b_3)] \varDelta T \qquad (5.5)$$

where $[(-b_3/(1 - b_3)]$ is the tax (or transfer) multiplier since it relates a change in output to a change in taxes (or unilateral government transfers).[3] Since the marginal propensity to consume out of disposable income is less than one, the tax multiplier must be smaller in magnitude than the simple multiplier of (5.3).

The economic rationale for the different magnitudes of these multipliers is readily illustrated by the following example. Suppose the government increases spending by $10 billion. If the marginal propensity to consume is 0.8, then total output will increase by $50 billion, according to (5.4). Ten billion of this increase is due to the first-round government purchases, and the remaining $40 billion is the result of increased consumption resulting from the increase in disposable income.

If taxes are reduced by $10 billion, then, according to (5.5), total output will increase by $40 billion. The initial (first-round) tax cut of $10 billion does not affect gross output or income but disposable income increases by the size of the tax cut. This increase in after-tax income induces an increase in consumption spending on the next round of $8 billion. This induced increase in employment and income leads to a third-round spending increase of $6.4 billion. At a limit, consumption rises by $40 billion.

If taxes and government spending are both simultaneously increased by the same amount, i.e. an incremental balancing of the budget, then the resulting increase in output is obtained by summing the effects of (5.4) and (5.5):

$$\Delta Y = [1/(1-b_3)]\Delta G + [-b_3/(1-b_3)]\Delta T \qquad (5.6)$$

and since $\Delta G = \Delta T$, therefore

$$\Delta Y = [(1-b_3)/(1-b_3)]\Delta G. \qquad (5.7)$$

If there is an incremental balanced change in the government budget, then the change in total output will just equal the change in government spending, $\Delta Y = \Delta G$.

IMPLICATIONS OF THE BALANCED BUDGET THEOREM

The unit value of this 'balanced budget multiplier' is independent of the marginal propensity to consume. This surprising result stems from a host of simplifying assumptions including (1) the marginal propensity to consume of the people who pay the taxes is the same as the marginal propensity to consume of those who receive income as the result of the additional spending of government, (2) the tax payment is independent of income and (3) there is no concomitant change in interest rates and investment spending. The extent to which these assumptions are not realistic implies that the balanced budget should not be taken literally as equal to unity. Instead, it should be interpreted as indicating that there is a larger employment and output effect per dollar of government spending compared to the employment effect per dollar of exogenous change in taxes.

Decisions on spending, taxation and the 'acceptable' level of the public debt can affect the magnitude of government fiscal policy needed to achieve a target rate of employment. For example, if the Council of Economic Advisers tells the president that there is a projected shortfall of $50 billion in aggregate demand from the necessary level to achieve full employment, then there are three possible functional finance policies available. Assume the marginal propensity to consume is 0.8. The first option is that the government could spend $10 billion on investment in infrastructure (without an increase in taxes) to achieve the objective.[4] The result will be a deficit of $10 billion and an increase in the size of the gross national product that is allocated to government investment projects such as highways and harbours.

The second option, the government could cut taxes by $12.5 billion to achieve the target employment goal. The deficit will be $12.5 billion and the increase in aggregate output will be in the form of additional consumer goods. The second option achieves the same employment objective with less government absorption of output, but with a higher government deficit.

The third option is to increase government expenditures by $50 billion and simultaneously increase taxes by $50 billion. The employment objective will still be met without a government deficit, but the whole increase in gross national product will be absorbed in the government investment in infrastructure.

The choice among these alternatives should rest on a national discussion about the relative merits or demerits of additional infrastructure spending versus additional consumption to create jobs. If the existing level of aggregate demand is insufficient to create employment opportunities for all who are willing to work at the going real wage, then the government has a responsibility to assure sufficient profit opportunities for full employment. To the extent that the public fears the size of the public debt *per se*, the government should opt for an incremental balanced budget to achieve full employment whenever there is a lack of effective demand. If fear of larger government absorption of output is an overriding constraint, then a tax cut alternative can be pursued. If fear of too much 'wasteful' consumption ranks high in the public mind, then a modest increase in government spending financed by an equal increase in the deficit might be the alternative choice. None of the aforementioned fears should encourage the government to do 'nothing' in the hope that a free market economy will soon right itself.

This is the basic message of Keynes's *General Theory*. This

theory is moderately conservative in its implications. For whilst it indicates the vital importance of establishing certain central controls in matters which are now left in the main to individual initiative, there are wide fields of activity which are unaffected. The State will have to exercise a guiding influence on the propensity to consume partly through its scheme of taxation, partly by fixing the rate of interest, and in other ways. Furthermore, it seems unlikely that the influence of banking policy on the rate of interest will be sufficient by itself to determine an optimum rate of investment. I conceive, therefore, that a somewhat comprehensive socialisation of investment will prove the only means of securing an approximation to full employment: though this need not exclude all manner of compromises and devices by which the public authority will co-operate with private initiative. But beyond this no obvious case is made out for a system of State Socialism which would embrace most of the economic life of the community. It is not the ownership of the instruments of production which it is important for the State to assume. If the State is able to determine the aggregate amount of resources to augment the instruments and the basic reward to those who own them, it will have accomplished all that is necessary.[5]

THE TAX MULTIPLIER WHEN TAX RECEIPTS DEPEND ON INCOME

To analyse the effect of a simple system of taxation geared to income levels, assume a simple proportionate income tax

$$T = rY \qquad (5.8)$$

where r is the income tax rate. Substituting (5.8) into (5.2) and the resulting into (5.1), we obtain

$$Y = a_3 + b_3(Y - rY) + I + G. \qquad (5.9)$$

If we assume a given change in government expenditures with no change in the tax rate, then the change in income is

$$\Delta Y = [1/(1 - (1 - r)b_3]\Delta G \qquad (5.10)$$

where the term in the square brackets is the tax multiplier associated with a proportional income tax.

Equation (5.10) indicates that a change in government expenditures[6] will still affect output, but the multiplier will be less than with a tax system where revenues are fixed and independent of income. The economic rationale is that with an income tax system, after-tax income does not change as much. The induced consumption of the second-round, third-round, etc., effects are, therefore, less.

Any change in the tax rate will change disposable income out of any level of gross income and therefore be the equivalent of a change in the a parameter in (5.2). This will not only initiate some change in consumption on the first round, but since the multiplier in (5.10) will be larger with a smaller tax rate, there will be an expanded multiplier effect.

With rising income accompanying a tax cut, the loss in total tax receipts might not be as large as expected. Nevertheless, it is unlikely that a tax rate cut will 'pay for itself' in the sense of not causing an additional government deficit. If for example the tax rate is reduced by 20 per cent (from $r = 0.3$ to $r = 0.24$), then income would have to increase by 25 per cent for there to be no increase in the deficit.[7]

Although most government tax receipts are geared to income, a proportional income tax is rare. Most systems are either regressive or progressive. A regressive tax is one where the proportion paid in taxes declines as income rises, even if the absolute amount of tax paid increases. A progressive income tax is one where both the absolute amount and the proportion of income paid in tax increases as income increases. Either of these latter forms of taxation could be introduced in a more complicated algebraic relationship in (5.8). This would alter the magnitudes involved but not the principle inherent in this balanced budget multiplier theory.

AUTOMATIC VERSUS DISCRETIONARY FISCAL POLICY

The discussion so far has assumed that functional finance decisions are made anew every time the level of economic activity varies. Government receipts and expenditures will vary as aggregate income changes even if no new legislative or executive actions are undertaken. If, for example, economic activity declines, then receipts from income, payroll and sales taxes are reduced while government expenditures on unemployment compensation automatically increase. Legislation that has the predetermined effect of altering government spending and receipts in a way that tends to offset changes in private spending is called an automatic stabilizer. The most important automatic stabilizers in most modern economies are the progressive income tax and unemployment compensation. If incomes rise rapidly, then tax revenues increase even more rapidly under the progressive income tax while unemployment compensation spending will decline. This reduces the ability of the private sector to have a large multiple of induced spending. If the economy turns down, then tax receipts fall off while government unemployment income transfers rise. As a result, purchasing power in the private sector does not decline as much as it might have if a head tax raised all the revenue and no unemployment compensation was paid. These and similar automatic stabilizers make modern economies less susceptible to the large fluctuations that many experienced before the 1940s. Automatic stabilizers have not been able to stabilize the economy at full employment.

Discretionary stabilizers are government actions taken at specific points of time to affect the change in the level of effective demand from one considered to result in an undesirable effective demand to a full employment effective demand. Tailoring fiscal policy to the events of the moment, what some economists have called 'fine tuning', has proven difficult to accomplish since (1) it requires the ability to make accurate predictions about the future, (2) it requires convincing legislators to act solely on the basis of the priority of achieving full employment over other political or economic aims, (3) it requires agreement on the part of economist advisers to policy decision makers as to what the appropriate policy is at a point of time, and (4) it requires convincing legislators that these policies are the appropriate ones.

The message of this book is that mainstream economics has not developed the appropriate theory for a real world, entrepreneurial economy. Economic advisers have failed in 'fine tuning' the economy through discretionary policies. Until we get our theory right, we will not get our functional finance policies correct.

NOTES

1. A.P. Lerner, 'Functional Finance and the Federal Debt', *American Economics Association Readings in Fiscal Policy*, edited by A. Smithies and J.K. Butters, Irwin, Illinois, 1955, p. 469.
2. With a change in government spending, the new level of output is given by:

$$\cdot Y + \Delta Y = [1/(1-b_3)][a_3 - b_3 T + I + G + \Delta G]. \tag{5.3a}$$

   Subtracting equation (5.3) from (5.3a) yields equation (5.4).
3. With a change in taxes the new level of income is:

$$Y + \Delta Y = [1/(1-b_3)][a_3 - b_3(T + \Delta T) + I + G]. \tag{5.3b}$$

   Subtracting equation (5.3) from (5.3b) yields equation (5.5).
4. Spending on infrastructure does not require significant increases in government-hired workers. The government can let contracts to private sector entrepreneurs to produce the highways, harbours, etc. required.
5. J.M. Keynes, *The General Theory*, pp. 377–8.
6. Actually a change in any exogenous spending (e.g. investment) will be associated with this multiplier if there is a proportionate income tax.
7. The so-called 'supply-side' economics rationale that was the rationale for President Reagan's tax cut in 1982 promised that so many more people would work that income would rise more than proportionately to the cut in the tax rate. The historical facts prove this claim to be wrong.

6. Money and uncertainty

THE NATURE OF MONEY

'Money', Hicks declared, 'is defined by its functions ... money is what money does'.[1] Harrod has written that 'Money is a social phenomenon, and many of its current features depend on what people think it is or ought to be'.[2] 'Money', Scitovsky adds, 'is a difficult concept to define, partly because it fulfils not one but three functions, each of them providing a criterion of moneyness ... those of a unit of account, a medium of exchange, and a store of value'.[3]

While economists have probably spilled more printers' ink over the topic of money than any other, and while monetary theory impinges on almost every other conceivable branch of economic analysis, confusion over the meaning and nature of money continues to plague the economics profession. Pre-Keynesian economists tended to emphasize the medium of exchange aspect of money, as the early quantity theorists stressed the neutrality of money and strict relationship between the money aggregate and total nominal transactions or income.

In a classical world of perfect certainty and perfect markets, with a Walrasian auctioneer assuring simultaneous equilibrium at a given point of time, it would be irrational to hold money as a store of value as long as other assets provide a certain positive yield.[4] In the absence of uncertainty, economic theory cannot explain why utility-maximizing, rational people hold money rather than goods as a store of value. The tâtonnement process implies that no transactions occur[5] until equilibrium is attained (recontracting is essential and the enforcement of existing contracts superfluous). Anyone holding money either during the auction or until the next market period is simply irrational since possessing money yields no utility. In equilibrium goods trade for goods.[6] The essential nature of money is disregarded in all general classical equilibrium systems since there is no asset whose value as a store of liquidity (i.e. whose liquidity premium) exceeds its carrying cost.[7] Even advocates of general equilibrium analysis admit that the 'economy that we have been considering, although one where the auctioneer regulates the terms at which goods shall exchange, is essentially one of barter'.[8]

Keynes described the classical view of the neutral nature of money as foolish. Keynes wrote:

> Money, it is well known, serves two principal purposes ... it facilitates exchanges.... In the second place, it is a store of wealth. So we are told, without a smile on the face. But in the world of the classical economy, what an insane use to which to put it! For it is a recognised characteristic of money as a store of wealth that it is barren.... Why should anyone outside a lunatic asylum wish to use money as a store of wealth?[9]

Keynes's answer to this rhetorical question was clear and unequivocal. 'Our desire to hold money as a store of wealth is a barometer of the degree of our distrust of our own calculations and conventions concerning the future ... the possession of actual money lulls our disquietude'.[10] Distrust? Disquietude? These are states of mind that are impossible in a world of certainty.

It is in a world where people cannot reliably predict future outcomes that

> expectations are liable to disappointment and expectations concerning the future affect what we do today. It is when we have made this transition that the peculiar properties of money as a link between the present and the future must enter into our calculations.... Money, in its significant attributes is above all, a subtle device for linking the present to the future and we cannot even begin to discuss the effect of changing expectations on current activities except in monetary terms. We cannot get rid of money even by abolishing gold and silver and legal tender instruments. So long as there exists any durable asset, it is capable of possessing monetary attributes and therefore, of giving rise to the characteristic problems of a monetary economy.[11]

Forward contractual commitments provide the necessary intertemporal links. It is the synchronous existence of money and money contracts over an uncertain future that is the basis of a monetary system whose maxim is 'Money buys goods and goods buy money; but goods do not buy goods'.[12]

CONFUSING RISK FOR UNCERTAINTY

Despite the apparent victory of the Keynesian Revolution immediately after World War II, subsequent developments in monetary theory by Patinkin, M. Friedman, Tobin, Lucas, B. Friedman and many others have regressed on this crucial nexus of tying money to uncertainty and the use of contracts to organize economic activities. The concept of quantifiable, statistical risk has been substituted for Keynes's uncertainty notion where the latter recognizes that people may be ignorant about the future.

Risk can, by probability statements, be reduced to an actuarial certainty, uncertainty cannot. Classical theorists fail to detect this crucial difference. Keynes insisted that uncertainty was the sole intelligible reason for holding money, and by uncertainty he meant that there 'was no scientific basis on which to form any capable probability whatever. We simply do not know'.[13]

UNCERTAINTY AND EXPECTATIONS

Time is a device that prevents everything from happening at once. The production of commodities takes time; and the consumption of capital goods and consumer durables takes considerable time. Decision makers recognize that the outcomes in terms of profit and/or utility to be obtained from engaging in production and exchange activities require a significant amount of historical time to pass between the point of time a decision is made and the time the consequences are experienced. Each of us, when faced with an economic decision whose costs and benefits are embedded in future events, has had to decide whether the economic environment concerning this prospective action can be characterized as falling into one of the following three mutually exclusive environmental categories:

An objective probability environment. In this situation, the decision maker believes that an immutable real objective probability distribution governs past, current, and future market outcomes. A rational decision maker will analyse past relative frequencies of outcomes to calculate a statistically reliable probability analysis of future prospects.

This is the economic environment in which the New Classical rational expectations hypothesis (REH) is embedded. REH presumes that rational knowledge regarding future consequences of today's decisions involves a confluence of the estimated (subjective) probabilities and objective (given by immutable laws) probabilities that governed past and current economic events.

A subjective probability environment. At the moment of choice, the decision maker believes he or she can order or array all possible future outcomes in terms of subjective probabilities.[14] In this situation, there is no necessary requirement that the short-run subjective probabilities must coincide with the presumed to exist long-run immutable objective probability distributions.[15] In the individual's mind, only his or her subjective probabilities regarding future prospects govern the choice made. In Social Darwinian style, classical economists proclaim that those decision makers who succeed will act 'as if' their subjective probabilities correctly reflect the objective probabilities that are presumed to prevail. Those who make wrong decisions because their subjective probabilities are in conflict with the ruling objective probabilities will fail – and like the dinosaur, perish from the economic earth. In the long run, the subjective probability environment collapses into the REH analysis of the objective probability analysis.

An uncertainty environment. The decision maker believes that during the lapse of calendar time between the moment of choice and the date(s) of payoff, unforeseeable changes can occur. In other words, the decision maker believes that reliable information regarding future prospects does not exist today. The future is not calculable, even if the decision maker is competent to perform the mathematical operations necessary to calculate probabilities of conditional events given the necessary information. This is uncertainty (or ignorance about future consequences) in the sense of Keynes and the Post Keynesians.[16] The longer the lapse of time between decision and consequence, all other things being equal, the more likely the individual is to believe he or she is making a decision in this uncertain environment.

OBJECTIVE PROBABILITIES, STOCHASTIC THEORY AND THE ERGODIC AXIOM

A majority of mainstream economists argue 'as if' all economic observations are part of time series realizations generated by stochastic processes.[17] This 'as if' condition is rationalized by the necessity of developing economics as an empirically based hard science.[18]

Samuelson has made the acceptance of the 'ergodic hypothesis'[19] regarding stochastic economic processes the *sine qua non* of the scientific method in economics. In an ergodic system, future events are always reliably predictable by using a probabilistic analysis of past and current outcomes. Lucas insists that it is no longer acceptable to develop models where expectations are not based on a probability analysis of a market time-series realization. In other words, Lucas insists that any analysis involving an uncertainty (nonergodic) environment is, in his view, unacceptable.

Ergodic Processes and Space versus Time Averages

To comprehend (a) Samuelson's association of the ergodic assumption with economics as a hard science, and (b) why REH proponents believe that rational expectations provide forecasts without persistent errors, it is important to distinguish between space averages and time averages. The former are calculated from cross-sectional data (a fixed point in time) and the latter are computed from time-series data (a fixed realization).

If the stochastic process is *ergodic*, then for an infinite realization, the time and space averages will coincide. For finite realizations of ergodic processes, the space and time averages tend to converge (with the probability of one). The ergodic axiom presumes that space or time averages calculated from past data are reliable estimates of the space average that will exist at any specific future date.

In an ergodic environment, knowledge about the future involves the projecting of calculated averages based on the past and/or current cross section and/or time-series data to forthcoming events. *The future is merely the statistical reflection of the past.* Economic activities are timeless and immutable.[20] There can be no ignorance of upcoming events for those who believe the past provides reliable statistical information (price signals) regarding the future, and this knowledge can be obtained if one is willing to spend the resources to examine the existing evidence regarding past patterns.

Some economists have confused the concept of an ergodic stochastic process with that of a stationary stochastic process. If a stochastic process is *stationary*, then the probability distributions from which time averages are calculated are unchanged over calendar time. In other words, in a stationary process, estimates of time averages do not vary with the historical calendar period under observation. *Nonstationarity is a sufficient but not a necessary condition for nonergodicity.* If a stationary process is nonergodic,[21] then probabilities calculated from past data cannot provide a reliable estimate for any prospect at any specific future date.

The necessary and sufficient conditions for the REH to provide a theory of expectational formation of future space averages without persistent errors at any future date(s) are:

a. the subjective and objective distribution functions must be equal at any given point of time, and
b. these functions must be derived from an ergodic stochastic process.

Under the ergodic axiom, probability is knowledge, not uncertainty.

If, in the real world, some economic processes are *not* ergodic, then conditional expectations based on past distribution functions can persistently differ from the probabilities that will be generated as the future unfolds and becomes historical fact. If people believe that the economic environment is uncertain (nonergodic) then it is perfectly sensible for them to disregard past and present market signals. The future is not statistically calculable from past data and therefore is uncertain. Or as Hicks succinctly put it 'One must assume that the people in one's models do not know what is going to happen, and know that they do not know just what is going to happen. As in history'.[22]

In conditions of uncertainty, people may realize they just 'don't have a clue' about what the future will bring. Entrepreneurs may follow their 'animal spirits' for positive investment action in a 'damn the torpedoes, full speed ahead' approach. The possibility of nonergodic economic conditions means that (1) the REH cannot be a general case and (2) Samuelson's presumption of ergodicity is inappropriate for any 'general theory' of economics unless one is sure that nonergodic processes can never occur in economics.

Keynes laid great stress on the distinction between uncertainty and probability, especially in relation to decisions involving the accumulation of wealth and the possession of liquidity. Keynes's[23] claim that some future prospects cannot have probability ratios assigned to them can be interpreted as either (a) rejecting the belief that particular observed economic phenomena are the outcomes of any stochastic process, or (b) if economic stochastic processes exist, they are nonergodic.

If observed economic events are not the result of stochastic processes then objective probability structures do not even fleetingly exist. Nevertheless, mechanical use of formulas still permits one to calculate a value for an arithmetic mean, etc., for any data set collected over time. If we do not possess, never have possessed, and conceptually never will possess an ensemble of macroeconomic worlds, then it can be logically argued that a distribution function cannot be defined. The application of the mathematical theory of stochastic processes to macroeconomic phenomena would therefore be questionable, if not in principle invalid.

Hicks reached a similar judgement and wrote: 'I am bold enough to conclude from these considerations that the usefulness of "statistical" or "stochastic" methods in economics is a good deal less than is now conventionally supposed. We have no business to turn to them automatically; we should always ask ourselves, before we apply them, whether they are appropriate to the problem at hand. Very often they are not'.[24]

If the existence of stochastic processes is presumed, then Keynes's uncertainty concept would be applicable whenever these processes are non ergodic. Some economists have suggested that the economy is a nonstationary process moving through historical time and societal actions can permanently alter economic prospects.[25] Indeed Keynes's famous criticism of Tinbergen's econometric methodology was that economic time series are not stationary for 'the economic environment is not homogeneous over a period of time (perhaps because non-statistical factors are relevant)'.[26]

Whenever economists talk about 'structural breaks' or 'changes in regime', they are implicitly admitting that the economy is, at least at that stage, not operating in ergodic circumstances. Most orthodox economists admit that important macroeconomic (and microeconomic?) events tend to evolve in nonergodic circumstances. Nevertheless, mainstream economic theory clings to the presumption of a predictable ergodic economic future. To abandon the ergodic axiom, it is feared, is to abandon one's claim to being a hard-headed scientist.

If, in the world of experience, people 'do not know what is going to happen and know they do not know', then they make decisions under conditions of Keynesian uncertainty or ignorance. Orthodox theory will be unable to describe behaviour correctly in the real world and economic policy prescriptions will be misleading and possibly disastrous.

SUBJECTIVE PROBABILITY AND NONERGODIC CIRCUMSTANCES

The concept of a subjective probability that in the short run may differ from any existing objective probability environment has been developed from Savage's Expected Utility Theory (EUT).[27] In EUT terminology a *prospect* is defined as a list of *consequences* with an associated list of probabilities, one for each consequence, such that these probabilities sum to unity. Consequences are to be understood to be *mutually exclusive* possibilities. A prospect comprises an exhaustive list of the possible consequences of a particular course of action. Each individual's preferences are defined over the set of all conceivable prospects.

Using these EUT definitions, an uncertain environment (i.e., nonergodic circumstances) occurs whenever an individual cannot *specify* and/or order a *complete* set of prospects regarding the future. This may be because the decision maker either is ignorant as to when the list of prospects is complete, or cannot assign probabilities to all conceivable consequences. If a decision maker cannot order all possible prospects, then EUT's *ordering axiom* is violated. Hicks has associated the violation of the ordering axiom with Keynes's concept of liquidity. According to Hicks, 'liquidity is freedom' to delay action that commits claims on real resources whenever the decision maker is ignorant regarding future consequences.[28]

Savage, in laying down the necessary conditions for justifying EUT's ordering axiom, admits that the idea of a human being able to specify, in advance, all possible future prospects 'is utterly ridiculous . . . because the task implied in making such a decision is not even remotely resembled by human possibility . . . [it is] preposterous. This theory is practical in suitably limited domains. . . . At the same time, the behavior of people is often at variance with the theory'.[29] Savage therefore admits that his subjective probability analysis is not a general theory, for it does not deal with Keynes's uncertainty environment. Savage admits that his approach is only applicable to a 'small world'.[30]

RATIONALIZING PROBABILITY IN MAINSTREAM THEORY

In a Keynes–Post Keynesian large world, 'the behavior of people is often at variance' with that attributed to decision-making agents in EUT. For Keynes and the Post Keynesians, the use of either subjective or objective probability concepts implies that the decision maker believes that he or she possesses complete knowledge about future events. Uncertainty involves ignorance about forthcoming prospects. In mainstream theory there is no concept equivalent to Keynes's uncertainty, i.e. ignorance of the future. Only under the fig-leaf subterfuge of Milton Friedman's positivistic methodological approach can the ubiquitous ignorance of the real world's future outcomes be banished from theory by presuming that decision makers act 'as if' they have knowledge – risky though it may be – about the future.

Orthodoxy often pays lip service to the 'crucial property of money . . . being a store of value'[31] even as they emphasize 'Liquidity Preference as A Behavior Towards Risk'[32] (*rather than uncertainty*). Yet, by defining money as 'anything that serves the function of providing a *temporary abode of purchasing power*',[33] Friedman is suggesting that money's role is a temporary, or short-run one. In the long run, money has no effect on the real economy, it is neutral. In Friedman's concept of equilibrium there is no need for money. All permanent anticipated real values are unchanged during the period under analysis, i.e., all long-run changes are foreseen.[34] There can be no uncertainty in long-run equilibrium.

The well-known real balance effect of Patinkin's model is based on a single market-period store-of-value aspect of money that disappears between periods. The flexibility of money wages and prices, which is essential to the generation of a real balance effect and the equilibrium position, requires certainty conditions.[35] The clearing of all payments before the next market period removes the need to use money as a store of value from period to period. Patinkin readily admits that his

concern . . . is with the demand for money that would exist even if there were perfect certainty with respect to future prices and interest. Uncertainty does play a role in the analysis, but only uncertainty with respect to the timing of payments. Thus one byproduct of the following argument is the demonstration that dynamic or uncertain price and/or interest expectations are not a *sine qua non* of a positive demand for money. . . . The general approach of the following argument is in the Keynesian spirit of analyzing the demand for this asset as one component of an optimally chosen portfolio of many assets.[36]

How can an analysis that irretrievably dispenses with long-run (period to period) uncertainty and the possibility of faulty expectations – as does much of what passes for advanced monetary theory in the professional literature – be in the spirit of Keynes? The music of this lively if mislabelled Keynesian gavotte emphasizing portfolio balance in a world of certainty or at least predictable risk may be the melody to which most modern monetary theorists trot, but surely it is not attuned to Keynes's majestic monetary dirge for Say's Law. It is only in a world of uncertainty and disappointment that money comes into its own as a necessary mechanism for deferring decisions; money has its niche only when we feel queasy about undertaking actions that will commit our claims on resources onto a path that can only be altered, if future events require this, at very high costs (if at all).

THE ESSENTIAL PROPERTIES OF LIQUID ASSETS

Recognition of this desire of income-earners to avoid committing all earned claims on resources provides the insight necessary to describe the social institutions associated with money as well as the elemental and peculiar properties of money essential to fulfil the two equally important liquidity functions of money, namely, a generally accepted *medium of contractual settlement* and a *liquid store of value* (or a *time-machine vehicle* to move purchasing power to the future) in a modern, monetary, market-oriented, but uncertain world.

The necessary properties (or attributes) of anything that can fulfil these functions are:

1. A zero (or negligible) *elasticity of production*. This elasticity attribute implies that money and other liquid assets are not readily reproducible by the use of labour in the private sector. In layman's language this means that 'money does not grow on trees'. Unemployed workers can neither be hired nor self-employed in the private sector to harvest money, even if the marginal productivity of picking fruit from a classical money tree exceeds the marginal disutility of reaching for the fruit. Or, as Keynes noted, unlike the producible goods and services that make up the gross national product of an economy 'labour cannot

be turned on at will by entrepreneurs to produce money in increasing quantities as its (spot) price rises'[37] in response to an increase in the demand for money.

2. A zero (or negligible) *elasticity of substitution for liquidity purposes* between all liquid assets and easily producible goods. Whenever individuals want to avoid increasing their commitment to use resources today and thereby preserve options for action for the future, they will reallocate their spending from producible goods and services to money and other liquid assets. The increase in demand for liquidity raises the liquidity premium and, therefore, the demand price of liquid assets. If the elasticity of substitution is zero, then this relative price rise of nonproducible liquid assets will not divert people into substituting producible goods as a store of value.

It is the existence of these two elasticity properties that creates the possibility of underemployment equilibrium in monetary economies. For example, suppose because the future suddenly appears more uncertain, people decide to buy fewer space vehicles (automobiles) to transport themselves geographically and instead demand more time vehicles to convey their purchasing power to an unspecified future time to meet possible liquidity needs. The decreased demand for space vehicles causes unemployment in the economy's auto factories. The increased demand for liquidity does not induce an offsetting increase in employment in the production of money or any good producible in the private sector.

Of course, if peanuts were money (as Abba Lerner long ago suggested in his analysis of general equilibrium), then unemployment in the auto industry would be offset by increased employment in the peanut farms. The change in the relative price of peanuts *vis-à-vis* autos would cause the invisible hand of the market-place to induce the reallocation workers and equipment from auto factories to peanut farms. Say's Law would hold and the economy would have no barrier to achieving full employment.

The cost of transferring money from its medium of contractual settlement function to its store of value function or vice versa must be zero (or negligible) so that individuals do not find it expensive to defer decisions or to change their minds. Minimizing these transaction costs requires a *civil law of contracts* stipulating that money is the thing that discharges all contractual obligations and that the State will enforce these contracts whenever either party to the agreement is unwilling or unable to meet the agreed upon terms.

An additional contribution to the minimizing of such transaction costs is the presence of an institution, a clearing system, which encourages the use of private debts in the settlement of transactions as long as it is expected that the private debt can be promptly converted into the form of legal tender money that is enforceable in the discharge of contracts.

In sum then, in an uncertain world, a monetary system is associated with at least two and usually three institutions – namely, contracts, enforcement, and clearing. The thing that becomes the money commodity will have two essential properties, a zero (or negligible) elasticity of production and a zero (or negligible) elasticity of substitution between it and any other good that has a high elasticity of production.

Uncertainty and unwillingness to commit earned income to current purchases of producibles (a process that the layperson terms savings) will cause unemployment, if, *and only if*, the object of the savers' desire is a resting place for their savings that is nonproducible and not readily substitutable for producibles – even if prices are flexible.

If prices are flexible and producibles were good substitutes for nonproducibles as liquidity time machines, then an increased propensity to save by the members of a community cannot, *ceteris paribus*, cause unemployment. In other words, if producible durables are capable of 'doing money's duty equally well',[38] then involuntary unemployment cannot be a significant problem for market-oriented, monetary economies. Any increase in the demand for liquid stores of value would, as Friedman's monetary framework suggests, rapidly spill over into an increase in the demand for producible goods.[39]

It is a failure by many able but wrong-headed economists to comprehend the importance of these three institutions and two properties that are peculiar to money and the need for liquidity in a monetary economy that has led to the shunting of much of modern monetary analysis onto a wrong line. Any model of a modern, monetary, market-oriented economy that attempts to provide insights about the real world should have the following characteristics:

1. Decision making by firms and households who are fully aware that human judgement is fallible.
2. The existence of contractual agreements, enforceable by the State, which permit the sharing of some of the burdens of uncertainty between the contracting parties.
3. Different degrees of organization of spot and forward markets for all sorts of real goods and financial assets. In many cases, either only a spot or a forward market exists for a particular item because of difficulties in organizing a market in a world of incomplete information. In markets that do exist, there may be significant and increasing transactions, search, and information costs.
4. Money buys goods in these markets, and goods can buy money, but

except for some relatively small – but not necessarily unimportant – markets, goods never trade directly for goods. In a monetary economy, *demand involves want plus the ability to pay*. Liquidity is defined as being able to meet all contractual payments as they come due. Financial conditions, by affecting the quantity of money in the hands of the public, can affect the public's ability to pay and the resulting use of real resources.

5. The various institutions that develop in organizing a market can affect the price path in the market as it reacts to a disequilibrium situation.
6. There is a clearing mechanism for private debts that permits the existence of a fractional reserve banking system. There are also non-bank financial institutions which because they lack a generally available clearing mechanism independent of the banking system cannot create a medium of contractual settlement. Nevertheless, these financial intermediaries can affect financial flows and therefore market demands.
7. There is confidence in the monetary and financial system.

Thus the main characteristics of real world monetary economies are Uncertainty, Fallibility, Covenants, Institutions, Commerce, Finance, and Trust. These are the Seven Wonders on which the Modern World is based. Simultaneously, these are the sources of the outstanding faults of a modern, monetary, free market economy, namely 'its failure to provide for full employment and its arbitrary and inequitable distribution of wealth and incomes'.[40]

CONTRACTS AND MONEY

All living organisms have to solve the basic economic problem of what to produce, how to produce it, and how the fruits of production are distributed amongst the members of the group. Most life forms solve these problems as members of an organizational and societal structure (e.g., beaver and ant colonies, schools of fish, herds of elephants). The survival of these life forms depends on their ability to solve the basic economic problem. Yet, except for some developed human societies, none of these life forms interact through contracts, money, and markets to solve the economic problem. Moreover, only in relatively recent times and only in developed societies have humans created and utilized the institutions of money, markets, and legally binding contracts as the primary tools for organizing production and exchange transactions that take place through time.

The standard of living of any life form that has not developed these human institutions of money and contracts (including some isolated human communities, e.g., jungle tribes, South Sea Islanders) are closely tied to their natural environment by Malthusian principles. When nature is bountiful, these life forms thrive; and when the environment turns bleak, the population declines.

For centuries, from Biblical times till the end of Feudalism, all human economies were similarly constrained by their natural environment. Beginning with the Renaissance, and the development of money, financial institutions, contracts, and markets as we know them, human beings created for themselves the ability to sever the direct Malthusian link between the size of the population and the generosity or frugality of the conditions of supply provided by Mother Nature. As markets, contracts and money use developed, the residents gained the means to thrive with ever rising standards of living even during periods of harsh natural supply conditions.

Of all life forms, only humans seem to suffer from the problem of maintaining the full employment of available resources in the production processes necessary to solve the economic problem of ensuring the survival of the species and/or its current standard of living. The existence of contracts and monetary institutions is important in explaining the economic evolution of *Homo Sapiens* and their superior economic level relative to other life forms. This superiority is a double-edged sword; it permits rising standards of living, but, under certain *man-made* conditions, it can subjugate much of the population to poverty and even starvation while at the same time society possesses idle resources that could alleviate this poverty if only these resources were fully and voluntarily employed.

This then is a paradox resulting from the human development and the use of money, contracts, and markets. When wisely directed, a market-monetary system can provide living conditions well above subsistence levels as scarce resources are fully and cleverly employed. When left to the vagueness of a *laissez-faire* environment, money-using market systems have shown a propensity, at times, to break down and fail to provide the prosperous standards of living that the system is capable of delivering. Resources that would be scarce if the economy was operating efficiently are allowed to lie idle.

Money is first a human institution – making liquidity a peculiarly human problem associated with developed market economies. In the world we live in, money is not shells or beads, or peanuts, or bananas or any other commodity easily produced by labour in the private sector. In our world, money supply is inextricably tied to society's laws governing the banking system and the use of money contracts to purchase goods and to hire labour on a time-use basis for productive purposes. With the legal abolition of slavery in modern economies, labour is employed primarily through the use of money-wage contracts.[41]

Business managers know that in a world of uncertainty 'to err is human'. Entrepreneurs realize that their expectations of sales and profits may be wrong in both the short run and the long run. If human nature does not experience the temptation to take a chance, to possess the 'animal spirits' that urge action rather than inaction, to 'damn the torpedoes and move full speed ahead', then real world entrepreneurial activities will quickly wither away. The courage of the entrepreneur to act in the face of ignorance regarding the future is the essential characteristic of successful and prosperous economies. As Davidson and Davidson proclaim, 'Society admires this courage; that is why we admire the entrepreneur more than we admire the actuary'.[42]

Only a fool would rush in to challenge the unknown future without some strategy to protect against error and failure. Smart and successful entrepreneurs are not fools. They only undertake challenges when they can enter into long duration forward money contracts with workers and suppliers, where the date(s) of deliveries and money payments – and therefore where liabilities – are fixed in advance. As long as entrepreneurs feel they have sufficient liquidity to meet these forward contractual obligations as they come due, they can adopt the 'damn the torpedoes' philosophy safe in the knowledge that their entrepreneurship cannot sink before the final output has been produced and is available for sale.

Modern society has developed the institution of legally enforceable forward money contracts to permit the contracting parties to possess a measure of control over future performance and cash flows, even in the face of ignorance regarding future real economic conditions. All legal contractual agreements among parties are enforceable solely by monetary payments under the civil law.

Time is of the essence of any contract. Each party to a contract believes, at the time of signing of the contract, that carrying out the contractual terms will enhance his or her own well-being. (This mutual beneficial agreement is known as 'the contract curve solution' in economics or a 'meeting of the minds' in law.) If, as classical economics assumes, the future was either certain or calculable in a probabilistic sense, then there would be no need to require legal enforcement of forward contracts since it is in the best interests of both parties to carry out the agreed upon terms of the contract.

Yet, as long as the future is uncertain (in the sense of Keynes), each party also 'knows' that when tomorrow becomes today, one or the other party may be unable and/or unwilling to carry out the terms of the contract.[43] Each contracting party is also aware that if the other fails to perform as specified in the contract, the State will enforce, in lieu of performance, a monetary payment for any damages to be made to the aggrieved party. When the law of contracts is enforced by the governments of all civilized societies, contracting parties are provided legal assurances regarding cash flows even if an unpredictable future event occurs.

The organization of production and exchange transactions on a money-contractual basis permits the seller and the buyer to maintain control over future cash flows in an otherwise unpredictable future. For example, contracts assure entrepreneurs future performance from workers and suppliers, or at least the ability to avoid pecuniary damages. Even if from hindsight today's decision to purchase inputs proves to be a terrible error, the business manager limits his maximum liability to his monetary contractual commitment. If each contracting party possesses enough liquidity to meet these future cash commitments, then each 'knows' that he or she can economically survive any future disaster involving this transaction.

In contrast, for classical economic theory to demonstrate logically and rigorously the benefits of a *laissez-faire* market system, it requires that **all** *contractual payments be made at the initial instant of time*.[44] The conclusion that a free market economy will automatically achieve a full employment, inflation-free utility-maximizing output equilibrium, not only requires the presumption of a statistically reliable, calculable future but it also has as a logical prerequisite that all payments for goods and services must be made at the initial instant of time – even if delivery is not expected until tomorrow, next year, or even next century. For example, Radner has characterized the circumstances involved in the fundamental contractual situation required for orthodox classical theory as follows:

> An elementary contract in this market will consist of the purchase (or sale) of some specified number of units of a specified commodity to be delivered at a specified location and date, if and only if a specified elementary event occurs. Payment for this purchase is to be made now (at the beginning).[45]

Professor Radner's summary of the classical view of contracts and payments is '[i]n the above interpretation of the economy, all accounts are settled before the history of the economy begins'.[46] In a sense, this is the classical 'Big Bang Theory of the Economic Universe'. Once the Big Bang occurs as all contracts are signed and settled, the future path of the economic universe is completely determined.

If all accounts are settled at the Big Bang 'before the history of the economy begins', then neither managers nor households need worry about liquidity. By assumption, there are no contractual obligations outstanding that will come due at any future date. Mainstream economists deal with the problem of liquidity as they have dealt with all the issues raised by Keynes in differentiating his 'general theory' from the classical analysis. Orthodoxy defines away the problem.

Yet, liquidity is a problem that every one of us has to deal with almost every day of our lives – and certainly every time we try to balance our chequebook. The problem of trying to maintain a liquid position is a universal one in modern society. It colours almost every major economic decision we make in the real world that we inhabit. Yet it is banished from the process of decision making in classical analysis.

ROBINSON CRUSOE – THE CLASSICAL ANALOGY OF A MONEY ECONOMY

Nonmonetary primitive human economies can exist (a) when the economic environment is expected to be unchanged (e.g., tribes in the Brazilian rain forests who have no contact with developed societies) or (b) in a strictly regimented economy where all production and exchange activities are decided either by a central authority, or by a communal agreement, or by pre-ordained customs, e.g. the military, a kibbutz, a monastery or nunnery, or a feudalistic society. In these economies there may be poverty but there is never involuntary unemployment. These economies do not operate through markets and use money to organize production and exchange activities; the complicated interdependent entrepreneurial economies of the modern world do. To speak of a nonmonetary market-oriented interdependent economy is a contradiction in terms.

Barro claims that 'the primitive environment of Robinson Crusoe contains the essence of choice problems that arise in complicated market economies'.[47] Barro characterizes a Robinson Crusoe economy as one where 'each person has no opportunity to exchange commodities or anything else with other households . . . each household's only option is to consume all the goods it produces'.[48] In the original Robinson Crusoe economy, there is only one inhabitant. There can be no transactions and there is never a need for contracts to organize production or money or liquidity to meet contractual obligations. Even with the introduction of Friday into the Robinson Crusoe world, there is no need for money. Friday is a slave and his production activities are organized by a central authority who solves the economic problems of what to produce, how to produce it and for whom it is produced.

A Robinson Crusoe economy is a nonmonetary economy where money does not matter, i.e. is neutral. Barro epitomizes the error of mainstream economics when he claims that the findings of his analysis of a Robinson Crusoe economy 'remains valid when we extend the analysis . . . to settings that look more like modern industrialized economies'.[49] Nothing can be further from the truth. No wonder so much that passes in the mainstream literature for macroeconomics has no applicability to the real world in which we live.

THE NATURE AND IMPORTANCE OF STATE MONEY

Hicks observed that although 'monetary theory is less abstract than most economic theory, it cannot avoid a relation to reality'.[50] Yet, much of the current literature on monetary theory, based on classical general equilibrium microfoundations (to which Professor Hicks has provided much impetus), is unrealistic. In the real world, money is not created as the manna from heaven of a Patinkinesque world or dropped by helicopter as in Friedman's construction. In the real world, money 'comes into existence along with debts, which are contracts for deferred payment, and price-lists, which are offers of contracts for sale or purchase'.[51]

In a world of uncertainty, the existence of a State organization that enforces the discharge of contractual commitments is essential in providing the public with assurances of the continuity of contractual arrangements between the present and the future; an assurance that is necessary if one is going to hold money as a store of value.

With the development of the civil law of contracts, the government appropriated to itself the right to define what is the unit of account and what *thing* should answer that definition. The State 'claimed the right to not only enforce the dictionary but also to write the dictionary'.[52] If the community loses complete confidence in the ability of State institutions to enforce contracts, then the monetary system breaks down and the community reverts to barter practices.[53] These are so costly that most members of society will cling to any ray of hope in the government's ability to enforce contracts into the future. Most communities reveal a preference to use even a crippled monetary system rather than revert to barter. It is only when the situation has deteriorated to such an extent that everyone is completely uncertain of the meaning of contractual commitments, that a catastrophic breach in the continuity of the system is inevitable. Such a catastrophe, by wiping out all existing contracts simultaneously, provides a foundation for developing a new monetary unit of account that can be used in denominating new contractual commitments.

Money is *not* merely a numéraire, i.e., a neutral device to help the classical economist specify the relationship among diverse goods – it is not merely a lowest common denominator. The very institution of money as a unit of account is the result of the existence of contracts that combine the offer of one party to sell goods for money with the offer of the other party to sell money for goods. If money was simply a classical numéraire, then goods could buy goods without the intermediation of money.

> The numéraire is not money; it is not even a partial money; it is not even assumed that it is used by the traders themselves as a unit of account. It is not more than a unit of account which the observing economist is using for his own purpose of explaining to himself what the traders are doing.[54]

It is the synchronous existence of money as a unit of account and the presence of 'offer contracts' and 'debt contracts' which are denominated in money units that forms the core of a modern monetary production economy. Money can function as the medium of contractual settlement only if the community believes that acceptance of the monetary intermediary as a liquid store of general purchasing power involves no risks (only uncertainties), since the State will enforce enactment of all future offer contracts in terms of the monetary unit of account. Trust in the ability of money to be a stable store of generalized purchasing power over producible goods depends on people believing that no matter how far the current spot price for any producible be momentarily displaced by spot market conditions, the market price for the good at some future date is anchored in a forward price constrained by money flow-supply prices whose principal component is the money-wage rate.

As long as flow-supply prices are expected to be sticky,[55] each individual 'knows' he or she can, at any time, find an entrepreneur who will offer a contract for future delivery of producible goods at a money price that does not differ significantly from today's flow-supply price.[56] In a production-specialization, money-using economy, expectations of money wages (sticky relative to productivity changes) combined with the public's belief in the sanctity of money contracts for future performance encourages the public to accept money today as a means of settling obligations.[57]

Any economy that uses money as a medium of contractual settlement and abides by a civil law of contracts has a tremendous advantage over a similarly endowed hypothetical economy that permits only barter transactions – for the cost of anticipating the needs of trading partners and then searching out such partners greatly exceeds the resources used in bringing buyers and sellers together in a money economy. It is only the presumed existence of the costless Walrasian auctioneer and/or a tâtonnement process that permits general equilibrium models to reach an equilibrium solution. The assumption of zero transaction costs, Hicks reminds us:

is hopelessly misleading when our subject is money. Even the simplest exchanges are in fact attended by some costs. The reason why a well-organized market is more efficient than a badly organized market . . . is that in the well-organized market the cost of making transactions is lower.[58]

The desire on the part of humans to minimize costs, including transaction costs, has led them to the discovery that while the introduction of a medium of contractual settlement reduces transaction costs over a barter system, the process of clearing claims to legal tender money rather than taking delivery of legal tender instruments themselves can lower transaction costs even further.

Bank money is, of course, simply evidence of a private debt contract, but the discovery of the efficiency of 'clearing', that is the realization that some forms of private debt that is regulated by the Monetary Authority can be used in settlement of the overlapping myriad of other private contracts immensely increases the efficiency of the monetary system. Three conditions are necessary in order for such a private debt to operate as a medium of contractual settlement: (1) private debt must be denominated in terms of the monetary unit; (2) a clearing institution for these private debts must be developed; and (3) a belief that uncleared debts are convertible at a known parity into the legally enforceable medium of contractual settlement.[59]

In a classical general equilibrium system the quantity of money is conceived to be independent of the volume of contracts.[60] The logically consistent classical theorist cannot find any secure anchor for the level of absolute prices in this system. The price level is indeterminate. Having cut the connection between money, labour offer contracts, and flow-supply prices, these modern Walrasians conclude that the level of prices is whatever it is expected to be. If it were not, money holders would, with the cooperation of the ubiquitous Walrasian auctioneer, simply bid up or down the price level until the purchasing power of money was at the level they wanted it to be while resource utilization (full employment) would be unaffected.[61]

NOTES

1. J.R. Hicks, *Critical Essays in Monetary Theory*, Clarendon Press, London, 1967, p. 1.
2. R.F. Harrod, *Money*, Macmillan, London, 1969.
3. T. Scitovsky, *Money and the Balance of Payments*, Rand, McNally, Chicago, 1969, p. 1.
4. See P.A. Samuelson, *Foundations of Economic Analysis*, Harvard University Press, Cambridge, 1947, pp. 122–4.
5. Some have introduced *ad hoc* transactions costs in an effort to explain why people in the real world are found with currency in their pockets (e.g. the shoe leather costs of walking to the bank to deposit the money into their accounts). With the growth of ubiquitous Automatic Teller Machines, one suspects that the transactions costs are now the wear-and-tear on the fingertips of typing information into the ATMs.

6. The introduction of production into a Walrasian model requires that all future prices of all possible quantities that could be bought or sold be known with certainty; otherwise, production involves an irreducible uncertainty since there must be a current contractual commitment to hire resources to produce products that will be available for sale to the market at some future date at an unknown price.

7. See Keynes's definition of a nonmonetary economy, *The General Theory*, p. 239.

8. F.H. Hahn, 'Some Adjustment Problems', *Econometrica*, **38**, 1970, p. 3.

9. J.M. Keynes, 'The General Theory of Employment', *Quarterly Journal of Economics*, **51**, 1937, reprinted in *The Collected Writings of John Maynard Keynes*, 14, ed. by D. Moggridge. Macmillan, London, p. 115. All references are to reprint.

10. Ibid., p. 187.

11. Keynes, *The General Theory*, pp. 293–4. A footnote associated with the phrase 'monetary attributes' indicates that Keynes is referring to his Chapter 17 essential properties – a zero elasticity of production and substitution. For a further discussion of these essential properties, see *infra*.

12. R.W. Clower, 'A Reconsideration of the Microfoundations of Monetary Theory', *Western Economic Journal*, **6**; reprinted in *Monetary Theory*, ed. R. Clower, Penguin, Middlesex, 1969, pp. 207–8. All references are to reprint.

13. Keynes, *The Collected Writings of John Maynard Keynes*, 14, pp. 114–15. Thus, uncertainty, in the Knight–Keynes sense, does not obey the mathematical laws of probability.

14. J. Von Neumann and O. Morgenstern, *Theory of Games and Economic Behavior*, 3rd edition, Princeton University Press, Princeton, 1953, believe that the subjective probabilities are in terms of relative frequencies, while L. Savage, *The Foundation of Statistics*, John Wiley, New York, 1954, defines subjective probabilities in terms of degrees of conviction.

15. If the subjective and objective probabilities tended to be the same, then the decision maker would believe he or she is operating in the objective probability environment explained above.

16. Keynes conceived of a 'life without probabilities' as conceptually quite different from life with probabilities in the classical sense. Keynes indicated that by uncertainty he did '... not mean merely to distinguish what is known for certain from what is only probable. The game of roulette is not subject, in this sense to uncertainty.... The sense in which I am using the terms is that ... there is no scientific basis on which to form any calculable probability whatever. We simply do not know'. (J.M. Keynes, 'The General Theory', *Quarterly Journal of Economics*, 1937, reprinted in *The Collected Writings of John Maynard Keynes*, 14, p. 113). Moreover, Keynes added, 'the hypothesis of a calculable future leads to a wrong interpretation of the principles of behaviour' (ibid., p. 122).

     For Keynes, the 'long period employment' need never be equal to the long-run equilibrium level of full employment predicted by Say's Law. This difference in employment outcomes was attributed, by Keynes, to agents demanding money, not to spend, but to hold to obtain sufficient liquidity to protect themselves from an uncertain and unpredictable future.

17. In the theory of stochastic processes, a realization constitutes a single time series, whereas a process makes a universe of such time series.

18. R.E. Lucas and T.J. Sargent, *Rational Expectations and Econometric Practices*, University of Minnesota Press, Minneapolis, 1981, pp. xi–xii.

19. Samuelson (p. 184) indicated that he uses the term ergodic 'by analogy to the use of this term in statistical mechanics'. By so doing Samuelson claims (pp. 184–5) 'Technically speaking, we theorists hoped not to introduce *hysteresis* phenomena into our model, as the Bible does when it says "we pass this way only once" and in so saying, takes the subject out of the realm of science into the realm of genuine history'. (See P.A. Samuelson, 'Classical and Neoclassical Theory', in *Monetary Theory*, edited by R.W. Clower, London, Penguin, 1969.)

     Thus from Samuelson's technical viewpoint presuming ergodicity removes economics from the socio-humanistic elements of history and makes it a science on a par with (18th century) physics. The renowned biological scientist Ernst Mayr (*The Growth of Biological Thought*, Harvard University Press, Cambridge, 1982), however, has noted that biologists, unlike physicists, deal with phenomena unknown to inanimate objects and therefore 'the assumption of the sameness of physical and biological sciences is naïve and misleading ... [in that] one loses the real significance of the respective biological phenomena' (p. 34). Since economists, like biologists, deal with phenomena associated with animate rather than inanimate objects, the desire to make economics over in the image of the physical sciences can also be naïve and misleading, often resulting in the inability of Samuelson's economist-cum-scientist to comprehend the significance of important economic phenomena such as the non-neutrality of money.

20. As Billingsley (*Ergodic Theory and Information*, Kreiger Publishers, Huntington, 1978, pp. 1–2) stated, if 'the laws governing ... change remain fixed as time passes ... [then] ergodic theory is a key to understanding these fluctuations'. Whenever the 'passage of time does not affect the set of joint probability laws governing experimentation (outcomes), then the assumption of ergodicity permits regularities to be perceived from what might at first sight be patternless fluctuations' (also see pp. 60–65). This perceived past pattern of regularities can then be reliably projected into the future.

21. For example, mathematical constructions called *limit cycles* produced stationary, nonergodic processes. In economic theory, the mathematical models of a multiplier–accelerator interaction with exogenously imposed ceilings and floors are limit cycles. The business cycle model developed by J.R. Hicks, *A Contribution to the Theory of the Trade Cycle*, Clarendon, Oxford, 1950.

22. J.R. Hicks, *Causality in Economics*, Basic Books, New York, 1979, p. vii.

23. J.M. Keynes, *The General Theory*, pp. 148–50, 161.

24. J.R. Hicks, *Causality in Economics*, p. 129.

25. Solow has argued that there is an interaction of historical–societal circumstances and economic events. In describing 'the sort of discipline economics *ought* to be', Solow has written, 'Unfortunately, economics is a social science' and therefore 'the end product of economic analysis is ... contingent on society's circumstances – on historical context. ... For better or worse, however, economics has gone down a different path'. (See R.M. Solow, 'Economic History and Economics', *American Economic Review Papers and Proceedings*, **75**, 1985, pp. 328–9.) Had the Keynes uncertainty concept been better understood by economists, then the discipline Solow thinks economics 'ought' to be might have developed in the last half century – and mechanical applications of eighteenth century physics concepts avoided.

26. *The Collected Writings of J.M. Keynes*, 14, edited by D. Moggridge, Macmillan, London, 1973.

27. L. Savage, *The Foundation of Statistics*, John Wiley, New York, 1954.

28. Hicks, *Causality in Economics*, pp. 94, 113, 115.

29. Savage, *Foundations of Statistics*, p. 16.

30. Savage, op. cit., pp. 82–6.

31. J. Tobin, 'Notes on Optimal Growth', *Journal of Political Economy*, **76**, 1968, p. 833.

32. J. Tobin, 'Liquidity Preference As a Behavior Towards Risk', *Review of Economic Studies*, 1958.

33. M. Friedman, *Dollars and Deficits*, Prentice-Hall, New Jersey, 1968, p. 186.

34. M. Friedman, 'A Theoretical Framework for Monetary Analysis', *Journal of Political Economy*, **78**, 1970, p. 223; also see M. Friedman, 'Monetary Theory of Nominal Income', *Journal of Political Economy*, **79**, 1971, pp. 326–9.

35. D. Patinkin, *Money, Interest and Prices*, 2nd ed., Harper & Row, New York, 1965, p. 275. Patinkin permits uncertainty to enter the front door via the assumption that during the 'period' the individual is uncertain as to when he or she receives payments or is required to make payment *during the period*, while simultaneously kicking uncertainty out of the back door by asserting that all market participants know that there will be a complete synchronized clearing of *all* payments by the end of the period in equilibrium (e.g. pp. 14, 80).

36. Ibid., pp. 80–81.
37. J.M. Keynes, *The General Theory*, p. 234. Keynes pointed out that 'A zero elasticity is a more stringent condition than is necessarily required' (ibid., 236, n. 1). As long as money and its close substitutes are not readily producible by labour in the private sector, i.e., money does not grow on trees, money possesses this unique station.
38. J.M. Keynes, *The General Theory*, p. 234.
39. Friedman has always asserted that the elasticity of substitution between financial assets and producible durables is very large. (See M. Friedman and A.J. Schwartz, 'Money and Business Cycles', *Review of Economics and Statistics Supplement*, 1963, p. 60; also M. Friedman, 'A Theoretical Framework For Monetary Analysis', in *Milton Friedman's Monetary Framework: A Debate With His Critics*, edited by R.J. Gordon, University of Chicago Press, Chicago, 1974, p. 27.) By putting the rabbits of high substitutability and flexible prices into his hat, it is not surprising that Friedman's analytical framework demonstrates that full employment is an inevitable outcome; by assumption, there is no way that society, in the aggregate, can defer using all its currently earned claims on resources. Supply therefore creates its own demand.
40. Keynes, *The General Theory*, p. 372.
41. Legal enforcement of labour-hire contracts cannot require performance, only the payment of a nominal sum to compensate the employer for damages due to nonperformance.
42. G. Davidson and P. Davidson, *Economics For A Civilized Society*, Norton, New York, 1988, p. 23.
43. This is logically impossible in a world where the future is calculable and each individual is motivated by his or her own self-interest in a *laissez-faire* environment.
44. Delivery is, somewhat anticlimactically, permitted to occur in the future, but the possibility that the delivering party may be unable to perform is never contemplated.
45. R. Radner, *American Economic Review Papers and Proceedings*, **60**, May 1970, p. 451.
46. Ibid., p. 456.
47. R.J. Barro, *Macroeconomics*, 4th Edition, Wiley, New York, 1993, p. 41.
48. Ibid., p. 44.
49. Ibid., p. 41.
50. J.R. Hicks, *Critical Essays*, p. 156.
51. J.M. Keynes, *A Treatise on Money*, I, p. 3.
52. J.M. Keynes, *A Treatise on Money*, I, p. 5.
53. In nations where the public loses confidence in State money, some may opt for using foreign money to settle spot contracts, while long-duration forward contracts are abandoned.
54. J.R. Hicks, *Critical Essays*, p. 3.
55. Sticky flow-supply prices mean that the rate of change in the money-wage rate relative to the rate of change in productivity is expected to be comparatively small.
56. By definition the price that buyers are offering to pay for forward delivery can never exceed the flow-supply price since the latter is the money-price required to call forth the exertion necessary to produce any given amount of the commodity for any given delivery date. (Cf. N. Kaldor, 'Speculation and Economic Activity', reprinted in *Essays on Stability and Growth*, pp. 34–5.)

    If, for example, the public were suddenly to change its views about the rate of inflation in future flow-supply prices and if they acted on the basis of such anticipations, they would immediately bid up the current spot price of all durables and they would place additional orders for forward delivery (of producible goods) at the current flow-supply price associated with the greater production flow. In other words, changes in the expected rate of inflation of producible goods will affect the current spot prices of all assets and the marginal efficiency of capital goods, while the resulting forward price of output will not exceed the current flow-supply price associated with the induced greater effective demand. (Cf. Keynes, *The General Theory*, pp. 142–3, 231.)
57. 'In other words, expectation of a relative stickiness of wages in terms of money is a corollary of the excess of liquidity-premium over carrying-costs being greater for money

than for any other asset'. (Keynes, *The General Theory*, p. 238).

58. J.R. Hicks, *Critical Essays*, p. 6. What Hicks fails to realize is that, in an uncertain world, there will only be an accidental matching of buyers and sellers in any spot market at any point of time – no matter how well organized. Thus, unless there is a residual buyer or seller who is willing to step in and make a market whenever one side or the other of the market temporarily falls away, the spot price can fluctuate violently. Such fluctuations are incompatible with individuals' desires to hold such items as a store of value. In other words, one necessary condition for any well-organized market is the existence of a market maker.

59. Bank money is a 'tap issue'. As long as bankers obey the Monetary Authority's regulations, the Central Bank will make the market in the bank's deposit liability issue at a fixed price. This assures holders (depositors) of bank debt that this particular form of private debt is a fully liquid asset – as long as the Monetary Authority assures the public that the bank is solvent, *or*, the bank's deposits are 'insured' (i.e., guaranteed as a fully liquid asset) by the government or its Monetary Authority.

60. Since recontracting is not only permitted but is required for equilibrium to occur.

61. See D. Patinkin, *Money, Interest, and Prices*, 2nd edition, pp. 44–5. Also Hicks, *Critical Essays*, pp. 9–10. Many theorists are in essence providing a bootstrap theory of the price level of goods in place of a bootstrap theory of the price level of bonds.

7. Liquidity preference – the demand for money

Why do people hold money which is barren rather than interest-bearing securities or 'productive' physical goods? This is the fundamental question for any monetary theory applicable to the real world. The answer involves uncertainty about future outcomes and the consequent need of economic decision makers to maintain a liquid position to avoid the malady of insolvency or the gallows of bankruptcy. There will be a demand for liquidity,[1] as long as members of the economy believe that future events are not actuarially predictable and they expect the existing money contractual system for organizing production and exchange to continue.

In *The General Theory*, Keynes distinguishes three motives for holding cash:

> (i) the transactions-motive, i.e. the need for cash for the current transaction of personal and business exchanges; (ii) the precautionary-motive, i.e. the desire for security as to the future cash equivalent of a certain proportion of total resources; and (iii) the speculative-motive, i.e. the object of securing profit from knowing better than the market what the future will bring forth.[2]

Keynes recognized that

> money held for each of these three purposes forms, nevertheless, a single pool, which the holder is under no necessity to segregate into three watertight compartments for they need not be sharply divided even in his own mind, and the same sum can be held primarily for one purpose and secondarily for another. Thus we can – equally well, and perhaps, better – consider the individual's aggregate demand for money in given circumstances as a single decision though the composite result of a number of different motives.[3]

In essence, there is only a *single* demand for money. For purposes of exposition it is desirable to study each motive for holding money 'as if' it was separate and independent of the others, even though in reality it need not be. In 1936 Keynes suggested that the three aforementioned categories formed an exhaustive set and that all other reasons for holding money (e.g. the income motive or the business motive) are merely subcategories of these three major divisions. By 1937 Keynes was forced to admit that one of the three motives, the transactions demand for money, was misspecified in *The General Theory*. He rectified this error by adding a fourth category for demanding money, *the finance motive*.

Unfortunately, this respecification of the demand for money went unnoticed as most economists were still trying to understand Keynes's liquidity preference theory as it had been set out in *The General Theory*. Keynes's 1936 triumvirate analysis of the demand for money was hailed by Keynesians as 'a study in depth of a magisterial quality not matched in the present century'.[4] Yet, by ignoring Keynes's 1937 finance motive correction to the theory of liquidity preference, many admirers of Keynes fostered a retrograde analysis that was incompatible with Keynes's earlier *Treatise on Money* where Keynes's 'views about all the details of the complex subject of money are . . . to be found'.[5] By the 1960s, what had evolved as mainstream Keynesianism was so different from Keynes's corrected monetary analysis that Milton Friedman could correctly accuse Keynesians of championing a theory in which money does not matter.

As Harrod pointed out 'it is a paradox that the man whose worldwide fame during most of his lifetime arose from his specific contributions to monetary theory, which were rich and varied, should be studied mainly in one of his books which contains little about money as such'.[6] Keynes quickly admitted that his brief discussion of money contained in the 1936 volume was incorrect. Mainstream 'Keynesians' ignored Keynes's 1937 correction as they regressed into classical analysis. The Keynesian Revolution was aborted by those who claimed to be Keynesians but who disregarded Keynes's *Treatise on Money* and his finance motive revision. The Post Keynesian research agenda has been directed to reviving Keynes's revolutionary analysis by judiciously blending Keynes's monetary analysis presented in his *Treatise on Money* with his 1937 corrected version of liquidity preference.

THE DEMAND FOR MONEY AS A MEDIUM OF CONTRACTUAL SETTLEMENT[7]

Keynes explained the transactions demand for money as the need 'to bridge the interval between the receipt of income and its disbursement'.[8] This time interval is determined by institutional contractual sales and payments arrangements. For example, hourly wage workers are often paid at the end of each week, while salaried employees are paid at the end of each month, credit card balances are due on a certain date each month, the rent is due at the beginning of the month, etc.

Households hold transactions balances to avoid the possibility of insolvency between the point of time they expect to receive money as a result of contracting for the sale of their labour services or to receive property income and the date(s) that they have contractually agreed upon to pay for purchase of goods. Similarly, entrepreneurs hold transactions balances to meet the contractual obligations for the purchase of productive inputs that come due between dates of sales receipts.

In *The General Theory* Keynes referred to this behaviour of households as the income motive; the behaviour of entrepreneurs was designated the business motive. In the *Treatise* he refers to the money being held for these motives as income deposits and business deposits respectively.[9] The quantity of income deposits held by households depends on (a) the length of time between well-established contractual pay intervals, and (b) the *planned* household spending during the pay interval. The quantity of business deposits held depends on (a) the sales receipts period, (b) the degree of vertical integration of firms, and (c) the *planned* spending of firms during the period.

Keynes, while defining the transactions motive as the 'need for cash for the current transaction of personal and business exchanges',[10] encouraged viewing this transactions demand for money for transactions balances solely from the householders' position to the neglect of the business motive. In *The General Theory*, planned household expenditures are identified with D_1 expenditures. Consequently, many 'Keynesians' (and, in 1936, Keynes himself[11]) were misled by this cursory treatment into incorrectly specifying the demand for transactions balances as being uniquely and directly related to the level of aggregate income. Thus the popular, but improperly specified, generalized demand for money for transactions purposes is written as

$$D_m^t = f1(Y, T) \qquad (7.1)$$

where Y represents the aggregate income of the community, and T is the average contractual payments interval. Assuming that the time interval is part of the institutional setting and invariant during the period of analysis, equation (7.1) reduces to

$$D_m^t = f1(Y). \qquad (7.1a)$$

Hansen, an early expositor of what became the basis of mainstream Keynesianism, specified the demand for transactions balances as

$$L_t = k_t Y \qquad (7.1b)$$

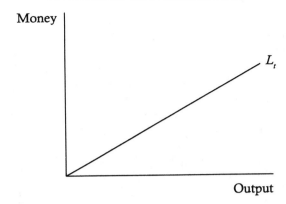

Figure 7.1   Hansen's graph of L$_t$

where k_t is a constant.[12] Hansen plotted equation (7.1b) as a straight line, L_t emanating from the origin (Figure 7.1).

Equation (7.1b) is still the standard specification for the transactions demand for money in most textbooks *and* professional articles written for learned journals.

Keynes's precautionary motive for holding cash balances is usually given perfunctory treatment. Typically, the precautionary motive is assumed to be directly related to society's aggregate income. Thus the precautionary demand for money is specified as

$$D_m^p = k_p Y. \tag{7.2}$$

In mainstream macroeconomics, the only significant difference between the transactions and precautionary motives is that the former involved planned transactions while the latter involved contingency transactions that could be foreseeable in general even if unplanned in specifics.[13]

Combining equations (7.1c) and (7.2) we obtain the demand for transactions and precautionary balances. This combined demand is often labelled the demand for active balances:

$$D_m^{t+p} = k_3 Y \tag{7.3}$$

where $k_3 = k_t + k_p$. This demand for active balances is typically as a straight line emanating from the origin.

This seemingly innocuous mis-specification is consistent with a misrepresentation of Keynes's system in the textbook 45-degree diagram[14] (Figure 7.2) where the latter, by definition, prohibits the analysis of nonequili-

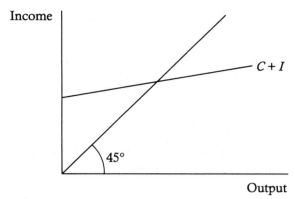

Figure 7.2 The 45-degree and C + I *lines*

brium positions (i.e., positions off the 45-degree line). In many textbooks, the 45-degree line is depicted as representing aggregate supply, while the $C + I$ line represents aggregate demand.

In mis-specifying the demand for active balances, Hansen and his innumerable followers were merely following a simplification of Keynes's when, for the purpose of analysing a specific situation, Keynes decided it was a 'safe first approximation' to write the demand for transactions (and precautionary) balances as $L_1(Y)$.[15] This specification implies that the aggregate demand for active money balances to buy goods in the current period is directly related to and solely a function of aggregate income or supply (the 45-degree line of Figure 7.2) rather than a function of planned spending (the $C + I$ demand curve).[16] Equation (7.3) is incompatible with Keynes's taxonomy where there is, at least, one category of spending, D_2, that is not related to aggregate current income or supply. It is this incompatibility that Keynes attempted to rectify with his 1937 finance motive analysis.

Before discussing the finance motive correction, it will be helpful to discuss the third motive for demanding money in *The General Theory* – the speculative demand for money.

THE SPECULATIVE MOTIVE – THE DEMAND FOR A TIME MACHINE[17]

Chapter 4 *supra* indicated that all income earners had to make two decisions regarding their currently earned claims on resources. These decisions are (1) the time preference decision of how to allocate current income between current planned consumption and planned non-consumption (savings) and (2) the liquidity preference decision of how to allocate savings out of current income among various time machines (liquid assets) to transport purchasing power to the indefinite and uncertain future. This time-machine allocative decision where savers choose among many possible liquid assets (including money) involves the speculative demand for money.

By definition, liquid assets are durables that are traded on well-organized, orderly spot markets. Since such assets can be readily resold at a market price tomorrow that can differ from today's spot market price, these assets are potential objects of speculation and possible alternatives to money as a time machine for transferring liquidity to the future.[18] In making a choice as to which time machines to use as liquid stores of value, savers face two potential uncertainties: (a) an income uncertainty and (b) a capital value uncertainty. Both uncertainties are vexatious. In an uncertain world, savers must choose how much of each uncertainty they wish to bear.

The income uncertainty. The issuers of most liquid assets have either contractually agreed or conditionally quasi-contractually agreed to pay income at specific future dates to the holders (e.g. interest payments on bonds, dividends on equity securities). The longer the saver holds a liquid asset, the more total income he or she may expect to receive. Savers must evaluate the promised potential future income stream minus any carrying cost of holding the asset and whether the issuers will be able to meet these future obligations. They must compare this uncertain future cash income with the certainty of receiving no income if one holds currency[19] instead.

The capital uncertainty. Since the spot market price of liquid assets can change over time, savers must contemplate the possibility of an appreciation or depreciation in the asset's market price at a future date when the holder wishes to liquidate his or her holdings. This potential capital gain or loss is obtained by subtracting today's spot price (p_s^{t0}) from the expected spot price at a future date (p_s^{t1}) when the asset will be resold. If $(p_s^{t1} - p_s^{t0}) > 0$, a capital gain is expected from holding the asset till $t1$; if $(p_s^{t1} - p_s^{t0}) < 0$, a capital loss will be expected. If the saver holds money instead, there will be no capital uncertainty. The price of money in terms of itself can never change.

Both uncertainties are vexatious to savers. Savers can avoid these uncertainties only if they hold all their store of value in the form of money. The cost of this option is to give up all possible income earnings on one's savings as well as the possibility of capital gains.[20] Buying liquid assets with one's savings exposes the saver to the uncertainty of possible capital loss.

Moreover, there are usually transactions costs (T_s) incurred in both buying and reselling any liquid asset. These transactions costs are usually independent of the time interval that the liquid asset is held.[21] If an unforeseen liability should come due in the immediate future, then the transactions cost of taking a position and then liquidating it can easily swamp any income flow received from holding the asset for such a short time. It is, therefore, normal to prefer to hold some saving in the form of money to cover planned and some possible unforeseen obligations that can come due in the very near future.[22]

The more uncertain the future appears, the more unforeseeable liabilities that may come due. The more desirable, therefore, it will be to minimize transactions costs by storing saving in the form of money rather than other liquid assets. Some saving is therefore always held in the form of money to meet contractual payments in the very near future. This soothes our fears of becoming illiquid if anything unpredictable occurs during the period.[23]

All savers find a capital loss repugnant. To induce a saver to exchange money (or any other fully liquid asset) for a liquid asset whose spot market resale price can change over time, the saver must expect to receive a liquidity premium in terms of promised future income payments less carrying costs that exceed the possible capital loss plus transactions costs of getting into and out of the liquid asset. Let q be the future expected income to be received over a period of time, and c be the carrying costs. If one holds money there is no income $((q-c)=0)$, no capital gain or loss $((p_s^{t1} - p_s^{t0})=0)$, and no transactions costs $(T_s = 0)$. Savers will estimate the expected future income plus capital gain or loss plus transactions costs associated with holding a liquid asset. They compare the result with that of money. If, for a specific liquid asset the saver expects

$$(q - c) + (p_s^{t1} - p_s^{t0}) - T_s > 0,$$

then the saver is a 'bull' and will buy all the asset that he or she currently can afford. If it is expected that

$$(q - c) + (p_s^{t1} - p_s^{t0}) - T_s < 0,$$

then the saver is a 'bear' and would prefer to hold money rather than the liquid asset for these speculative purposes. Of course, in a world of uncertainty, most people are unlikely to have absolute confidence in any expectation of future capital gains or losses they might hold. Few savers are likely to be a complete bull or a complete bear. Most sensible people will hold a mixed portfolio of money and other liquid assets – rather than putting all their liquidity eggs in one basket. The larger the positive

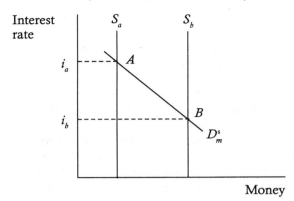

Figure 7.3   The speculation demand curve for money

evaluation a saver puts on $(p_s^{t1} - p_s^{t0})$, the more bullish he or she is and the more he or she will alter his or her portfolio from money towards other liquid assets.

This bull–bear evaluation applies to any easily resalable durable. In *The General Theory*, Keynes used bonds as the only alternative liquid asset to money. This simplification permitted Keynes to provide an easy explanation of how the nominal rate of interest was determined in the market place.

For long-term bonds, the rate of interest is inversely related to the spot price of the bond, i.e. $i = f(1/P_B)$ where i is the market rate of interest and P_B is the spot price of the bond. If most participants in the bond market think today's interest rate is 'high' (bond prices are 'low'), then they will tend to be bullish on bonds. Since the term 'high' connotes the expectation that the interest rate is normally lower and therefore bond prices are normally higher, the market must think bond prices should rise and the interest rate fall. In Figure 7.3, at the 'high' interest rate of i_a, the quantity of money demanded will be relatively small (i.e., close to the ordinate axis) as most bond market participants are bullish. Point A in Figure 7.3 represents this bullish position on the speculative demand curve for money.

If more people believe interest rates are 'low' at the interest rate i_b in Figure 7.3 (bond prices are high), then more savers will expect interest rates to increase. They will be bearish on bonds. The quantity of money demanded for speculative purposes will be greater than at interest rate i_a. Connecting points A and B, the result is the downward-sloping demand for money for speculative purposes curve D_m^s in Figure 7.3.

A linear algebraic representation of this speculative demand for written money function can be written as

$$D_m^s = a_4 - b_4 i \tag{7.4}$$

where b_4 is the slope of the demand curve for speculative balances and a_4 is the intercept where the curve intersects the abscissa.

If the money supply is determined exogenously by the actions of the Central Bank, then the supply of money can be represented as the vertical curve, S_a, in Figure 7.3. Any exogenous increase in the supply of money will shift the money supply curve outward, say from S_a to S_b. If there is no change in the demand for money for transactions, precautionary or speculative purposes, then the rate of interest will decline from i_a to i_b.

In *The General Theory*, Keynes argued that any lower interest rate below the rate deemed normal reduces the income to be earned from an investment while increasing the possibility of a capital loss. If the interest rate is 4 per cent, it is worthwhile to invest as long as the saver does not think the price of bonds will fall more rapidly than 4 per cent per annum. If the interest rate is 2 per cent, the purchase of a bond will be worthwhile as long as the price of bonds is not expected to decline by more than 2 per cent per annum (assuming $T_s = 0$). This implies that the speculative demand for money curve is a downward-sloping rectangular hyperbola that approaches the abscissa asymptotically.[24]

Mainstream Keynesians claim that the demand curve for speculative money balances becomes infinitely elastic (horizontal) at some low but positive interest rate.[25] This horizontal segment of the speculative demand curve was designated the liquidity trap by Old Keynesians. If the economy is enmeshed in the liquidity trap, then Old Keynesians argued that the Monetary Authority is powerless to lower the rate of interest to stimulate the economy no matter how much they exogenously increased the supply of money.

Mainstream Keynesians made the liquidity trap the hallmark of their neoclassical synthesis Keynesian theory when they proclaimed that fiscal policy was necessary to pull an economy out of a recession. The idea that the Central Bank was powerless to push the economy onto a road to recovery was succinctly summarized in the motto 'you can't push on a string'. This became a major policy theme for many who called themselves Keynesians, even though Keynes had never claimed there was a liquidity trap.

Econometricians searched in vain to demonstrate the existence of a liquidity trap where monetary policy could not affect the interest rate. This failure to provide empirical evidence of the existence of a liquidity trap permitted Monetarists such as Milton Friedman to denigrate Keynesian economics and use the motto 'Money Matters' as an anti-Keynesian weapon. As the discussion in the next chapter indicates, this controversy between Monetarists and Old Keynesians could have been avoided had the followers of Keynes recognized that the finance motive was necessary to specify correctly Keynes's liquidity preference theory.

HICKS'S IS–LM MODEL; A FAILED REPRESENTATION OF KEYNES

While Keynes was still working to specify correctly his liquidity preference analysis, J.R. Hicks published what he claimed was a complete equational representation of Keynes's central argument. Hicks's equational system, which became known as the IS–LM model, has become entrenched in textbooks and the professional literature as the correct depiction of Keynes's *General Theory*. By 1967, Hicks was expressing second thoughts when he admitted IS–LM is a 'potted version'[26] of Keynes. By 1980, Hicks went even further in his repudiation of the IS–LM as a proper representation of Keynes.[27] Despite this disavowal by Hicks of his model, variants of the IS–LM system still represent mainstream macroeconomic models. In this chapter, this IS–LM basic model will be developed. In the next chapter, the limitations of this model and why the introduction of Keynes's 1937 finance motive radically changes the implications of the model will be discussed.

The mainstream three-equation model of Chapter 4 representing the real side of the economy is:

$$Y = C + I \tag{7.5}$$

$$C = a_1 + b_1 Y \tag{7.6}$$

$$I = a_2 - b_2 i \tag{7.7}$$

Substituting equations (7.6) and (7.7) into the accounting identity (7.5), and rearranging terms produces an equation that Hicks labelled IS:

$$Y = (1/[1 - b_1])(a_1 + a_2 - b_2 i) \tag{7.8}$$

This IS equation is depicted as showing all possible combinations of equilibrium values for the interest rate and the aggregate level of income in the real sector. The negative sign on the parameter associated with the independent variable i in (7.7) indicates that the IS curve (e.g. IS_0) is downward sloping in Figure 7.4. At lower interest rates, investment and therefore income is greater.

The monetary sector is described by a demand for active balance equation

$$D_m^{t+p} = k_3 Y \tag{7.3}$$

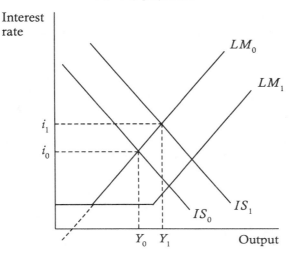

Figure 7.4   The IS–LM system

plus the linear speculative demand function (ignoring for the moment the liquidity trap) of equation (7.4)

$$D_m^s = a_4 - b_4 i \qquad (7.4)$$

and an exogenous supply of money, M. Combining equations (7.3) and (7.4) with the given money supply and rearranging terms, the LM equation of Hicks's system is:

$$i = a_5 + b_5 Y - c_5 M \qquad (7.9)$$

where $a_5 = (a_4/b_4)$, $b_5 = k_3/b_4$ and $c_5 = 1/b_4$.

In Figure 7.4, this LM equation is upward sloping as the plus sign in front of the parameter b_5 indicates that as output rises the quantity of money demanded for active balances increases.

To represent the liquidity trap, at some positive but low rate of interest, the bottom portion of the LM curve becomes horizontal rather than continuing to be downward sloping (as the dashed portion of the LM curve in Figure 7.4 illustrates).

Solving IS_0 and LM_0 simultaneously yields the equilibrium values of i and Y as i_0 and Y_0. Any hypothesized exogenous increase in aggregate spending will shift the IS curve to the right, from IS_0 to IS_1, increasing income from Y_0 to Y_1. If, in Figure 7.4, the economy is not initially in the liquidity trap, the hypothesized rightward shift of IS induces a rise in the interest rate from i_0 to i_1. In the liquidity trap, on the other hand, a rightward shift of the IS curve raises output but leaves the interest rate unchanged.[28]

An exogenous increase in the money supply shifts the LM curve downward to the right (reflecting the negative sign associated with the exogenous money variable) from LM_0 to LM_1 in Figure 7.4. Outside the liquidity trap, this reduces interest rates and induces additional investment and output. In the liquidity trap, however, the shift of the LM curve has no effect on the rate of interest and therefore no change in output will be forthcoming. Accordingly, we have the 'can't push on a string solution'.

NOTES

1. In the absence of these conditions, the economy would operate as a *nonmonetary economy* in which there would be no asset whose liquidity premium exceeded its carrying costs. In a nonmonetary economy, no asset exists whose ability to carry purchasing power over time exceeds the carrying cost associated with the asset's physical and value deterioration and/or inventory storage costs. (See J.M. Keynes, *The General Theory*, p. 239.)
2. J.M. Keynes, *The General Theory*, p. 170.
3. Ibid., p. 195.
4. R.F. Harrod, *Money*, Macmillan, London, p. 151.
5. R.F. Harrod, *The Life of John Maynard Keynes*, Macmillan, London, 1951.
6. R.F. Harrod, 'Themes in Dynamic Theory', *Economic Journal*, **73**, 1963, p. 442.
7. This section is based on P. Davidson, 'Keynes's Finance Motive', *Oxford Economic Papers*, **17**, 1965.
8. J.M. Keynes, *The General Theory*, p. 195. Also see *A Treatise on Money*, I, Ch. 24.
9. Keynes, *The General Theory*, p. 195, *A Treatise on Money*, I, pp. 34–5. Actually Keynes subdivides business deposits into two categories – A and B – and only business deposits A are used for transactions purposes, ibid., p. 244.
10. J.M. Keynes, *The General Theory*, p. 170.
11. J.M. Keynes, *The General Theory*, p. 199.
12. See for example, A. Hansen, *Monetary Theory and Fiscal Policy*, McGraw-Hill, New York, 1949, p. 61.
13. For example, you may not know whether, during the period, your child will get hurt and need medical attention, or you will smash your car fender and need to get it repaired, etc. but actuarially speaking you 'know' that some unforeseen contingency will arise which will require cash to make a payment during the period.
14. Had an alternative geometrical apparatus using aggregate supply and demand functions (as developed by Weintraub) been adopted, the omission of the finance motive and the incorrect specification of the transactions demand for money function would probably not have occurred. With Weintraub's scheme, it would have been obvious, I believe, to relate the demand for money schedule with the demand for goods function. See S. Weintraub, *An Approach To The Theory of Income Distribution*, Chilton, Philadelphia, 1958, Chapter 2.
15. J.M. Keynes, *The General Theory*, p. 199.
16. Consequently, this specification is applicable to a Say's Law special case where aggregate demand is coincident with aggregate supply rather than Keynes's general case.
17. In *The General Theory*, Keynes emphasized the speculative motive for holding money, because, at the time, it was less understood than the demand for active balances. It is

particularly important in understanding how central banks can transmit an exogenous change in the quantity of money (e.g., obtained through open-market operations) to the rate of interest (or the exchange rate in an open economy).

18. In an economy without any organized spot market for reselling assets the precautionary motive for holding money would become more prominent.

19. The holders of currency receive no income, but the holders of bank money may receive income.

20. For those individuals who are afraid to bear any capital losses – the complete bear – saving will be held entirely in money or other fully liquid assets. For those savers, sometimes characterized as widows and orphans – who would never 'live off their capital', except for transactions and precautionary balances, saving will be invested entirely in income-bearing securities where the fear of default is at a minimum.

21. The transactions costs of taking and then liquidating a position are usually independent of the length of time the position is held (and often increase at a decreasing rate as the value of the purchases rises). The expected cash inflow received from holding securities is normally closely related to the passage of time.

22. Cf. J.R. Hicks, 'A Suggestion for Simplifying the Theory of Money', *Economica*, **2**, 1935, reprinted in *Critical Essays in Monetary Theory*. All references are to the reprint.

23. Transactions costs (of holding alternative liquid assets) in the broadest sense – that is including the *fear* of rapid *unpredictable* changes in spot prices, or operating in a thin spot market where no financial institution will act as a residual buyer and seller – are basic to determining the magnitude of transactions, precautionary and speculative demands for money in the current income period. If all assets were instantaneously resaleable without any costs, there would never be a need to hold 'barren money' rather than a productive asset, except for the necessary nanosecond before it was necessary to meet a contractual commitment that came due. In the real world, the magnitude of actual costs of moving between liquid assets and the medium of contractual settlement is related to the degree of spot market organization and the existence of financial institutions that 'make' spot markets and that thereby assure reasonable moment-to-moment stickiness in spot prices.

24. J.M. Keynes, *The General Theory*, p. 202.

25. In terms of Figure 7.3, the liquidity trap would be represented by the linear downward-sloping curve becoming horizontal at some low but positive interest rate.

26. J.R. Hicks, *Critical Essays in Monetary Theory*, Oxford University Press, Oxford, 1967, p. vii.

27. J.R. Hicks, 'IS–LM: An Explanation', *Journal of Post Keynesian Economics*, **3**, 1980–81, p. 139.

28. The multiplier analysis of Chapter 3 implied that output would rise with an increase in exogenous spending without any change in the interest rate. Hence, if the money supply is unchanged, the multiplier effect is applicable only to the liquidity trap situation or an accommodating monetary authority who maintains the rate of interest.

8.   The finance motive and the interdependence of the real and monetary sectors

Keynes had searched for a simplification of his *Treatise on Money* when he concluded that his critics 'simply failed to grasp' his elaborate monetary analysis.[1] The result was a less rigorous monetary specification in *The General Theory* where 'money enters into the economic scheme in an essential and peculiar manner, [but] technical monetary detail falls into the background'.[2] As the last chapter indicated, this deliberate ensconcement of monetary analysis led Keynes into incorrectly specifying the transactions demand. This error encouraged mainstream 'Keynesians' to develop a Bastard Keynesian model that was a perversion of Keynes's own system.

In 1937, Ohlin quickly spotted the error of Keynes's 1936 simplification of the transactions demand. In reply to Ohlin's criticism, Keynes introduced a new and what appeared to be a somewhat novel purpose for demanding money, namely the *finance motive*.[3] Keynes argued that if contractual commitments to buy new capital per period were unchanged, then the money held to 'finance' investment expenditures was more or less constant and could be lumped under a subcategory of the transactions motive where capital-goods transactions are involved. Entrepreneurs must hold some cash balances between payments periods to assure themselves that when they enter into forward contracts for the hiring of inputs for production of capital goods they will be able to meet these obligations. The quantity of cash balances needed each period to meet these forward contracts for producing investment goods will be unchanged as long as planned investment is unchanged.

'But', Keynes argued, 'if decisions to invest are (e.g.) increasing, the extra finance involved will constitute an additional demand for money'.[4] If, for example, profit expectations exogenously increase, then at the initial flow of output and rate of interest, entrepreneurs will demand additional investment goods and be willing to enter into more forward contracts to produce capital providing they can obtain finance. The demand for money to pay for the production of these additional investments at any given interest rate will increase even before any additional employment and income are generated.[5]

To clarify the essence of the finance motive, and to indicate why it is not properly taken into account in his 1936 discussion of the transactions motive, Keynes wrote:

> It follows that, if the liquidity-preferences of the public (as distinct from the entrepreneurial investors) and of the banks are unchanged, an excess in the finance required by current ex-ante output (it is not necessary to write 'investment', since the same is true of *any* output which has to be planned ahead) over the finance released by current ex-post output will lead to a rise in the rate of interest; and a decrease will lead to a fall. I should not have previously overlooked this point, since it is the coping-stone of the liquidity theory of the rate of interest. I allowed, it is true, for the effect of an increase in *actual* activity on the demand for money. But I did not allow for the effect of an increase in *planned* activity, which is superimposed on the former. . . . Just as an increase in actual activity must (as I have always explained) raise the rate of interest unless either the banks or the rest of the public become more willing to release cash, so (as I now add) an increase in planned activity must have a similar, superimposed influence'.[6]

Since Keynes felt that the finance motive was the coping-stone of his liquidity preference theory, it is surprising that the concept was never adopted in the mainstream Keynesian economic literature.

There was a very clear practical illustration of this finance motive analysis offered by Keynes in 1939 when his attention was devoted to the imminent rearmament programme and the prospect of war. In a letter printed in the 18 April 1939 edition of *The Times*, Keynes elucidated his reasoning still further. The immediate question was how to finance the pending additional government expenditures for rearmament. Keynes argued that 'If an attempt is made to borrow them [the savings which will result from the increased production of non-consumption (war) goods] before they exist, as the Treasury have done once or twice lately, a stringency in the money market must result, since pending the expenditure, the liquid resources acquired by the Treasury must be at the expense of the normal liquid resources of the banks and of the public'. In other words, an increase in planned governmental expenditures will normally result in an increase in the aggregate demand for transactions balances, even before the expenditures are undertaken.[7]

It is evident from the *Treatise on Money* and Keynes's finance motive notes in the 1937 issues of *The Economic Journal* that specifying the demand for money as a direct function of current income is a gross and somewhat misleading simplification of his liquidity analysis. The introduction of the finance motive concept involves relating the demand for transactions balances to planned, contractual spending propensities during the payments period. The demand for transactions balances must be a

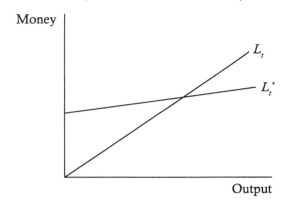

Figure 8.1   The graphs of L_t *and* L_t^*

function of the aggregate planned demand for goods (the $C + I$ line in Figure 7.2) rather than the 45-degree (aggregate supply) line.

The finance motive represents shifts in the transactions demand function for money associated with shifts in the aggregate demand function of Figure 7.2. Any exogenous planned increase in the demand for goods requires people to hold additional money balances to meet the resulting additional contractual commitments that will come due during the period. If the quantity of money is unchanged, this requirement for additional finance will increase the rate of interest even *before* there is any additional output flow as the additional borrowers tend to crowd out others in the market. If the Monetary Authority and the banking system attempt to maintain the interest rate in response to an increased demand for additional finance, then the money supply will endogenously expand *before* there is any change in the rate of flow of production and the level of employment.

Using the mainstream equation model of Chapter 3, a correctly specified Keynesian transactions demand concept is a function of the summation of the consumption (income-related D_1) spending plus investment demand (income-unrelated D_2). If the quantity of money demanded for transactions and precautionary balances is equal to some constant fraction action of the aggregate planned demand for goods $(D_1 + D_2)$ at each level of output, then the demand for active balances function would be drawn as L_t^*, rather than L_t, in Figure 8.1 (since it is related to the $C + I$ line rather than the 45-degree line in Figure 7.2).[8]

Much more is involved here than merely a geometric misrepresentation of the demand for transactions balances. The relationship between the quantity of money demanded for transactions and the level of output is a function of a function of current output, rather than directly related to current output. Given the customary contractual payments period in the economy, it follows that if consumers and/or investors decide to spend more at any given flow of income (an upward shift of the aggregate demand function), then there will be an increase in the demand for money for the purchase of goods at every level of income (an upward shift of the L_t^* function).

On adding an exogenous government spending (G) component to both our D_2 expenditures category and the aggregate demand for transactions balances, L_t^*, can be written as:

$$L_t^* = \alpha C + \beta I + \epsilon G; \qquad (8.1)$$

C, I, and G are the planned consumption, investment, and government spending commitments to purchase goods and services during the period. The α, β, and ϵ are constants whose magnitudes depend primarily on the frequency of payments and the overlapping of payments and receipts in the system. Assuming linear functions (for algebraic simplicity), we have the consumption function:

$$C = a_1 + b_1 Y \qquad (8.2)$$

where a_1 is a constant and b_1 is the marginal propensity to consume. The marginal efficiency of investment function is:

$$I = a_2 - b_2 i \qquad (8.3)$$

where a_2 and b_2 are constants and i is the rate of interest. Government spending, G, is assumed to be exogenous. Substituting for C, I and G in equation (8.1), the demand for active balances is rewritten as:

$$L_t^* = \alpha(a_1 + b_1 Y) + \beta(a_2 - b_2 i) + \epsilon G. \qquad (8.4)$$

Assuming a given interest rate,[9] then the last two terms on the right hand side of equation (8.3) are both constants[10] and equation (8.4) reduces to:

$$L_t^* = J + \alpha b_1 Y \qquad (8.4a)$$

where $J = \alpha(a_1) + \beta(a_2 - b_2 i) + \epsilon G$.

Equation (8.4a) is algebraically similar to Hansen's equation (7.1b) except that the former does not emanate from the origin. There is a significant analytical difference between equations (7.1b) and (8.4a).

Hansen's representation of the demand for active balances equation is independent of the behavioural a_1, a_2, b_1, and b_2 parameters of the real sector. In Hansen's equation the parameter k depends only on the (given and presumed unchanging) customary length of the payments period in the economy. Hansen's demand for active balances is, therefore, stable, even if the parameters of real aggregate demand change.

Once the finance motive analysis provides the correct specification of Keynes's demand for active balances, then the latter is not as stable as the Hansen specification implies. The behavioural a_1, a_2, b_1, and b_2 parameters of the consumption and investment functions and the level of government planned spending are also parameters of Keynes's demand for money (equation (8.4)). Any exogenous change in government spending or the behavioural parameters associated with consumption and investment spending will shift the aggregate demand for goods function *and* simultaneously shift (change) the demand for money function. This is the macroanalogue of the microeconomic maxim 'Demand means want plus the ability to pay'.

As Keynes noted, any 'increase in planned activity' will result in an increased demand for money *at each level of income*. The demand for money is *not* independent of demand in the real sector.

If there is an increase in planned investment (or planned spending of any kind[11]), then the equilibrium quantity of money demanded increases for two reasons. First, there is a shift in the L_t^* function (i.e., the finance motive). Second there is a movement along the new L_t^* function as output increases and induces further spending through the multiplier. It is the shift in the L_t^* function that puts additional pressure on the rate of interest.[12]

THE FINANCE MOTIVE AND THE INCOME VELOCITY OF MONEY

Classical monetary theorists presume that there is an invariant relationship between the demand for money and the level of current aggregate income known as the income velocity of money. Since Keynes's properly specified demand for money function shifts concomitantly with the aggregate demand function, and since neither function necessarily emanates from the origin, there is no reason to expect to observe a constant income velocity of money over any length of calendar time. The recognition of the 'finance motive' concept produces some clearer understanding of monetary phenomena that have been confusing to classically trained theorists.

For example, Friedman, recognizing that the income velocity of money is a demand-oriented phenomenon, has attempted to estimate the income elasticity of demand for money. He found that observed short-run variations in income velocity imply an income elasticity less than unity, whereas secular evidence indicates an elasticity that exceeds unity. In a novel (and forced) explanation, Friedman reconciles these conflicting short-run and secular estimates of elasticity by imputing differences between 'permanent' income and prices and measured income and prices.[13]

The finance motive concept suggests a much simpler explanation that is entirely consistent with Friedman's different short-run and secular estimates. If the short-run demand for transactions balances function has a positive intercept and is either a straight line or concave to the abscissa, then:

$$[dL_t^*/dY] < [L_t^*/Y]$$

It therefore follows that the income elasticity of demand for transactions balances will be less than unity along the entire function.[14] Given the normal aggregate consumption and investment functions and the rate of interest, short-run movements in output will be accompanied by less than proportional changes in the quantity of money demanded by spending units as the economy moves towards equilibrium.

Observed secular changes in the quantity of money demanded, on the other hand, are most likely the result of viewing particular demand points on different L_t^* functions as the latter shifts through time in response to changes in the parameters of the aggregate demand for goods function. The income elasticity calculated from observations that cut across short-run L_t^* functions will obviously be larger in magnitude than the elasticity measured along any one short-run L_t^* function and might easily result in estimates that exceed unity. This secular elasticity measurement has little or no relationship to the usual concept of income elasticity that assumes a given preference scheme (i.e., given behavioural parameters).

Friedman has made the assumption that 'the elasticity of demand for money with respect to real income is approximately unity' the foundation for his 'superior ... method of closing the theoretical system for the purpose of analyzing short-period changes'.[15] If the demand for transactions balances is related to aggregate supply (or the 45-degree line), then demand for money will be a straight line emanating from the origin. This straight line will possess an income elasticity of unity. The unity income elasticity of demand for money can only belong to the world of Say's Law where the aggregate demand function coincides with the 45-degree aggregate supply line. In such a world, the aggregate demand function is linear and homogeneous with respect to aggregate income and money is a neutral veil. There is a dichotomy between the real and monetary sectors so that there can be no monetary obstacle to full employment – the real and monetary factors are completely independent. In other words, Friedman's 'superior method of closing the theoretical system' invokes the nonmonetary economy of Say's Law to support his claim that 'money matters'.

If the demand for transactions balances is a function of aggregate demand, which, because of the existence of D_2 spending, is not homogeneous with respect to output, then the demand for transactions money balances is also not homogeneous with respect to output. The system cannot be dichotomized into independent monetary and real subsets since the scale of activity is an important determinant of the level of planned aggregate demand and Say's Law is not applicable.

Keynes believed that any model that presumed an analytical separation of independent real and monetary sectors could not explain the existence of unemployment in the real world.[16] A long-run unit elasticity of demand for money is incompatible with Keynes's finance motive analysis – and is inimical to the Keynes–Post Keynesian belief in the non-neutrality of money, and the importance of an endogenous money supply in facilitating economic expansion in the real sector.

Since Friedman based his analytical model on a unit income elasticity of demand for money, it is not surprising that he asserts that all changes in the quantity of money 'can be regarded as completely exogenous'.[17] When members of the Monetarist school observe a statistically significant relationship between changes in the quantity of money and changes in aggregate income, they insist that the former must have (by hypothesis) caused the latter. Recognition of Keynes's finance motive concept means that causality cannot be determined by any empirical relation between these variables.

When Keynes linked the finance motive with changes in the decision to invest, he was, as he readily admitted, discussing 'only a special case' of the finance motive. Keynes's justification for linking the finance motive to changes in planned investment was his belief that planned investment is 'subject to special fluctuation of its own'. In his discussion of war finance Keynes generalized the application of the finance motive to other exogenous components of aggregate demand.

Any change in exogenous planned spending behaviour will result in a shift in the transactions demand for money function, and if the banking system responds, changes in the money supply will be endogenously determined. Keynes believed that an endogenous monetary supply system was an ideal one. He wrote that bank 'credit is the pavement along which production travels, and the bankers, if they knew their duty, would provide the transport facilities to just the extent that is required in order that the productive powers of the community can be employed at their full capacity'.[18] An overdraft system 'is an ideal system for mitigating the effects on the banking system of an increased demand for *ex ante* finance'.[19]

THE FINANCE MOTIVE AND THE INTERDEPENDENCE OF THE REAL AND MONETARY SECTORS

The inappropriateness of attempting to dichotomize the system into independent real and monetary subsets and the question of whether deficit government spending to stimulate the economy will 'crowd out' private investors from the market for borrowing funds can be clarified by using an IS–LM model modified to include the finance motive.

The basic IS function (equation (7.8) in Chapter 7) augmented to include an exogenous government spending component to obtain an ISG equation:

$$Y = (1/[1-b_1])(a_1 + a_2 - b_2 i + G). \tag{8.5}$$

To the demand for money equation (8.4) add a linear speculative demand for money function, $D_m^s = a_4 - b_4 i$ (while ignoring the possibility of a liquidity trap) to obtain the total demand for money (L) as:

$$L = a(a_1 + b_1 Y) + \beta(a_2 - b_2 i) + \epsilon G + (a_4 - b_4 i). \tag{8.6}$$

Equating the demand for money with an exogenous money supply (M) yields:

$$a(a_1 + b_1 Y) + \epsilon G + \beta(a_2 - b_2 i) + (a_4 - b_4 i) - M = 0. \tag{8.7}$$

Rearranging terms

$$(\beta b_2 + b_4) i = a a_1 + \beta a_2 + a_4 + a b_1 Y + \epsilon G - M. \tag{8.8}$$

Letting $\pi_1 = [1/(\beta b_2 + b_4)]$ and $\pi_2 = a a_1 + \beta a_2 + a_4$, then the LM equation is

$$i = \pi_1(\pi_2) + \pi_1 a b_1 Y + \pi_1 \epsilon G + \pi_1 M. \tag{8.9}$$

The ISG equation $(I_1 SG$ in Figure 8.2) traces out all the values of output and the rate of interest that are compatible with the planned investment,

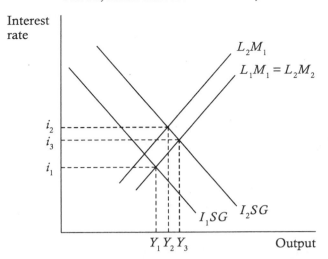

Figure 8.2   The interdependence of the real and monetary subsectors

consumption, and government spending. In Figure 8.2 the I_1SG is downward sloping.

Except in the omitted liquidity trap, the LM equation (8.9) is upward sloping (L_1M_1 in Figure 8.2) since, as Y increases, the rate of interest rises. The values of i and Y that satisfy the I_1SG and L_1M_1 equations simultaneously are i_1 and Y_1 in Figure 8.2.

The interdependence of the money market and the real sector is easily demonstrated. Assume an exogenous increase in expected profit opportunities leads to an increase in a_2. At each rate of interest, the Y ordinate of the ISG function will increase by an amount equal to the change in a_2 multiplied by $1/(1 - b_1)$, i.e., the ISG function moves outwards to I_2SG in Figure 8.2.

In Hansen's system, the LM function would remain unchanged when the IS curve shifts. Equation (8.9), however, indicates that when a_2 increases, the ordinate of the LM function will increase by an amount equal to the change in a_2 multiplied by π_1 at each output level. The whole L_1M_1 function shifts upward to L_2M_1 in Figure 8.2. The new equilibrium level of output and rate of interest (Y_2 and i_2 respectively) are higher than before.[20] Whenever any of the parameters of aggregate demand change, simultaneous shifts in the ISG and LM functions occur.

The inevitable conclusion is that this macro system cannot be dichotomized into independent real and monetary subsets. The classical dichotomy based on the neutrality of money does not hold. The interdependence of the real and monetary sectors does not require the fine theoretical point (which may have little practical significance) of a real balance effect or even the fixity of product prices. That so much of mainstream macroeconomics still assumes the independence of the real and monetary subsectors is surprising. Keynes warned that the 'division of Economics between the Theory of Value and Distribution on the one hand and the Theory of Money on the other hand is, I think, a false division'.[21] Had the interconnection between the finance motive, the transactions motive, and the aggregate demand function been understood originally, much of the barren development of macroeconomics in recent decades could have been avoided.

Once the finance motive concept is understood, it is easy to demonstrate the correctness of Keynes's *obiter dictum* that an overdraft system is an 'ideal system for mitigating the effects on the banking system of an increased demand for ex-ante finance'.[22] If there is an outward shift of the ISG function from I_1SG to I_2SG as profit expectations rise, and if the resulting increase in demand for cash to finance the additional investment plans can be furnished by overdrafts, then the supply schedule of money will endogenously increase *pari passu* with the increase in the demand for money function. The L_1M_1 function will not shift upwards as the endogenous increase in the quantity of money just offsets the increase in the demand for money generated by the finance motive. LM will remain firm as L_1M_1 ($= L_2M_2$) so that the equilibrium level of output will expand to Y_3, while the equilibrium rate of interest increases only to i_3 in Figure 8.2. As Keynes noted, 'to the extent that the overdraft system is employed and unused overdrafts ignored by the banking system, there is no superimposed pressure resulting from planned activity over and above the pressure resulting from actual activity. In this event the transition from a lower to a higher scale of activity may be accomplished with less pressure on the demand for liquidity and the rate of interest'.[23]

CROWDING OUT

Keynes's finance motive analysis highlights the fact that if the money supply is unchanged, *any* exogeneous increase in planned spending will create 'congestion' (to use Keynes's term) in the market for loans. In this situation, Keynes wrote:

> if there is no change in the liquidity position, the public can save ex-ante and ex-post and ex-anything-else until they are blue in the face, without alleviating the problem in the least – unless, indeed, the result of their efforts is to lower the scale of activity to what it was before. . . . The banks hold the key position in the transition from a lower to a higher scale of activity. If they refuse to relax, [i.e. to

provide additional endogenous money supplies] the growing congestion of the short-term loan market or the new issue market, as the case may be, will inhibit the improvement, no matter how thrifty the public purpose to be out of their future income. On the other hand, there will always be *exactly* enough ex-post saving to take up the ex-post investment and so release the finance which the latter has been previously employing. The investment market can become congested through a shortage of cash. It can never become congested through a shortage of savings. *This is the most fundamental of my conclusions within this field.*[24]

In the 1970s this 'most fundamental' conclusion regarding congestion in the money market was resurrected (without recognizing its origin in Keynes's analysis) in a debate between Monetarists and neoclassical synthesis Keynesians. The former claimed that any attempt by the federal government to deficit finance an increase in government spending to stimulate the economy would 'crowd out' private sector investors from the market for loans. The result would be that the government stimulus would be offset by a contraction in gross private investment spending. Neoclassical synthesis Keynesians denied that crowding out would occur.

The debate tended to boil down to the question of the slope of the LM function in the textbook model (i.e., without the finance motive) of the IS–LM system where the IS and LM equations are independent.[25] Any increase in exogenous spending will shift the IS curve to the right. If the unchanged LM curve is vertical, the result will be complete crowding out as the planned increase in demand spends itself entirely on an increase in the equilibrium interest rate without any increase in output.

Tobin tends to see the difference between Monetarism and Keynesianism in terms of the slope of the independent LM function. In a debate with Friedman, Tobin claimed that the 'main issue' separating Monetarists such as Milton Friedman from Tobin's Keynesianism is 'the shape of the *LM* locus'[26] and therefore the degree of crowding out. Tobin associated the Monetarist position with an independent vertical LM curve and complete crowding out. If the LM curve is perfectly horizontal (as in the liquidity trap), then there will be no crowding out. Tobin indicated that his view was between these two polar cases. His position is that 'the *LM* locus is upward sloping because $\delta L/\delta Y$ is positive and $\delta L/\delta i$ is not zero but negative'.[27]

Friedman responded that 'the main issue between us clearly is not and never has been whether the *LM* curve is vertical or has a positive slope'.[28] In an analysis that is superficially similar to Keynes's finance motive congestion case, Friedman argues that under certain circumstances the IS and LM equations are interdependent. A rightward shift of the ISG curve can induce a concomitant shift in the LM curve. Although Friedman has not perceived all the ramifications of the interrelationship between IS and LM functions, in this debate he at least opens up the question of the possibility of the interdependence of the real and monetary subsectors. This interdependence is basic to Keynes's approach, yet it has so far escaped the perception of the proponents of mainstream Keynesian analysis.

Friedman, accepting the crowding-out effect (without realizing its origin in Keynes's finance motive analysis), sketches his position with the following example. Assume a permanent, once-for-all increase in the ISG function due to a deficit-financed increase in government spending from G_0 to G_1. The deficit (D) equals the increase in government expenditures

$$D = (G_1 - G_0). \qquad (8.10)$$

According to Friedman, the entire deficit must be financed by a concomitant increase in the supply of money (to avoid 'crowding out'), i.e.

$$D = (G_1 - G_0) = (m_2 - m_1) \qquad (8.11)$$

where $(m_2 - m_1)$ is the resulting increase in the money supply in the period between t_0 and t_1 when government spending increases from G_0 to G_1. This increase in the money supply *with no change in the demand function for money* means that the LM curve shifts rightward *pari passu* with the rightward shift in the LM curve. Friedman warns that although the ISG has (by hypothesis) a once-for-all shift, the LM curve

is not a once-for-all shift. So long as the deficit continues . . . the nominal stock of money continues to grow and the LM . . . continues to move to the right. Is there any doubt that this effect must swamp the once-for-all shift of the IS curve?[29]

In Friedman's analysis a permanent government deficit leads to a once-for-all shift in ISG and an increase in aggregate income, from Y_0 to Y_1. In each future period the government deficit must remain at G_1 to maintain the Y_1 income level. Friedman asserts that a permanent $(G_1 - G_0)$ deficit in each future period must be monetized to avoid crowding out in each future period. The result is a perpetual outward shifting of the LM function as long as the government deficit continues.

Friedman's explanation of LM's interdependence with IS relates an increase in real demand with an endogenous *supply side* for money, while Keynes's interdependence of the money and real sectors is based on the *demand side* for money being parametrically tied to any increased demand for goods independent of what happens to the supply of money.

Friedman has *not* recognized the aggregate real demand–money demand interdependence, where an initial outward shift of the IS curve induces an *inward* shift of the LM curve. If he had, then Friedman would recognize that an increase in the money supply to avoid 'crowding out' *in the initial period* by monetizing the initial increase in government deficit spending would avoid congestion by offsetting the inward shift of the LM function due to the finance motive. Whether the LM curve must continue to shift outward in each subsequent future period to keep the interest rate unchanged and avoid crowding out depends on the flow demand for securities out of the current savings in each income period.

This securities flow-demand depends on the magnitude of what we may call the marginal propensity to purchase securities out of savings, μ. Mainstream Keynesian theory assumes that $\mu = 1$, i.e. that at the initial level of interest all *ex post* saving in each period is used to purchase securities as time machines.[30] If $\mu = 1$, then as income increases from Y_0 to Y_1 in the initial period, the change in aggregate savings (S) is

$$S = (S_1 - S_0). \qquad (8.11a)$$

This change in aggregate savings must be equal, *ceteris paribus*, to the government deficit,[31]

$$D = (G_1 - G_0) = (S_1 - S_0). \qquad (8.12)$$

After income has risen to its new equilibrium level of Y_1, there is sufficient saving to fund fully the deficit in each future period. Thus if the marginal propensity to buy securities out of savings equals unity, the public will buy all the additional government bonds issued in every future period, and there is no need to monetize each future period's deficit. Friedman is in error when he claims that a once-for-all shift in the IS due to a rise in deficit financed government spending $(G_1 - G_0)$ leads to more than a once-for-all increase in the money supply equal to the increase in government deficit-spending on goods and services in each period. There is no shifting of either IS or LM after the initial period.

If, however, $\mu = 0$, then at the initial interest rate each period's saving is held completely in the form of money. In this case Friedman is correct in arguing that each future period's deficit must induce an equal increase in the quantity of money. The public exhibits an incremental bear position in the sense they do not want to buy any of the additional government bonds necessary to finance the annual deficit even as the public's savings and wealth increase. The LM curve will continue to shift out in every future period. (Surprisingly, the validity of Friedman's argument requires people to behave 'as if' they are in a liquidity trap as far as increments in bond supplies are concerned. Yet Friedman claims that it is Keynes's system that requires a liquidity trap to achieve its predictions.[32])

There is no reason to believe that μ equals either zero or unity. Keynes argued that $0 < \mu < 1$.[33] For a once-for-all increase in deficit-financed government spending, the money supply will increase $(1/(1-\mu))$. The interest rate will remain unchanged. The outward shift in the LM function due to increases in the money supply is limited.

Keynes's finance motive analysis emphasizes the importance of banking and financial institutions in facilitating expansion in the real world. In the absence of an endogenous money supply system

> a heavy demand for investment can exhaust the market and be held up by the lack of financial facilities on reasonable terms. *It is to an important extent the 'financial' facilities which regulate the pace of new investment.* Some people find it a paradox that, up to the point of full employment, no amount of actual investment, however great, can exhaust and exceed the supply of savings. . . . If this is found paradoxical, it is because it is confused with the fact that *too great a press of uncompleted investment decisions is quite capable of exhausting the available finance*, if the banking system is unwilling to increase the supply of money and the supply from existing holders is inelastic. It is the supply of available finance which, in practice, holds up from time to time the onrush of 'new issues'. But if the banking system chooses to make the finance available and the investment projected by the new issues actually takes place, the appropriate level of incomes will be generated out of which there will necessarily remain over an amount of saving exactly sufficient to take care of the new investment. *The control of finance is, indeed, a potent, though sometimes dangerous, method for regulating the rate of investment* (though much more potent when used as a curb than as a stimulus).[34]

ENDOGENOUS VS. EXOGENOUS MONEY

Money does not enter the system like manna from heaven, nor is it dropped from a helicopter, nor does it come from the application of significant additional labour to produce the money commodity. The supply of money can increase only through two distinct institutional processes – both of which are related to the institution of money contracts.

The income generating–finance process. Whenever entrepreneurs expect demand to increase, they will have a profit incentive to increase borrowing from the banking system to purchase more plant, equipment and working capital.[35] If the banking system is designed to make additional bank-debt contracts available, then the bankers will respond positively to these 'needs of trade'. Bank money supply will expand endogenously with the increase in demand.[36] Depending on the short-run production flow-supply elasticities of the industries thus stimulated, changes in real income and/or prices will follow (with varying time lags) this endogenous increase in the money supply. Once a new higher level of equilibrium output is reached there is no further need to increase the money supply (due to the finance motive) as the needs of trade are no longer expanding.

Of course, if entrepreneurs expect demand for producible goods to decline, then the finance process can work in reverse. Firms will use some of their current sales proceeds to reduce the annual volume of working capital loans. In the absence of other borrowers willing to expand loan obligations, the total supply of money will endogenously decline.

The portfolio change process. The Monetary Authority can exogenously initiate action (open-market operations) to induce the public to hold more or less money balances. By bidding up the price of outstanding government debt (lowering the rate of interest), the Monetary Authority makes it profitable for bondholders to sell some government securities and substitute additional bank deposits as an alternative liquid store of value. Alternatively, by selling bonds and depressing their price, the Monetary Authority can raise the interest rate sufficiently to induce the public to reduce its holdings of money.

In sum, under the income generating–finance process, an increase in the demand for money induces an endogenous increase in supply *if bankers are willing and able to expand under the rules of the game* that regulate banking operations. This endogenous money supply increase occurs *pari passu* with additional purchase orders for resources and goods. Changes in the money supply and changes in resource utilization can be directly correlated though the income generating–finance process. Because production takes time, changes in measured output flows will tend to lag behind changes in the volume of outstanding bank loans. This calendar sequence of events has led some empiricists to infer incorrectly that an increase in the money supply 'causes' an increase in output.

In the portfolio change process, increases in the supply of money are immediately used by the receiving public as a substitute for securities as a liquid store of value. If both money and securities have zero elasticities of production, and if they are good substitutes for each other but poor substitutes with respect to producibles, then this exogenous increase in the quantity of money will not necessarily be associated with any increased demand for output and resource utilization. An exogenous increase in the money supply initiated by the Monetary Authority can increase the demand for producible capital goods either by (a) the Keynes effect of lowering the discount rate used by firms to evaluate an exogenously unchanged expected stream of future quasi-rents associated with investment projects, or (b) reducing the amount of credit rationing to a previously unsatisfied fringe of borrowers, or (c) inducing an improvement in the expected flow of quasi-rents.[37] There is no requirement that increases in the money supply must induce a *pari passu* increase in aggregate demand.

APPENDIX: KEYNES'S REPUDIATION OF NEOCLASSICAL MARGINAL PRODUCTIVITY THEORY: A DIGRESSION

In his discussion of liquidity preference theory Keynes traced the initial impact of an exogenous open-market change in the money supply on the money rate of interest and only then on income and employment through the effect of discount rates on the demand (price) of real capital relative to its production flow-supply price. This view is fundamental not only to Keynes's attack on Say's Law but also to his rejection of a purely physical or technological concept such as the marginal product of capital as *the* determinant of either (a) the earnings of capital, or (b) the rate of return on capital, or (c) the rate of interest.

In a series of revealing footnotes excoriating classical theory, Keynes insists that:

1. The rate of investment per period depends directly on the spot demand price compared to the flow-supply price of capital goods. Keynes noted that

    > [t]he equality between the stock of capital goods offered and the stock demanded will be brought about by the *prices* of capital goods, not by the rate of interest. It is equality between the demand and supply of loans of money, i.e. of debts, which is brought about by the rate of interest.[38]

2. The effect of a fall in the rate of interest on the rate of investment flow per period depends on the elasticity of the short-period flow-supply schedule of the capital goods-producing industries. Keynes illustrates this argument as follows:

    > Suppose, for example, that the extensive increase in the demand for capital in general is due to a *fall* in the rate of interest. I would suggest that the sentence be rewritten: In so far, therefore, as the extensive increase in the demand for capital goods cannot be immediately met by an increase in the total stock, it will have to be held in check for the time being by a rise in the supply price of capital goods sufficient to keep the marginal efficiency of capital in equilibrium with the rate of interest without there being any material change in the scale of investment. . . .[39]

3. The traditional views of the importance of the rate of return on the existing capital stock as the determinant of the rate of interest is misleading, circular, and confused. Keynes approvingly quotes Marshall's warning 'It cannot be repeated too often that the phrase "the rate of interest" is applicable to old investment of capital only in a

limited sense'.[40] Keynes continues, 'In fact, we cannot speak of it at all. We can only properly speak of the rate of interest on *money* borrowed for the purpose of purchasing investments of capital, new or old (or for any other purpose)'.[41]

Nevertheless, this classical view of the importance and relevance of the marginal physical productivity of capital as a determinant of the earnings of capital *in a monetary economy* has been resurrected and made the keystone of modern growth analysis.[42] Energies and intellectual resources have been drained into barren controversies involving the malleability of capital, choices of techniques of production, reswitching, and the existence and role of an *ex ante* real rate of interest. If economists had followed Keynes's lead these discussions involving the marginal physical product of capital could have been dislodged from the focal point of economic models of monetary economies a long time ago. Alternative constructs providing relevant insights into economic problems and policies based on the operations of a non-neutral, modern monetary economy would have come to the forefront. We would not be trapped into formulating theories analysis relying on the real marginal physical products as the sole determinate of the demand for the factors of production and their earning.

Marshall was well aware that profit maximization required the condition that the annualized cash flow value of the marginal product of capital would just equal the rate of interest. Marshall warned that this condition 'cannot be made into a theory of interest, any more than into a theory of wages, without reasoning in a circle'.[43] This section has indicated why the marginal product of capital is not the demand curve for capital in Keynes's system. Chapter 11 will explain why the marginal product of labour is not the demand curve for labour.

NOTES

1. R.F. Harrod, *The Life of John Maynard Keynes*, p. 435, also see p. 437.
2. J.M. Keynes, *The General Theory*, p. vii.
3. J.M. Keynes, 'Alternative Theories of the Rate of Interest', *The Economic Journal*, **47**, pp. 141–52.
4. Ibid., p. 147.
5. J. Robinson, *The Rate of Interest and Other Essays*, Macmillan, London, 1952, pp. 20–22.
6. J.M. Keynes. 'The Ex-Ante Theory of the Rate of Interest', *The Economic Journal*, **47**, 1937, p. 667.
7. Thus Keynes anticipated and explicitly responded to the so-called 'crowding-out' argument almost three decades before it was developed as an anti-Keynesian argument by Monetarists in the 1970s.
8. Keynes, of course, recognized that the demand for transactions balances was not only related to the aggregate demand function, but also via the business motive to the

parameters of the aggregate supply function (i.e. to the price of inputs, production functions, degree of industry integration, and the degree of monopoly). To make the following analysis comparable to the usual Keynesian treatments of liquidity preference, however, we shall make the explicit assumption (which is implicit in the works of others) that, either (1) there is no change in the aggregate supply function, or (2) any change in the quantity of money demanded for the business motive occurs *pari passu* with changes in the aggregate demand function. Accordingly, we can focus our attention entirely on aggregate demand.

9. This assumption is implicit in the usual two-equation (45-degree diagram) model presented in textbooks.

10. Introducing a simplified speculative demand for money function, $D_m^s = a_4 - b_4 i$ to equation (8.4), a correctly specified demand for money function is:

$$L^* = a(a_1 + b_1 Y) + \epsilon G + \beta(a_2 - b_2 i) + (a_4 - b i_4). \tag{8.5}$$

If the interest rate is assumed unchanged, then the last three terms on the right-hand side of equation (8.5) are constants.

11. In the case of war finance, discussed by Keynes in 1939, what was involved was an increase in the government component of aggregate demand which was to be financed by borrowing before the actual spending occurred.

12. It was this aspect that led D.H. Robertson to utter the triumphal note that Keynes had at last restored productivity 'to something like its rightful place in governing the rate of interest from the side of demand'. See D.H. Robertson, 'Mr. Keynes and Finance', *The Economic Journal*, **48**, 1938, p. 317.

13. M. Friedman, 'The Demand for Money: Some Theoretical and Empirical Results', *Journal of Political Economy*, **67**, 1959, pp. 327–8. Permanent incomes and prices represent expectational levels that, in the long run, will be realized since there is no uncertainty in Friedman's model. Permanent values can never be measured. They can only be inferred from the way the investigator interprets the results of his or her observations. Permanent values are, therefore, in the eye of the beholder.

14. Letting *Em* represent the income elasticity of demand for money, this elasticity can be defined as

$$Em = [dL^*/dY][Y/L^*].$$

It therefore follows that the income elasticity of demand for money is greater than (equal to, less than) unity, when $[dL^*/dY]$ is greater than (equal to, less than) $[L^*/Y]$.

Keynes believed that the income velocity was not constant, and furthermore, he suggested that the elasticity of demand for money would normally be less than unity at less than full employment. See *The General Theory*, pp. 201, 299, 304–6.

15. M. Friedman, 'A Monetary Theory of Nominal Income', *Journal of Political Economy*, **80**, 1971, pp. 324–5.

16. 'I am saying that booms and depressions are phenomena peculiar to an economy in which ... money is not neutral. Accordingly I believe the next task is to work out in some detail a monetary theory of production. ... At any rate that is the task on which I am now occupying myself, in some confidence that I am not wasting my time'. J.M. Keynes, 'A Monetary Theory of Production' (1933), in *The Collected Writings of John Maynard Keynes*, XIII, edited by D. Moggridge, Macmillan, London, 1973.

17. M. Friedman, loc. cit., p. 329.

18. J.M. Keynes, *Treatise on Money*, II, p. 220.

19. J.M. Keynes, 'The Ex-Ante Theory of the Rate of Interest', *The Economic Journal*, **47**, 1937; reprinted in *The Collected Writings of J.M. Keynes*, 14, ed. by D. Moggridge, Macmillan, London, 1973.

20. Since normally $b_2 > 1$, while $1 - b_1 < 1$, a change in a_2 will have a larger impact on the ISG function than on the LM equation, that is the ISG curve will shift more than the LM curve so that the new intersect will always be to the north-east of the original intersection.

In Hansen's traditional system, since the LM curve is not displaced, the new equilibrium level of output and rate of interest are Y_3 and i_3 respectively.

21. J.M. Keynes, *The General Theory*, p. 293.
22. J.M. Keynes, 'The Ex-Ante Theory of the Rate of Interest', *The Economic Journal*, **47**, 1937, p. 669.
23. Ibid., p. 669.
24. J.M. Keynes, 'The Ex-Ante Theory of the Rate of Interest', *The Economic Journal*, **47**, 1937, pp. 668–9. Italics added.
25. For example, D. Colander, *Macroeconomics*, Glenview, Scotts Foreman, 1986, p. 198. The flatness of the IS curve is also mentioned.
26. J. Tobin, 'Friedman's Theoretical Framework', in *Milton Friedman's Theoretical Framework: A Debate With His Critics*, edited by R.J. Gordon, University of Chicago Press, Chicago, 1974, p. 77. Tobin admits that he takes an 'eclectic nonmonetarist view' which 'certainly contains many elements not in *The General Theory*. Perhaps it should be called Hicksian'. Ibid., p. 77.
27. Ibid., pp. 77–8.
28. M. Friedman, 'Comments on His Critics', *Milton Friedman's Monetary Framework: A Debate With His Critics*, edited by R. J. Gordon, University of Chicago, Chicago, 1974, p. 142.
29. M. Friedman, op. cit., p. 141.
30. See F.P.R. Brechling, 'A Note On Bond-Holding and the Liquidity Preference Theory of Interest', *Review of Economic Studies*, **24**, 1957, pp. 195–6.
31. Since $\Delta Y = \Delta C + \Delta I + \Delta G$, while $\Delta S = \Delta Y - \Delta C$ and, in the absence of any crowding out, $\Delta I = 0$, therefore $\Delta S = \Delta G$.
32. Friedman, op. cit., pp. 21–9.
33. J.M. Keynes, 'The Ex-Ante Theory of the Rate of Interest', *The Economic Journal*, **47**, 1937, p. 668.
34. J.M. Keynes, 'Alternative Theories of the Rate of Interest', *The Economic Journal*, **47**, 1937, p. 248. Italics added. Of course, if there was some queueing initially (before the increase in the demand for finance), then the length of the queue will increase as planned transactions rise as a result of entrepreneurs attempting to finance more investment projects than before.
35. To the extent that final buyers currently do not possess enough liquidity to meet these hypothesized increased contractual purchase obligations they will have to obtain commitments from their bankers (via either credit card lines of credit, overdraft facilities, direct bank and mortgage loan commitments and investment banker commitments etc.) to meet their expected increased flow of purchases.
36. Sometimes it is claimed that this endogenous money supply must be done at an unchanging rate of interest. See B.J. Moore, *Horizontalists and Verticalists*, MIT Press, Cambridge, 1988.
37. A vivid illustration of the possibility that an exogenous increase in the money supply will not stimulate additional spending for producibles was provided in the 1990–92 period. During that period, the Federal Reserve lowered interest rates over 20 times, but aggregate demand in the private sector increased less than 2 per cent in real terms, while real investment declined. Apparently, lower interest rates were accompanied by lower entrepreneurial expectations of future quasi-rents, and therefore the demand for investment goods fell, while real consumption increased slightly as real income increased by 2 per cent.
38. J.M. Keynes, *The General Theory*, p. 186, n. 1.
39. J.M. Keynes, *The General Theory*, p. 187, n. 2.
40. A. Marshall, *Principles of Economics*, 8th Edition, London, Macmillan, 1920, p. 593. In the previous sentence, Marshall, anticipating the Cambridge controversy involving the malleability of capital and the determination of the rate of profit, wrote 'It is only on this [malleability] supposition that we are at liberty to speak of capital in general as being accumulated under the expectation of a certain net interest which is the same for all forms'.

41. J.M. Keynes, *The General Theory*, p. 187, n. 3.
42. For example, see P.A. Samuelson and F. Modigliani, 'The Pasinetti Paradox in Neoclassical and More General Models', *Review of Economic Studies*, **33**, 1966.
43. A. Marshall, *Principles of Economics*, 8th edition, Macmillan, London, 1956, p. 430.

9. Three views of inflation

The main focus of public concern in discussing inflation is not rising spot prices of non-reproducible goods such as rare paintings or sculptures, or the prices of securities listed on the New York Stock Exchange. The public focuses on inflation as a problem only when the prices of *currently producible goods and services* that bulk significantly large in consumers' budgets are continuously increasing. In an economy where production is occurring, the spot price can exceed the forward (or flow-supply) price by an amount limited only by the unwillingness of the buyer to pay the higher spot price rather than to wait for forward delivery. The price that buyers are willing to pay for forward delivery can never exceed, and will normally equal, the short-run flow-supply price since the latter is defined as the money price required to call forth the exertion necessary to produce any given amount of the commodity for any given delivery date.[1]

For redundant commodities, the spot price will be less than Marshall's short-run flow-supply price – a contango – by an amount sufficient to compensate the buyer for the expected carrying costs of the commodity until some future date when it is no longer expected to be superfluous. Then the spot price will again exceed the short-run flow-supply price.[2] Marshall's short-run flow-supply price is the anchor around which the spot price swings, as the spot market is either in backwardation or contango. While today's spot price is immediately responsive (perfectly flexible) to changes in circumstances, nevertheless it is the components of the short-run flow-supply price that ultimately determine the prices at which current production flows will be offered to buyers.

Keynes labelled changes in spot prices relative to the flow-supply prices *Commodity or Capital Inflation (or Deflation)*,[3] or what can be called *Spot Price Inflation*. Holders of existing assets can obtain capital gains or losses as today's changes in demand for immediate delivery impinge on today's spot prices. Spot price inflation primarily affects capital values of pre-existing durables rather than the flows of money income.

Keynes called changes in flow-supply prices or forward prices of producible goods, an *Income Inflation (or Deflation)*.[4] This terminology highlights the obvious but oft neglected fact that, given productivity relations, changes in the money costs of production are always a change in someone's money income.

Inflation in the flow-supply prices of producibles is everywhere and always a rise in somebody's income. This does not mean that demand factors cannot affect the price of output. Excess demand can induce spot price inflation. The latter can affect, or be affected by, changes in flow-supply prices.[5]

If an exogenous increase in the money supply finances unexpected increases in demand for goods for immediate delivery, then actual (or notional) spot prices will rise instantaneously. Any excess demand in today's spot market will be eliminated. These immediately increasing spot prices relative to flow-supply prices will induce some demand to spill over into the forward market. Some buyers will wait until tomorrow for the goods they wanted at the original spot price today.[6] If, despite the increase in spot prices, the flow-supply prices are unchanged as additional forward market demand occurs, then no matter how far today's spot price may be momentarily displaced from the offer price for forward delivery, tomorrow's spot price will return to a normal backwardation with the current flow-supply price. The belief that flow-supply prices are sticky permits money to be a vehicle for transferring a stable volume of purchasing power as long as buyers are willing to wait for delivery.[7]

THE THREE KINDS OF INCOMES INFLATION[8]

Any rise in the short-run flow-supply price of output is due to three possible causes: (1) diminishing returns, (2) increasing profit margins, and (3) increasing money wages (relative to productivity increments).[9]

Diminishing returns inflation. For more than a century, economists have taught that every expansion of the flow of output and employment will normally involve increasing costs and increasing supply prices because of the law of diminishing returns. Diminishing returns, it is held, are inevitable – even if all labour and capital inputs in the production process are equally efficient – because of the scarcity of some input such as raw materials or managerial talent.

Economic expansion can lead to increasing costs not only because of the classical law of diminishing returns but also because labour and capital inputs are really not equally efficient. Increasing production flows often involve the hiring of less-skilled workers, and the utilization of older, less-efficient standby equipment. These factors are an additional cause of increasing marginal costs. This phenomenon of *hiring path diminishing returns*, was emphasized by Keynes as a main reason 'for rising supply prices before full employment'.[10]

The importance of diminishing returns inflation will vary with the level of unemployment. When the rate of unemployment is high, idle capacity will exist in most firms, so that diminishing returns are likely to be relatively unimportant. As full employment is approached an increasing number of firms will experience increasing costs, and diminishing returns inflation will become more important. Short-run diminishing returns inflation of either the traditional or the hiring path variety is ultimately an inevitable consequence of expansion in employment. It represents a once-over real cost to society required to obtain an increased flow of output. It cannot, in the short run, be avoided. No public policy need be devised to avoid the once-for-all price increase it entails.[11] In the long run, improvements in technology, government-sponsored training and educational programmes, and increases in capital equipment per worker can offset diminishing returns inflation.

Degree of monopoly or profits inflation. When entrepreneurs believe that the market conditions have changed sufficiently so that it is possible (or even necessary) for them to increase the mark-up of prices relative to costs, the economy will experience a profits inflation. There is no theoretical reason to suggest that changes in profit margins are necessarily related to changes in aggregate effective demand.

Harrod hypothesized a law of diminishing price elasticity of demand[12] that implies the possibility of rising profit margins with income growth. Kalecki assumed a greater collusion amongst firms during a slump thereby suggesting an inverse relation between profit margins and the level of employment.

The Cambridge views of Joan Robinson, Kaldor, and Pasinetti tend to associate higher profit margins with economic systems that possess higher rates of accumulation. This reflects an updating of Keynes's belief in the importance of a Profits Inflation in providing the wherewithal for a more rapid rate of capital accumulation.[13] In the *Treatise*, Keynes permitted, as Kaldor and Pasinetti do in their models, profit margins to vary relative to money wages in response to changes in demand. The resulting income redistribution from wage-earners to profit recipients frees resources and makes them available for more rapid accumulation[14] and the long-run enrichment of human life.[15] This redistribution also provides some internal finance that, Kaldor claims, is a prerequisite to the firms' ability to borrow externally.

Wage inflation. Every increase in money-wage rates not offset by productivity improvements raises production costs. If profit margins are maintained, the result must be an increase in flow-supply price schedules. If unemployment rates shrink significantly, it is easier for workers to obtain (collectively and individually) more liberal wage increases.[16] Wage inflation can occur even without a significant reduction in unemployment rates if labour is able to secure increases that exceed productivity increments.

'Since each group of workers will gain, *cet. par.*, by a rise in its own wages, there is naturally for all groups a pressure in this direction, which entrepreneurs will be more ready to meet when they are doing better business'.[17] To the extent that workers view their well-being relative to the income of others, the struggle about money wages becomes a struggle for those on the bottom of the wage ladder to reduce wage differentials, and for those on the top to maintain or increase them.[18]

The growth of economic and political power by groups of workers plus the increasingly available information on the earnings of others creates pressures that made wage-price inflation the most dangerous of economic problems during the decades immediately following World War II. The full employment policies actively pursued by governments encouraged an increase in the truculence of wage-earners (both collectively and individually) and the acquiescence of managers. As fears of wage inflation increased, many governments and central bankers adopted the view that planned recessions are necessary to keep labour in its place.

REAL WORLD INFLATION

Observed rises in the price level of domestic output as a whole can be due to some combination of these inflationary processes.[19]

Every significant expansion in economic activity will induce some price increases because of diminishing returns. With rising prices and stronger employment opportunities, workers will try to seek, at a minimum, cost-of-living wage increases. As pools of unemployment dry up, workers can become more impenitent in their wage demands. Managers are more willing to grant wage increases in a rising market.

If government demands augmenting policies to produce full employment, entrepreneurs can be reasonably confident that they will be able to pass the higher labour costs on by way of higher prices. Management will find that as they hire more workers to meet rising demand for their products, the cost of searching out and training the remaining unemployed will increase. They will create additional wage inflation pressures as they attempt to bid workers away from other employers rather than to recruit from the remaining unemployed. If management also believes that the growth in demand is sufficiently strong they may be encouraged to attempt to increase profit margins and thereby add a profits inflationary tendency.

Legislators may find that the legal minimum money wage becomes substandard as inflation occurs. In a humanitarian spirit, they may legislate an increase in the legal minimum. This can encourage better-paid workers to increase wage demands to restore previous income differentials.

All these factors can feed back on each other to create mounting wage-profit margin-price pressures for as long as the economic expansion is permitted to continue.

Since the rate of diminishing returns, the rate of increase in money-wage rates, and increases in profit margins may be related to *either* low unemployment rates and/or to rapidly decreasing employment rates, orthodox anti-inflation policies are oriented towards maintaining a sufficiently high unemployment rate to constrain inflationary wage demands of workers and profit margin increases of firms.

Any monetary and/or fiscal policy aimed at preventing *all* price increases before full employment is reached can be successful only if they perpetuate significant unemployment. Even this may not be sufficient, for as Keynes warned over forty years ago, 'If there are strong social or political forces causing spontaneous changes in the money-rates of efficiency wages [i.e., unit labor costs], the control of the price-level may pass beyond the power of the banking system'.[20]

DIFFERING VIEWS ON THE PRIMARY CAUSE OF INFLATION

Three schools of economic thought have suggested differing primary causes of inflation and therefore three different policies for fighting inflation. These three schools are: (a) the Monetarists, (b) the neoclassical synthesis Keynesians, and (3) the Post Keynesians.

The Monetarist view. Milton Friedman, the Nobel Prize winning Monetarist economist, is usually credited with coining the motto 'inflation is always and everywhere a monetary phenomenon'. The basis of this claim is the truistic equation of exchange

$$MV = PY \tag{9.1}$$

where M is the money supply, Y is the real income or output of the community, P is the market price level associated with selling the existing output, and V is the velocity of money (defined as equal to $[PY]/[M]$). This price equation is usually added to some variant of the IS–LM system to obtain the basic Monetarist model of the economy.[21]

The Monetarist view is that inflation will occur if, and only if, the rate of growth of the money supply exceeds the exogenously determined rate of growth in real income.[22] Monetarists assume that the magnitude of the velocity variable is both exogenous and stable over time, so that increases in the quantity of money cause the price level to rise. Restrictive money supply growth policy is required to subdue the inflation.

Table 9.1 Money supply growth and price level changes

Period	Money (% increase)	Price level (% increase)
1977–1981	32	40
1982–1986	40	12
1983–1992	97	40

Unfortunately, as Table 9.1 demonstrates, the historical data do not always support the Monetarist contention that restrictive money supply growth is a necessary condition to reduce the inflation rate. During the period 1977 to 1981, data support the Monetarist contention that increases in the money supply and inflation are closely related. Since 1982, however, the money supply increased much more rapidly than between 1977 and 1981, while price level increases have been more modest. Monetarists attribute these disturbing statistics to an unexplained exogenous decrease in velocity since 1982.[23]

The neoclassical Keynesian view. The original Keynesian IS–LM model did not possess any price-determining equation. Most early 'Keynesian' formulations, assumed money wages were fixed and prices moved only to the extent that there were diminishing returns before full employment. Since, for industrial economies, diminishing returns is not an important phenomenon, Old Keynesian models were fixprice systems that presumed no price increases occurred before full employment. Any increase in aggregate demand after full employment would directly increase prices.

In 1958, the empirical evidence contradicted this naïve early 'Keynesian' view. In that year, the consumer price index increased 2.7 per cent, while the unemployment rate climbed from 4.3 to 6.8 per cent. The unusual nature of these events was in sharp contrast to the previous postwar recessions of 1949 and 1954, when as unemployment declined, the price level either stabilized or showed a small concomitant decline. The 1958 experience forced neoclassical 'Keynesians' to search for an explanation of why prices could increase in the face of rising unemployment rates.

Fortuitously in 1958, A.W. Phillips published a study showing that for over 100 years the rate of change of money-wage rates in Britain was inversely related to the level of unemployment.[24] Since changes in unemployment rates are associated with aggregate output flows and

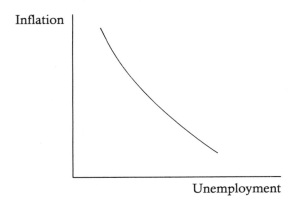

Figure 9.1   The Phillips curve

changes in money wages could be related to inflation, Phillips's research provided an easy explanation of inflation. In industrial societies, the Phillips curve as drawn in Figure 9.1 indicates that there is a tradeoff between the rate of unemployment and the rate of inflation.

By 1960, two eminent neoclassical synthesis Keynesians, Samuelson and Solow, proclaimed that the data for the United States indicated a Phillips curve tradeoff where 'price stability is seen to involve about $5\frac{1}{2}$ per cent unemployment; whereas ... 3 per cent unemployment is seen to involve a price rise of about $4\frac{1}{2}$ per cent per annum'.[25] The Phillips curve equation had become *the* price equation for Keynesian IS–LM models.

Unfortunately for these Keynesians, the 1970s produced an upward-sloping Phillips relationship as higher unemployment rates were correlated with higher rates of inflation. The Keynesian's heralded Phillips curve tradeoff was inapplicable. Bereft of an explanation of inflation in a period of rapidly rising prices, the neoclassical Keynesian analysis fell into ill-repute among economists.

Theoretical groundwork for the *coup de grâce* to the Phillips curve had already been laid by Milton Friedman[26] when he argued that once workers expected future inflation they would build this anticipation into their wage contract demands. Friedman claimed that the long-run Phillips curve is vertical at the 'natural rate of unemployment'. If policy makers tried to trade off unemployment and inflation along a short-run downward-sloping Phillips curve they would merely exacerbate inflationary expectation pressures that would then require higher rates of unemployment to prevent workers from making truculent wage demands. When the data of the 1970s showed a positive relationship between unemployment rates and inflation rates, the Friedman natural rate of unemployment hypothesis seemed to be validated and the Phillips curve was buried.

The Post Keynesian distribution view. The Post Keynesians accept a variant of the Friedman aphorism that inflation is always a monetary phenomenon. For Post Keynesians, inflation can only occur in economies that use money (and money contracts) to organize production and exchange processes. Inflation then is always the result of attempts to alter the existing distribution of money income among inhabitants of the same region, and/or interregionally, and/or internationally. In other words, inflation is a symptom of a fight over the distribution of current income.

In 1961, Sidney Weintraub[27] was able to simplify the analysis of the price inflation of currently produced goods by a bit of simple algebra:

$$Z = PQ = kwN \qquad (9.2)$$

where Z is current aggregate output of the private sector (business) in money terms, P is the price level, Q is the real business output, w is the money-wage rate, N is the level of employment, and k is a multiple of the wage bill (wN). Dividing both sides of equation (9.2) by Q, we obtain:

$$P = k \, (w/A) \qquad (9.3)$$

where A is the average physical productivity of labour, w/A is unit labour costs of production (or efficiency wage), and k is the gross profit mark-up. Weintraub concluded that the price level associated with the private sector's producible goods and services is related to the profit margin mark-up and the efficiency wage. To eliminate inflation then requires preventing increases in (i) the gross profit margin *and* (ii) limiting the rate of change in money wages to the change in labour productivity.

As an empirical fact, the value of k for the gross business product of the United States had shown no secular trend for the period from 1890 to 1960. If k remained stable over time, Weintraub argued, then inflation could be tamed if money-wage rate increases were geared to productivity increases.[28]

Weintraub recognized that it was not sufficient for economists to be good, i.e., to identify the correct overriding principle governing a policy problem. To achieve a successful policy solution, economists also had to be clever. Using the proper overriding principle, economists had to develop a specific policy that would encourage voluntary compliance by most of the population, while avoiding prohibitively high administrative costs.

In 1970, Weintraub developed a 'clever' anti-inflation policy that he called TIP or a tax-based incomes policy. The basic philosophy of TIP is that wage increases in excess of productivity growth harm most members of society. TIP required the use of the corporate income tax structure to penalize the largest firms in the economy if they granted money-wage increases more than a socially acceptable non-inflationary norm based on average labour productivity increases. Firms that accede to inflationary wage demands are inflicting a cost on the entire society, similar to the social costs inflicted by firms that discharge pollution above some socially acceptable norm into the air or public waterways.

TIP involves disincentives through higher taxes levied directly on those whose demand for higher money incomes foster inflation. To offset the potential deflationary aspects of the extra tax revenues paid by those penalized under TIP, Weintraub recommended that those firms and workers whose behaviour was not inflationary could receive incentive rewards in the form of a tax cut. As a consequence, total tax revenues due to the institution of TIP would not be increased.

TIP is aimed at directly punishing those who unleash inflationary forces while rewarding those whose money income demands are socially acceptable. By comparison, a Monetarist 'tight money' anti-inflation policy inflicts punishment on most workers and firms. Monetarist policy can fight inflation only if it indiscriminately reduces aggregate demand sufficiently to inflict widespread economic losses to convince entrepreneurs that they must fight workers' wage demands for they will not be able to pass along inflationary wage demands. Simultaneously, enough workers have to be thrown out of jobs (what Marx called the 'industrial reserve army of the unemployed') so that all the remaining workers are intimidated sufficiently to prefer job security to attempting to obtain higher wages.

TIP has to be a permanent policy institution if the inflationary dragon is to be permanently tamed. There must always remain on the books a civic statement as to what is acceptable non-inflationary income demand behaviour as a constant reminder that inflating one's income is always contrary to the governing social interest. If a specific future date for the end of TIP was to be announced, its effectiveness would diminish as that date approached. As the end of TIP approached, everyone would know that constraints on inflationary income behaviour would soon disappear. The existing social contract would erode as each member of society could no longer rely on the civilized behaviour of others. Self-interest alone would encourage each person to try to increase their own money income *before* others did so. The struggle over the distribution of income would be reignited – and could be dampened only by the dousing waters of another planned recession.

TIP relates anti-social behaviour with tax penalties. TIP also requires educating the public to understand their social responsibilities in preventing a social conflict over the existing distribution of income. TIP is similar to road regulations governing driving behaviour on the nation's highways. Speed limits setting socially acceptable driving behaviour are permanent but the magnitude of the speed limit can change depending on driving conditions, the need for energy conservation, etc. – factors whose *raison d'être* in achieving society's goals are clear to an educated driving public. Similarly TIP would be a permanent institution but the magnitude of the allowable wage increase could vary depending on economic conditions. Public education would be necessary to explain the factors affecting the magnitudes involved in TIP.

Speed limits, paying one's taxes, and similar civic behaviour, depend on voluntary compliance working in tandem with fines levied on those who excessively violate the rules. Governments never reward good drivers for obeying the speed limit – or taxpayers for paying their proper taxes. This behaviour is expected of all citizens – even if it is not in their own self-interest. Similarly, those whose wage and income increases are non-inflationary should not be expected to be directly rewarded – such social behaviour would be expected. In other words, a reward-based TIP policy would be costly and probably ineffective.

Entrepreneurial fears of massive government regulation and additional record-keeping requirements must be assuaged. Weintraub recommended that TIP be applied to only the top 2 000 firms in the United States. These firms produce over half of the GDP and are key to the general wage level and profit margins set in the rest of the economy. Managerial control of such large enterprises already requires extensive record-keeping. TIP would not add significantly to this record keeping burden as compliance could be calculated from existing records and shown on an additional three or four lines on corporate income tax forms. Smaller businesses – and especially new enterprises – on which the vitality of the entrepreneurial system depends would not be affected at all.

The public would be educated to understand that TIP is inexorably linked to a set of expansionary fiscal and monetary policies. Planned recessions would be a thing of the past. Acceptance of TIP guarantees maximum production and the highest standard of living possible for the community. The only anti-inflation alternative to a permanent incomes policy is permanent high unemployment (to limit inflation) and low rates of economic growth or even stagnation.

THE POST-WAR INFLATION AND UNEMPLOYMENT RECORD

In the absence of an explicit public consensus on an acceptable distribution of income, a fully employed but 'free' economy is apparently unable to harmonize the conflicting income demands of people motivated solely by self-interest. Indeed in a world devoid of civic constraints on income demands, conservatives have recognized that the only way to fight inflation requires incomes losses, unemployment, the destruction of profit opportunities, and a resulting reduction in the total size of the economic pie to impoverish everyone sufficiently to keep people's income demands in their place.

The historical record shows that only during the period 1961 to 1968, and again briefly in 1972 to 1973, when the government developed a political consensus supporting a policy of directly limiting money income growth (with some form of 'incomes policies') did the economy approach full employment without suffering inflation.

During the Kennedy–Johnson years of 1961 to 1968, prices were held in check by a wage-price 'guideline' policy that urged that money-wage increases be geared to productivity increases. These guidelines were entirely voluntary. There were no monetary rewards or punishments to force workers and managers to behave. These guidelines, relying solely on the community accepting responsibility for its money income demands, were enhanced by President Kennedy's stirring inaugural motto 'Ask not what the country can do for you, ask what you can do for the country'. For eight years, these voluntary guidelines worked.

During the period 1961–67, real GNP increased by 34 per cent (real GNP per capita by 24 per cent) as the economy was stimulated by a tax cut in tandem with increased military expenditure. In the same six-year period, the Consumer Price Index rose only 12 per cent. With the growth of the unpopular Vietnam war under Johnson the civic cohesion generated by the Kennedy charisma and challenge was shattered. Compliance with the guidelines disappeared in the last year of the Johnson Administration as civic values were degraded and self-interest became dominant.

From 1969 to 1980, part of the public agenda was a continuing search for an acceptable incomes policy to replace the 'guidelines' to control inflation and to provide for an equitable sharing of the economic largess of a fully employed society. In August 1971, President Nixon successfully instituted an incomes policy through wage and price controls. (This approach was, of course, in direct conflict with the expressed conservative philosophy of his Administration.) This freed the Federal Reserve of responsibility for controlling inflation. The Fed immediately eased monetary policy while additional federal government spending stimulated the economy. The result was a vigorously growing non-inflationary economy. Real GNP rose more than 5 per cent between 1972 and 1973, while inflation dropped from 4.5 per cent to 3.3 per cent. This vigorous recovery with less inflation contributed to the Nixon landslide election victory. After reelection, Nixon removed most of the controls. Prices climbed by 6.2 per cent in 1973 and by 11 per cent in 1974. The Federal reserve raised interest rates from 4 per cent to over 7 per cent as a planned recession was thought to be required to reduce inflation.

By 1975, President Ford felt the necessity to hold a 'White House Conference on Inflation'. Approximately 700 leading US economists engaged in a two-day discussion of what to do about inflation. The only tangible result from this meeting was President Ford's WIN (Whip Inflation Now) Campaign that tried to emulate Kennedy's example of appealing to civic values. The public saw the WIN campaign as a stunt, not a policy. The erosion of individuals' feelings of civic responsibility was fostered by Johnson's unpopular Vietnam war policies and Nixon's Watergate. The resulting environment was not sufficient for 'catchy' advertising slogans to whip up public support.[29]

Unemployment increased from 4.9 to 8.2 per cent between 1972 and the planned recession of 1974–5. Inflation dropped to 5.8 per cent by 1976. With a recovery in the early years of the Carter Administration the inflation rate again rose to 6.5 per cent in 1977 and 7.7 per cent in 1978. Inflation was getting out of hand. President Carter therefore proposed a new incomes policy that he labelled a 'real wage insurance' scheme. Carter proposed to reduce taxes for those workers who limited wage demands to a socially acceptable level. The Carter proposal, however, was abandoned by the President even before Congress could act.

Except for the 17-month period of Nixon's wage and price controls beginning in August 1971 the main tool used to fight inflation was planned recessions induced by restrictive monetary policy. Between 1969 and 1980 each tight money episode increased unemployment rates to what were thought to be politically unacceptable levels. With Congressional elections every two years and Presidential elections every four years, most politicians lost the political 'stomach' for the resulting unemployment and deserted the conservative cause. As soon as the inflation problem began to abate, political pressures built up to re-stimulate the economy. The 1970s was a period of on-again off-again restrictive monetary policies stringent enough to raise unemployment, but neither strong enough nor long enough to more than temporarily subdue the inflationary struggle over the distribution of income.

Restrictive monetary policy became the 'only game in town' to fight inflation. When inflation reached 11.3 per cent in 1979, the Federal Reserve – under a new chairman, Paul Volker – invoked a brutally restrictive monetary policy. Interest rates were pushed to unprecedented high levels, finance dried up, and loan defaults proliferated.

The result was to create a severe worldwide recession, the worst since the Great Depression of the 1930s. Unemployment soared from 5.8 per cent in 1979 to a peak of 10.8 per cent in mid-1982. The rate of inflation dropped from 13.5 per cent in 1979 to 4 per cent by the end of 1982. In August 1982, under the threat of a Mexican loan default, the Fed relented. At the same time, President Reagan persuaded Congress to legislate a massive tax cut, while total government spending increased. The economy revived. By 1986, despite a much looser monetary policy, inflation had fallen to less than 2 per cent per annum and the unemployment rate dropped to 7 per cent,[30] higher than it had been for decades before Monetarism had been officially adopted as Fed policy by Mr. Volker.

In the early years of the Bush Administration, inflation advanced from 4.4 per cent in 1988 to 6.1 per cent in 1990. The Federal Reserve again stepped on the Monetary brake, while the Bush Administration attempted to raise taxes and slow government spending. The economy again headed into recession. Inflation slowed to 2.9 per cent by 1992, while the unemployment rate jumped from 5.2 per cent in 1989 to 7.3 per cent in 1992. Capacity utilization declined from 83.9 per cent in 1988 to 77.8 per cent in 1992.

This evidence of recent decades indicates that the inflationary dragon can be temporarily stilled by traditional tight monetary and fiscal policies, but only at a great cost in terms of persistent high unemployment, unused industrial capacity, and stifling low rates of economic growth. Inflation has not been eliminated as an affliction for the United States or other modern economies that strive to obtain full employment. By early 1993, inflation had begun to accelerate towards a 4 per cent annual rate as President Clinton sent up a fiscal stimulus package to Congress.

Many have interpreted the evidence of the 1980s as demonstrating that our economy does not require direct controls on income as long as society apparently accepts a barbaric restrictive policy requiring permanently high levels of unemployment and unutilized industrial capacity to force people to restrict their money income demands.

Much of the real credit for the mid-1982–1988 recovery is due to the Reagan Administration's policy of reducing taxes while *increasing* total government spending on goods and services just as the Federal Reserve was relaxing its stringent monetary policy. This success was not related to the supply-side promise that the 1982 tax cuts would stimulate so much more additional work and investment that the cuts would pay for themselves. The huge and continuing federal deficit since 1981 is vivid evidence of the failure of supply-side economics.

Nor should credit for the 1982–88 recovery go to the Federal Reserve and the relaxation of the high interest rates foisted on the US and the rest of the world between 1979 and 1982. This 1979–82 tight money policy forced the United States into the second largest economic depression in the twentieth century. Between 1979 and 1985 alone, the loss of real income to Americans from not running a full employment economy has been estimated at almost 3 trillion dollars. Had the United States managed to maintain a close to full employment economy, the average American would have had at least a 12 per cent larger slice of the pie *in every year between 1979 and 1985*. This diminution in the relative economic well-being of the American people, due to the Fed's accepting the role of maintaining a natural rate of unemployment, is truly staggering. Of course had the Fed not relaxed its Monetarist policies in mid-1982, the resulting economic losses would have been even more staggering.

The primary fuel that stimulated the recovery between mid-1982 and the end of the decade has been the enormous federal deficits. Rather than constituting a new age of conservative economic policy based on 'sound' finance, the recovery of the US economy is primarily attributable to a repackaging of old Keynesian policy prescriptions of stimulating demand through deficit spending plus providing the economy with sufficient liquidity through a less restrictive monetary policy.

Whatever victory against inflation was achieved should be put into perspective. Inflation declined from 13.3 per cent in 1979 to between 3.8 and 4.0 per cent during the late 1980s (except for the unusual 1.1 per cent in 1986) – a decade of almost 4 per cent per annum. This inflation rate may look 'low' compared to the experience of the late 1970s, but inflation was only 4.2 per cent in 1971 when President Nixon was traumatized into imposing wage and price controls. Meanwhile unemployment remains above the level of the mid-1970s and economic growth between 1978 and 1992 was approximately 2 per cent per annum over the entire period – well below the post-war average. Even during the Reagan 'boom' years of 1982 to 1986 growth was only 3.3 per cent – about equal to growth averaged over prosperous times *and* slumps since 1946.

INCOMES POLICY AND RESOURCE ALLOCATION

Mainstream economists often criticize any incomes policy that limits wage changes as an impediment that does not permit markets to allocate labour resources optimally. This view implicitly assumes that present labour markets with their arbitrary and unequal bargaining power and supply restrictions are efficient allocators. The response to such a myopic faith in the operation of labour markets can be made on at least four different levels.

1. There is considerable empirical evidence that suggests existing labour markets with existing free collective bargaining arrangements and

institutional rules to limit growth in supply are not very good allocators.[31]

2. Even if labour markets could efficiently allocate, all that would be required for reallocation would be changes in relative prices and not in the general wage and price level. Different variants of incomes policy have been suggested which would permit these relative wage changes while restricting a general wage and price level change.[32]

3. Any possible loss in social welfare due to possible labour misallocation in the economy must be weighed against the welfare loss resulting from traditional restrictive monetary and fiscal policies that create unemployment and reduce the rate of accumulation. As long as there are millions of unemployed in the United States who are willing and able to work but who are kept unemployed to temper wage demands, then an economy that continuously utilizes these resources is less wasteful than one that requires them to be perpetually on the dole. (The latter system also ultimately fosters social antagonism.)

4. In an uncertain world, stickiness in the money-wage rate is necessary for the efficient operation of the monetary system.

An incomes policy obviously requires that the public interest be taken into account at the wage-bargaining table and when management is making its pricing decisions. This policy must be considered a necessary supplement to monetary and fiscal policies that would *guarantee* continuous full employment. In return for this guarantee of full employment and high production levels, labour would be required to restrict its wage demands to, at most, rises in average productivity, while business must hold profit mark-ups constant.

If money-wage rates and gross margins could be kept unchanged, then with technological progress, price levels would decline. This would allow consumers, including *rentiers*, to share in the gains of technology. This variant of an income policy (which is less likely to be politically acceptable) would provide the greatest degree of fairness. If some groups in society have their income fixed in money terms, then equity should require that all remuneration be somewhat fixed in money terms.[33]

The desirability of instituting a full employment policy in coordination with a permanent incomes policy is clear. The problem is to find a political leader who will advocate these policies that will be, at least initially, unpopular. (Many people might find themselves liking the results of such a policy, once they got over the shock of it.)

If the government were to adopt policies oriented towards stability in money-wage rates and growth in effective demand at full employment, then the remaining major economic problems would be related to (a) minimizing the effects of unavoidable errors of foresight, and (b) choosing whether expansion should be oriented towards a more rapid accumulation of capital goods or towards the provision of more current consumer goods at full employment production. Development of policies to address these remaining aggregate economic problems would be based on practical rather than theoretical judgements.

Stickiness in wages and the ability to avoid planned recessions to prevent inflation should in themselves reduce the uncertainty about the future. Nevertheless, to err is human, and government must be prepared to aid the innocent victims of the inevitable mistakes made by a prudent management in an uncertain world. Best that we should know the outcome of all decisions before we make them, but in the absence of such perfect certainty it would be unfair of a wealthy society to leave each individual's income to be entirely determined by demand quantities and flow-supply prices in an uncertain market. Government must develop 'guarantee' programmes for insuring against uninsurable economic uncertainties so that no group suffers grievously because of outcomes that were not predictable (acts of God?) when sensible decisions and production commitments were undertaken. Practical and political judgements will determine the best means of providing adequate family income for unemployed workers, compensation for relocation costs, financial aids to producers who enter into reasonable contracts in good faith but who through *no fault of their own* find that the passage of events has caused past production decisions to be in error.

The decision on whether to increase the growth in consumption at the expense of accumulation as well as the decision as to the type of capital projects that are socially (as opposed to commercially) desirable could be resolved on a theoretical plane only if it is assumed that all interpersonal and intergenerational welfare comparisons could be made with complete certainty and with complete knowledge of the most desirable distribution of income at each point of time. Since such information will never be available in the real world, economists must leave it to responsible politicians to make these significant allocative decisions.

Economists should be neither the apologists nor the critics for any ideology *per se*. They should, of course, point out the errors in the economic arguments presented by one side or another. In a world of uncertainty, their most useful contribution to the policy makers will be to trace out as best they can the ramifications associated with the alternative paths of development implicit in each allocative decision without making implicit value judgements as to the relative desirability of the various alternatives. If economists would undertake these tasks, then as Keynes noted: 'economists could manage to get themselves thought of as humble, competent people, on a level with dentists, [and] that would be splendid!'[34]

APPENDIX ON SPOT INFLATION

Spot prices require immediate delivery. Since production takes time, only goods that have already been produced and are currently being stored as shelf inventory can practically be sold in spot markets. Any sudden increase in demand for immediate delivery (or decline in shelf-inventory supplies) will cause a *spot or commodity price inflation*. The result will be a windfall change in the wealth of those possessing the existing commodities.

Buffer stocks. Since a spot or commodity price inflation occurs whenever there is a sudden and unforeseen change in demand or available supply *for immediate delivery*, this type of inflation can easily be avoided if there is some institution that is not motivated by self-interest but which will maintain a 'buffer stock' to prevent unforeseen changes from inducing wild spot price movements. A buffer stock is nothing more than some commodity shelf inventory that can be moved into and out of the spot market to buffer the market from disruptions by offsetting the unforeseen changes in spot demand or supply.

For example, since the oil price shocks of the 1970s, the United States has developed a 'strategic petroleum reserve' stored in underground salt domes on the coast of the Gulf of Mexico. These oil reserves are designed to provide emergency market supplies to buffer the oil market if it is suddenly cut off from foreign supply sources. In such a situation, the spot price of oil would not increase as much as it otherwise would; a spot oil price inflation could be avoided as long as the buffer stock remained available. In 1986 spot oil prices dropped from $20 to almost $10 per barrel as the result of worldwide excessive inventories of crude oil. If the United States had increased its purchases for the strategic oil reserves during this period, then the commodity price deflation and its devastating impact on the income of domestic oil producers in the oil patch of the Southwestern States could have been mitigated.

In the absence of such buffer stocks of commodities, every unexpected change in spot demand or available supply will produce an immediate change in spot prices. In times of great uncertainty about the future use and/or availability of important commodities, e.g., oil, metals, etc., the spot price can fluctuate dramatically in short periods of time – as they did during brief periods in the 1970s and 1980s.

Rising spot prices signal an inventory shortage, thereby encouraging an output expansion. The resulting rebuilt inventories will end the spot price inflation. Falling spot prices signal producers that inventories are excessive. Managers will cut back future production to work off the existing inventories, thereby stopping the price decline. Essentially spot price inflation (or deflation), provided it does not induce change in the future costs of production, should subside as it encourages entrepreneurs to take on inventory adjustments. To the extent that the spot price of commodities is rising it may take too long for new supplies to come to market. Buyers may not be able to wait for a return to more normal supply–demand conditions, or they may be stampeded by fears of an uncertain future into thinking that the current spot price inflation will permanently affect future costs of production, thereby encouraging producers to raise supply contract prices.

The policy solution to spot price inflation that threatens to outlive the buyers' patience is as old as the biblical story of Joseph and the Pharaoh's dream of seven fat cows followed by seven lean cows. Joseph – the economic forecaster of his day – interpreted the Pharaoh's dream as portending seven good harvests where production would be much above normal followed by seven lean harvests where annual production would not provide enough food to go around. Joseph's civilized policy proposal was for the government to store up a *buffer stock* of grain during the good years and release the grain to market, without profit, during the bad years. This would maintain a stable price over the fourteen harvests and avoid inflation in the bad years while protecting farmers' incomes in the good harvest years. The Bible records that this buffer stock policy was a resounding economic success.

The idea of using buffer stocks to stabilize commodity prices is not new. It was used briefly by the United States during World War I. It was revived as part of the agricultural policy of the New Deal to maintain farm income. In the period from the end of World War II until the 1970s, an expressed government policy was to maintain significant buffer stocks of agricultural products and other strategic raw materials to support prices that adequately rewarded producers for efficiently organizing the production process. This policy helped stabilize commodity prices worldwide even as world demand for foodstuffs and other basic commodities exploded under the stimulus of global economic growth.

The other side of the coin of stable commodity prices was stable incomes for farmers and other commodity producers. The result was (a) prosperity for raw material producers, (b) the encouragement of continuing productivity enhancing investment in these areas, and (c) a non-inflationary price trend for the food and basic commodity component of consumers' budgets despite a soaring global population and rapid worldwide economic growth. From hindsight it is clear that the stability of commodity prices during the period 1947 to 1972 was an essential aspect of the unprecedented prosperous economic growth of the world's economy over a quarter of a century.

The success of this post-World War II buffer stock programme over several decades was its ultimate undoing. As productivity in food and other primary products increased (encouraged by a guaranteed price), some taxpayers began to object to the cost of carrying the buffer stock. Objections were also raised that the income of farmers and other commodity producers was being guaranteed at what appeared to be the consumers' expense. After all, if the existing surplus buffer stock was dumped onto the market, spot prices would fall, providing the consumer with a 'bargain' – at the expense of producers.

Public attention was not drawn to the fact that the urban taxpayer as a consumer received the benefit of a plentiful food supply at stable non-inflationary prices. Moreover, as workers and entrepreneurs in the industrial sector, urban taxpayers found plenty of job opportunities producing the many industrial products that only prosperous raw material producers could demand.

When the Nixon Administration dismantled these buffer stock programmes to save warehousing costs and to use these savings to help finance the war in Vietnam, world spot commodity markets were left to the mercy of unforeseen events. The result was the violent commodity price fluctuations that occurred in the 1970s and 1980s. In the early 1970s – even before the first oil shock – spot food prices began to soar as a result of some natural disasters that reduced harvests and fishing catches. Since world commodity supplies were no longer buffered, prices swung widely in response to these unforeseen disasters. As buffer stocks disappeared, cartels of foreign producers had the freedom to raise prices by restricting supplies. Cost-of-living escalator clauses in many wage contracts were triggered by this commodity inflation thereby causing this spot price inflation to spill over into production costs (incomes) inflation for industrial goods. This process was already well under way in 1972 even before the OPEC oil cartel's embargo drove oil prices through the roof, and exacerbated the situation.

As a result, many foreign nations who were net importers of agricultural products and petroleum were especially hard hit by the ongoing worldwide commodity inflation. In the absence of any significant international buffer stock, each nation attempted to become more self-sufficient in these basic commodities rather than pay the 'exorbitant' prices to the traditional foreign producers. This policy of self-sufficiency meant subsidizing less efficient domestic raw material producers. This self-sufficiency movement was encouraged when, for political reasons, President Carter ordered a grain embargo in 1979. This signalled foreign grain importers that for political reasons they could no longer count on United States production to feed their population at any price.

The politically motivated actions by the Nixon and Carter Administrations eliminated the United States as the world's major buffer stock operator who had, for decades, maintained international spot commodity price stability. When the United States publicly abandoned the role of the world's non-profit buffer stock operator, commodity producers and consumers were given a clear signal their future prosperity could no longer be secured on the civilized post World War II international institutions.

If we have learned anything from this history of commodity price gyrations, it is that wild commodity spot price swings in free markets create havoc, inefficiencies and misery – sometimes among producers and sometimes among buyers. At any point of time these volatile spot price movements produce some winners and offsetting losers between producer and consumer groups, giving the impression that it is the zero-sum game. From a longer perspective, the whole world has been a loser as a result of the unbuffering of commodity prices under the Nixon presidency compared to the world's economic performance from 1947 to 1970 when spot price stabilization was an explicit policy goal.

NOTES

1. A. Marshall, *Principles of Economics*, 8th Edition, Macmillan, London, 1949, p. 142.
2. Keynes, *A Treatise on Money*, 2, p. 144.
3. Ibid., 1, pp. 155–6.
4. Ibid., 1, p. 56. Keynes separated a profit inflation which raised the gross margin from an incomes inflation which involved increasing money wages and 'normal' profits. For present purposes, any increase in gross profit margins can be referred to as a profits inflation.
5. Classical theories of inflation always associate inflation with immediate spot price movements. That is why classical theory is linked to exogenous 'demand-pull' explanations of inflation, while the Keynes–Post Keynesian analysis of incomes-inflation is simplified into an exogenous 'cost-push' supply-side inflationary view.
6. Cf. J.M. Keynes, *A Treatise on Money*, 1, p. 156.
7. Even if the retail market is conceived as a spot market, in the sense that purchasers do not order for forward delivery, the retail price will not fall below the flow-supply price, if the retailer operates as a going concern, for he will have to replace shelf inventory with new output. (The obvious exception is at the end of a model year – a clearance sale – when the market is in a contango.) For consumer goods that have short production gestation periods, the retail 'spot' price is not likely to rise much above the flow-supply price because any shortages that develop can be quickly alleviated by increased production flows.
8. This section is derived from S. Weintraub, *An Approach To The Theory of Income Distribution*, Chilton, Philadelphia, 1958, pp. 162–4.
9. If imports are a significant component of the producible goods that residents of a nation buy, then rising import prices can affect the flow-supply prices. (See Chapter 13 *infra*.)
10. J.M. Keynes, *The General Theory*, pp. 42–3, including footnotes, pp. 299–300.
11. Unless the economic rents which accrue to enterprises are deemed to be socially undesirable. In that case, a tax may have to be levied on such rents.
12. R.F. Harrod, *The Trade Cycle*, Clarendon Press, Oxford, 1936, pp. 21–2.

13. Keynes, *Treatise on Money*, 2, pp. 162–3, especially;

     Thus, if we consider a long period of time, the working class may benefit far more in the long run from the forced abstinence which a *Profit Inflation* imposes on them than they lose in the first instance in the shape of diminished consumption . . . *so long as wealth and its fruits are not consumed by the nominal owner but are accumulated*, the evils of an unjust distribution may not be so great as they appear.

14. This 'forced savings' assumes the propensity to save out of profits is greater than the propensity to save out of wages.

15. Keynes, only half jokingly, suggested that as a result of the profit inflation in Elizabethan England, 'We were just in a financial position to afford Shakespeare at the moment when he presented himself!' Keynes, *A Treatise on Money*, 2, p. 154.

16. This phenomenon led to the popularization of the Phillips curve (see *infra*).

17. J.M. Keynes, *The General Theory*, p. 301.

18. J.M. Keynes, *The General Theory*, p. 14.

19. In an open economy, it is also possible to import inflationary tendencies from abroad. For a further discussion of import inflation see Chapter 12 *infra*.

20. Keynes, *A Treatise on Money*, 2, p. 351.

21. See M. Friedman, 'A Theoretical Framework for Monetary Analysis', in *Milton Friedman's Monetary Framework: A Debate With His Critics*, edited by R.J. Gordon, Chicago University Press, Chicago, 1974.

22. Friedman states that 'The simple quantity theory adds the equation $[Y/P] = y = y_0$, that is, *real income is determined outside the system*'. M. Friedman, 'A Theoretical Framework for Monetary Analysis', in *Milton Friedman's Monetary Framework: A Debate With His Critics*, edited by R. J. Gordon, Chicago University Press, Chicago, 1974, p. 31.

23. Only the assertion that, for some exogenous reason, the short-run value of the velocity variable declined dramatically in 1982 can rescue the Monetarist view. Unfortunately, this reliance on unexplained short-run velocity variability converts the Monetarist view into a metaphysical vision. Whenever the historical facts diverge from the Monetarist argument, the salvation will be an unexplained change in velocity. Since velocity is *defined* in terms of the ratio of nominal income divided by the money supply, there can never be data to disprove the Monetarist view, as long as short-term velocity variability is permitted to be an adjusting explanation.

24. 'The Relation between Unemployment and the Rate of Change of Money Wage Rates in the United Kingdom, 1861–1957', *Economica*, **26**, 1958.

25. P.A. Samuelson and R.M. Solow, 'Analytical Aspects of Anti-Inflation Policy', *American Economic Review Papers and Proceedings*, **50**, 1960, pp. 192–3.

26. M. Friedman, 'The Role of Monetary Policy', *American Economic Review*, **58**, 1968, pp. 1–17.

27. S. Weintraub, *Classical Keynesianism, Monetary Theory, and the Price Level*, Chilton, Philadelphia, 1961.

28. In the 1960s, other studies by students of Weintraub indicated a similar historical stability for the variable *k* for other nations. Hence the problem of changes in the profit margin appeared to be relatively unimportant. The inflation problem between the end of World War II and the 1960s appeared to be primarily one of controlling wages relative to productivity. In the 1970s and 1980s, however, the profit margins tended to rise (especially after the oil price shock of 1973 – which was a gross profit margin increase forced by the OPEC cartel).

29. President Carter experienced a similar disappointment when he tried to enlist public support for energy conservation by declaring it the 'Moral Equivalent Of War' without any positive leadership actions. The cynical public labelled the Carter moral equivalent policy 'M.E.O.W'.

30. Inflation in Europe had also subsided but unemployment remained at a post-war high.

31. See S. Weintraub, *Some Aspects of Wage Theory and Policy*, Chilton, Philadelphia, 1963, Ch. 5.

32. Ibid., ch. 6. Also see A.P. Lerner, 'Employment Theory and Employment Policy', *American Economic Review Papers and Proceedings*, **57**, 1967, pp. 1–18.
33. J.M. Keynes, *The General Theory*, p. 268.
34. J.M. Keynes, *Essays in Persuasion*, Norton, New York, 1963, p. 373.

10. Keynes's aggregate supply and demand analysis

Keynes argued that money value and employment are the two 'fundamental units of quantity'[1] to be used when dealing with macroeconomic relationships. The aggregate sales proceeds and intended demand purchases in Keynes's aggregate supply and demand functions are always measured either in money value terms or in a money value deflated by the money wage. This deflated money term Keynes called the wage unit.

DERIVING THE AGGREGATE SUPPLY FUNCTION

Keynes's aggregate supply function is derived from ordinary Marshallian micro flow-supply functions.[2] The aggregate supply function relates the aggregate number of workers (N) that profit-maximizing entrepreneurs would want to hire for each possible level of expected sales proceeds (Z) – given the money-wage rate, technology, the degree of competition (or monopoly), and the degree of integration of firms.

For any given degree of integration, GDP is directly related to total sales proceeds. If each firm is fully integrated from raw material production to finished product sales then aggregate sales proceeds equals GDP.

The aggregate supply function is specified as:

$$Z = f_1(w, N) \tag{10.1}$$

or

$$Z_w = f_2(N) \tag{10.2}$$

where Z is measured in money units and Z_w is in terms of wage units, while N is hiring in terms of employment units and w is the money wage.

For purposes of simplicity and ease of comparability with the ordinary Marshallian micro-supply function, only the form of equation (10.1) will be developed. (Equational form (10.2) of the aggregate supply function can be derived by dividing all money sums expressed in equation (10.1) by the money-wage rate.)

The Marshallian flow-supply curve for each firm indicates the profit-maximizing output possibilities for alternative market demand conditions facing the firm. The profit-maximization condition is

$$p[1 - 1/E_{df}] = MC_f \qquad (10.3)$$

where p is the market price, E_{df} is the absolute value of the price elasticity of demand facing the firm for any given level of effective demand, $1/E_{df}$ is the firm's degree of monopoly (μ_f) and MC_f is the marginal cost schedule facing the firm. The supply schedule of any profit-maximizing firm (s_f) is related to its marginal cost and its degree of monopoly,

$$s_f = f_1(MC_f, \mu_f). \qquad (10.4)$$

Assuming labour is the only variable input in the production process, the firm's marginal cost equals the money wage (w) divided by the firm's marginal productivity of labour (mp_f) where the latter is a function of hiring by the firm and the laws of returns involved in the technology of the firm, i.e.,

$$MC_f = w/mp_f \qquad (10.5)$$

For any given 'law of returns' facing the firm, there will be a different marginal production cost structure. With diminishing returns, marginal production costs increase with increasing output. With constant returns to labour, marginal production costs are constant. With increasing returns, marginal costs decline with increases in output and employment.[3] Figure 10.1 represents the traditional marginal costs under diminishing returns situation.

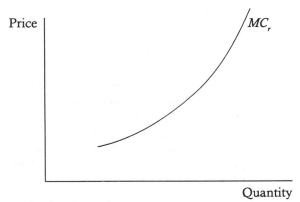

Figure 10.1   The firm's marginal cost curve

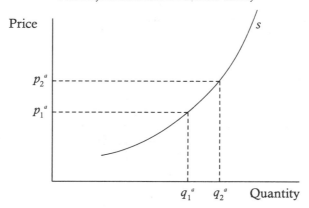

Figure 10.2a   Marshallian industry supply function

For a perfectly competitive firm, $E_{df} = \infty$, and therefore the firm has no monopoly power $(\mu_f = 0)$. In this case, the marginal costs schedule of the firm is its flow-supply curve. For conditions of less than perfect competition, the degree of monopoly will vary between zero and one as $1 > E_d < \infty$. Whenever $0 > \mu_f < 1$ both marginal costs and monopoly power affect the firm's supply curve offerings at alternative market prices.[4] If the firm is in a purely competitive market then the marginal cost curve in Figure 10.1 represents the firm's supply function. If the firm has some degree of monopoly power, the supply function would be the marginal cost schedule of Figure 10.1 multiplied by some scalar equal to $[1/\mu_f]$.

The Marshallian industry flow-supply schedule (s) is simply obtained by the usual lateral summation of the individual firms' supply curves. The industry supply schedule is, therefore, related to the average industry mark-up or 'average' degree of monopoly (μ) *and* the industry's marginal costs schedule (mc), i.e.

$$s = \Sigma s_f = f_4[mc, 1/\mu] \qquad (10.6)$$

Given (a) each firm's production technology, (b) the money wage, and (c) average degree of monopoly based on specified market conditions for any given potential output and employment level, a unique industry supply function can be derived as depicted in Figure 10.2a.

Output across firms in the same industry may be homogeneous and therefore can be aggregated to obtain the industry supply schedule in Figure 10.2a. Keynes rejected this homogeneity of output assumption as the basis for summing across industries to obtain the aggregate supply function.[5] It is necessary to convert the Marshallian industry supply function, s, which

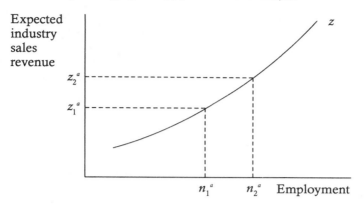

Figure 10.2b   Keynes's industry supply function

relates prices (p) and quantities (q) to a function (that we may call Keynes's industry supply function) whose units can be aggregated across industries to obtain an aggregate supply function. Keynes's industry supply function in Figure 10.2b relates total industry sales proceeds in money terms (z) with total industry employment hiring (n), i.e.

$$z = f_3(n) \tag{10.7}$$

Given productivity, the money wage, and the degree of monopoly, every point on the Marshallian industry supply function is associated with a unique profit-maximizing price-quantity combination whose product equals total expected sales proceeds (i.e. $pxq = z$). Every industry output level (q) can be associated with a unique industry hiring level, i.e. $q = f(n)$. Given industry A's supply curve in Figure 10.2a, if entrepreneurs of that industry expect a price of p_1^a, they will produce q_1^a and expect a total sales revenue of $z_1^a (= \text{to } p_1^a q_1^a)$. To produce q_1^a output, n_1^a workers will have to be hired in the A industry. Consequently, z_1^a and n_1^a describe the coordinates of one point on Keynes's industry supply function in Figure 10.2b.

In a similar manner, every point of the Marshallian industry supply function in the p vs. q quadrant (e.g. p_2^a, q_2^a in Figure 10.2a) can be transformed to a point on the Keynes industry supply curve in pq vs. n space (e.g. z_2^a, n_2^a) in Figure 10.2b.

For every industry where a traditional Marshallian flow-supply function can be formulated, a Keynes industry supply function can also be uniquely specified. All of Keynes's industry supply functions can then be aggregated together to obtain the aggregate supply function of Figure 10.2c in terms of aggregate money proceeds (Z) and the aggregate quantity of employment

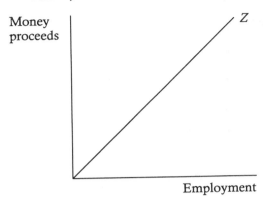

Figure 10.2c   The aggregate supply function

units (N), provided one reasonably assumes that corresponding to any given point of aggregate supply there is a unique distribution and employment between the different industries in the economy.[6]

INCOME DISTRIBUTION AND AGGREGATE SUPPLY

If all firms in each industry are fully integrated, then the aggregate expected sales proceeds of Figure 10.3 is equal to the Gross Domestic Product (GDP) of the economy.[7] The distribution of GDP between workers and capitalists will reflect the average distribution of the total revenue of each of the firms in the economy. The distribution for each firm can be obtained if we combine equations (10.3) and (10.5):

$$p(1 - 1/E_{df}) = w/mp_f. \qquad (10.8)$$

Rearranging terms

$$w/p = (mp_f)(1 - 1/E_{df}). \qquad (10.9)$$

The fraction of the total revenue of the firm paid to wage earners is called the wage share. The wage share for each firm is the total wages bill of the firm (wn_f) divided by total sales proceeds (pq). It is $[(wn_f)/(pq)]$. The average product of labour (ap_f) in the firm is equal to (q/n_f). If both sides of equation (10.9) are multiplied by the reciprocal of the average product of labour (n_f/q),

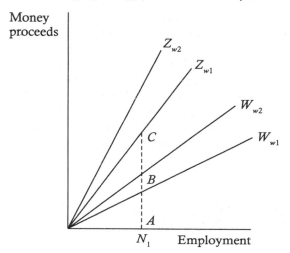

Figure 10.3   Aggregate wage bill lines and aggregate supply functions

$$(w/p)(n_f/q) = (mp_f)(1 - 1/E_{df})(n_f/q)$$

then the wage share is obtained as

$$[wn_f/pq] = [mp_f/ap_f][1 - 1/E_{df}].   (10.10)$$

If all firms in the economy are fully integrated, then the wage share in GDP, at any level of employment, is

$$W/Z = [MP/AP][1 - M]   (10.11)$$

where W is the aggregate wage bill, Z is GDP, MP is aggregate marginal product of labour, AP is the aggregate average product of labour, and M is the average degree of monopoly in the economy. In a purely competitive economy, $M = 0$, and the aggregate wage share is equal to the economy's MP/AP ratio.

The aggregate wage bill (W) is total money wages (wN) paid to workers at any level of aggregate employment. Given a money-wage rate of w_1, the aggregate wage bill line, W_1 $(= w_1 N)$ can be drawn as a straight line emanating from the origin in Figure 10.3. The slope of this wage bill line is w_1. Given the MP/AP ratio as determined by productivity relations, and the economy-wide average degree of monopoly, the aggregate supply function associated with W_{w1} is Z_{w1}. The distribution of income for any given level of employment can be derived from Figure 10.3. If, for example, aggregate employment is N_1, then the wage bill will be equal to AB, and the wage share will be AB/AC. The vertical distance between the wage bill line and the aggregate supply curve at each employment level in Figure 10.3 depends on the economy-wide MP/AP ratio and degree of monopoly. (In a purely competitive economy, the vertical distance between the Z curve and the wage bill line depends only on the MP/AP ratio.) If the MP/AP is a constant at each level of employment,[8] then the aggregate supply curve is a straight line emanating from the origin, e.g. Z_{w1} in Figure 10.3. If the MP/AP ratio declines (due to diminishing returns), then the Z curve will be convex to the wage bill line.

CHANGES IN THE MONEY-WAGE RATE AND THE AGGREGATE SUPPLY FUNCTION

The aggregate wage bill line W_{w1} and aggregate supply curve Z_{w1} are associated with a specific money-wage rate, w_1. If the money wage was w_2, where $w_2 > w_1$, then the slope of the wage bill line W_2 would be steeper. In Figure 10.3, the W_2 wage bill line would be higher than the wage bill line W_1 in exactly the same proportion as the money-wage rate w_2 is greater than w_1. Since at the higher money-wage rate, the wage bill shifts up proportionately, and since the distribution of income between workers and capitalists depends only on the MP/AP ratio and the economy-wide degree of monopoly, then the aggregate supply curve (Z_{w2}) associated with a wage rate of w_2 will be proportionately higher than the aggregate supply curve Z_{w1} associated with the money-wage rate w_1.

A change in the money wage results in a proportionate shift in the aggregate supply function. This proportionate effect will be an important factor when, in the next chapter, the shape of the aggregate demand for labour curve is investigated.

DERIVING THE AGGREGATE DEMAND CURVE

Given the discussion of the aggregate demand categories D_1 and D_2 in Chapters 3 and 4, for any given money wage w_1, the aggregate demand curve can be drawn as the upward-sloping curve D_{w1} in Figure 10.4. The slope of the aggregate demand curve will depend on the marginal propensities to consume of the various income recipients.[9]

Our Z_{w1} function from Figure 10.3 can be redrawn in Figure 10.4. The point of effective demand, E, is given by the intersection of the aggregate

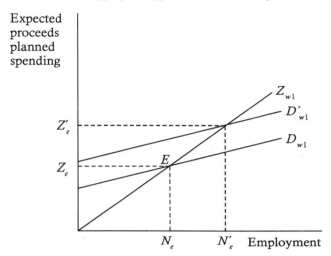

Figure 10.4   Aggregate demand and supply

demand curve D_{w1} and aggregate supply curve Z_{w1}. The equilibrium level of employment and GDP is N_e and Z_e.

If, *ceteris paribus*, there is an exogenous increase in D_2 spending the aggregate demand curve will shift from D_{w1} to D'_{w1} in Figure 10.4. Employment will rise from N_e to N'_e and GDP will increase from Z_e to Z'_e.

THE AGGREGATE DEMAND CURVE DERIVED AND MARSHALLIAN MICRO-DEMAND CURVES

Unlike the upward-sloping aggregate demand curve, the Marshallian micro-demand curve facing an industry is normally downward sloping. Despite these different slopes, the aggregate demand curve can be derived from a Marshallian micro-demand and supply analysis.

At an expected price of p_1, entrepreneurs in industry a will produce q_1 output, will hire n_1 workers, and expect a total revenue of z_1 $(=p_1q_1)$. A Marshallian demand curve is based on the assumptions of given tastes, given other industry demand and supply conditions, and *given the aggregate demand schedule*. The demand schedule for this industry 'can only be constructed on some fixed assumption as to the nature of demand and supply in other industries and as to the amount of the aggregate effective demand'.[10] In Figure 10.5, the upward-sloping Marshallian industry supply curve, s_a, is drawn. If entrepreneurs in industry a expect a price of p_1 they will choose to produce q_1 as shown on S_a in Figure 10.5. Given concomitant

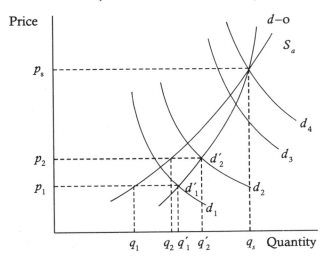

Figure 10.5   Deriving the demand–outlay curve for industry a

prices and outputs of all other industries there will be a given level of aggregate income so that the demand curve facing industry a is d_1 in Figure 10.5.

At the supply price of p_1 in Figure 10.5, the quantity buyers demand would be q_1'. Buyers' intended demand–outlay is d_1' $(=p_1 q_1')$. As drawn in Figure 10.5, at the supply price of p_1, intended demand–outlay exceeds expected sales $(d_1' > z_1)$. The supply price p_1 is less than the equilibrium price, given the implicit assumption regarding demand and supply in other industries and the level of effective demand this assumption entails.

At an alternative expected supply price of p_2, entrepreneurs in representative industry a expect to sell q_2 output for a total revenue of z_2 $(=p_2 q_2)$ and will hire n_2 workers. This increased output and employment in representative industry a will be associated with similar increases in all other industries. The result will be larger factor incomes throughout the economy associated with supply price p_2 compared to supply price p_1. The larger aggregate factor payments imply that a new Marshallian demand curve, d_2 in Figure 10.5, is the relevant demand curve facing industry a. At the supply of p_2, consumers intend to purchase q_2' output and intended demand–outlay is d_2' $(=p_2 q_2')$. Intended spending still exceeds expected sales revenue $(d_2' > z_2)$.

In this way, an intended demand–outlay can be developed from a family of Marshallian demand curves[11] for each supply price in Figure 10.5. Connecting the relevant demand–outlay points at alternative supply prices, the demand–outlay curve d–o in Figure 10.5 is obtained. This upward-sloping demand-outlay function is the industry analogue of Keynes's aggregate demand curve. At any level of aggregate employment, aggregate demand is the summation of intended demand–outlays over all industries.

Implicit in this analysis is the recognition that if employment and output expands in each industry, then aggregate factor incomes rise and the quantity of D_1 aggregate demand increases. Every movement up the given aggregate demand curve associated with an alternative higher level of employment and output generates a higher member of the Marshallian family of industry demand curves. As long as the marginal propensity to consume is less than one, the increase in aggregate demand–outlay will rise slower than the increase in aggregate factor incomes. At some supply price (p_5 in Figure 10.5), the demand–outlay function intersects the industry supply curve and intended outlay just equals expected sales. This point of intersection is the industry analogue to the point of effective demand for the economy as a whole.

NOTES

1. J.M. Keynes, *The General Theory*, p. 41.
2. J.M. Keynes, *The General Theory*, pp. 44–5. The following derivation of the aggregate supply function has its origins in Keynes, *General Theory*, 1936, as elucidated by Weintraub, *An Approach To The Theory of Income Distribution*, Chilton, Philadelphia, 1957 and further developed by P. Davidson, 'More On The Aggregate Supply Function', *Economic Journal*, **72**, 1962, and P. Davidson and E. Smolensky, *Aggregate Supply and Demand Analysis*, Harper & Row, New York, 1964.
3. The latter two cases are incompatible with perfect competition; they require some degree of monopoly and hence some positive mark-up, ($k > 0$) over marginal costs, so that market price covers average unit costs. If marginal user costs (MUC) are not negligible, then $MC_f = [w/MP + MUC]$.
4. In the simplest case when aggregate demand changes, the demand curve facing the firm shifts without altering the degree of monopoly of the firm. For example, for the purely competitive case, shifts in the firm's demand curve do not alter the competitive market conditions. In more complex cases the degree of monopoly may vary as aggregate demand changes and the firm's demand curve shifts, i.e.,

$$\mu_f = f_2(N). \tag{10.2'}$$

5. J.M. Keynes, *The General Theory*, Chapter 4.
6. J.M. Keynes, *The General Theory*, p. 282.
7. Implicit in this statement is the assumption that all production firms are organized by profit-making entrepreneurs in the private sector, i.e., there are no charitable or government-organized firms.
8. Assuming diminishing returns, the MP/AP ratio will be a constant at each level of employment if the marginal product and average product decline at the same rate. This would occur, for example, in a Cobb–Douglas production function of the form $q = an\beta$. Otherwise the marginal product falls faster than the average product and the aggregate supply function will be convex relative to the wage bill line. For a further explanation of

the shape of the aggregate supply function, see P. Davidson and E. Smolensky, *Aggregate Supply and Demand Analysis*, Harper & Row, 1964, pp. 126–8.

9.   A fuller derivation is given in P. Davidson and E. Smolensky, op. cit., Chapter 10.
10. J.M. Keynes, *The General Theory*, p. 259.
11. Each member of the family of Marshallian demand curves represents a different level of aggregate factor income.

11.   The demand and supply of labour

According to classical theory, unemployment is the result of the money wage being too high to clear the labour market. If money wages were perfectly flexible, then in a recession the resultant fall in money wages would induce entrepreneurs to hire more workers. In classical theory, the reduction in the wage rate implies that the marginal cost (and therefore micro flow-supply) curves of all firms and industries shift outwards. All Marshallian industry-wide demand curves are presumed to be unchanged despite the economy-wide decline in the wage rate. The resulting decline in marginal cost and industry supply curves induces downward movements along all the presumed unchanged industry demand curves. Entrepreneurs can make additional profits if they hire additional workers to expand production to meet the presumed induced increases in quantities demanded from every industry.

The fatal logical defect in this classical argument is that it assumes all industry supply curves can shift simultaneously while all industry demand curves remain unchanged. 'The demand schedules for particular industries can only be constructed on some fixed assumption . . . as to the amount of aggregate effective demand',[1] Keynes insisted. It is proper to claim that a change in supply conditions in a single industry can shift the industry's supply curve without altering the demand schedule facing this industry. 'It is invalid', Keynes wrote, 'to transfer the argument to industry as a whole unless we also transfer our assumption that the aggregate effective demand is fixed. Yet this assumption reduces the argument to an *ignoratio elenchi*'.[2]

Underlying the classical analysis of the labour market is the conflation of money wages with real wages. The money-wage rate is a veil behind which real wage forces operate to induce changes in entrepreneurs' hiring of workers. These real wage forces are derived from the marginal physical product of labour curve which is classical theory's aggregate demand curve for labour[3] in a money-using economy. If diminishing returns are prevalent in the production process, then the marginal product of labour (MPL) curve is downward sloping (Figure 11.1).[4] Since this marginal product curve is the classical demand curve for labour, then in classical theory if the wage is reduced from w_a to w_b, entrepreneurial demand for workers will increase from N_a to N_b.

175

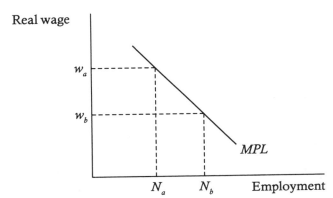

Figure 11.1   The marginal product of labour curve

The classical use of a downward-sloping marginal product of labour as evidence that in a purely competitive economy lower wages will always induce entrepreneurs to hire more workers is irrelevant in analysing the effect of an economy-wide change in wages on the aggregate level of employment. It is a fallacious argument that is apt to deceive with an appearance of algebraic truth. Stiglitz, for example, insists that the downward-sloping marginal product of labour curve must be the demand curve for labour because it is the algebraic equivalent of equating price to marginal cost.[5] If Stiglitz is correct, profit-maximizing entrepreneurs in competitive markets will always increase the number of workers they will hire at alternative lower wage rates. Unfortunately, Stiglitz's claim does not respond to the relevant question that if there is an exogenous decline in demand causing unemployment, then can a reduction in wages *per se* restore full employment in a purely competitive economy with profit-maximizing entrepreneurs.

Keynes argued that a reduction in the wage rate

> will have no lasting tendency to increase employment except by virtue of its repercussions either on the propensity to consume for the community as a whole, or on the schedule of marginal efficiencies of capital, or on the rate of interest. There is no method of analysing the effect of a reduction in money-wages, except by following up its possible effects on these three factors.[6]

The classical view of labelling the marginal product curve as the aggregate labour demand curve is an oversimplification that assumes that economy-wide shifts in industry supply curves due to a change in the aggregate money-wage rate can occur without any 'repercussions' on the components of the aggregate demand function. This classical simplification cannot be presumed, it must be demonstrated.

The proper way of deriving an aggregate demand for labour curve requires analysing the effects of a change in the wage rate on both the aggregate demand and the aggregate supply functions. The aggregate demand for labour curve must relate every alternative wage rate with its associated point of effective demand.[7]

The derivation of the aggregate demand for labour is discussed in Chapters 19 and 20 of *The General Theory*. Keynes specifically analyses the implications of 'Changes in Money-Wages' and 'The Employment Function'. It is unfortunate that the placement of these chapters followed Chapter 18 entitled 'The General Theory of Employment Restated'. Apparently mainstream macrotheorists believe that all the essential aspects of Keynes's *The General Theory* must have been developed by the time they reach a chapter indicating it is a restatement.

This permits most economists to characterize the analysis in Chapters 19–24 as not essential to *The General Theory*. Friedman, for example, argues that the entire book following Chapter 18 should be considered 'strictly peripheral to the main contribution of the *General Theory*'.[8] By labelling Keynes's analysis of relating changes in wage rates with alternate points of effective demand as peripheral to Keynes's analytical framework, mainstream economists rationalize their ignorance of the analytical contents of these chapters.

CAN UNEMPLOYMENT EXIST IN A CLASSICAL SYSTEM?

Classical economists insist that a downward-sloping marginal product curve (*MPL* in Figure 11.2) is the aggregate labour demand curve. The aggregate labour supply curve (*SL* in Figure 11.2) is conceived as upward-sloping in order to reflect increasing marginal disutility of labour as employment increases. At the point of equilibrium, E in Figure 11.2, the real wage equals w_e and the level of employment is N_e. The marginal product equals the marginal disutility and all who want to work are employed. There can be no unemployment in equilibrium in the classical system. Equilibrium is synonymous with a clearing of the labour market.

Yet, Keynes claimed that the most important outcome of his *General Theory* was to show that there could be an 'insufficiency of effective demand' creating an unemployment equilibrium where 'the marginal product of labour still exceeds the marginal disutility of employment'.[9] This equilibrium result of Keynes is impossible in Figure 11.2. That fact

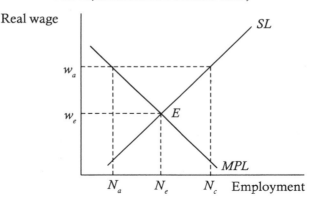

Figure 11.2   The aggregate labour supply curve

alone should have alerted mainstream theorists to the fact that the
marginal product-demand for labour analysis of Figure 11.2 is not compatible with Keynes's *General Theory*.

To force compatibility, mainstream Keynesians use some *ad hoc*
assumption that makes the wage rate (and/or prices) inflexible or rigid.
New Keynesians insist that fluctuation in employment 'requires nominal
wage and/or price rigidity'.[10] Thus if the wage rate is w_a in Figure 11.2,
entrepreneurs will hire N_a workers, while N_c will be seeking jobs. The
difference $(N_c - N_a)$ will be the number of unemployed. To obtain full
employment equilibrium, classical theory suggests that the wage rigidity
should be removed. In the classical system, as long as the rigidity remains,
unemployment can occur because of the failure of the market.

In classical theory, individuals are acting voluntarily when they are all
on their supply and demand schedules simultaneously. The very notion of
involuntary unemployment conjures up in the mind of classical theorists
the idea that workers are off their supply schedule.[11] Unemployment is
therefore a disequilibrium rather than an equilibrium situation[12] as long as
entrepreneurs do not reduce their wage offer to obtain all the workers they
need at the equilibrium wage, which equals w_e.

Keynes demonstrated that involuntary unemployment involved an
equilibrium in the labour market without labour market clearing. Keynes
used the term equilibrium in the Marshallian sense. Equilibrium is a state
where no forces are at work to alter the position of the economy as long as
the specified conditions remained unchanged.

Mainstream economists have confused market clearing, i.e., where the
quantity demanded exactly equals the quantity supplied, with market
equilibrium, where nothing changes in the system's position. Market

clearing is a sufficient condition for market equilibrium, it is not a necessary condition.

Properly interpreted within a Keynes aggregate supply and demand framework, the concept of an aggregate marginal product of labour curve represents, in Patinkin's terminology, *a market equilibrium curve*. This market equilibrium curve shows the real wage that corresponds to each equilibrium level of employment (as determined by the point of effective demand).[13] The next section of this chapter illustrates how the aggregate demand for labour curve is derived (independent of the marginal product of labour curve) in Keynes's *General Theory*. Once Keynes's analysis of the labour demand function is derived, it is possible to explain why a classical labour supply analysis,[14] which is often incorporated in New Classical macromodels, is logically incompatible with Keynes's real world monetary analysis.

DERIVING THE AGGREGATE DEMAND FOR LABOUR FUNCTION

A Marshallian demand curve is the geometric expression of the functional relationship showing at alternative market prices what quantity buyers demand. An aggregate demand curve for labour represents the volume of labour hiring profit-maximizing entrepreneurs will demand at every alternative possible wage rate. The aggregate equilibrium hiring of workers is determined by the point of effective demand.

Given the stock of equipment, technology, and the degree of competition in the economy, the aggregate supply function is represented as

$$Z = f_z(w, N). \tag{11.1}$$

Given the preferences of households, the distribution of income, and investment demand (in a two-sector model[15]), the aggregate demand function is represented as

$$D = f_d(w, N) \tag{11.2}$$

where w is the money wage, N is the level of employment, and D and Z are respectively aggregate demand and aggregate supply magnitudes measured in nominal values. In equilibrium aggregate supply equals aggregate demand, so that once the money wage is specified, the equilibrium level of employment is determined by the point of effective demand. For example, when the money-wage rate is w_a, the aggregate demand and supply curves

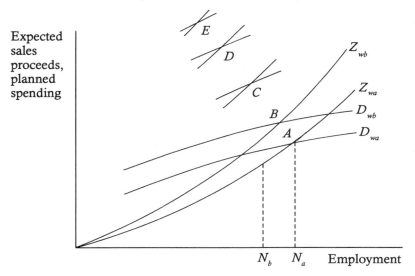

Figure 11.3   Effective demand with alternative money wage rates

can be represented as D_{wa} and Z_{wa} respectively in Figure 11.3. The point of effective demand associated with money-wage rate w_a is point A. The equilibrium level of employment is N_a.

The demand for labour curve is developed in the wage rate versus employment quadrant of Figure 11.4. Since, in Figure 11.3, the equilibrium level of employment associated with a money wage of w_a is N_a, then the coordinate (w_a, Na) is one point on an aggregate demand curve for labour. It is represented by point A' in Figure 11.4.

A different pair of aggregate demand and supply curves in Figure 11.3 will be associated with every alternative money-wage rate. By varying the money wage rate and observing the resulting shifts in the aggregate demand and supply curves, the resulting effective demand point for each money-wage rate can be obtained. These alternative effective demand points are used to derive the coordinates for each point on the aggregate demand for labour curve. Thus if Z_{wb} and D_{wb} are the aggregate demand curves associated with the money wage w_b, then effective demand is at point B where N_b workers are hired. The coordinates (w_b, N_b) provide a second point, B', on the aggregate demand for labour curve in Figure 11.4.

Repeating this conceptual experiment for every conceivable money-wage rate produces shifts in both Z and D. The resulting locus of effective demand points $(A, B, C, D, E$ in Figure 11.3) can then be used to derive the points on the aggregate demand curve for labour $(A', B', C', D', E'$ in Figure 11.4).

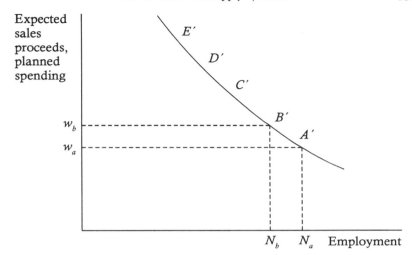

Figure 11.4   Aggregate demand for labour curve

As drawn, Figure 11.4 suggests that the demand curve for labour is downward sloping. The quantity of labour demanded declines at alternative higher money wage rates if the higher wage induces a greater upward shift in the Z-curve than in the D-curve in Figure 11.3.

There is no obvious compelling reason why the aggregate supply curve must shift more than the aggregate demand curve at each alternative wage rate. If the shift in the aggregate supply curve associated with changing money-wage rates is equal to (less than) the shift in aggregate demand, then the aggregate labour demand curve is vertical (upward sloping). In these latter cases, the aggregate demand curve for labour would not be downward sloping, even if labour is subject to diminishing returns and therefore the marginal product of labour curve decreases as employment increases.

Three labour demand curves are conceptually possible.

The classical demand curve. Figure 11.5a depicts the classical demand curve for labour since its downward slope is what most classical economists believe is the appropriate one. This downward slope is not a direct result of the downward slope of the marginal product of labour curve. Rather it depends on the presumption that each alternative wage rate will have a greater relative impact on the aggregate supply function than it has on aggregate demand.

The Keynes demand curve. If, at alternative money-wage rates, the Z and D curves shift by the same proportion, the resulting aggregate demand curve for labour is perfectly inelastic as represented in Figure 11.5b.

The underconsumptionist demand curve. There has always been a small

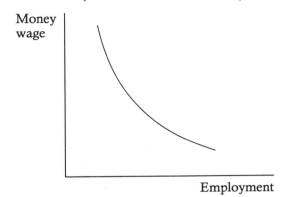

Figure 11.5a   The classical demand curve for labour

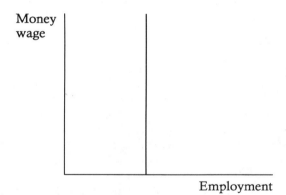

Figure 11.5b   The Keynes demand curve for labour

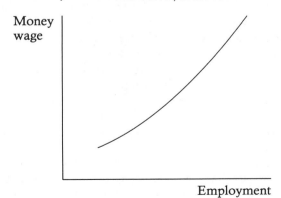

Figure 11.5c   The underconsumptionist demand curve for labour

group of unorthodox economists who have argued that increases in money wages will lead to an increase in the quantity of labour demanded. This occurs if the aggregate demand curve shifts proportionately *more* than the aggregate supply curve, for every alternative wage rate.[16] The resulting aggregate demand for labour curve is upward sloping in the money-wage–employment quadrant, as illustrated in Figure 11.5c.

DERIVING THE RELEVANT DEMAND CURVE FOR LABOUR

'At issue', Keynes noted, 'is whether a reduction in money-wages will or will not be accompanied by the same aggregate effective demand as before measured in terms of money, or at any rate, by an aggregate effective demand which is not reduced in full proportion to the reduction in money-wages (i.e., which is somewhat greater measured in wage-units)'.[17] In other words, to determine the effect of a change in the wage rate on employment, it is necessary to analyse the effect on the shifts in the aggregate supply and demand curve.

In the last chapter it was demonstrated that for a money-wage reduction, the aggregate supply curves shift downwards by the full proportion of the reduction in the money wage. If, and only if, the aggregate demand curve shifts down by a smaller proportion then 'aggregate effective demand . . . is not reduced in full proportion to the money wage' then the classical conclusion is applicable. If the aggregate demand function shifts by an equal amount to or more than the aggregate supply function, then the classical conclusion is not applicable. Until the effect of changes in the money wage on the components of the aggregate demand function and the resulting shift in the aggregate demand curve is explicitly analysed, no conclusion about the relevant shape of the aggregate demand curve for labour can be obtained.

It is possible to analyse the conditions that would be necessary to support choosing one shape of the demand curve for labour over the others. Some relevant conditions to consider include: (1) expectations as to whether the change in the money-wage rate is a once-for-all change, or whether additional future money-wage changes are expected; (2) the distribution of income and the difference in marginal propensities to consume amongst different income groups; and (3) the effect of different wage rates on the rate of interest.[18]

Case 1. A once-for-all change in money wages. Assume that

1. production techniques are given and unchanged during the period of analysis;

2.   the Monetary Authority takes whatever steps are necessary to maintain the existing rate of interest; and
3.   people expect that any changes that occur in the current period are once-for-all changes, i.e. no further changes in wages will occur in future periods.

If the money-wage rate increases by x per cent, then, as demonstrated in Chapter 10, the aggregate supply curve will shift upwards by x per cent at each level of employment. The effect of an x per cent rise in the money-wage rate on the aggregate demand function is more complex. The impact on the marginal efficiency of capital and on the propensity to consume must be evaluated separately.

The marginal efficiency of each investment project involves the rate of discount that makes any future expected stream of quasi-rents equal to the current flow-supply price of capital. Equation (11.3a) represents the marginal efficiency of investment formula if no change in the money-wage rate has occurred.

$$SP = q_1/(1+r) + q_2/(1+r)^2 + \ldots + q_n/(1+r)^n \qquad (11.3a)$$

where SP is the supply price of investment goods, q is the expected quasi-rent in each period, and r is the marginal efficiency of investment.

Assume labour is the only variable factor of production. If the money-wage rate is increased by x per cent, then the current period's marginal cost curves for every industry will be x per cent higher. The flow-supply price of all new investment goods is x per cent higher. This once-for-all wage increase implies that in every future period, expected factor and product prices will be x per cent higher than if wages remained constant. Expected quasi-rents will be x per cent greater in each future period compared to expectations if no wage increase has occurred. Equation (11.3b) presents the marginal efficiency of investment after the once-for-all wage increase.

$$(1+x)(SP) = [(1+x)(q_1)]/(1+r) + [(1+x)(q_2)]/(1+r)^2 +$$
$$[(1+x)(q_3)]/(1+r)^3 + \ldots + [(1+x)(q_n)]/(1+r)^n. \qquad (11.3b)$$

Since the current flow-supply price of capital and the expected future flow of quasi-rents both increase by x per cent under these hypothesized conditions, then the rate of discount that equalizes the sum of the quasi-rents and the supply price is the same in both equation (11.3a) and (11.3b). The marginal efficiency associated with any investment project is unchanged after the once-for-all wage change. If (by assumption) there is no change in the interest rate, then entrepreneurs will want to undertake the same level of *real* investment spending as before the money-wage increase.

Since the market price of new investment after the money-wage increase is *x* per cent higher, then the investment demand component of the aggregate demand curve (in money terms) in Figure 11.3 must shift up by *x* per cent. There will be no change in the equilibrium level of employment associated with the investment component of aggregate demand. If there is to be an impact on the equilibrium level of employment, it must operate through the aggregate propensity to consume causing the aggregate demand curve to shift up more, or less than *x* per cent.

The major effect of a change in the money-wage rate at any level of employment will be on the distribution of income. Since money wages and product prices rise proportionately (at each level of employment), real wages, and therefore the real consumption behaviour of workers, are unchanged. Since prices of all consumption goods are *x* per cent higher, spending in money terms by workers will be *x* per cent higher.

If there are fixed money income recipients, i.e. *rentiers*,[19] a consequence of an increase in money wages (and prices) is to redistribute real income (at each level of employment) from *rentiers* towards the profits of firms and their stock-holders. Real consumption by rentiers will decline at each employment level by an amount given by the *rentiers'* marginal propensity to consume. Real consumption by profit recipients will rise based on their marginal propensity. Any change in aggregate consumption spending will depend on the difference in the marginal propensity to consume of *rentiers* compared to profit recipients. If there is no difference, then the redistribution will not affect real consumption at any level of employment and the aggregate demand curve will shift proportionately with the aggregate supply curve.

If the marginal propensity to consume out of gross profits is less than the *rentiers'* marginal propensity,[20] then real consumption will be lower at each level of employment. With prices higher by *x* per cent, money spending by all consumers will rise by less than *x* per cent. The aggregate consumption demand component of the *D*-curve will shift proportionately less than the aggregate *Z*-curve. There will be some decrease in the quantity of labour demanded for this hypothesized once-for-all increase in the money wage. The downward slope depends on the difference between the marginal propensities of *rentiers* and profit recipients. The demand curve should not deviate too much from the vertical unless there are very large differences in the marginal propensities.

Case 2. Inflationary expectations. A change in money-wage rates today may affect people's expectations regarding future wages and prices. In particular, if the money-wage rate rises *x* per cent today, people may expect wages and prices to rise an additional x per cent in each future period. This inflationary psychology can have an impact on aggregate demand.

If inflation is expected to continue in future periods, then today entrepreneurs will anticipate a constant rate of growth each period in future quasi-rent from any investment project. By hypothesis, today's marginal costs and therefore flow-supply prices will only reflect the increase in money wages occurring today. The future stream of expected quasi-rents will increase more than today's flow-supply price for an x per cent rise in money wages today and the marginal efficiency of each project will rise.[21] Equation (11.3c) represents this situation.

$$(1 + x)SP = [(1 + x)(q_1)/(1 + r)] + [(1 + x)^2(q_2)/(1 + r)^2]$$
$$+ [(1 + x)^3(q_3)/(1 + r)^3] + \ldots + [(1 + x)^n(q_n)]/(1 + r)^n. \quad (11.3c)$$

In equation (11.3c) the future stream of quasi-rents accelerates at x per cent per annum while the current supply price rises only by x per cent. The resulting rate of discount that equalizes the accelerating future stream of quasi-rents with the current higher supply price is larger than the rate of discount that created equality in equations (11.3a) and (11.3b) *supra*. Expectations of continuing inflation will improve the expected rate of return on new investment. Total investment spending in real terms, at the (assumed) unchanged rate of interest will increase. Investment spending in money terms will rise by more than the current increase in the money wage.

This increase in real investment demand will tend to offset any decline in real consumption demand resulting from the redistribution in income away from *rentiers* and towards profit recipients. If consumers expect further inflation in the future, then they will tend to move their planned future consumption expenditures forward to today. Inflationary expectations tend to move future consumption forwards in time, as long as households can afford the extra inventory costs involved *and* are certain of which consumption goods they will want in future periods.[22]

Inflationary expectations, therefore, are likely to cause the aggregate demand curve to shift at least proportionately with the aggregate supply curve (assuming no change in the interest rate). The result is that the demand curve for labour will closely emulate the vertical Keynesian demand curve for labour of Figure 11.5b.

Case 3. The real balance effect. Mainstream economic literature suggests that real consumption depends on the real wealth of individuals (rather than on today's measured real income). If wages and prices rise, then the real wealth of those who hold money or interest bearing government debt will decline without any concomitant increase in the real wealth of other individuals in the economy. Holders of money and government bonds will feel poorer. They should cut real consumption at any level of real income.[23]

The magnitude of the real balance effect depends critically on the price rise (fall) necessary to make creditors feel sufficiently poorer (richer) so that, *ceteris paribus*, they reduce (increase) real consumption. If prices fall sufficiently so that possession of a penny today permits one to purchase the same amount of goods as $1 million bought before the price (and wage[24]) fall, then those lucky enough to have pennies would spend like millionaires. Price changes of this magnitude are likely to wreck the banking system (whose nominal liabilities would not be altered while bankers would find few borrowers who did not go bankrupt) and destroy confidence in the monetary system. For less violent, but more realistic price movements, there is little empirical evidence of a real balance effect.[25]

Case 4. The open economy. In an open system the aggregate demand curve includes an export component net of the imports for consumption and investment. If there is a reduction in money wages *relative* to the money wage abroad when both wages are reduced to a common nominal unit, then domestic employment can increase in (a) the domestic economy's export industries, and (b) local industries to the extent they produce a close substitute to imported goods and services.

A reduction in domestic wages relative to foreign wages can have a larger proportionate effect in shifting the aggregate demand curve relative to the shift in aggregate supply. The result will be to provide a downward slope in the aggregate demand for labour curve. This improvement in domestic effective demand and employment is a result of the local economy *exporting its unemployment*. The improvement in sales and jobs by domestic firms and workers is bought at the expense of foreign entrepreneurs and labour. As long as global aggregate demand is not increasing there cannot be a gain in global employment. Any downward slope in the domestic economy's aggregate demand for labour curve is gained at the expense of an inward shift in each trading partner's demand for their own labour.

A reduction in money wages (relative to foreign money wages) will worsen the terms of trade.[26] A deterioration in the terms of trade means a reduction in domestic real income for all (except the newly employed) as imports become more expensive. Aggregate domestic consumption spending on both foreign and domestic goods at each level of employment is likely to be depressed. This tends to offset somewhat the upward shift in aggregate demand for domestic labour due to the export–import changes.[27]

If the nation with the falling relative money wage is a small one, the absolute volume of unemployment is likely to be small. It can export its unemployment without expecting retaliation by its larger trading partners. If the nation exporting its unemployment is a large one, the impact on the workers in other nations is likely to be significant. It is unlikely that its trading partners will stand idly by and import a significant volume of unemployment from this large economy. Especially in periods of large-scale global insufficiency of effective demand, the trading partners are likely to retaliate by raising import tariffs and quotas, or even by exchange rate depreciation to re-export the unemployment to others. As the experience of the Great Depression has shown the resulting trade wars add to the forces depressing aggregate demand curves for workers in all nations in which the export sector is important.

Case 5. The Keynes interest rate effect. If a fall in money wages is accompanied by a fall in product prices, then the public's demand for transactions cash balances at any level of employment will decline. *Given an exogenous* money supply, this reduced demand for liquidity will lower interest rates. To the extent that the marginal efficiency of capital is unchanged in the face of falling wages and prices, a lower interest rate will stimulate additional investment spending and labour hiring. Given the many provisos in the preceding sentences necessary for an all-round decline in money wages to pull interest rates down *relative* to the marginal efficiency of capital (what the mainstream literature labels the 'Keynes effect'), it is obvious that there can be many a slip twixt the cup and the lip if one is hoping that the Keynes effect will induce a downward slope in the aggregate demand curve for labour.[28]

GENERALIZING ABOUT THE SHAPE OF THE DEMAND CURVE FOR LABOUR

The five cases analysed *supra* are not a complete catalogue of all possible effects of a change in money wages on employment. Nevertheless they probably include many of the most relevant cases – certainly most of the ones that have been widely discussed in the economic literature. Leaving aside for the moment the open economy situation, the most favourable conditions for a downward-sloping demand for labour curve involve circumstances where the interest rate falls relative to the marginal efficiency of investment. This view led Keynes to proclaim that if people were advocating falling money wages as a way of stimulating employment by lowering the interest rate, they should advocate an increase in the money supply instead. The resulting fall in interest rates will not have an adverse impact by inducing a reduction in expectations regarding the marginal efficiency of investment. Decreasing money wages can cause a lowering of profit expectations.[29]

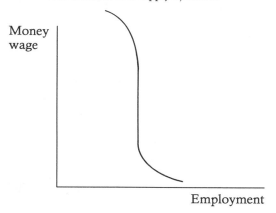

Figure 11.6   *A real balance effect augmented demand curve for labour*

Any claim that there must always exist a downward-sloping aggregate demand curve is false, given the array of possible cases *supra*. Given all the possible effects of changing wages on both the investment and consumption components of aggregate demand, it is probably safe to assume that the demand for labour curve is likely to be almost vertical (if not completely inelastic) through most of its relevant range. If there are significantly large changes in prices, the real balance effect might become significant. As a result there might be a tendency to have non-vertical downward-sloping sections at the top and bottom segments of the demand curve for labour.

Figure 11.6 represents a real balance effect augmented demand curve for labour. The reader should be warned that in the non-vertical portions at the top and bottom of this curve in Figure 11.6, the price and money level changes relative to the middle of the curve are so large that they would probably cause a complete breakdown of the monetary system. In other words, the cure might work, but only by killing the patient.

KEYNES'S LABOUR DEMAND CURVE AND THE MARGINAL PRODUCT OF LABOUR CURVE

In Keynes's analytical framework the marginal product of labour (*MPL*) curve is a market equilibrium curve that specifies the real wage (*w/P*) outcome associated with any given equilibrium level of employment. The real wage is determined as:

$$(w/P) = MPL = f_1(M, g) \tag{11.4}$$

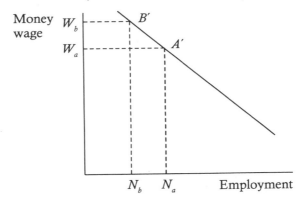

Figure 11.7   Aggregate demand for labour

where w is the money-wage rate, P is the price level, M is the economy-wide measure of the degree of monopoly,[30] and g $[=f_2(N)]$ is the physical productivity returns to labour. The market equilibrium *MPL* curve in Figure 11.8 is drawn as downward sloping to represent 'the familiar proposition that industry is normally working subject to decreasing returns',[31] i.e.

$$(\delta g/\delta N) < 1. \tag{11.6}$$

For ease of exposition, assume that the labour supply is simply an increasing function of the real wage and is represented by the curve *Ns* in Figure 11.8.[32]

Keynes's demand curve for labour is given a downward slope in Figure 11.7, although a completely vertical or even upward sloping labour demand curve could be analysed. The point A' on the labour demand curve is associated with the equilibrium level of employment, N_a, determined by the point of effective demand when the money-wage rate is w_a (point A on Figure 11.3). Given the N_a equilibrium level of employment, equation (11.5) indicates that the associated real wage is w_a/P_a, and the relevant point on the *MPL* curve is A'' in Figure 11.8. Point R'' on the labour supply curve represents the (full employment) quantity of labour that is being offered at the market equilibrium real wage of (w_a/P_a). The amount of involuntary unemployment is the horizontal distance $A''R''$ in Figure 11.8.

Assume a *ceteris paribus* money-wage increase from w_a to w_b. The point of effective demand, B in Figure 11.3, indicates that the equilibrium level of employment N_b is less than N_a, and therefore the marginal product of labour is higher when N_b workers are hired. With an effective demand of B

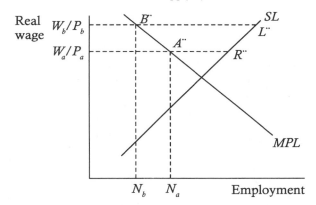

Figure 11.8   Marginal product and supply curves of labour

in Figure 11.3, the associated point on Keynes's labour demand curve is B' in Figure 11.7. The market equilibrium curve in Figure 11.8 indicates that at an employment level of N_b the real wage is w_b/P_b. Point L'' on the labour supply curve indicates the number of people willing to work at the real wage w_b/P_b. The horizontal distance $C''L''$ in Figure 11.8 represents the amount of involuntary unemployment when N_b workers are hired at a money wage of w_b and the corresponding real wage of w_b/P_b.

THE LABOUR SUPPLY FUNCTION

Lucas argues that there is no way to explain real world unemployment patterns except by an analysis of intertemporal substitutability of leisure and work effort by optimizing households.[33] Today's unemployed workers are revealing a preference for leisure rather than working for income in the current period. The unemployed believe that the real wage will be higher tomorrow and therefore prefer to take more leisure today for the possibility of working for higher wages tomorrow.

Keynes's real wage–labour supply analysis assumes that, at the going real wage rate, unemployed labour wants to work but cannot find a job. The unemployed are suffering. They are not enjoying their self-enforced leisure. Keynes's concept of involuntarily unemployed workers is logically incompatible with specification of the intertemporal substitutability of labour supply as developed by Lucas and Rapping.[34]

The existence of involuntary unemployment during a recession does not require workers to be off the long-run supply curve or to enjoy leisure as in the Lucas–Rapping analysis. In a Keynes–Post Keynesian analytical framework, the quantity of labour supplied for any given labour market equilibrium real wage is given by the N_s function of Figure 11.8. The involuntarily unemployed, e.g., $A''R''$ in Figure 11.8, know that they are suffering a permanent loss in real income. They are not engaging in a Lucas-optimizing decision to take more leisure today in the expectation that by so doing they will obtain significantly more income and consumption goods tomorrow when they expect to be rehired at a higher (normal) real wage than today's market real wage.[35]

Workers can be involuntarily unemployed whenever the marginal propensity to spend (from income earned in the production process) on producible goods is less than one. The income saved is stored in nonproducible assets such as money, bonds, collectibles, etc. Hahn has shown that if there are 'resting places for savings other than reproducible assets', then this is all that is 'required to do away with a Say's Law-like proposition that the supply of labour is the demand for goods produced by labor'.[36] The peculiar but essential properties of money and other liquid assets assure that there can be a long-run deficiency in effective demand. As long as people prefer liquidity to producible economic goods in a recession, there are no actions that can be taken by workers to bring 'their real wage into conformity with the marginal disutility of the amount of employment offered by employers at that wage ... [there is no] tendency towards equality between the real wage and the marginal disutility of labour'.[37]

Whenever there is an insufficient effective demand, actual behaviour in the goods, assets, and labour markets cannot be logically consistent with Lucas's contention that all households maximize utility solely in terms of the things that require labour supply. These four items specified by Lucas are: (1) today's consumption, (2) today's labour supply, (3) tomorrow's consumption, and (4) tomorrow's labour supply.[38] For households to be able to achieve utility maximization solely in terms of these four arguments of the Lucas-specified utility function, Lucas must assume that households have an intertemporal marginal propensity to spend on producible goods of one.

Given the classical assumption that substitution effects dominate (negligible) income or asset effects[39] in the Lucas equilibrium system, it is the expected changes in tomorrow's real wage relative to today's that motivate households to intertemporally allocate all their time this period either in (i) planned leisure or (ii) planned work to earn income. For households to achieve intertemporal utility maximization they must plan to spend, either today or tomorrow, *all* the income they expect to earn in their lifetime on producible goods. Producible goods and leisure time are the only significant gross substitutes in the households' utility function assumed by Lucas.

Lucas's claim[40] that this intertemporal substitution of labour and leisure is the only correct way to explain unemployment patterns is true only in a Say's Law world. In this classical environment, in the long run (i.e., over two periods called today and tomorrow) and on the statistical average, optimizing households have a marginal propensity to spend of one as the intertemporal long-run labour supply function assumed by Lucas is also the intertemporal demand for goods produced by labour.[41] Of course in a world where Say's Law is assumed to prevail, Keynes's policy prescriptions are irrelevant.[42] Lucas and other modern mainstream macroeconomists, by assuming Say's Law prevails, have solved the real world's unemployment problems, by assumption, not by analysis.

APPENDIX: THE LOGICAL CATCH-22 IN THE REAL BALANCE ANALYSIS

There is a fundamental logical problem underlying the claim that, at least as a theoretical matter, full employment is assured as a result of a real balance effect where there is a coordinated fall in all wages and prices in the presence of a fixed stock of financial assets (including money). This real balance effect requires

1. a commodity money (e.g., gold) whose excess flow supply is negligible and therefore whose physical volume is independent of economic activity, and/or
2. some financial asset whose nominal value remains unchanged in the face of a coordinated fall in all prices, and
3. the absence of a substantial number of bankruptcies despite the fall in wages and prices.

In real world modern money-using entrepreneurial economies, conditions (1), (2), and (3) cannot occur.[43] When production processes are primarily organized by forward money contracts, a coordinated fall in all wages and prices large enough to induce a significant real balance effect will induce enough bankruptcies to jeopardize the possibility that a full employment equilibrium can exist.

In a world where bank money and the outstanding liabilities of the Monetary Authority are the medium of contractual settlement, if there is a coordinated fall in money wages and product prices, it is impossible to maintain an unchanging stock of money and/or financial assets. The total of all outstanding financial assets (including money) will fall *pari passu* with the hypothesized coordinate drop in wages and prices of producibles.

The nominal market value of all financial (equity and debt) securities depends on the expected future net (nominal) cash inflows associated with each security. If all product prices fall, then the future net cash inflow associated with any equity security must decline. The 'real' value of equity assets cannot increase and cause a real balance effect in the face of a coordinated price fall.

A similar decline in the market value for all debt securities will occur. If the debtors' nominal contractual obligations are included in the hypothesized 'coordinated fall of all prices' then the market value of debt security holdings (by creditors) falls proportionately. If, on the other hand, the debtors' obligations in nominal terms remain unchanged while debtors' money incomes are dependent on the declining wages and prices, then debtors will be unable to meet the contractual interest and principle repayments obligations. In the latter case, debtors must declare bankruptcy, thereby wiping out the market value of these debts. In either case, the real wealth of creditors based on the value of outstanding debt holdings will fall so that the real balance effect of outstanding debt cannot occur.

The final fallback position of those who claim the existence of a real wealth effect is that even in the face of a coordinated fall in all product prices and wages, there is an unchanged stock of money, i.e. the money supply is completely exogenously determined. Whenever the money of an economy is primarily bank money based on a fractional reserve system (as in all modern economies), the outstanding stock of money cannot remain unchanged as all prices fall.

A coordinated fall in all money wages and product prices must ultimately involve a coordinated collapse of the nominal asset side of the banking system's balance sheet. The value of assets in banks' portfolios will collapse when borrowers cannot service their outstanding nominal loan obligations to the banking system. A coordinated fall in all wages and prices by depressing the money incomes of all private sector households and firms will force private sector borrowers to default *en masse* on obligations to the banks. This, in turn, will significantly impair, if not wipe out, the banks' net worth, thereby inducing massive banking system bankruptcies. As banks go 'belly up' on a significant scale, the outstanding nominal stock of bank money will decline and the real wealth value of the remaining money stock will show little or no gain.[44] Only government or Monetary Authority bank deposit 'guarantees' can prevent the stock of money from collapsing and thereby maintain the volume of bank money held by the public.[45]

With the inevitable bankruptcies induced by a fall in all wages and prices in a monetary economy, all existence proofs of a full employment general equilibrium are jeopardized. In other words, it is not possible to demonstrate that any set of new lower relative prices will clear all markets simultaneously (and therefore eliminate involuntary unemployment by a real balance effect) once bankruptcies occur. It is impossible to demonstrate that even the extreme top and bottom segments of the aggregate demand curve for labour will have a downward slope. The classical claim of a downward-sloping demand for labour function due to a real balance effect is unproven, and unlikely.

NOTES

1. J.M. Keynes, *The General Theory*, p. 259.
2. J.M. Keynes, *The General Theory*, p. 259.
3. For example, see A. Meltzer, 'Keynes's General Theory: A Different Perspective', *Journal of Economic Literature*, **19**, 1981.
4. For an example of this argument see A.B. Abel and B. Bernake, *Macroeconomics*, pp. 357–8.
5. See J. Stiglitz, *Economics*, Norton, New York, 1992, p. 367.
6. Keynes, *The General Theory*, p. 262.
7. Keynes, *The General Theory*, p. 280.
8. M. Friedman, 'Comments on the Critics', in *Milton Friedman's Monetary Framework: A Debate With His Critics*, edited by R.J. Gordon, University of Chicago Press, Chicago, 1974, p. 149.
9. J.M. Keynes, *The General Theory*, p. 31.
10. L. Ball, N.G. Mankiw, and D. Romer, 'The New Keynesian Economics and the Output-Inflation Tradeoff', *Brookings Papers on Economic Activity*, 1988, p. 1. Tobin argues that all that is necessary for unemployment is 'the Absence of perfect flexibility'. See J. Tobin, 'Price Flexibility and Output Stability: An Old Keynesian View', *Journal of Economic Perspectives*, **7**, 1993, p. 48.
11. D. Patinkin, *Money, Interest and Prices*, 2nd edition, Harper & Row, New York, 1965, pp. 313–15.
12. For example, see R.J. Barro and H.I. Grossman, *Money, Employment, and Inflation*, Cambridge University Press, Cambridge, 1976, or D. Patinkin, *Money, Interest and Prices*, 2nd Edition, Harper & Row, New York, 1965.
13. In Keynes's words 'real wages and the [equilibrium] volume of output (and hence of employment) are uniquely correlated ... [and without] disputing the vital fact which classical economists have (rightly) asserted ... [that] the real wage has a unique (inverse) correlation with the volume of employment. ... This is simply the obverse of the familiar proposition that industry is normally working subject to decreasing returns'. See Keynes, *The General Theory*, p. 17.
14. See R.E. Lucas, *Studies in Business Cycle Theory*, MIT Press, Cambridge, 1983.
15. In an expanded model, aggregate demand would consist of the propensity to consume domestically produced goods, the spending of entrepreneurs and government on domestically produced goods, and export sales.
16. A possible explanation for this phenomena would be if any money-wage rate increase shifted income, at each level of employment, from low marginal propensity to consume rentiers and/or profit recipients to high marginal propensity to consume workers. The result would be to shift upwards the aggregate consumption function (in real terms).
17. J.M. Keynes, *The General Theory*, pp. 259–60.
18. In an open economy, the domestic income elasticity of demand for imports compared to the rest of the world's income elasticity of demand for the exports of the domestic nation, and the exchange rate is also relevant. We shall discuss these aspects in Chapters 12–16 *infra*.

19. The fixed income of the *rentiers* is, from the entrepreneur's perspective, the fixed money costs of production.

20. This is likely to be true since some of the transferred real profits will remain the property of the firm and will not be distributed out as dividends. To the extent that only dividends are available for consumption spending out of gross profits, profit recipients are not likely to increase their purchases by an amount sufficient to offset the reduction in *rentier* consumption.

21. 'The expectation of a fall in the value of money [inflation] stimulates investment and hence employment. . . . *If* the rate of interest were to rise *pari passu* with the marginal efficiency of capital, there would be no stimulating effect from the expectation of rising prices'. J.M. Keynes, *The General Theory*, pp. 141–3.

22. Accordingly, this borrowing of demand from the future will tend to be concentrated in foodstuffs that do not spoil readily (since food purchases are repetitive) and consumer durables that are easily storable and which were expected to be replaced in the near future.

23. Holders of private debt (creditors) would, of course, also feel poorer, and as a consequence might reduce their real consumption at any level of employment. Private debtors, whose money incomes increase at each level of employment (wage earners and profit recipients) would find the real burden of their debt reduced and might consequently expand their real consumption at any level of employment. The action of these private debtors would offset the action of the creditors so that, in the aggregate, the existence of private debt should not give rise to any aggregate real balance effect.

24. If, before the price fall, the average worker earned approximately $961 per week (equal to $50 000 per year, or lifetime earnings of $1 million (assuming a 50-year working life)), then after the price fall the average weekly wage would be approximately $0.000004, or an annual wage of $0.0002 – two-tenths of a mill per year or a total lifetime earnings (assuming a 50-year working life) of one penny.

25. Even one of the leading advocates of the theoretical importance of the real balance effect has suggested that, for all practical purposes, it is insignificant. Patinkin (in his *Money, Interest and Prices*, Harper & Row, New York, 1956) indicates that it would take a major price decline to significantly increase the quantity of labour demanded and 'it is precisely this necessity for a major price decline which makes this process unacceptable as a primary ingredient of a modern full-employment policy' (p. 233). Moreover, expectations of further price declines would offset 'the stimulating real-balance effect' (p. 235).

26. J.M. Keynes, *The General Theory*, pp. 262–3.

27. Of course, the terms of trade will improve for each of the trading partners.

28. If money wages decline while firms use bank loans to finance payrolls, then working capital loan repayments can exceed new loans causing the money supply to endogenously decline *pari passu* with wages. 'If the quantity of money is itself a function of the wage- and price-level, there is indeed, no hope in this direction' (Keynes, 1936, p. 266) for wage declines to stimulate employment.

29. J.M. Keynes, *The General Theory*, pp. 265–7.

30. The degree of monopoly for each firm is defined as equal to $[(p - mc)/p]$ where p is the price of the product and mc is the marginal cost of the product when firms are producing at the profit-maximizing level. The average degree of monopoly in the economy (M) is the average of the degree of monopoly of each firm weighted by the importance of the firm in the aggregate economy.

31. J.M. Keynes, *The General Theory*, p. 17. A horizontal (constant returns) marginal product curve, or even a rising (increasing returns) marginal product curve could also be analysed without changing any fundamental principles.

32. Vertical or even backward-bending labour supply curves could be analysed.

33. R.E. Lucas, *Studies in Business Cycle Theory*, MIT Press, Cambridge, 1983, p. 4.

34. R.E. Lucas and L.A. Rapping, 'Real Wages, Employment, and Inflation', *Journal of Political Economy*, **77**, 1969, pp. 24–5; reprinted in Lucas's 1983 *Studies in Business Cycle Theory*. All page references are to this reprint.

35. See Lucas and Rapping, op. cit., p. 32.
36. F.H. Hahn, 'Keynesian Economics and General Equilibrium Theory: Reflections on Some Current Debate', in *The Microfoundations of Macroeconomics*, edited by G.C. Harcourt, Macmillan, London, 1977, p. 31.
37. J.M. Keynes, *The General Theory*, p. 11.
38. Lucas and Rapping, op. cit., p. 24.
39. Lucas and Rapping, op. cit., pp. 25, 49.
40. R.E. Lucas, *Studies in Business Cycle Theory*, p. 4.
41. This requirement is due to the seemingly innocuous assumptions that 'future goods and leisure are substitutes for current leisure, that leisure is not inferior, and that the asset effect is small' (Lucas and Rapping, op. cit., p. 25). Thus by assuming no significant income effects and all the 'commodities' in the consumer utility function are either gross substitutes producible by labour (or labour itself), Lucas has reintroduced Say's law.
42. J.M. Keynes, *The General Theory*, pp. 25–6.
43. In fact, a fixed quantity of a commodity money would be incapable of sustaining a growing, interdependent monetary system. It is not just a historical accident that with economic growth since the Renaissance, the monetary systems of the industrializing world have evolved into a more elaborate fractional reserve system which requires double-entry bookkeeping and the clearing of debts to settle contractual commitments.
44. A microcosm of the type of phenomena that is contemplated in this paragraph was the systemic failure of the Savings and Loan Associations in the 1980s. As inflation slowed down and unemployment and idle capacity increased, borrowers *en masse* were unable to service their outstanding debt and massive S and L failure followed. The only thing that prevented the collapse of the money supply in this case, was that the government was willing to increase its outstanding nominal debt obligations to guarantee that each depositor would not lose money as these depository institutions failed. In the absence of such deposit 'insurance' and the federal government's willingness to undertake additional debt as prices in this subsector of the economy were falling, the money supply would have shrunk endogenously.
45. A comparison of the banking and monetary supply collapse in 1932–33 with the S and L collapse with a sustained money stock illustrates the difference.

12. Money in an international setting

THE TAXONOMY OF OPEN VS. CLOSED AND UMS VS. NUMS SYSTEMS

A precise taxonomy is a necessary precondition for all scientific inquiry. In this chapter, clear distinctions are made between open and closed economies and between unionized monetary systems (UMS) and non-unionized monetary systems (NUMS). Table 12.1 presents the four possible combinations of these features.

Table 12.1   A classification of economic systems by trading patterns and monetary systems

Monetary System	Closed Economy $(\phi = 0)$	Open Economy $(\phi > 0)$
Unionized Monetary System (UMS) $(\Theta = 0)$	(1) no external trading partners (2) single money for contracts	(1) external trading partners (2) single money for contracts
Non-Unionized Monetary System (NUMS) $(\Theta > 0)$	(1) no external trading partners (2) various monies for contracts, no fixed exchange rate	(1) external trading partners (2) various monies for contracts, no fixed exchange rate

The closed UMS cell of this table is the equivalent of the traditional closed economy model that was used with great success by Keynes in *The General Theory* to demonstrate the possibility of underemployment equilibrium. If it is possible in this simplest model to show why market-oriented, entrepreneurial economies could obtain an unemployment equilibrium, then it was reasonable to believe that the more complicated open economies (in the second column of the table) were even less likely to achieve a socially desirable level of output, employment and price stability

198

without some governmental and private institutional planning and control. The open-economy UMS cell in Table 12.1 can be associated with an analysis of a home (local) regional economy trading with other regions (usually in the same nation). The trading partner regions have a legal (or customary) currency union so that, either by law or by practice, transactors use the same monetary unit to denominate all private contracts.

The closed-economy NUMS cell in Table 12.1 is applicable to a global analysis where the various trading partners use one monetary unit for denominating contracts between internal residents and different monetary units for contracts between foreigners and domestic residents. The exchange rate is expected to vary over the life of the contract. Finally, the last cell of Table 12.1 (open NUMS) is applicable to the analysis of an individual real world national economy that has foreign trading partners with different currencies and variable exchange rates.

The four-way classification scheme of Table 12.1 depends on:

1. the theory of aggregate accounting to distinguish between open and closed economies; and
2. the laws and customs of society that determine the medium of contractual settlement to distinguish between UMS and NUMS.

AGGREGATE ACCOUNTING AS A BASIS FOR THE CLOSED–OPEN CLASSIFICATION

For the most part, aggregate economic income measures can have no meaning other than that assigned to them by Aggregate Accounting Theory. The aggregate (or social) accounts do not measure conventionally existing items – rather, they are a way of accounting for particular abstract theoretical concepts.[1]

In theory, a closed economy is one where there are no transactions between individuals in the domestic economy and others outside the economy's accounting system. There are no external trading partners who either (a) sell raw materials, labour, or finished goods to domestic firms and residents or (b) purchase the products of domestic industries, or (c) buy and/ or sell assets from/to domestic economic agents. In a closed system, the aggregation of the accounting records of all transactors is included in the aggregate or national accounts. All payments (except currency transactions) are entirely recorded in the books of the economy's banking and clearing-house system.

For a closed economy, a double-entry record-keeping system[2] of aggregate accounts ensures that the total money expenditure of domestic residents on new goods and services equals the total gross money income receipts of residents. This accounting definition of income was used by Keynes in *The General Theory*.[3]

An open economy, by its very nature, involves a significant volume of transactions between domestic residents in nation A and inhabitants of the rest of the world. The accounting system for open economy A will provide information regarding the division of income and wealth among A and its trading partners, as well as indicating the size and growth of the aggregate income of A.

In the aggregate accounting system of an open economy all the simple equalities between aggregate expenditures and income receipts of domestic residents no longer necessarily hold. The market value of production of final goods by domestically located enterprises need not equal either the gross income earned by domestic residents or the total expenditures of domestic residents on final goods and services. The following accounting relationships are useful in sorting out the differences between closed and open economies where

V_c = the market value of domestically produced final consumer goods purchased for domestic use net of the value of foreign components,[4]

V_i = the market value of domestically produced investment goods for domestic use, net of foreign components,

V_g = the market value of domestically produced government-purchased goods for domestic use, net of foreign components,[5]

V_x = the market value of domestically produced goods for export net of foreign components,

V_m = the market value of all foreign-produced goods imported into the domestic economy net of domestically produced components.

All values are expressed in terms of the domestic monetary unit. The value of aggregate expenditures on all final goods by domestic residents (E_D), or gross domestic purchases is

$$E_D = V_c + V_i + V_g + V_m. \qquad (12.1)$$

The value of aggregate domestic production emerging from domestically located enterprises (V_{GDP}) or income generated domestically is called Gross Domestic Product (GDP). It is

$$V_{GDP} = V_c + V_i + V_g + V_x. \qquad (12.2)$$

GDP measures all income produced within the borders of a nation whether that income is to be received by foreigners or by domestic residents.

Gross National Product (GNP) is the gross aggregate income earned by domestic residents, whether from domestic production or foreign production. To obtain the value of GNP one must add to GDP the foreign-generated income earned by domestic firms and residents $(Y_{f \to d}^g)$ and subtract the domestically generated income earned by foreign firms and residents $(Y_{d \to f}^g)$ to obtain *aggregate income earned by domestic residents* (V_{GNP}), i.e.

$$V_{GNP} = V_{GDP} - Y_{d \to f}^g + Y_{f \to d}^g. \qquad (12.3)$$

When a nation earns more than it produces domestically (GNP > GDP) this difference is accounted for by presuming an export of a productive service (capital) to foreigners who paid for it either by profit repatriation (from equity capital) or interest (on debt capital). Income earned by residents of a nation may therefore be more (or less) than income generated domestically because of foreign ownership of business enterprises located in the domestic region.[6]

In a closed economy, $V_X = 0$, $V_M = 0$, $Y_{d \to f}^g = 0$, $Y_{f \to d}^g = 0$, so that

$$V_{GDP} = V_{GNP} = E_D. \qquad (12.4)$$

The difference between the aggregate output produced by domestic firms (or GDP) and aggregate expenditures by domestic residents is obtained by subtracting equation (12.1) from (12.2). In an open economy, this difference is equal to the exports minus imports, or the economy's savings on foreign account

$$V_{GDP} - E_D = V_x - V_m = B \qquad (12.5)$$

where B is the balance of goods and services trade.

Income available (Y^a) for spending by domestic residents is obtained by adding income earned by domestic residents plus transfer payments to domestic residents from foreigners minus transfer payments from the domestic economy to foreigners. The difference between aggregate income available and aggregate expenditures is equal to the balance of payments on current account (B_{CA}), i.e.,

$$Y^a - E_D = B_{CA}. \qquad (12.6)$$

The current account balance is a measure of international payments imbalances. The current account balance measures the value of home-owned output of goods and services (whether produced domestically or abroad) placed at the disposal of foreigners minus the value of foreign-owned output (produced at home or abroad) placed at the disposal of domestic residents.[7]

Transfer pricing. Multinational corporations are firms with their own production facilities in different countries. If a multinational transfers goods from one of its subsidiaries in country A to another in country B, then there is the question of what price should be put on this shipment. The transfer price will affect the value of exports from A and imports to B in the balance of payments accounts. The transfer price that is recorded in the multinational corporation's accounting books need not be a market price. Rather it can reflect a valuation picked by the multinational's comptroller. Transfer prices can be arbitrarily set to avoid national tax liabilities or avoid currency and capital export restrictions or other government regulations.[8] If shipments by multinationals are significant in a nation's balance of payments, then transfer prices can bias the national income measurements of trade and current account balances. Caution must be exercised before interpreting any balance of trade statistics as symptomatic of a fundamental national disequilibrium, rather than as an accounting imbalance due in some part to decisions of a multinational comptroller to take advantage of different regulations or tax laws in various national jurisdictions.

Finally, foreign lending can be defined as financial contractual commitments by domestic residents that places the domestic currency or claims to it at the disposal of foreigners in return for some form of either an IOU from a foreigner or a title to property owned by foreign residents. Net foreign lending, the balance of transactions on capital account is equal to the excess of foreign lending by domestic residents over the value of similar transactions by foreigners in their purchase of domestic IOUs, titles, etc.

THE BALANCE OF PAYMENTS ACCOUNTING STATEMENT

The items that make up a Balance of Payments Accounting Statement are illustrated in Table 12.2. This Balance of Payments statement involves a double-entry bookkeeping system. For the United States, every item in the statement that puts the United States into debt to foreigners is recorded in the debit column, and every item that provides the United States with a claim on foreigners is recorded as a credit entry. (A simple formula for remembering where to place any item is: credit is for claims, and debit is for debts.)

Table 12.2   A balance of payments statement

Credits (Claims on Foreigners)	Debits (Debts To Foreigners)
1. Merchandise exports	Merchandise imports
2. Exports of services	Import of services
3. Investment income on US assets abroad	Income payments on foreign assets in the US
4. Unilateral transfers to US from abroad	Unilateral transfer from US to foreigners
5. Short-term credit from foreigners	Short-term credit to foreigners
6. Long-term investment of foreigners in the US	Long-term investment of US residents abroad
7. Foreign Reserve changes	

Line 1 on Table 12.2 indicates that all United States exports of merchandise during the accounting period provide the United States with claims on foreigners while all merchandise imports put the United States into debt to foreigners. Except for smuggling, the import and export of merchandise goods can be readily recorded at ports of entry and exit. The value of merchandise credits minus debits on line 1 is often referred to as the *balance of trade*.

Line 2 records the exports and imports of services. Exports of services (e.g., foreigners flying on United States airlines) produce claims on foreigners, while the import of services (e.g., United States residents purchasing insurance from Lloyd's of London) puts the United States in debt to foreigners.

Line 3 records income received by United States residents from production abroad (claims), and income payments to foreigners (debts) from production occurring in the United States.

The net value of the sum of lines 1, 2, and 3 is called the *balance on goods, services and income account*. It is a measure of the savings of the nation on its foreign account. A positive balance indicates that the nation is spending less than it is earning from transactions with its foreign trading partners. If the balance is negative, the domestic nation is spending more than it is earning (during this accounting period).

Line 4 records unilateral transfer payments between residents of different nations during the accounting period. A *unilateral transfer payment* is payment made from one person to another residing in a different country without any offsetting sales of goods, services or assets. For example, if a foreign student is studying at the University of Tennessee and he or she receives money from his or her parents overseas to pay for his or her living expenses in the United States, that transaction is a unilateral transfer credit in the United States balance of payments. Similarly, if a Mexican working in the United States sends part of his or her wages back to his or her family in Mexico that gives rise to a debit unilateral transfer payment for the United States.

Unilateral transfer payments can be between either individuals or governments. For example, when Germany and Japan paid their contribution to the United States war against Iraq ('Desert Storm') in 1991, these payments were recorded as unilateral government transfer credits on line 4 of the United States balance of payments statement.

Lines 1, 2, 3, and 4 together are called the *Current Accounts*. If the current account balance is negative, then the domestic nation is spending more than its earnings plus unilateral transfers. A negative current account balance is often characterized as evidence that a nation is 'living beyond its means'. The 'means' is defined as the net export earnings on goods and services plus net investment income plus net transfer payments. If the deficit in the current account balance persists, conventional wisdom suggests that the nation must 'tighten its belt' and lower its 'riotous' living by reducing dependence on imports.

Lines 5, 6, and 7, below the line in Table 12.2, represent the *Capital Accounts*. If the current account is in deficit then the capital account must be in surplus. Changes in the capital accounts indicate how any current account deficit or surplus is being financed – by either (a) short-term credits, (b) direct investments (by buying or selling assets), (c) or sales or purchases of foreign reserves.

MEASURING THE DEGREE OF OPENNESS

Weintraub has suggested that the degree of 'closeness' of any economy can be empirically measured by a variable n, which is defined as the domestic content component of each money unit of final product making up aggregate domestic production during an accounting period.[9] In Weintraub's analysis, as n approaches unity, the economy becomes more closed.

For our purposes, it is preferable to measure the degree of openness as ϕ $[=f(1-n)]$. This degree of openness (ϕ) is equal to the ratio of the market value of imports denominated in local currency terms to the total amount of domestic expenditure on final goods and services,[10] i.e.

$$\phi = [V_M/E_D]. \tag{12.7}$$

If $\phi = 0$, the economy is closed and there are no purchases by domestic residents from any foreigners. The greater the value of ϕ, the more open is

Table 12.3 Degree of openness (φ)

	Year							
	1970	1973	1975	1980	1982	1985	1986	1988
United States	.06	.07	.08	.11	.09	.10	.10	.10
Mexico	.11	.10	.11	.13	.11	.11	.13	.14
Japan	.10	.11	.14	.16	.16	.13	.09	.09
Australia	.16	.14	.15	.18	.18	.19	.18	.17
France	.15	.17	.18	.23	.23	.23	.20	.21
Greece	.16	.22	.23	.25	.26	.29	.28	.26
Philippines	.19	.19	.24	.25	.22	.18	.20	.22
Venezuela	.20	.22	.28	.28	.28	.18	.21	.22
Indonesia	.15	.20	.22	.24	.24	.21	.22	.24
Italy	.18	.19	.22	.26	.23	.22	.18	.18
New Zealand	.25	.25	.29	.29	.32	.33	.28	.27
Canada	.22	.23	.25	.27	.23	.26	.27	.26
F.R. Germany	.20	.20	.24	.29	.31	.32	.29	.28
South Africa	.25	.24	.30	.30	.27	.25	.24	.22
United Kingdom	.21	.25	.27	.26	.25	.28	.27	.27
Denmark	.31	.30	.31	.33	.36	.36	.32	.30
Sweden	.25	.26	.30	.31	.32	.34	.31	.31
Switzerland	.33	.31	.28	.39	.35	.39	.36	.35
Austria	.31	.32	.33	.40	.37	.40	.36	.35
Iceland	.46	.40	.44	.39	.36	.41	.37	.36
Norway	.43	.44	.46	.44	.42	.42	.40	.37
Saudi Arabia	.41	.44	.52	.51	.53	.45	.42	.38
Netherlands	.48	.48	.51	.53	.56	.62	.52	.51
Belgium	.42	.46	.47	.61	.67	.71	.65	.64
Israel	.42	.50	.52	.54	.48	.52	.47	.49
Ireland	.40	.42	.47	.56	.52	.60	.55	.57

Source: International Monetary Fund, *International Financial Statistics*, October 1977, February 1981, March 1986, September 1989.

the economy. At the limit, when $\phi = 1$, the economy is completely open and residents do not purchase any home-produced goods. They buy only imported products.

Table 12.3 presents estimates of ϕ for a number of nations for selected years from 1970 to 1988. This table indicates the relative degree of openness in modern economies and their trend over the recent past. Despite the rapid growth in total international trade, most countries are only slightly more open than they were a decade or two ago.

THE PRICE LEVEL IN AN OPEN ECONOMY

The degree of openness is a measure of the economy's susceptibility to importing inflation. Concerns about inflation involve the price level of the things residents buy. The more open the economy, the less the overlap of the price level of the things residents buy with the things residents produce.

It follows from equation (12.1) that

$$E_D = P_D Q_D + P_M Q_M = PQ \qquad (12.8)$$

where P_D is the price level of domestically produced goods (Q_D). P_M is the price level of imported goods (Q_M), P is the price level of all purchases of domestic residents, Q is the quantity of final goods bought by domestic residents. P is a weighted average of P_D and P_M where the weights represent the importance of domestic goods and imports in the total purchases of the local inhabitants, i.e.

$$P = [P_D][1 - \phi] + P_M[\phi]. \qquad (12.9)$$

Equation (12.9) implies that the price level of goods and services that make up domestic aggregate expenditure is a function of several factors:

1. the rate of money wages (w) to average labour productivity (AP) in domestic industries,
2. the profit margin or mark-up (K) of these domestic industries,
3. the price of imports (P_M) in terms of domestic money, and
4. the degree of openness (ϕ) of the economy.

In other words

$$P = f(w, AP, K, \phi, P_M) \qquad (12.10)$$

where

$$[dP/dw] > 0, \ [dP/dAP] < 0, \ [dP/dK] > 0, \ [dP/d_\phi] > 0, \ [dP/dP_M] > 0.$$

The effect on changes in w, K, and AP on the price level has been discussed in Chapter 9. An open economy introduces new factors ϕ and P_M which can affect the price level of what domestic residents buy.

The greater the degree of openness of the economy, the greater the potential for importing inflation. For example, if $\phi = 0.2$, then a 10 per cent rise in the price level of imports (P_M) in terms of domestic currency will lead to a 2 per cent increase in the average price level (P) of things residents buy.[11] If P is to remain unchanged, then the price level of domestically produced goods (P_D) has to decline by 2.5 per cent to offset the imported inflation. If P is directly related to unit labour costs and if domestic productivity was rising by, say, 3 per cent per annum, then price stability would require that money wages increase by no more than 0.5 per cent per annum. In other words, if import prices rise over time, domestic money wages must rise by less than the growth in productivity to offset this imported inflationary force.

During the twelve months of 1979, for example, the price of imported Saudi marker crude oil in terms of dollars increased approximately 65 per cent. The value of oil imported into the United States at that time was approximately equal to 2.3 per cent of United States aggregate domestic expenditure so that ϕ in terms of oil was equal to 0.023. Assuming the increase in Saudi prices is representative of the price of all imported crude, then the contribution of the 1979 oil price shock to US inflation was 1.5 per cent (i.e. $0.65 \times 0.023 = 0.015$). The price of domestic goods would have had to decline by 1.5 per cent during 1979 if the price level of all things purchased by United States residents (P) were to remain unchanged in 1979. This means that if labour productivity had been rising at its traditional post-war 3 per cent per annum during 1979, domestic money wages would have been able to rise by no more than 1.5 per cent on average if inflation in the United States was to be avoided.

Labour productivity declined by approximately 3 per cent in 1979. Consequently, if the inflationary impact of the OPEC oil price increase in 1979 was to be offset in the United States, money wages would have had to decline by approximately 4.5 per cent. Even if it were possible to convince American workers that an 'across the board' reduction of 4.5 per cent in money wages would have eliminated inflation and hence would not affect real wages (other than through the real adverse effects of lower productivity and the adverse change in oil terms of trade *vis-à-vis* OPEC, both of these factors being taken as parameters in this case), American workers would not have accepted a decline in their money wages.

This refusal to accept lower money (not real) wages would not be due to a money illusion, i.e., to workers confusing a money-wage decline for a further decline in real wages. Instead, workers' resistance to money wage cuts is because in entrepreneur economies production and purchase of long-lived durables are organized on a forward money contracting basis. Most American workers have long-term cash outflow commitments in terms of mortgages on their houses, rental leases on their apartments, and even loan obligations to finance children's college education. Any reduction of workers' cash (wage) inflows, even if it does not imply a further reduction in real wages, would immediately create a serious liquidity shortage threatening families with insolvency. Lower cash inflows, even when they do not mean further reduction of purchasing power, are not willingly accepted by households and firms operating in an entrepreneur economy that organizes production and consumption activities on a forward contracting basis,[12] and that does not permit recontracting without capital or income penalties.

THE UMS–NUMS CLASSIFICATION

As has already been stressed, money is that thing that discharges legal contractual obligations. In modern societies money is anything 'the State or the Central Bank undertakes to accept in payments to itself or to exchange for compulsory legal-tender money'.[13] If things other than legal tender instruments are customarily accepted in discharge of debts to the State or the Central Bank, they will be accepted to discharge private contractual obligations, and therefore these other things are money.

There are two basic types of monetary systems – *a unionized monetary system (UMS)* and a *non-unionized monetary system (NUMS)*. If all spot and forward contracts between transactors (in either a closed or open economy) are denominated in the same nominal unit, such a contracting system is a pure UMS. The system is still essentially a UMS even if various nominal units are used in different contracts between different transactors, as long as the exchange rates among the various nominal units are (a) fixed (with negligible conversion costs) *and* (b) expected to remain unchanged over the life of the contracts. Any system that permits different contracts denominated in various nominal units while maintaining a fixed exchange rate amongst these units can be considered a UMS where the various currencies are fully liquid assets.

If there is more than one fully liquid asset and if law or custom permits contractual settlement of any contract with any of the available fully liquid assets at the option of the payer, then the system can be considered a pure UMS. If law or custom requires fully liquid assets to be converted into the money of contractual settlement at the option of the payee, then the system is one step removed from a pure UMS where the size of the step depends on the cost of conversion.[14]

Where different contracts are denominated in different nominal units, expectations of fixed exchange rates are therefore a necessary requirement for any system to approach UMS status. Moreover, since forward contracts for production, hiring, investment, and other economic activities do not have any uniform duration, and since an ongoing economy is always operating under a myriad of existing catenated spot and forward contracts, the exchange rate must be expected to remain unchanged for the foreseeable (contracted for) future.

For example, one can conceive of the State of Tennessee as an open economy ($\phi > 0$) dealing with the rest of the United States in a pure UMS since all contracts between Tennessee residents and trading partners throughout the United States are in dollar terms. Each Federal Reserve District Bank issues its own bank notes. Until the mid-1970s, Federal Reserve notes found circulating in the United States but outside the district of issue were sent back to the issuing Federal Reserve District Bank for redemption. Nevertheless, notes from any Federal Reserve District Bank are legal tender for paying any contractual obligations within the United States. Furthermore, the exchange rate between one Federal Reserve District Bank's dollars and any other Federal Reserve District's dollars are fixed and unchanging no matter what the payment flow imbalance between these districts. Thus, the twelve Federal Reserve districts are part of one single UMS, even though each district can be considered an open economy trading with the other eleven districts in a UMS (and with the rest of the world in an NUMS).

Similarly, Scotland and England can be looked upon as open economies trading with each other (and others), even though the Scots use different-looking bank notes compared to English currency. These two 'nations' are part of the UMS of Great Britain and even if devolution ultimately comes to Scotland and the political openness of the two nations increases, this should not *per se* affect either the magnitude of the degree of openness or the basic UMS of Great Britain.

In an NUMS, regional or national contracts are denominated in local monetary units, while interregional or international contracts are denominated in various nominal units. The exchange rate between units is expected to exhibit significant variability over the contract period. In essence, then, the UMS can be thought of as a limiting case of an NUMS when any domestic currency can be used as the means of contractual settlement, for the exchange rates are expected to remain absolutely unchanged during the period.

Since unionization of the monetary system depends on expectations about the fixity of future exchange rates, it cannot be measured directly. The degree of 'non-unionization' (Θ) of the monetary system could be measured *ex post*. The variability of exchange rates between trading partners over past periods (looking back) need not reflect what past populations expected the future to be (looking forward). Of course, if for a significant period of calendar time the historical record showed $\Theta = 0$, as in the case of the exchange rate between the English and Scottish pounds, then it seems reasonable to suppose that past populations considered the two nations to be in a UMS. If the historical record shows $\Theta > 0$, it may also be reasonable to believe that in the past people thought they operated in a less than perfect UMS. The degree of non-unionization that was expected in the past is unknown. Only if the unlikely rational expectations assumption is accepted will the historical record accurately track the average expectations of the population in the past.[15]

EXCHANGE UNCERTAINTY

The most obvious advantage for decision makers residing in a UMS over those in an NUMS is that there is one less uncertainty (unpredictability) that economic agents in the former need worry about when they undertake long-term contractual commitments across regions. In an NUMS possible changes in exchange rates (and/or conversion cost changes) can wipe out any expected profit for an entrepreneur *vis-à-vis* the same contractual arrangement if the firm operated in a UMS. The uncertainty regarding possible exchange rate changes in an NUMS represents a real cost of operating in NUMS that does not exist in a UMS. The possibility of forward contracting in one currency or the other may protect one party to a transaction, but it exposes the other party entirely to the real cost of exchange uncertainty.

Thus the existence of an NUMS inflicts a real cost to the economic system that would not exist otherwise. This real cost, which is due solely to the way economies organize the medium for discharging a contract in an NUMS, must be borne by someone.[16] Organized forward exchange markets permit the shifting of uncertainty from the entrepreneur to the speculator, but at a cost to the entrepreneur to enter the forward exchange market. Moreover, since most forward exchange markets are limited to a 90 or 180 day duration, exchange uncertainties associated with longer-term contracts cannot be shifted but must be willingly borne by at least one of the original transactors if they are to consummate a 'deal'.

WAS THE GOLD STANDARD A UMS?

Under the gold standard the exchange rate between domestic currencies was fixed except for the movements between gold export and gold import points. As long as each nation's central bank defined the domestic monetary unit in terms of a weight of gold and was obligated to 'make' a market in gold, i.e., to maintain two-way convertibility between domestic money and gold, the gold price of each currency could fluctuate only between the gold points. These gold points depended on (a) the difference between the buy and sell prices of gold at the Central Bank, and (b) the cost of transporting gold.[17] As long as two-way convertibility was maintained, the exchange rate could never fall below the gold export point in A (above the gold import point in B). If the public was confident that existing parities would be maintained under the gold system, then as soon as the market exchange rate moved close to the gold export point in economy A, commercial banks and business firms that deal in international trade could move in to buy the relatively 'weak' domestic currency of A by selling some of the 'strong' currency of B. Hence, the private sector's liquidity desires provide helpful exchange movements provided 'there is a fixed rate of exchange and complete confidence that it will not be altered'.[18] The gold standard, except for fluctuations between the gold points, was a UMS. The closer the gold points were to each other, the more the trading partners linked into a UMS.

NOTES

1. For a complete discussion of the importance of theory before measurement, see P. Davidson and E. Smolensky, *Aggregate Supply and Demand Analysis*, Harper & Row, New York, 1964, Chapter 15.
2. It is not an exaggeration to suggest that the most important invention ever made by man was double-entry bookkeeping! This system provides a method of control over complex economic production and exchange activities. Without such controls, modern economies could not survive. Many societies have developed other important inventions such as the wheel, gunpowder, etc., but it was only after the development of double-entry bookkeeping in the Italian merchant states that Western European nations (and later their territorial positions) led the world into the Commercial and Industrial Revolutions. After centuries of economic stagnation, those economies that adopted a double-entry bookkeeping system to organize and control production and exchange processes enjoyed tremendous rates of growth in living standards. Those economies that do not use a double-entry bookkeeping system (e.g., tribes in Africa and the Amazon) continue to stagnate.
3. J.M. Keynes, *The General Theory*, p. 54: 'the income of the rest of the community [in a closed system] is the entrepreneurs' factor costs, while gross entrepreneurial income is defined as the excess of market value of final output over entrepreneurial factor costs. Hence, aggregate income is the sum of gross entrepreneurial income plus factors costs and therefore aggregate income ... thus defined, is a completely unambiguous quantity'.
4. For example, suppose someone purchased an IBM personal computer in New York for $1 000. The value of the computer chips component produced in Japan (say $300) plus the value of the parts produced and assembled overseas (say $400) should be subtracted from the purchase price to obtain the V_c of this computer. In this case $V_c = \$1\,000 - \$700 = \$300$.
5. Calculations involved in estimating such items can be very complicated. For example, the costs of US personnel that staff the embassy in Mexico, is part of V_g, but the cost of

the Mexican cleaning help for this embassy is a foreign component which would not be computed here, but rather as an import.

6. For example, in 1988, the United States earned \$20.7 billion more from overseas investments than it paid to foreigners who owned US investments.
7. *The Collected Writings of John Maynard Keynes*, 5, p. 118.
8. Multinational corporations have sometimes set up what has been labelled a 'daisy-chain' of transfer prices. In a daisy-chain, if nation A has high corporate profit taxes, then the multinational can transfer price the export at a loss and send it to a subsidiary in country B, a 'tax-haven' country (i.e., a country that has very low or negligible corporate profit taxes). The subsidiary in B can then send the product at a high price to a subsidiary in country C where the product is sold to the public at a loss. All the profits have been transferred to the tax haven country. Moreover losses have been inflicted on the subsidiaries in countries A and C. These losses can be used to offset profits on strictly domestic operations in countries A and C and thereby avoid most of the corporate profit liabilities. In reality the product can be conveyed from A to C and never physically landed in country B. As long as the subsidiary in B takes legal title to the product while it is in international waters and resells to the subsidiary in C, the daisy-chain has been operative.

    During the period of price controls under President Nixon in 1972–73, multinational oil companies set up daisy-chains in order to bring oil imports into the United States at high prices in an attempt to circumvent domestic oil price controls.
9. S. Weintraub, 'The Price Level in an Open Economy', *Kyklos*, **30**, 1970, p. 27.
10. (ϕ) is not quite the complement of Weintraub's n, for the latter would use V_{DP} rather than E_D in the denominator of any ratio of equation (4.11) (V_{DP} will equal E_D only when $B = 0$). Thus, strictly speaking, the complement of Weintraub's n would be $\phi' = [V_M/V_{DP}]$ and $\phi = \phi'$ only if $V_X = V_M$.
11. As all price indices do, we are measuring price level changes for a given market basket of goods. The composition of this initial market basket was determined in part by the initial ratio (P_D/P_M). We are not accounting for any substitution effects that may occur after the initial instant due to a change in relative prices. (Nor would we account for an exogenous change in relative demands and, hence, the composition of the original market basket.)
12. If cash flow problems become pervasive in the economy, then a cumulative debt deflation process can occur which will threaten the very structure of capitalist financial institutions. See H.P. Minsky, *John Maynard Keynes*, Columbia University Press, 1975.
13. *The Collected Writings of John Maynard Keynes*, V, p. 6.
14. In a modern, bank money economy, the ability to write sight drafts for the immediate transfer of ownership of particular fully liquid assets through the clearing mechanism of the national banking system in effect 'monetizes' the fully liquid assets known as bank demand deposit liabilities.
15. Of course, the same degree of unionization need not exist between the domestic economy and all its trading partners, since the exchange rate could be unchanged between some trading partners (e.g. the US and Mexico in the 1960s) while in the same period it varied with others (e.g. the US and Canada).
16. Thus there is *ceteris paribus* potential for a 'free lunch' in international trade if nations would organize their laws of contract on a UMS basis.
17. Keynes argued that it was the spread between the gold points which permitted interest differential between financial centres in different countries. The greater the spread between the points, the greater the possible differential interest rates; hence the greater the leeway for some independence of interest rate policies in the two countries. Keynes recommended a spread of at least 2 per cent between bid and ask prices for gold.
18. R.F. Harrod, *Money*, Macmillan, London, 1969, p. 75.

13. Trade imbalances and international payments

A Keynes–Post Keynesian monetary approach indicates that any international payments imbalance creates a *liquidity* problem. When a nation cannot pay for imports with export earnings (plus net investment income), then its initial problem is how to finance the excess of international purchase obligations. Typically this problem is resolved temporarily by an extension of net short-term trade credit by the exporting surplus nation(s). This gives the deficit nation time to obtain long-term funding of these international liabilities. For the export surplus nation(s), the less pressing liquidity problem is to choose which vehicle(s) it should use to store its surplus international earnings (claims).

Classical theory argues that international payments deficits cannot persist. Some real adjustment mechanisms will automatically eliminate imbalance. The free market solves all deficit problems in the long run while perpetuating global full employment.

Classical trade theory denies that there can be any liquidity approach to adjustment processes. In discussing classical adjustment mechanisms to the balance of payments, Johnson claims that 'In fact the difficulty of monetary theory can be seen as [merely] an extra complication of a problem in "real" or "barter" theory that has always given economists trouble'.[1] Classical theorists focus on real adjustment mechanisms where both surplus and deficit nations share equally in the mechanism of adjustment.

The current international financial arrangements and institutions, however, place the major onus for adjusting to international imbalances on the partner faced with a shortage of liquidity; i.e. the deficit nation. Moreover, this one-sided pressure on the deficit nation to solve the problem produces a deflationary bias that can reduce the well-being of the surplus trading partner(s) as well.

In this chapter, the classical adjustment mechanisms are discussed and compared to an adjusting process developed from Keynes's liquidity preference theory where monetary changes are not viewed as mere 'complications' and money is not neutral in both the domestic and international economies.

Where change in a nation's export–import balance occurs without any

213

change in global effective demand, this liquidity approach will focus on monetary factors by emphasizing the demand for transactionary and precautionary international reserves. When changes in global effective demand induce a change in international payments, this Keynes–Post Keynesian adjustment mechanism emphasizes the income-generating finance process (which has been developed since *The General Theory*).[2]

CLASSICAL REAL ADJUSTMENT PROCESSES

Classical trade theory has always relied on some variant of Hume's specie (gold)-flow mechanism to resolve trade imbalance problems. Under the gold standard, an excess of imports over exports is financed by an outflow of specie (gold)[3] from the deficit to the surplus nation. This redistribution among the nations' gold holdings alters the money supply in each nation. The loss of gold by deficit nations forces them to reduce the domestic money supply. The inflow of gold to the surplus trade nations increases the supply of money. According to the classical 'quantity theory of [neutral] money', relative changes in money supply cause relative changes in national price levels and/or cost levels (in terms of a single currency) between the surplus and deficit nations. The rising price level in surplus (gold-importing) nation B reduces A's demand for imports from B and increases B's demand for imports from A until the deficit is eliminated without altering the global level of real income.

The 'monetary approach to the balance of payments' adjustment explanation was developed by classical economists primarily at the University of Chicago. This 'monetary approach' relies on a mechanism similar to Hume's specie-flow analysis, but it is not necessarily tied to nations operating on the gold standard. Johnson succinctly summed up this monetary approach by claiming that *all* 'balance of payments deficits or surpluses are by their nature *transient and self-correcting*, requiring no deliberate policy to correct them. ... The reason is simply that deficits reduce money stocks whose excessive size underlies the deficit, and surpluses build up the money stocks whose deficiency underlies the surplus'.[4]

This 'monetary approach' assumes that it is the 'excessive size' of the domestic money supply that is the initiating cause of a payments imbalance. Given an initial price level, this excess issuing of money causes households to believe their real wealth has increased. This real wealth effect induces an increase in demand in A for *all* goods including imports. The rise in imports causes the trade deficit.

By postulating that trade deficits are always and only the result of an excessive supply of money, and by assuming that there must exist a (Walrasian) price vector that assures the simultaneous clearing of all markets when goods trade for goods, Johnson has loaded the deck. An observed trade imbalance must be a *temporary* phenomenon readily resolved through an unfettered market system. Given the aforementioned conditions, trade imbalances are always eliminated by relative price level movements between the trading partners. The entire problem is resolved by assuming gross substitution adjustments and the absence of any income effects.

Given the gross substitution axiom, the relative price of imports declines compared to domestically produced goods in the surplus country. In the deficit economy, the relative price of imports rises compared to home production. If all goods are gross substitutes and income effects are negligible, then residents in the surplus country will increase their import purchases. Residents in the deficit country will reduce imports. In the long run, exports will pay for imports, without changing the long-run global real income or wealth total.

This 'monetary approach to the balance of payments' is firmly based on the classical axioms of gross substitution and the neutrality of money. These postulates assure that flexible prices (and exchange rates) can always resolve the problem without any significant effect on the combined aggregate real income and wealth of the trading nations. All of this is accomplished in the name of a monetary approach that analyses the operation of a real or barter economy in which (a) money has no real role to play and (b) liquidity considerations are irrelevant.

TRADE ADJUSTMENTS, PAYMENTS ADJUSTMENTS AND THE MARSHALL–LERNER CONDITION

In an NUMS system, an exchange rate devaluation is another classical mechanism for invoking relative price adjustments as the trade adjustment mechanism. The advantage of an exchange rate devaluation is that it permits an immediate alteration in relative prices rather than a slow continuing process of adjustment where A endures a slow deflation and B experiences a relative price inflation until a long-run adjustment is completed.

The fear of running out of gold (or any other international reserve asset) can force the government of trade deficit nation A to devalue its exchange rate immediately. This raises the costs (in terms of A's currency) of A's imports relative to substitutes produced at home. For households in B, it simultaneously reduces the costs of purchasing A's exports compared to buying goods from B's factories. The result will be an increase in export quantities and a reduction in import quantities for A, and *vice versa* for B.

A devaluation will usually lower the physical volume of imports and increase exports. It will reduce the payments deficit only if the *resulting change in the monetary value* of exports is greater than the change in the monetary value of imports. This change in monetary values depends on the magnitude of the absolute sum of the price elasticity of demand for imports plus the price elasticity of demand for exports. Assuming no change in aggregate income, if the sum of these elasticities exceeds unity (the Marshall–Lerner condition), then the total monetary value of A's imports will decline relative to the market value of exports and the balance of payments will improve.

For example, in the extreme case where A's elasticity of demand for imports is zero so that there is no change in the real volume of imports coming into A but the value of imports *in monetary terms* increases by the full percentage of depreciation, then elasticity of demand for A's exports must be greater than unity, so that the monetary value of total exports increases by more than the percentage depreciation in the exchange rate. If, on the other hand, each elasticity is less than unity but the sum exceeds unity, then the expansion of exports in local currency value will exceed the expansion of imports.

Classical theorists usually presume that the Marshall–Lerner condition will always prevail in the long run when everything becomes a good substitute for everything else. The implicit acceptance of the classical axiom of gross substitution is the foundation of the neoclassical claim that the depreciation of the exchange rate will always cure the international payments imbalance without affecting the long-run global real income of trading partners.

Orthodox economists have admitted that in the short run, the Marshall–Lerner conditions may not hold. In the short run, consumers and business firms may not have a chance to adjust their spending patterns in response to an exchange rate change. As one popular textbook puts it, 'a fall in the exchange rate tends to reduce [the value] of net exports in the very short run. . . . After consumers and firms have had more time to change the quantities of imports bought and exports sold, the Marshall–Lerner condition is more likely to hold, and a fall in the exchange rate is likely to lead to an increased net exports'.[5]

Orthodox economists suggest that the typical response of net exports to an exchange rate depreciation is in the form of a 'J-curve', where, for an unspecified length of time, the deficit in the balance of payments worsens (the downward slope of the J-curve), before an improvement (upward movement on the J-curve) can be expected. This short-run worsening in the payments balance can force another devaluation. A new J-curve will be encountered with a further immediate decline in the value of net exports. In a series of short runs it is possible that devaluation provokes continued devaluation, and an improved trade balance is never achieved. For who knows how long a period of calendar time is required until the consumers and firms make sufficient adjustments so that the Marshall–Lerner conditions prevail?

To avoid this perverse and unsettling possibility, orthodox macroeconomists merely 'assume that the time period is long enough so that Marshall–Lerner conditions holds'.[6] In other words, mainstream macroeconomists solve the problem of an adverse trade deficit by *assuming* conditions in which gross substitution effects are sufficiently strong to solve the problem. In a moment of candour, Abel and Bernanke remind the reader, 'Keep in mind, though, that this assumption [that the Marshall–Lerner conditions prevail] may not be valid for shorter periods – and in some cases, even for several years'.[7]

In 1985, after three years of large import surpluses, classical economists in the United States claimed that only a devaluation of the US dollar would resolve this persistent payments problem. In late September of 1985, under public pressure fermented by the persistent demands of classical economists for a devaluation, Treasury Secretary James Baker launched an initiative to 'talk down' the value of the dollar in the foreign exchange market. Secretary Baker's economic advisers spoke about a 'soft landing' where a 35 per cent devaluation of the dollar would cure the US trade deficit without unleashing any inflationary or depressionary forces.

One week before this Baker initiative, testimony[8] presented to the Joint Economic Committee of the US Congress indicated why a deliberate lowering of the dollar exchange rate by 35 per cent would not, by itself, significantly reduce the US trade deficit. Table 13.1 provides the data on the US payments balance since 1981. Unfortunately, the facts since 1985 when the United States deliberately undertook to talk down the dollar tend to support the testimony presented to the Joint Economic Committee rather than the orthodox argument that a devaluation would provide a soft-landing solution to the persistent US trade deficit. In 1986, despite a drop of more than 30 per cent in the value of the dollar, the value of imports grew by 11 per cent while the value of exports rose less than two per cent. In 1987 with another 10 per cent drop in the dollar, exports and imports both expanded by 11 per cent. In 1988 the dollar dropped again, bottoming out at almost 50 per cent below its 1985 peak value. Only by 1988–89, when the dollar price of imported oil collapsed on world markets (imported oil equalled almost half of the total dollar value of all US imports) did the value of US exports rise significantly more than the value of US imports. Thus it

Table 13.1   United States international payments balances

Year	Merchandise Balance	Goods, services income balance	Current account balance
		(in billions of dollars)	
1981	− 28.0	16.7	5.0
1982	− 36.5	5.6	− 11.4
1983	− 67.1	− 25.9	− 43.6
1984	− 112.5	− 78.2	− 98.8
1985	− 122.2	− 98.8	− 121.7
1986	− 145.1	− 123.4	− 147.5
1987	− 159.6	− 140.4	− 163.5
1988	− 127.0	− 101.8	− 126.7
1989	− 115.7	− 75.5	− 101.1
1990	− 108.8	− 57.5	− 90.4
1991	− 73.4	− 11.7	− 3.7
1992	− 96.1	− 31.5	− 66.4

Source: Economic Indicators, Council of Economic Advisers, Washington, May 1993.

took more than 2½ years after the dollar was 'talked down' by almost 50 per cent, and a fall in the dollar price of international oil, before there was *any* reduction in the US import trade deficit.

In 1991, the US experienced a big improvement in its current account imbalance. Unfortunately most of this reduction in the deficit is traceable to two factors. First, the US slipped into recession in 1991, causing imports to decline, while exports continued to rise. Second, the current account balance improved dramatically as Japan, Germany, and some other nations made large unilateral transfer payments to the United States as their contribution to financing the short war against Iraq – 'Desert Storm' – in 1991. In 1992, these one-time unilateral transfers disappeared. Also by mid-1992 the United States began to expand while Europe and Japan slipped towards recession. The result was that the current account balance significantly worsened.

This historical record suggests that the substitution effects implied in the Marshall–Lerner condition necessary to cure a payments imbalance was not applicable for the United States after 1981. Indeed income effects involving changes in differential growth rates between the United States and its major trading partners appear to have a more significant impact on the payments balance than substitution effects.[9]

In the real world, trade between nations does not always involve the large gross substitutes presumed by classical theory. Income (and liquidity) effects can have major impacts on a nation's international payments balance. Sole reliance on changes in relative prices to end trade deficits can be misplaced even in the long run. Changes in income can have significant effects on trade. Income effects on the payments balance are immediate, direct, and unambiguous (unlike substitution effects that rely on Marshall–Lerner conditions prevailing).

INCOME EFFECTS AND PAYMENTS BALANCES

In 1933, Harrod[10] demonstrated that if the only component of autonomous demand was exports, then there could be a foreign trade multiplier such that

$$y_a = [1/mpm][x_a] \qquad (13.1)$$

where y_a is the change in aggregate income in nation A, x_a is the change in A's exports, and *mpm* is the marginal propensity to import of A's residents.

Since this Harrod insight preceded Keynes's *General Theory*, Harrod had not made consumption a function of income, and therefore the marginal propensity to consume was implicitly assumed to be zero. After the *General Theory* this Harrod formulation was recast into a Keynesian foreign trade multiplier mechanism.[11] It was presumed that in each nation the marginal propensity to import is normally less than the marginal propensity to consume.

In the resulting Keynesian trade multiplier analysis, the Harrod emphasis on exogenous exports was lost. Instead the focus was placed on an exogenous increase in some internal component of A's aggregate demand function inducing, through the propensity to import, an increase in import demand. The Keynesian foreign trade multiplier literature indicated that a domestic policy to stimulate effective demand would induce some increase in imports relative to exports, thereby creating a balance of payments problem. The expansion of domestic effective demand spilled over into a demand for imports. This growth in imports would stimulate some economic expansion in the nation's trading partners, thereby inducing some expansion of the nation's exports. This feedback effect merely reduced the magnitude of the balance of payments problem. It did not solve it, even in the long run.

THIRLWALL'S LAW: EXTENDING THE HARROD
TRADE MULTIPLIER ANALYSIS

Thirlwall[12] developed a demand driven model of international payments
from Harrod's trade multiplier insight. His analysis provides guidelines on
the rate of economic growth a nation can achieve without suffering
deterioration in its payments balance. A demand driven model is a Keynes
model where employment is determined by the point of effective demand.
It does not employ the classical presumption of continuous global full
employment. Demand driven models do not assume that long-run economic growth is exogenously determined by technological progress and
labour force growth.

In Thirlwall's model, export and import functions are represented by:

$$X_a = (P_d/P_f)^z Y^{erw} \tag{13.2}$$

$$M_a = (P_d/P_f)^u Y^{ea} \tag{13.3}$$

where

X_a and M_a are exports from nation A and imports into A;
(P_d/P_f) is the ratio of domestic prices to foreign prices expressed in terms
of the domestic currency of A;
z is the price elasticity of demand for A's exports, u is A's price elasticity
of demand for imports;
e_a is A's income elasticity of demand for imports; and
e_{rw} is the rest of the world's income elasticity of demand for A's exports.

If z and u are small and/or relative prices do not change significantly, then
substitution effects can be ignored. The analysis concentrates on income
effects.

Using the natural log form of equations (13.2) and (13.3) and ignoring
substitution effects, one obtains Thirlwall's Law of the growth of income
that is consistent with an unchanged trade balance as:

$$y_a = x/e_a \tag{13.4}$$

where y_a is the rate of growth of nation A's GNP, x is the rate of growth of
A's exports, and e_a is A's income elasticity of demand for imports. Since the
growth of exports for A depends primarily on the rest of the world's growth
in income (y_{rw}) and the world's income elasticity of demand for A's exports
(e_{rw}), i.e.

$$x = (e_{rw})(y_{rw}) \tag{13.5}$$

then equation (13.4) can be written as

$$y_a = [e_{rw}y_{rw}]/e_a. \tag{13.6}$$

If a nation starts from a position of international payments balance, then there is only one rate of growth that a nation can sustain without running into a balance of payments deficit. This sustainable growth rate, as shown in equation (13.6), depends on the rest of the world's growth and the relevant income elasticities for imports and exports.

If the growth in the value of imports is to exactly equal the growth in the value of exports, i.e.

$$e_{rw}y_{rw} = y_a e_a \tag{13.7}$$

then

$$[y_a/y_{rw}] = [e_{rw}/e_a]. \tag{13.8}$$

Equation (13.9) is called Thirlwall's Law. This law indicates that the ratio of the growth of income in nation A to the growth rate in the rest of the world is equal to the ratio of the income elasticity of demand for A's exports by the rest of the world to A's income elasticity of demand for imports. *If $e_{rw}/e_a < 1$, and if growth in A is constrained by the need to maintain a balance of payments equilibrium, then nation A is condemned to grow at a slower rate than the rest of the world.*

For example, if less-developed nations (LDCs) of the world have a comparative advantage in the exports of raw materials and other basic commodities (for which Engel's curves suggest that the developed world will have a low income elasticity of demand) while the LDCs have a high income elasticity of demand for the manufactured products of the developed world, then, for these LDCs

$$[e_{rw}/e_{ldc}] < 1. \tag{13.9}$$

If economic development and the balance of payments equilibrium is left to the free market and a balance in the current account is required, then the LDCs are condemned to relative poverty, and the global inequality of income will become larger over time.

Moreover, if the rate of population growth in the LDCs (p_{ldc}) is greater than the rate of population growth in the developed world (p_{dw}), that is if $p_{ldc} > p_{dw}$, then the future of the LDCs is even more dismal. The rate of growth of GNP per capita of the LDCs will show a greater relative decline (or slower increase) compared to the standard of living of the developed world, i.e.

$$[y_{ldc}/p_{ldc}] \ll [y_{dw}/p_{dw}]. \tag{13.10}$$

In the absence of Keynesian policies to stimulate growth, the long-term growth rate of the developed world taken as a whole tends to be in the 1 to 2.5 per cent range. As long as the developed world's population growth rate is less than this long-term economic growth rate, these nations will enjoy a rising living standard.

If reasonable values for the parameters in inequality (13.9) are assumed, then since $(y_{ldc} < y_{dw})$, while $1 < y_{dw} < 2.5$, a dreary prognostication for the global economy emerges. If the free markets are permitted to determine the balance of payments constraints on every nation, then a shrinking proportion of the world's population may continue to get richer (or at least hold their own), while a growing proportion of the earth's population is likely to become poorer. Moreover, the slower the rate of growth in income of the rich developed nations, the more rapidly the poor are likely to sink deeper into poverty. In an unfettered global market environment, an improvement in the standard of living of the poor depends on the rich increasing their standard of living faster than any improvement the poor will experience.

Life may not be fair, but surely a civilized global society should not permit such regressive economic laws to operate freely without attempting to change these dismal implications. Surely it is the responsibility of the rich nations to explore the analysis to see if there are policy interventions that can be developed to prevent market-determined balance of payments constraints from condemning the majority of the world's population to increasing poverty.[13]

Keynes's *General Theory* was explicitly an analysis of a demand-driven, non-neutral money, closed economy. If Keynes's monetary analysis emphasizing the liquidity motives of firms and households in the operation of an entrepreneur production economy is expanded to analyse an open economy, it should be possible to develop Keynes-like policy proposals to avoid the potential dire outcomes of a free market Thirlwall's Law model.

THE DEMAND FOR MONEY – DOMESTIC OR INTERNATIONAL

Money has been defined by its two primary functions, namely (a) a medium of spot and forward contractual settlement, and (b) a liquidity time machine, i.e. a store of generalized purchasing power. In the absence of uncertainty over time, the liquidity functions of money over time would be superfluous.

Keynes's powerful dual-purpose classification of money led to the two essential properties of money (zero or negligible elasticities of production and substitution) which are 'significant attributes' for money in an uncertain world where 'expectations are liable to disappointment and expectations concerning the future affect what we do today'.[14] Using this Keynesian approach, the demand for money (in a closed UMS) via the transactions, precautionary, speculative, and financial motives has been developed to a fine edge.[15]

The role of money and liquidity relationships in an open NUMS, on the other hand, has not been similarly developed. Practical complications create perplexing theoretical problems especially for classical analysis where money is a mere numéraire. Classical theory treats international trade as if it were a barter process where goods trade for goods, and monetary theory is just an 'extra complication' (to use Johnson's phrase) in a real or barter analysis.

In the real world of open entrepreneurial economies, each nation has its own money for denominating and settling private contracts between domestic residents. Different monies may be used to settle private contracts between residents of one country and residents of other countries. Central Banks may use yet another medium (often not available to the private sector) to settle claims against each other, or against other national banking systems. Financial arrangements and institutions are an essential element in the determination of the level of the international flow of production and exchange of real goods and services. Money really does matter in the determination of real international trade levels and patterns.

What determines the medium of contractual settlement that will be used in international transactions? The money in use, an essential element of all economically developed civilizations, depends upon both law and custom. Arching over all civilizations is the civil law of contracts. In the absence of law-abiding economic agents committed to obeying this civil law, there can be no significant transactions, freely made, among independent economic agents. In all modern economies the State enforces both law and custom in the case of contractual disputes between residents of the same country. Thus as long as transactors are law abiding, the internal medium of contractual settlement is not only whatever is declared to be legal tender by the State, but also anything the State or the Central Bank undertakes to accept from the public in payment of obligations or in exchange at a fixed rate for legal tender money.[16]

Unfortunately, no such simple chartalist prerogatives exist to determine the money of settlement when contractual disputes occur between residents of different nations. Thus, custom and voluntary cooperation between governments are important factors in encouraging entrepreneurs to engage in international trade. Specifying a particular nation's money as the means of settlement in an international contract immediately determines the nation in whose courts an aggrieved party to an international contract can seek restitution.

In general, local currency cannot be directly used to settle an international obligation denominated in terms of another currency. Thus, the payer of a foreign money contractual commitment will normally have to sell the domestic currency in either a spot or forward exchange market to obtain the means of contractual settlement.[17] How and who organizes the foreign exchange markets will determine the degree of international liquidity that any domestic money is thought to possess. In a UMS among nations, each nation's Central Bank operates as a market maker in foreign exchange to guarantee a fixed exchange rate. Confidence in the ability of the State to maintain the announced exchange rate makes the domestic money a fully liquid international asset capable of being converted immediately into the medium of settlement of any other national currency. In an NUMS, on the other hand, the local currency has varying degrees of international liquidity depending on the confidence the public has as to the ability of the market maker(s) of the foreign exchange market to maintain an orderly market price.

It was essential to comprehend the liquidity motives of economic agents holding cash and other liquid reserve assets in a closed UMS economy facing an uncertain future (Keynes's theory of liquidity preference). A parallel theory of international liquidity and reserve asset holdings for agents operating in an open NUMS must be developed.

THE NEED FOR RESERVES

When the future is uncertain, the possibility of changing one's mind and altering one's activities as time passes is part of the human condition.

In such a world there can be a sequential causality of events. For example, entrepreneurs are continually examining outcomes over time to see if they match previous expectations. Unexpected outcomes at time t_0 are inspected for possible evidence of new, different, and previously unforeseen trends. When surprising events are (correctly or incorrectly) perceived to have significantly altered the economic environment, then entrepreneurs will alter their expectations about the future. These revised expectations will induce agents to recast their decisions at time t_1. These changed decisions will affect economic actions and activities at time t_2.

The calendar time that passes between t_0 when 'surprise events' are discovered and t_1 when decisions are altered, depends largely on how long it takes agents to collect and analyse data, and, in the context of their historical and current experiences, identify what they believe is a new expected pattern that will not be an ephemeral event. The period between t_0 and t_1 is a data-collecting, processing, and identification period. Its calendar length (which cannot be specified in advance) is mainly determined by perceptual and psychological factors.

The calendar distance between t_1 and t_2 (between revising decisions and changing activities) is constrained by two economic factors. The length of time each agent is bound by previous forward contractual commitments and the real costs of buying oneself out of these commitments will necessarily limit changes in decisions that could bring t_2 closer in time to t_1. The more uncommitted liquidity one has, or can obtain, to meet new contractual obligations that will be incurred by any new actions undertaken at a point of time, the closer t_2 can be brought to t_1. The possession of sufficient liquidity is freedom in the sense that it permits new actions to be taken quickly, and often shortens the distance between t_1 and t_2 when entrepreneurs perceive past errors and desire to embark on new and different activities. The duration and magnitude of existing contractual commitments (for any given degree of liquidity possessed) force a posterior calendar time lag on new actions.

The holding of liquid reserve assets gives decision makers time to sort out and interpret the myriad of market and other signals that they are continuously receiving. They may then decide whether a change in plans is required while they continue to meet contractual obligations not only during the period of signal interpretation but also during the period of posterior lag while the decision maker plans alterations in his original activities. *Thus, the possession of liquidity is essential for the continuity of economic activity in a free market entrepreneurial economy where everyone recognizes that the economic future is statistically unpredictable and full of potential surprises,* i.e., in a nonergodic environment. In a nonergodic real world 'liquidity is freedom'.[18]

Hicks has invented a taxonomic scheme for classifying asset holdings in an uncertain world.[19] *Running assets* are those required for the normal operations of economic processes. In an entrepreneurial economy, contracts are used to organize most production and exchange processes. These contracts lead to a stream of money obligations. The holding of cash balances or other fully liquid assets to meet the contractual obligations coming due in the very near future are the running financial assets to support the normal expenditure activities of buyers.[20]

Reserve assets are assets that are similar to running assets but are not normally required for the current level of planned activities. Instead, reserve assets are held for exigencies that can occur during normal economic activities. Precautionary and speculative holdings of money and other liquid assets are financial reserve assets.

The quantity of reserve financial assets the public wishes to hold at any time depends on the magnitude of the future cash flow problems that the public expects to encounter. The quantity of international reserve assets that are fully liquid at any point of time is determined by the Central Bank and, in an international system, by the organization of foreign exchange markets.

In an international UMS, the domestic rate of interest on loans in a nation 'will be dragged up to a parity with the *highest* rate (highest after allowing for risk) prevailing in any country belonging to the international system',[21] while in a flexible exchange rate system the risk allowances will be greater and therefore permit greater differences in domestic interest rates.

In his perceptive analysis of *Reforming the World's Money*, Harrod noted that the management of international financial assets is 'the most important problem confronting those responsible for economic affairs in the free world'.[22] The need to manage and maintain adequate levels of international running assets and reserve assets is essential in promoting economic prosperity in developed trading nations.

Just as for each individual there is a level of transactions and precautionary balances perceived as necessary to meet upcoming contractual obligations, so for each nation there is a level of international asset holding (the foreign reserves of the Central Bank as running or reserve assets) which are held as a balance to bridge the gap between foreign receipts and upcoming foreign payments obligations. Individuals and nations face similar cash flow or running-reserve asset liquidity management problems.

If it were possible with perfect certainty to coordinate exactly the time payment of all cash inflows and outflows, individuals or nations would have to hold transaction balances only momentarily, if at all. Such coordination is, of course, impossible. Financial assets must be held to bridge significant periods of calendar time. The greater the lack of planned coordination between contractual cash inflows and outflows, *ceteris paribus*, the greater the need to hold stocks of running and reserve liquid assets. In international transactions this need manifests itself in the need for foreign exchange holdings that are positively related to (a) the flow level of foreign contractual obligations coming due, (b) the lack of coordination between international inflows and outflows, and (c) a need for precautionary or reserve assets to cover possible but unpredictable emergencies in foreign transactions cash flows.

In a closed UMS, an individual's cash holdings can increase at the expense of others; but, in the aggregate, an expansion of cash balance holdings by the public requires an increase in the domestic money supply (i.e., the liabilities of the bank and/or the Central Bank or the non-interest paying liabilities of government). Similarly, each nation can individually increase its foreign exchange holdings at the expense of others, but from a global view all countries cannot on average simultaneously increase their total holdings of running and reserve liquid assets unless new international liquid assets are created.

In a closed UMS system every increase in planned expansion of economic activity requires an increase in the money supply through the income-generating finance process[23] if congestion in the money market (which can constrain expansion) is to be avoided. In a similar manner international liquid assets must increase concomitantly with planned international trade expansion.[24]

In domestic money affairs, the Central Bank is usually given the responsibility of providing for an elastic currency to meet the 'real bills' needs of trade. There is no existing financial mechanism that assures the confluence of the growth in the supply of international reserves and the needs for such balances as the volume of international trade expands. This, of course, was one of the great disadvantages of the automatic gold standard which in the nineteenth century made gold the international money for all contracts enforceable in nations honouring the gold standard. Shortages of gold could limit expansion of global production and trade.[25]

Some have argued that if exports and imports grow at identical rates over a period of time, there is no need to expand the international running reserve base – as if goods exchange for goods in international trade without the intermediation of money. Proponents of this barter view of international trade proclaim that the only time running and reserve financial assets are needed is if a nation's trade balance is unbalanced. This implies that there are no financial constraints to international trade as long as $B = 0$ in each accounting period for each trading partner, with exports and imports growing concomitantly over time.

Once uncertainty and the impossibility of perfect coordination of cash inflows and outflows are recognized as inherent characteristics of all trading relations, it is obvious that an increase in international reserve holdings (liquidity) becomes a necessary condition for expanding trade even in the event that expansion does not increase the size of trade deficits. Even if expansion of trade is balanced over a period of time, and even if cash inflows and outflows are only randomly distributed over time rather than perfectly coordinated, Bernoulli's Law of large numbers would suggest that as trade expands, the absolute discrepancy between cash inflows and outflows for each nation at any point of time increases. Larger international reserves would be needed to finance these temporary absolute cash flow imbalances even if, in the long run and on average, no nation ends up with a trade deficit or surplus.[26]

Of course, the history of the real world in recent years is that nations can suffer under persistent trade deficits. The United States has acted as the Central Banker of the world through the 1980s by persistently issuing liabilities (in true central banker fashion) to provide the additional international liquid running and reserve assets necessary to permit the rapid growth of the free world's production and trade. In the absence of the large persistent trade and payment deficits of the Reagan years, the free world and especially those who pursued an export-led growth policy, e.g. West Germany, Japan, and the newly industrialized countries of Taiwan, South Korea, Hong Kong, and Singapore would not have been able to sustain the economic growth that occurred.

The money supply is a necessary prerequisite for expanding economic activity in a closed UMS. Similarly, expanding the stock of international running and reserve assets is a necessary precondition for the orderly continuous growth of international economic activity. In the days of the automatic gold standard, if world gold supplies entering international asset holdings increased less rapidly than world trade, there was a tendency towards congestion in international financial markets that constrained the growth of trade.

In the period since World War II, gold augmented by 'hard-currency' holdings of Central Banks has played the role of international running and reserve assets. In the 1980s the large US current account deficits helped to provide additional liquidity to promote export-led economic growth in Western Europe and the Pacific Rim nations. The world cannot rely on the United States to supply additional international liquid reserves whenever the world needs it. In Chapter 16 *infra*, the question as to what international payments system Keynes would have recommended for the twenty-first century will be analysed.

First it is necessary to analyse the relationship between international liquidity and stability in the foreign exchange markets.

NOTES

1. H.J. Johnson, 'Money and the Balance of Payments', *Banca Nazionale Del Lavoro Quarterly Review*, March 1976, p. 5. Keynes, on the other hand, always argued that 'the theory which I desiderate would deal . . . with an economy in which money plays a part of its own and affects motives and decisions and is, in short, one of the operative factors in the situation, so that the course of events cannot be predicted either in the long period

or the short, without a knowledge of the behaviour of money between the first state and the last' (Keynes, *The Collected Writings of John Maynard Keynes*, 13, pp. 408–9). In other words, for Keynes and Post Keynesians, money is *not* just an 'extra complication' added to a real or barter theory analysis.

2. For a full analysis of the income-generating finance process (which is based on Keynes's post *General Theory* finance motive analysis) see P. Davidson, 'A Keynesian View of Friedman's Theoretical Framework for Monetary Analysis', in R.J. Gordon (ed.), *Milton Friedman's Monetary Framework: A Debate With His Critics*, University of Chicago Press, 1974, p. 103 and P. Davidson, *Money and the Real World*, Macmillan, London, 1972, Chapter 7.

3. The specie-flow mechanism involves the sale of a 'perfectly integrated' asset (gold) by residents of A to those in B, with a consequent change in relative production prices and costs (in terms of gold).

4. H.G. Johnson, 'Money and the Balance of Payments', op.cit., p. 16, italics added.

5. A.B. Abel and B.S. Bernanke, *Macroeconomics*, Addison-Wesley Publishing Company, New York, 1992.

6. Abel and Bernanke, *Macroeconomics*, p. 508.

7. Abel and Bernanke, *Macroeconomics*, p. 508.

8. Testimony of Professor Paul Davidson, Joint Economic Committee, September 18, 1985.

9. Although the question of whether the Marshall–Lerner conditions will be met for any country has to be made on a case-by-case basis, there is some reason to suspect its applicability for many less-developed countries. For those LDCs whose major export earner is an agricultural crop or mineral, international contracts are made in dollars. Devaluation of the local currency therefore will not affect foreign demand. To the extent that the major imports of the LDC are food and other raw materials that are priced internationally in dollars, devaluation lowers the real income of its inhabitants significantly and thus brings about an improvement in its trade balance via an income effect.

10. R.F. Harrod, *International Economics*, Cambridge University Press, Cambridge, 1933.

11. The simple foreign trade multiplier formula is

$$\frac{1}{[(mps) + (mpm)]}$$

where *mps* is the marginal propensity to save.

12. A.P. Thirlwall, 'The Balance of Payments Constraint As An Explanation of International Growth Rate Differences', *Banca Nazionale del Lavoro Quarterly Review*, 1979, **128**, pp. 45–53.

13. If equations (13.8) to (13.10) are permitted to govern outcomes then only if the rich can continue to achieve the historically high real rates of growth experienced during the first 25 years after World War II can we hope to significantly improve the economic lot of the poorer nations of the world. In that golden age of two and a half decades Keynesian rather than free market policies were actively pursued domestically and internationally by the developed world.

14. J.M. Keynes, *The General Theory*, pp. 293–4.

15. For example, see P. Davidson, *Money and the Real World*, Chapters 6–13.

16. Cf. J.M. Keynes, *A Treatise on Money*, I, reprinted as vol. 5, Macmillan, London, 1971, p. 6. The institutional relationship between the Central Bank and the national banking system determines which sight drafts for the transfer of ownership of private (bank) facilities the Central Bank will accept in exchange for legal tender and hence which private debts are the monies of contractual settlement in the domestic economy.

17. Alternatively one can directly sell a liquid asset in a market located in the foreign country whose currency is needed to settle the contractual commitment. (This assumes that well-organized spot markets exist for the sale of these assets.)

18. J.R. Hicks, *Causality in Economics*, Basic Books, New York, 1979, p. 94.

19. J.R. Hicks, *Critical Essays in Monetary Theory*, Oxford University Press, 1967, pp. 38–45.
20. Cf. Keynes's income and business motives for demanding money, *The General Theory*, 1936, p. 195.
21. Keynes, *The General Theory*, p. 203.
22. R.F. Harrod, *Reforming the World's Money*, Macmillan, London, 1965, p. 1.
23. See P. Davidson, *Money and the Real World*, pp. 159–84, 402–5.
24. Of course, to the extent that payment inflows can be better coordinated with payment outflows, fewer running assets are needed for any level of international activity. The rising demand for transaction balances as planned spending increases assumes that better coordination cannot be achieved.
25. Moreover, within the inelasticity of total gold reserves, the fact that the flow of specie among trade debtors and creditors failed to provide an easy adjustment mechanism to restore balance led to the inevitable abandonment of this form of international money.
26. This, of course, was exactly the problem that Harrod was concerned with.

14. International liquidity and exchange rate stability

FIXED VS. FLEXIBLE RATES AND ASSET HOLDINGS

In modern 'fixed' exchange rate systems, Central Banks agree to intervene in the exchange market only after the exchange rate moves by a specified (but usually small) per cent. For example, during the 1980s, in the currency arrangement known as the European Monetary System or EMS, France, West Germany, the Netherlands, Ireland, Belgium and Denmark pledged, at least in the short run, to prevent their currencies from rising or falling against each other by more than 2.25 per cent while Italy undertook to maintain a 6 per cent margin. In the late 1980s, the United Kingdom joined the EMS.

To maintain a fixed rate system such as the EMS, the Central Bank of each member nation must enter into an agreement to intervene in the market to limit the movement of the exchange rate. Ideally, the agreement should be that the Central Bank of the nation whose exchange rate is threatening to go above the ceiling price will buy the money of the nation with the falling exchange rate with whatever amount of its money necessary to bring the exchange rate back to its preagreed fixed rate. Since each nation can always create additional amounts of its own money, the Central Bank can aggressively continue to sell until the rate falls back to its preagreed upon fixed rate.

Under this 'ideal' system for fixing exchange rates, the nation with the appreciating currency has surrendered national control over its outstanding money supply. The nation has agreed to permit international forces to determine the amount of domestic money available to the public at home and abroad. Most nations fear giving up their sovereign right to control their domestic money supply. Instead, they will agree upon a system where the Central Bank of the nation with the currency that is declining will be required to step in and buy its own money with its foreign reserves. If the reserves are sufficient, then the exchange rate can be stabilized at the fixed rate. If the Central Bank is running out of either reserves or nerve, then, unless the nation can borrow reserves from other members, it will be forced to withdraw from the fixed rate system.[1]

Under the ideal system for operating the EMS if, for example, the German mark rose more than 2.25 per cent against the French franc in the market, then the German Bundesbank would be pledged to buy French francs in the market by selling Deutsche Marks (DMs) until the exchange rate fell back. The French could simultaneously cooperate by buying francs and selling DMs, but the primary onus would be on the German bank to fix the rate. Under the more orthodox system, the Bank of France has the primary responsibility of buying francs for DMs (by selling its foreign reserves), while the German Bundesbank may voluntarily cooperate by either lending the Bank of France DMs or buying French francs for DMs directly in the foreign exchange market.

The success of maintaining the fixed rate is unquestioned in the 'ideal' system if the public is convinced the Germans are willing to sell unlimited quantities of DMs if necessary to preserve the fixed exchange rate. The success in the second case depends on the adequacy of French reserves as a first line of defence. The second line of defence depends on the willingness of the German bank to sell DMs to help the French husband their reserves.

A publicly announced small range of exchange rate flexibility occurs in most fixed rate systems. Even under the gold standard, exchange rates could fluctuate by a few percentage points between the gold export point and the gold import point. In the normal course of events, slight imbalances in trade due to seasonality, random causes, variations in stockpiling, or phases of the business cycle can cause some oscillations in international payment inflows and outflows. These variations will affect the spot market demand and supplies of the currencies of the trading partners leading to some weakening of the exchange rate for nations running a payments deficit. If this weakening is perceived as a temporary aberration, then a spot rate decline will provide profit opportunities for comptrollers of multinational corporations (and others who engage in international trade and finance) to buy more of the weaker currency to hold and to sell some of their holdings of the stronger currency. These portfolio transactions create market forces that tend to move the price back towards the original fixed exchange rate after the 'temporary' decline.

The rationale for these profitable portfolio transactions is easily illustrated. Suppose currency A's exchange rate declines by 1 per cent. The comptroller of the XYZ Multinational, knowing he or she has a contractual payment in terms of A's currency in the near future, will have to decide whether to buy currency A spot or at the future commitment date. The weaker the exchange rate compared to the 'normal' rate, the greater the incentive to purchase currency A on the spot. This will mean substantial savings compared to the normal exchange rate as long as there is complete confidence in the ability of the Central Bank to maintain the normal rate.[2]

Whenever an actual exchange rate change is perceived to be temporary and short-lived, the elasticity of expectations will be approximately zero. Market perturbations that are expected to be temporary and short-lived set loose forces that restore the normal exchange rate with a minimum of Central Bank direct intervention.

In a flexible exchange rate system, on the other hand, if a 1 per cent weakness of currency A occurs, no one can be sure whether the rate will move further away from the original rate or in the reverse direction. If international transactors are on average split evenly (in terms of payment commitments) between those who think the weakness is temporary (inelastic expectations) and those who think it will worsen (elastic expectations), there will be no adjustments in the leads and lags of private trade payments. If the preponderant market view is that the current weakness in the exchange rate is a signal of still further larger declines to come, then the elasticity of expectations is elastic. The leads and lags in private sector payments will then tend to reinforce the current decline.

Elastic expectations create instability and induce a process of cumulative exchange rate decline. As Hicks has noted:

> Technically, then, the case where elasticities of expectations are equal to unity marks the dividing line between stability and instability. A slight disturbance will be sufficient to make it pass over to instability. ... Thus even when elasticities of expectations are equal to unity, the system is liable to break down at the slightest disturbance.[3]

If there is a perception of permanent weakness in an exchange rate in either a fixed or flexible rate system, then the public's uncertainty about the future value of the currency A tends to rise and the elasticity of expectations has a propensity to become more elastic. The public will reduce holdings of transactions and precautionary balances of the weakened currency and substitute either other currencies that are perceived as stronger or other internationally marketable assets (e.g., gold) whose value in terms of currencies in which future contractual commitments are denominated is expected to increase.

The more flexible the exchange rate system is perceived to be, therefore, the more likely an apparent weakness in a currency will induce perceptions of greater uncertainty about the ability of that currency to maintain its value relative to other currencies, and the more probable it is that private sector liquid asset holders will abandon the weakened currency as a running and reserve asset.

Individuals often abandon a currency for transaction and precautionary reasons, and not necessarily for the prime purpose of speculation. They may have no idea whether the market is properly evaluating the possibility of a further market decline in the weakened currency, but they will sleep better at night if they transfer more of their precautionary holdings to a safer liquidity time machine. The resulting movement to other currencies accentuates the weakness of the threatened currency and fosters a fear of further depreciation. This can lead to a bandwagon effect until either some event or some official pronouncement encourages individuals to believe that the winds of change are moving in a different direction.[4]

In an uncertain world where unforeseen changes are inevitable, an announced flexible exchange rate system must increase the extent of exchange rate movements for any given exogenous disturbance. This should create disincentives for long-duration international commitments by international traders. It also encourages short-term precautionary and speculative capital movements. According to Keynes's theory of markets, our current expectations are anchored only by conventions.

> The essence of this convention – though it does not, of course, work out quite so simply – lies in assuming that the current state of affairs will continue indefinitely, except in so far as we have specific reasons to expect a change. This does not mean that we really believe that the existing state of affairs will continue indefinitely. We know from extensive experience that this is most unlikely.[5]

The existence of credible State-sponsored institutions 'guaranteeing' continuity in economic affairs creates expectations of stickiness if not complete fixity in markets. This Keynes–Post Keynesian psychological view of markets implies that if dependable institutions are absent from a market, expectations can become unhinged by ephemeral (from hindsight) events, spot market prices can fluctuate violently, or temporarily pause at any value until the next agitating event happens.

THE EFFICIENT MARKET HYPOTHESIS

The classical efficient market hypothesis is in direct contrast to Keynes's belief that a flexible rate system can generate psychological beliefs that create additional volatility in spot market evaluations of prices. The classical view presumes that all relevant information about 'economic fundamentals' regarding future demand and supplies currently exists and is available to market participants. This information is embodied in the historical market data base and current market price signals.

This efficient market hypothesis claims that expectations of all rational agents are based on this available information. It is presumed that either all agents have the same expectations or else the dispersion of expectations about the average expectation does not affect future trends by causing a significant volume of false trades, bankruptcies, etc. In the absence of government interference in the market-place, these informed agents, acting in their own self-interests, will always perceive the future without making persistent errors. The actions of these rational agents will establish the equilibrium exchange rate. Observed variations around this market equilibrium rate can be attributed to random shocks that will quickly be dampened down by the alert action of informed agents.

The development of the efficient market hypothesis has driven Keynes's psychological approach to the formation of spot market evaluations from most academic discussions of financial market performance. Nevertheless, there is mounting empirical evidence of both a short-run and long-run nature that is incompatible with the efficient market theory. Shiller,[6] for example, has examined the long-run relationship between real stock prices and real dividends in the United States from 1889 to 1981 and concluded that 'the volatility of stock market price indices appears to be too high to accord with the efficient market model'.

Short-run analysis of exchange market data during periods of uncertainty is also incompatible with the efficient market hypothesis. For example, in 1985 *The Economist* magazine noted that during the first few months of that year the daily exchange rate volatilities of the D-mark and sterling 'have often swung 2–3% a day against the dollar. Not so the yen [because of Bank of Japan intervention]. . . . In terms of daily movement, European currencies have become more volatile this year than 1980–84'.

Table 14.1   *Daily volatility* of dollar exchange rates, %*

	1980–84	Jan–April 1985
D-mark	0.7	0.9
sterling	0.6	1.1
yen	0.7	0.5

Note: *Standard deviation of % change.

Since there was no obvious increase in random shocks or the amount of daily information flows regarding the future in the first four months of 1985 compared to 1980–84, the data in Table 14.1 appear to be inconsistent with the efficient market hypothesis. This observed increase in European currency fluctuations is compatible with unanchored expectations in the absence of governmental intervention. The daily stickiness of the Japanese exchange rate, on the other hand, can be associated with expectations secured on the more active interventionist role played by the Bank of Japan during that period to stabilize the dollar–yen exchange rate.

Once rapid movements in exchange rates become widely expected, any nation's currency can become subject to a 'flight of capital' – a real world phenomenon without an obvious counterpart in an Arrow–Debreu model. International flight capital is a readily understandable phenomenon. It is the open NUMS model equivalent of a bearish surge out of securities because of an expected decline in the spot price in a closed UMS system.

In the absence of financial institutions whose explicit function is to constrain the rate of change in the spot exchange rate, expectations can become so elastic that a current unexpected change in exchange rates can induce destabilizing views about the future. In these circumstances, the existence of an equilibrating price vector that includes foreign exchange rates cannot be demonstrated. Even if existence could be demonstrated, its stability would be threatened as long as the elasticity of expectations exceeds unity. Since the breakdown of the Bretton Woods Agreement, Central Banks have had to increase their active intervention in spot exchange markets to achieve some modicum of stability[7] and calm the market's possible fears.

WHO SHOULD 'MAKE' THE EXCHANGE RATE MARKET?

Defenders of freely flexible exchange rates implicitly assume that a *laissez-faire* market system must possess an equilibrium price vector that clears all markets simultaneously. Proponents of flexible rates argue that if only Central Banks would remove themselves as 'makers' of the foreign exchange market, then private sector entrepreneurs – presumably international bankers – would move in and stabilize the foreign exchange market. These international bankers are motivated solely by the profit motive (as opposed to nationalist pride or political myopia that, it is claimed, motivates Central Bankers). It is claimed these entrepreneurs will find the exchange rate that maintains a general equilibrium among all trading partners. If the original private sector market-makers in the exchange market do not do their job properly, then they will face bankruptcy. Other international bankers will spring up and do a better job in identifying the correct equilibrium prices over time. This orthodox view assumes that there exists a stable equilibrium price vector over time. Unexpected changes and the potential for bankruptcy by private sector international bankers who make the foreign exchange markets are incompatible with this assumption.[8]

Only if private sector bankers who make the spot exchange market can fully anticipate a stable future can the threat of bankruptcies and the ensuing discontinuities that threaten the existence of a general equilibrium solution be avoided. In an uncertain world, there is no reason to believe that private bankers are able to forecast future economic and political events with less persistent errors than Central Bankers and central government. Moreover only the latter, with cooperative effort, can create sufficient liquidity to quell almost any private sector liquidity shifts.

Even if a long-run equilibrium exchange rate could exist, why should profit-maximizing private sector bankers attempt to identify it? If these bankers believe that in the short run the expectational elasticities of others are elastic, there is more money to be made by swimming before the tide. For private sector financial market participants the lure of making short-term capital gains by anticipating even ephemeral fluctuation becomes paramount. As Keynes noted, 'life is not long enough; – human nature desires quick results, there is a peculiar zest in making money quickly. . . . Furthermore, an investor who proposes to ignore near-term market fluctuations needs greater resources for safety'.[9]

If there are private sector foreign exchange market makers who do attempt to maintain the long-run equilibrium exchange rate in the face of short-term disturbances, then these agents will need more liquid assets as reserves than Central Bankers require under a fixed exchange system.[10] Yet it is unlikely that, in the aggregate, private foreign exchange dealers would find it either possible or profitable to hold more reserve assets than Central Banks do.

If a private banker had sufficient reserves to swim against the short-term tide and take a position in defending an exchange rate, and by so doing promote the public interest, such a banker would be considered idiosyncratic or eccentric by the public and his professional colleagues. As Keynes pointed out, the long-term investor, i.e. the one who is not in and out for a quick turn of profit, who can be thought of as the one

> who most promotes the public interest [by providing stability to an otherwise potentially volatile system] . . . will in practice come in for the most criticism, whenever investment funds are managed by committees or boards or banks. For it is in the essence of his behaviour that he should be eccentric, unconventional and rash in the eyes of average opinion [otherwise, he would not be swimming against the tide of public opinion]. If he is successful, that will only confirm the general belief in his rashness; and if in the short run he is unsuccessful, which is most likely, he will not receive much mercy. Worldly wisdom teaches that it is better for reputation to fail conventionally, than to succeed unconventionally.[11]

Private sector international bankers and MNC comptrollers are required each day to demonstrate publicly their ability to augment the 'bottom line' in *each* accounting period. When these bankers are entrusted with the making of foreign exchange markets, they find it easier to achieve success by swimming in the lead of the tide of public opinion rather than trying to buck the short-term currents.[12] Under such circumstances instability rather than stability is likely to be the rule under any but the most stationary of economic environments.

A truly flexible exchange rate will not have any private or Central Bank market-maker to limit short-term exchange rate movements and thereby inspire some confidence in the stability of the current exchange rate. This flexible rate system is the equivalent of operating in a closed economy where forward money contracts for organizing production and trade are banned. The absence of forward contracts (including the labour contract) to organize production is inconsistent with the existence of an entrepreneurial economy. The necessity for entrepreneurs to limit future liabilities by forward money contracts (e.g., payrolls and raw material costs) before undertaking long-duration productive activities has already been noted. Moreover, 'The convenience of holding assets in the same standard as that in which future liabilities may fall due and in a standard in terms of which the future money cost of output is expected to be relatively stable, is obvious'.[13]

If there are orderly markets for foreign exchange, then entrepreneurs can engage in international production and trading transactions. They can store liquidity in either domestic or foreign assets with the full confidence that at any moment they can convert a marketable asset into the standard in which their expected international liabilities are falling due. Without the presence of a foreign exchange market maker who is willing to swim against short-run tides even if it means incurring significant short-run losses on occasion, orderly markets for foreign exchange cannot exist.

The trick of the entrepreneurial money economy game lies in the need to hold assets whose expected liquidity value is relatively stable in terms of the same units as future liabilities and future money costs of production. In a world of uncertainty and unpredictable changes, there can be no store of value over a period of calendar time in an entrepreneurial economy, unless liabilities are fixed in some nominal unit. Whatever the nominal unit of contractual obligation is, it has a unique role to play in an entrepreneur system.[14]

In an entrepreneurial economy, 'the firm is dealing throughout in terms of sums of money. It has no object in the world except to end up with more money than it started with. *That is the essential characteristic of an entrepreneur economy*'.[15] In an open NUMS entrepreneurial economy where multinational firms daily deal in production contracts denominated in different money units, the object of an ongoing business enterprise will be to end up with more money than it started with in terms of those monies in which most of its future liabilities and production costs are expected to be denominated. Thus expected stickiness of exchange rates over the life of the production period is a necessary condition to encourage entrepreneurs to engage in long-term production commitments that cross national boundaries.

The more flexible the exchange rate system, the greater the incentives to make 'more money' through financial currency speculation rather than through real production processes. Flexibility *per se* tends to expand international capital flows relative to production and trading payment flows. It is not therefore surprising to find exchange rate values are normally dominated by capital movements rather than purchasing power parities since the breakdown of the Bretton Woods agreement. If a fixed exchange rate system could be reinstituted before the end of the twentieth century and if the publicly announced rules convinced people that Central Banks are immutably committed to defending the exchange rate, then it would not be surprising to find purchasing power parities become more important in exchange rate determination in the twenty-first century.

NOTES

1. As the United Kingdom did in September 1992 when it is estimated the Bank of England lost almost $15 billion in foreign reserves in a few days before it withdrew from the EMS.
2. Those holding currency A and having a forward contractual commitment in terms of B will at the same time be trying to revise their financial arrangements in order to avoid selling currency A for as long as the exchange rate is weak. Those holding currency B and having a forward contractual commitment in currency B will purchase money of A to resell for B at the commitment date if the transaction costs of the foreign exchange market are less than the difference between the current spot price of A and the normal price, as long as the normal price is expected to prevail at the commitment date.
3. Cf. J.R. Hicks, *Value and Capital*, 2nd ed., Oxford University Press, 1946, p. 255. Also see pp. 205–6, 250–52, 264–6.
4. In September 1992, doubts about the ability of England to remain in the EMS led to huge movements out of the pound sterling which the Bank of England was unable to stop unilaterally until England abandoned the EMS and let the pound float. Later in the year when similar doubts were raised about the French franc, the outflow was stopped by cooperative actions to support the franc by the German Bundesbank and the Bank of France. This cooperative effort by alleviating fears kept the exchange rate between the franc and the Deutsche Mark fixed.
5. J.M. Keynes, *The General Theory*, p. 152.
6. R.J. Shiller, 'Financial Markets and Macroeconomic Fluctuations', mimeo, 1984.
7. See S. Weintraub, 'Flexible Exchange Rates', *Journal of Post Keynesian Economics*, **3**, Summer 1981.
8. The possibility of bankruptcy however creates discontinuities which endanger all existence proofs of general equilibrium. Thus if bankruptcy occurs, no general equilibrium may exist. See K. Arrow and F. Hahn, *General Competitive Analysis*, Holden-Day, San Francisco, 1971, pp. 355–61.
9. J.M. Keynes, *The General Theory*, p. 157.

10.   See S. Weintraub, 'Flexible Exchange Rates', *Journal of Post Keynesian Economics*, **3**, Summer 1981.

11.   J.M. Keynes, *The General Theory of Employment, Interest and Money*, pp. 157–8.

12.   Those who place their beach blankets at the edge of the surf during mid-tide in order to have easy access to the sea must surely know they will have to retreat in front of the advancing tide if they are not to be inundated – even if they know that more than half the time they will remain high and dry!

13.   Keynes, *The General Theory*, pp. 236–7.

14.   Since the money-wage contract is the most ubiquitous domestic forward contract in non-slave societies, the money wage plays a predominant and persistent role in the determination of employment and the domestic market prices of producible goods.

15.   *The Collected Writings of John Maynard Keynes*, XXIX, p. 89. Italics added.

15. Financing the wealth of nations

DOES TRADE ALLEVIATE A LACK OF AGGREGATE DEMAND OR AN AGGREGATE SUPPLY CONSTRAINT?

Adam Smith believed that the wealth of nations was constrained primarily by the extent of the market-place, i.e. by a lack of aggregate demand. By expanding the market through the introduction of trade between regions entrepreneurs could take advantage of economies of scale and therefore enhance the wealth of nations.

For Adam Smith economic growth was primarily demand driven. The expansion of demand was the key to overcoming existing production constraints. The obvious moral of Smith's analysis is that no nation aspiring to be wealthy can be an island unto itself. Implicit in the Smith analogy is that the internal market is already satiated with goods so that domestic market expansion is not possible. The ubiquitous classical law of diminishing returns has no significant role to play in Smith's inquiry into the conditions that limit the wealth of nations at any point of time.

Ricardo introduced the concepts of diminishing returns and comparative advantage to justify trade among nations. Increases in aggregate demand *per se* will not increase the growth of the wealth of nations. The law of comparative advantage claims that the key to economic growth depends on the industrial specialization of each nation to take advantage of its *unique* national environment (e.g., mineral deposits, climate, technical expertise).

The defence of free trade, under the law of comparative advantage, involves the idea of opening the domestic market to a foreign source that has a monopoly hold on lower real costs of production so that these 'real' advantages are not available to domestic entrepreneurs. 'Real' production costs divergences are obvious in agriculture, mining, and similar industries where climate and the geographical distribution of mineral deposits made certain commodities relatively cheaper to produce in one country than another. In the nineteenth century famous wine-cloth example, it was the climate that gave Portugal its absolute and comparative advantage in wine[1] and English technological monopoly of the steam engine that gave it the comparative advantage in weaving cloth.

Implicit in the gains from trade due to the law of comparative advantage argument is the assumption that although foreigners might have monopoly

241

access to climate, minerals, etc., there will be sufficient competition among foreign entrepreneurs to ensure that this real advantage will be passed on to domestic buyers.

During the nineteenth and early twentieth centuries, the law of comparative advantage was reinterpreted into a law of comparative 'real' costs where national differences in real production costs were attributed to disparities in 'real' productivity in the same industries operating with the same technology in different countries. These disparities were due to differing proportions of fully employed labour and capital supplies in each country.

Today, with the existence of multinational firms and the ease with which capital and technology can be transferred internationally, differences in relative 'real' costs of production in industries that are not climate or mineral deposit dependent reflects national differences in money wages (measured in terms of a single currency) and differences in what each society believes are 'civilized' working conditions for its labour force. In a *laissez-faire* international system, industrial trade patterns are likely to reflect differences in (a) nominal wages, (b) occupational safety and other labour expenses, (c) tax laws and (d) political stability among nations.

Mass production industries that can use unskilled or low-skilled workers are likely to locate operations in those countries where the value of human life (including working conditions) is the lowest. Encouraging unfettered competition among these mass production industries in international trade tends to reduce the standard of living of low-skill workers in each nation towards that of workers in the poorest nations having high population growth rates, lowest living standards, and little legislation protecting working conditions.

Growth industries whose technology requires workers with significant skills and educational levels will employ a labour force that still possesses some degree of monopoly power by virtue of the limited availability of such skills globally. These skilled workers have so far been able to insulate themselves from the inevitable forces of international competition that, in the last years of the twentieth century, are driving down the workers' standard of living to the lowest common denominator among trading partners.

This does not deny that Ricardo's law of comparative advantage argument regarding geographical differences in the real cost of production is still relevant for primary industries in which climatic conditions (e.g. agricultural crops) or the extraction of mineral deposits (e.g. crude oil) are important. Even some tertiary industries (e.g. tourism) may follow this law.[2] International production in many of these primary industries is often controlled by the market power of cartels and/or governmental policies that prevent market prices from falling sufficiently to reflect the purely competitive 'real' costs of production. In these real world industries where free trade arguments based on comparative advantage might still be applicable, consumers are likely to pay large monopoly rents as the entrepreneurs are sheltered from international competitive forces.

In earlier decades, high domestic unit labour costs often acted as a spur to encourage managers to search for innovative ways to improve productivity. With the growth of multinationals and the removal of many restrictions on the international trading of manufactured goods, high domestic labour costs now encourage managerial practices such as 'outsourcing', i.e. substituting unskilled cheap labour from poor countries to lower unit production costs and reducing the power of truculent union workers rather than searching for productivity-enhancing technological innovations. The short-run higher cost of searching for technological improvements in the production process is likely to reduce profits compared with the profit result from outsourcing, even if technological improvements, upon which growing living standards depend, are preferable for increasing the wealth of nations. The decline in domestic labour productivity growth in many developed nations since the 1970s can be related partly to this phenomenon of emphasizing the use of cheap foreign labour rather than searching for productivity-enhancing improvements.

If diminishing returns are not a problem, then the only important justification for the desirability of the expansion of international trade will be a lack of domestic aggregate demand. Export-led growth can explain the growth of the wealth of nations in both the Adam Smith sense of exploiting economies of scale and in the sense of John Maynard Keynes who saw the lack of effective demand as the main reason for poverty in the midst of plenty.

FINANCE AND GROWTH

In any economy where production is organized by entrepreneurs, real growth and money supply growth are intimately and inevitably related. Keynes's 1937 finance motive analysis demonstrated that in a closed UMS the national banking system held the key to facilitating the transition from a lower to a higher scale of economic activity.

These same finance and liquidity principles apply to an open economy. In the case of an open UMS, the 'openness' of the system creates no new monetary difficulties, since all contracts are denominated in a single currency unit. In an NUMS system the need to finance contractual commitments in different currency units compounds the liquidity difficulty of entrepreneurs. The international financial system must provide sufficient liquidity to meet the needs of entrepreneurs if trade-driven demand is pursued as the primary course for growth.

FINANCING INTERREGIONAL TRADE DEFICITS

Assume an exogenous increase in A's demand for imports from B at the expense of A's home-produced goods. Assume regions A and B are in a closed UMS system. If residents of A had idle cash balances (reserve money assets), then they could draw these down to finance the ongoing inter-regional trade deficit. There will be a cash outflow from banks in region A to banks in B.

If this interregional trade deficit persists, then the redistribution of bank balances creates a chronic cash outflow for A's banks at the interregional bank clearing house. Some banks in A (and their customers) will be threatened with a lack of liquidity. Assuming no policy actions by the Central Bank or the State to recycle funds from B to A, asset holders in the deficit A region (or their bankers) would have to sell marketable fully liquid (or liquid) assets to the residents in B. The resulting positive net 'foreign' lending of B will reflux money to A's banks so that A's residents will be able to continue their economic activities.

If the interregional trade deficit continues to persist (B's net foreign lending remaining positive), then A will ultimately run out of marketable assets and/or acceptable promises it can pledge to gain replenishment of its bank holdings and reserves. At that time, A will find that it is not able to finance its import deficit.

Even more serious, the illiquidity threat to bankers in A will make them less willing and able to finance the remaining payrolls for working capital production in A's remaining industries. Unemployment and depression will grow in region A until the residents are too poor to afford the imports from B. In the nineteenth century in the American west, the so-called 'ghost town' was often the result of persistent trade deficits between the community and the rest of the American economy.

The law of comparative advantage suggests that trade deficits will end long before the deficit economy becomes a 'ghost town' since the deficit region must have some productive activity for which it has a comparative advantage. The presumed existence of gross substitution and long-run Lerner–Marshall conditions provide the basis for this classical conclusion, despite the empirical evidence.

In the real world where involuntary unemployment is often a normal outcome of unfettered production and trading activities, long-run interregional trade deficits need not be cured by converting the deficit region into a ghost town, or even by impoverishing the region with additional unemployment. Existing trade deficits can continue and be a source of economic growth in the Adam Smith and Maynard Keynes sense if

1. a government fiscal policy deliberately recycles income and money balances from the surplus to the deficit region, or
2. unilateral grants (private or governmental) are provided as a reflux mechanism, or
3. the Central Bank creates additional reserves for the deficit region's bankers.[3]

In the real world these options for regional refluxing of cash flows to stimulate economic growth and prosperity for both regions are possible. If they are not exercised then even before A becomes a ghost town, the economy in B can slide into recession as its exports to A decline. In the real world, if liquidity refluxing and replenishing policies are not used to help finance a persistent interregional payments deficit, then poverty and recession can permeate the economies of both regions.

One way that these liquidity problems can be avoided is if the Central Bank acts to make an orderly market in commercial paper and other debt instruments issued by residents of the deficit region by acting as a lender of last resort. If the Central Bank is perceived to be willing to support local financial asset markets, deficits due to regional imbalances in export–import flows can be readily offset by reverse deficits in net interregional lending. In the short run, support by a Central Bank in spot markets for regional financial assets can prevent any interregional liquidity problems from depressing aggregate economic activity.

Secondly, if both regions A and B are within the same national boundaries, then the central government's taxation and spending policy can act as a transfer instrument to reflux liquidity and support economic activity in both A and B. Government-sponsored interregional transfers can finance at least some, if not all, of the deficit indefinitely. The amount of refluxing finance government will provide depends on the differences in regional tax burdens and the government's propensity to spend in the deficit region compared to the surplus region.

In the early decades after World War II, enlightened governmental fiscal policy continually financed regional payment imbalances. Typically the deficit region was one of high unemployment and poverty relative to the surplus region. An informed policy will reflux liquidity for as long as significant inequalities persist. The result will be to improve the level of employment and income of both regions. As the income of A's residents rise (or is at least prevented from falling), they become richer (or at least not poorer) customers of entrepreneurs in B. This creates additional (or at least supports existing) profit opportunities for B's entrepreneurs. Any resulting growth in B's income results in turn in expanding the markets for the products of A's industries. Properly designed the refluxing and expansion (as needed) of interregional liquidity enhances the well-being of all.

FINANCING TRADE DEFICITS BETWEEN NATIONS IN AN NUMS

There are two important additional complications to financing trade deficits if regions A and B are in different countries using different monies and possessing independent banking systems. First, there is no overriding central governmental authority that can engage in taxing and spending policies to recycle liquidity at an international clearing house to offset the trade deficit-induced losses in liquidity. Second, in the absence of an agreement between the governments of the trading nations that each will be willing to purchase liquid assets from the other at a fixed price without limit (i.e., a UMS), persistent trade deficits may encourage speculative forces that can cause a continuing devaluation in the exchange rate of the deficit nation. Foreigners will then reduce their estimates of the value of A's remaining collateral once the exchange rate starts to decline. This creates a further reduction in liquidity (market value of assets to turnover) for those banks in the deficit region that finance trade between the nations in the NUMS. This potential liquidity crunch can be avoided only if the deficit region's banking system holds sufficient reserve assets in terms of foreign-denominated assets or fully liquid international assets such as gold to squelch any speculation. This fear that trade deficits can induce speculative devaluation forces each nation to hold larger foreign reserves than otherwise.

Neither of these complications is inevitable. Grants and/or loans from the surplus nation's government to the deficit can prevent the latter from suffering from an international liquidity problem. In the 1940s, for example, the United States' Marshall Plan, and the Lend-Lease Agreement with England almost a decade earlier, were planned programmes by the surplus government (the United States) to recycle liquidity to finance the otherwise unfinanceable (under the classical rules of the game) huge trade deficits of England and Western Europe. This liquidity refluxing may have been undertaken for political rather than economic reasons. Nevertheless the results impressively demonstrate that there is no natural or national economic law that prevents authorities in trade surplus areas from redistributing (recycling) purchasing power and assets for as long a period as they wish, with obvious and widespread economic benefits to residents of *both* the surplus and the deficit regions.

Even in the absence of intergovernmental unilateral transfer payments to ease the financing problem of interregional trade imbalances, as long as the banks of each region are members of banking systems cooperating in an international clearing-house system possessing powers to cure excessive reserve holdings,[4] then the rules of the clearing house can be designed to permit creation of sufficient balance sheet reserves to promote expansionary conditions for international trade.[5]

Whenever classical economic theory has dominated the thoughts of Central Bankers, national Central Banks have not been willing to become members of a well-organized international clearing-house system possessing *pro bono* powers to provide sufficient international liquidity to promote global full employment. As a result the ability of any national Central Bank to provide liquidity in the face of an external trade deficit is closely circumscribed by its gold and other foreign reserve asset holdings. The ability of each nation's central banker to accommodate its residents' international liquidity needs is often less than that of regional bankers in a modern national banking system to meet their clients' domestic liquidity demands. In the absence of an international institution able to 'make' a market in international liquidity, each national Central Bank has to hold overwhelmingly large international reserves to assure that they will be able to finance clearing house deficits due to interregional trade imbalances.

In an NUMS system, there is no immutable fully liquid international reserve asset to finance international transactions, unless Central Banks make an agreement to convert some asset such as gold at a fixed rate of exchange. When the nations of the world cooperated by way of an automatic gold standard, gold was the fully liquid-running and reserve asset of international finance. The possession of gold provided liquidity, and liquidity is freedom to buy the time to make whatever economic adjustments are deemed necessary while sustaining a trade deficit.

THE ASSET OF ULTIMATE REDEMPTION IN A UMS

In the present state of the world, any attempt to form an international UMS (for at least some of the more developed nations) requires a cooperative agreement among the Central Banks of these nations. The Central Banks must agree on the 'rules of the game' that permit fixing of exchange rates. They must agree to accept either an existing asset (e.g., gold) as the international asset that ultimately redeems all contractual commitments or an invented asset of ultimate redemption. Each Central Bank must agree in advance to buy this asset of ultimate redemption with domestic currency under pre-specified price rules. This cooperative obligation of the Central Banks ensures that if any nation runs persistent deficits at the international clearing house, the deficit nation's Central Bank can sell (at its own option) some of its asset of ultimate redemption to discharge its clearing obligation while undertaking adjustments to phase out the trade deficit.

The desirable and necessary characteristics of an asset of ultimate redemption include:

i.   it must be convertible into any monetary unit in which any future liabilities are expected to fall due;

ii.   it must be fixed in a unit whose purchasing power in terms of future producible goods is expected to be relatively stable, and

iii.   it must possess relatively low carrying costs so that the cost of holding the asset of ultimate redemption does not, in itself, require the holders to give up significant claims of future real resources merely to meet the current costs of carrying an inventory of this asset;

iv.   it must be well distributed among the participants. There must be a simple preagreed upon method for refluxing this asset if its distribution becomes too unequal.

If an asset with these characteristics can be found, then the game of international trade can continue and flourish, with potential real gains to all who play. As in the famous Parker Brothers board game that children play named 'Monopoly', if any participant runs out of the means of settlement when he lands on a square that requires a payment to another participant, then that player defaults and is forced out of the game. In the Monopoly board game, play can continue for long periods of time because there are preexisting rules for replenishing one's liquid assets, e.g. 'When you pass Go, collect $200'. This arithmetic rule increases aggregate liquidity as economic development in terms of building houses and hotels on properties is being undertaken. Such an inflexible rule of collecting a fixed $200 each time one passes Go does not ensure that a player will never become insolvent and has to default. It only ensures that the medium of contractual settlement (liquidity) in the hands of the players increases as economic development occurs on the board.

This absolute rule for expanding the money supply as players pass 'Go' is not ideal in terms of providing for an elastic currency. The cost of landing on properties is designed to increase geometrically as economic development occurs, while the money supply increases arithmetically as players pass 'Go'. Ultimately the game of 'Monopoly' ends as each player except one overextends 'investments' and then experiences, by landing on someone else's property, an obligation that he or she is unable to finance by liquefying current asset holdings (i.e. when a liquidity shortage occurs). In the game of Monopoly there can be only one winner, but many losers.

In the real world game of 'Enterprise', on the other hand, it is a socially desirable objective that every possible player be a winner and that economic development continue forever. We hope the game of 'Enterprise' never ends. This goal of a perpetual game in which players' activity promotes increasing prosperity for all requires a more flexible rule for costlessly expanding liquidity than the one underlying the board game of 'Monopoly'. In the real world game of international enterprise, trade and finance, the participants need rules for replenishing liquidity through expansion of aggregate liquid holdings, and redistributing such assets from surplus to deficit players whenever a liquidity shortage threatens. Replenishment by expansion is essential with growth, while redistribution is required whenever holdings become so excessively concentrated as to threaten the end of the game. Humans can surely devise financial rules and institutions that continually provide the players with liquidity and thereby perpetuate the game of Enterprise and the resultant prosperity it provides.

To keep the game going and growing, any international UMS requires each Central Bank to relinquish some of its desire to engage in a completely independent domestic monetary and reserve holding policy. This perceived fear of loss of national autonomy due to joining a cooperative international clearing system is largely a bogus anxiety as long as the rules are designed to encourage adjustments by increasing aggregate demand to promote global full employment.

The loss of complete economic self-determination is always a cost of entering any continuous trading relationship. Economic independence can come only with complete economic isolation or with complete dominance of one's trading partners. Once a nation decides to join a community of nations for both political and economic reasons then interdependence and feedback effects among the trading partners are inevitable.

Trepidation over the loss of the current degree of national autonomy has been a fundamental factor preventing rational nations from organizing some international institution to coordinate more efficiently the liquidity-finance methods for generating additional income among trading partners. Nevertheless, it is obvious that a well-designed organization, staffed by a management that comprehends the need for additional liquidity as a prerequisite for generating additional income for entrepreneur economies, could contribute significantly to the more rapid global growth of real income and employment. Until national governments recognize this elemental truth, private sector banking interests will, in a *laissez-faire* environment, develop makeshift institutions (e.g., Eurocurrencies) which provide additional international liquidity for the expansion of world trade. Unfortunately, these private sector expedients often fail at the least propitious time as they are unable to weather a liquidity crunch, especially when cash flow imbalances inevitably develop with global economic expansion. In a crunch, Central Bankers will have to underwrite liabilities of these makeshift arrangements if a global liquidity crisis is to be avoided.

RESOLVING TRADE DEFICITS

Given the current economic environment, there is no international organization that can recycle finance from trade surplus nations to trade deficit nations through a deliberate policy of taxing the former and spending more in the latter. Nor is there any international institution that can readily recycle and/or replenish the running and reserve assets of trading partners. Thus, each nation must jealously guard and husband its international reserves. Each nation enhances its international liquidity position and its creditability by attempting to accumulate additional international liquid assets that may be used to finance a future trade deficit if one should occur. Of course, all nations cannot concurrently build up holdings of international reserve assets unless the global total of such reserves is growing concomitantly.

Export-led growth policies are a sure way of augmenting a nation's liquid international reserves. All nations cannot simultaneously achieve export-led growth. Those countries that successfully augment their international liquidity position by export-led growth will be rewarded with the freedom and time for the nation to adjust to any future international clearing-house deficit problems encountered. These creditor nations have the wherewithal to withstand a future deficit while devising a strategy to deal with it.

On the other hand, those nations who have not built up 'adequate' reserves[6] through export-led growth can face an overwhelming problem if they experience a trade deficit. Those who previously have not experienced sufficient export-led growth to build up adequate reserves will not have the luxury of contemplating alternative schemes for resolving the cash flow deficit.

In an interdependent global economy, nations must all hang together or they will all hang separately. In the next chapter, some guidelines will be developed for creating an international institution where nations can hang together and cooperate to promote the economic well-being of all their citizens.

NOTES

1. The abundance of capital in England could be used to alter climatic conditions via green-houses to make wine. Given Portugal's monopoly on 'cheap' i.e., free warm climatic conditions, however, Portugal had the comparative advantage in wine making compared to cloth making which does not require as much climate controls.
2. Although news reports from Japan indicate that one of the major consumer growth industries in recent years is the *indoor* beach resorts that have been built in large cities. These indoor facilities provide artificial sunlight, machine-made waves, and clean, safe, sandy beaches.
3. In a completely *laissez-faire* system, factors (1), (2) and (3), by definition, will be absent and, in the long run, persistent deficits cannot endure although the cost of ridding the system of the persistent trade deficit is the death of A's economy.
4. See Chapter 16 *infra*.
5. The international payments system proposal developed in Chapter 16 *infra* does not imply that it is the responsibility of the creditor nations to subsidize the improvident and impecunious regions of the world. If the standard of living any region aspires to exceeds its productivity capacity, then a reduction of this level of aspiration is not avoidable unless the 'richer' nations of the world agree that it is in global interests to more equitably redistribute global income. But if the real income of a country is compatible with an equilibrium in its balance of payments while there is a global lack of effective demand, then it is possible to improve the real income by creating real bills to additional international activities.
6. In a world of uncertainty and the absence of international cooperation to resolve deficit problems, no one can be sure what are adequate reserves holdings.

16. Export-led growth and a proposal for an international payments scheme

A consistent theme throughout this book has been that classical logic has assumed away the economic problems that are fundamental to a market-oriented, money-using entrepreneurial economy. These aspects neglected by classical theory are particularly relevant for understanding the international payments questions that plague modern economies involving liquidity, persistent and growing debt obligations, and the importance of stable rather than flexible exchange rates.

An example of the sanguine classical response to those raising these issues is Professor Milton Friedman's response to me in our 'debate' in the literature. Friedman stated: 'A price may be flexible ... yet be relatively stable, because demand and supply are relatively stable *over time*.... [Of course] violent instability of prices in terms of a specific money would greatly reduce the usefulness of that money'.[1] It is nice to know that as long as prices or exchange rates remain relatively stable, or 'sticky' over time, that there is no harm in permitting them to be flexible.

The problem arises when there are volatile movements in exchange rates. Should there be a deliberate policy to intervene in the market to maintain relative stability or should a *laissez-faire* market be permitted to determine the price? Keynes helped design the Bretton Woods Agreement to foster action and intervention to fix exchange rates and control international payment flows. Friedman sold the public on the beneficence of government inaction and the free market determination of exchange rates.

Nowhere is the difference between the Keynes–Post Keynesian view and the view of those who favour *laissez-faire* more evident than when concerned with questions of international capital movements and payments mechanisms; the desirability of a flexible exchange rate system; and the importance of the international debt problem. We shall explore these differences in this chapter.

CAPITAL MOVEMENTS

Little has been said in this volume about exogenous capital movements and their effects on the balance of payments. It is obvious that large speculative and precautionary capital flows can create serious international payments problems for nations whose current accounts would otherwise be roughly in balance. Unfortunately, in a *laissez-faire* system of capital markets there is no way of distinguishing between the movement of funds being used to promote genuine new investment for developing the world's resources and funds that take refuge in one nation's money after another in the continuous search for either speculative gains or hiding from the tax collector or laundering illegal earnings.

The international movement of significant amounts of speculative, precautionary, or even illegal funds can be so disruptive as to impoverish most, if not all, nations who organize production and exchange processes on an entrepreneurial basis. Keynes warned 'Loose funds may sweep round the world disorganizing all steady business. Nothing is more certain than that the movement of capital funds must be regulated'.[2]

One of the more obvious dicta that follow from Keynes's revolutionary vision of the importance of liquidity in open economies is that

> There is no country which can, in the future, safely allow the flight of funds for political reasons or to evade domestic taxation or in anticipation of the owner turning refugee. Equally, there is no country that can safely receive fugitive funds which cannot safely be used for fixed investments and might turn it into a deficiency country against its will and contrary to the real facts.[3]

Even in these days of global electronic communication, governments can monitor and control international capital flows if they have the will and the necessary cooperation of other governments. How to control capital fund movements is a technical matter involving the use of accounting records of each nation's banking system, the details of which need not detain us in this volume. As long as governments have the power to tax and central bankers have the power to audit and regulate their respective domestic banking systems, large international capital flows can be observed and controlled provided there is international cooperation in this matter. As long as currency is issued only in small denominations, the physical bulkiness of moving large sums secretly across borders cannot be a major threat to any capital controls policy.

In recent years, governments' desire to avoid capital controls has made it easy to hide not only legally earned income and wealth from tax collectors but also profits from drug and other illegal transactions from law enforcement agencies. This encourages uncivilized behaviour by self-interested economic agents – and thereby imposes an important, if often neglected, real cost on society.[4] What is more important, flight capital has often drained resources from the relatively poor nations towards the richer ones, resulting in a global inequitable redistribution of income and wealth, thereby increasing the immiseration of a majority of the people on this planet.

Cooperation between nations in detecting, reporting and controlling disruptive capital funds movements among nations can be readily accomplished through the international payments mechanism described in this chapter.[5] Moreover the successful implementation of our proposed international payments scheme assures inelastic expectational elasticities regarding the rates of exchange among various nations' monies. Within a very short span of calendar time after a new payments scheme like the one proposed here is implemented, problems of speculative and precautionary 'hot money' flows, as well as the international movements of income and wealth to avoid the tax collector or law enforcement officers, could quickly shrink to relative insignificance.

Since 1973, when the world embarked on its great classical experiment of floating rates, there have been periodic bouts of great inflation, increasing rates of unemployment, a persistent growth of international debt, and an increasingly inequitable international distribution of global income – as many of the rich nations got richer, while most of the poor nations got poorer on a per capita basis and suffered huge 'flight capital' losses to the wealthy.

Since 1982, one nation – the United States – appears to have been able to take advantage of the existing international payments system to obtain a 'free lunch', that is, to run massive persistent trade deficits. Although residents of most other countries may resent the ability of the United States to use the present system to obtain this 'free lunch', they are hesitant to change a system that is heralded by classical economists as the only mechanism that permits the freedom to choose through free markets. To be against the existing system is considered to be anti-free market. To be for some government constraints on market actions is an unpopular position in these days when planning has failed so spectacularly in Eastern Europe. In the absence of a complete collapse of the international monetary payments system, unless an attractive feasible alternative to the current system is put on the public agenda for discussion and development, the status quo will remain. It is an old adage in political science that 'you can't beat somebody with nobody!'

Any suggestion for reforming the international payments mechanism should build on whatever advantages the current system possesses, while providing rules to prevent any one nation from enjoying a free lunch –

unless a free lunch is available to all. It is possible to provide all with a free lunch if a new payments system has a built-in expansionary bias that encourages nations to operate closer to full employment than the existing system does.

Before developing our suggestion for an international payments scheme which provides this expansionary bias, it is necessary to explain why the existing flexible exchange rate system tends to encourage national policies that impart a slow-growth, deflationary bias.

FLEXIBLE EXCHANGE RATES AND EXPORT-LED GROWTH

The success of Keynes's Revolution in encouraging domestic full employment policies between the end of World War II and the mid-1960s created an endemic problem of wage-cost inflation for most of the developed countries of the world. Without the persistent threat of large-scale unemployment, workers in the developed world, and labour unions in particular, became more aggressive in their wage demands. By the late 1960s many developed nations were forced to pursue 'stop–go' policies that generated small planned recessions to reduce the market power of workers to demand inflationary wage increases. These temporary recessions were followed by expansionary Keynesian policies to move the economy back towards full employment until the next round of inflationary wage demands was tabled by workers.

With the breakdown of the Bretton Woods fixed exchange rate system and the movement towards a *laissez-faire* flexible exchange rate environment, some nations found that by pursuing an export-led growth policy, rather than a Keynesian policy of deliberately stimulating some component of internal effective demand, the nation could move towards higher employment levels without unleashing domestic inflationary wage demands. With export-led growth and flexible exchange rates, any latent inflationary forces can be exported to one's trading partners.

Unfortunately, all countries cannot achieve export-led growth simultaneously. If all nations attempt to adopt this method of fostering economic growth, either all will fail to expand (with the result of global stagnation), or else for each successful nation, there must be one or more other nations that fail to achieve satisfactory growth while experiencing growing international debt and higher inflation rates.[6]

A flexible exchange rate regime guarantees that for every 'successful' economy that pursues a mercantilist trade surplus policy for expansionary purposes, there must be offsetting failure nations plagued with persistent trade deficits and the problem of importing inflation. For every winner on the flexible rate system, there must be one or more losers. In a fixed exchange rate system, on the other hand, export-led growth does not provide a nation with an advantage by permitting more employment and growth with less inflation compared with Keynesian policies that stimulate internally generated demand. A fixed exchange rate regime operating in tandem with intelligent internal demand and incomes management policies will create an environment where all nations simultaneously can be winners and economic growth increases globally without any nation necessarily running into a balance of payments constraint. A fixed exchange rate system combined with intelligent international cooperative Keynesian policies, therefore, holds out the promise that all nations can be winners of a free lunch.

Since the breakdown of the Bretton Woods agreement, it has become increasingly unpopular for a government to use fiscal policy to directly stimulate increases in the domestic components of aggregate demand. Any nation foolish enough to attempt, on its own, to engage in Keynesian fiscal (and/or monetary) policies aimed at deliberately stimulating internal effective demand to lift its industries out of a recessionary or slow growth mode will become enmeshed in a balance of payments problem as imports rise relative to exports. Simultaneously, any resulting stronger domestic markets that significantly reduce unemployment can encourage inflationary wage and profit demands by domestic workers and firms.

In the 1980s, those nations that the economic and financial media have proclaimed 'successful', or even 'economic miracles', have won such appellations because they have been able to expand output and employment through export-led growth. This policy enhances their foreign reserve holdings and international creditor status without causing significant domestic inflation. Because of the requirements of double-entry book-keeping successful export-led growth economies force trade deficits, loss of international reserves, and increased international indebtedness on their trading partners. These export-led growth policies pursued by successful nations are nothing more than a late twentieth century form of 'beggar thy [trading] neighbour' activities.

In a world operated according to classical axioms export-led growth should be no more desirable in terms of generating employment without inflation than internally generated demand growth. Despite Adam Smith's claim that increasing exports was the initiating force underlying the growth of the wealth of nations, classical economic theory assumes that the economy will track the long-run full employment growth trend no matter what the primary source of demand growth.

The facts of the 1980s demonstrate that miraculously successful economies tend to pursue export-led growth rather than domestic demand-induced expansion. During the decade of the eighties, nations such as West Germany, Japan, Taiwan, Singapore, Hong Kong, and South Korea were not only applauded for their economic miracles by leading Monetarist and classical Keynesian scholars, but they were proclaimed to be shining examples of the proper functioning of a classical economy operating free from oppressive government intervention. Yet there is nothing in modern classical theory that justifies relying primarily on export-led growth.

WHY THE PREFERENCE FOR EXPORT-LED GROWTH?

In a flexible exchange rate world, governments have an incentive to pursue export-led growth policies rather than stimulating internal components of aggregate demand if growth without inflation is an objective. To demonstrate the existence of this incentive, let us, for simplicity, assume labour is the only variable factor of production. The money wage (w) divided by the marginal product of labour (MPL) is equal to the marginal cost of domestic industry (MC). In a purely competitive economy

$$[w/MPL] = MC = P_d \qquad (16.1a)$$

where P_d is the price level associated with domestic output. If there is a given degree of monopoly (M) at any level of employment, where $0 < M < 1$, then $P_d > MC$, and

$$(w/MPL) = MC = (P_d)(g) \qquad (16.1b)$$

or

$$P_d = w/[(MPL)(g)] \qquad (16.1c)$$

where g equals one minus the average degree of monopoly in the system.[7] In a purely competitive system where $M = 0$, $g = 1$, equation (16.1b) is reduced to the purely competitive case of equation (16.1a).

Equation (16.1b) can be rewritten as:

$$(w/P_d) = (MPL)(g). \qquad (16.2)$$

Classical economists claim that the aggregate marginal productivity of labour curve is the demand curve for labour when $g = 1$. Chapter 11 has

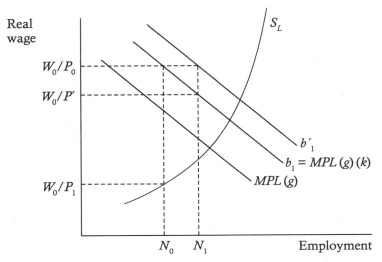

Figure 16.1   Diminishing returns marginal product of labour and labour supply

explained the Post Keynesian position that the marginal productivity of labour curve (multiplied by any value for the scalar *g*) can be envisioned as a real wage-determining curve, or in Patinkin's terms a 'market equilibrium curve', rather than a demand curve for labour.[8] Under either interpretation, the real wage at each level of employment is related to the marginal product of labour schedule.[9]

A downward-sloping MPL curve merely means that industry 'is subject to decreasing returns ... so that the marginal product ... necessarily diminishes as employment increases'.[10] Figure 16.1 presents a downward-sloping marginal product curve (multiplied by *g*) for domestic output. If production occurs instead under constant returns, then the marginal product and the *MPL* (*g*) curves will be horizontal (as shown in Figure 16.2).

Labour's real wage is determined by the money wage divided by the price level (P^c) of the consumer products (wage goods) bought by labour. The equation for the real wage, whether the economy is open or closed, is

$$w_r = (w/P^c) \qquad\qquad (16.3)$$

where w_r is the real wage. As a first approximation, one may assume that the price level of domestically produced consumer goods (P_d^c) is equal to (P_d), the price level associated with all the domestically produced goods (e.g., the

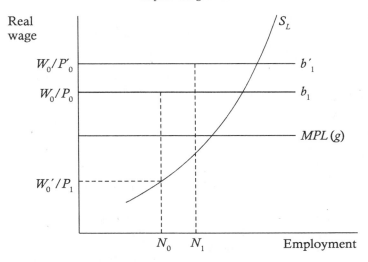

Figure 16.2   *Constant returns marginal product of labour and labour supply*

GDP price deflator).[11] For a *closed economy*, equation (16.3) can be written as

$$w_r = (w/P^c) = (w/P_d^c) = (w/P_d) = (MPL)(g).$$ (16.4)

In an *open economy* the price level associated with domestic consumption expenditures is explained in Chapter 12 as

$$P^c = (P_d^c)(1 - \phi) + (P_m^c)(\phi)$$ (16.5)

where P_m^c is the price of consumer good imports in terms of domestic currency and ϕ is the proportion of aggregate domestic consumption expenditures spent on imports. Assuming $P_d^c = P_d$, substituting equation (16.5) into equation (16.3), then the real wage in an open economy is

$$w_r = w/P^c = \frac{w}{[(P_d)(1 - \phi) + (P_m^c)(\phi)]}$$ (16.6)

$$= \frac{w}{(P_d)(1/k)}$$ (16.7)

where

$$(1/k) = [(1 - \phi) + (P_m^c/P_d)(\phi)].$$ (16.8)

The price of imported goods is necessarily lower than the price of the competitive domestic goods that they replace. P_m^c/P_d is necessarily less than one. From equation (16.8) it therefore follows that $1/k$ must be less than unity.

Substituting the equation (16.1c) for P_d in equation (16.7) and rearranging terms gives the real wage rate in an open economy as

$$w_r = MPL(g)(k) \qquad\qquad (16.9)$$

where $k > 1$.

In Figure 11.1, S_L is the aggregate supply curve of labour while the real wage-determining equation (16.4) in a closed economy is drawn as the $MPL(g)$. Comparing equation (16.4) with equation (16.9) indicates that the real wage-determining curve in an open economy (b_1 in Figure 16.1) will be some multiple (k) of $(MPL)(g)$. This b_1 curve lies above the $MPL(g)$ curve as the price level of imported goods is lower than the price level of domestic goods at any employment level and $\phi > 0$. Moreover the more open the economy, (the greater ϕ), the greater the vertical distance between $MPL(g)$ and $MPL(g)(k)$. If the exchange rate appreciates, then imported products are cheaper. The value of k will be increased and the real wage-determining curve will shift upwards to b_1'.

In Figure 16.1, at N_0, the real wage W_0/P_0 exceeds the minimum real wage W_0/P_1 required to bring N_0 workers[12] into the labour market. Given the existence of involuntary unemployment in the system, if the government (or the Central Bank) initiates a policy of stimulating domestic spending to increase employment to N_1 in Figure 16.1, then the real wage would fall to W_0/P_0' as the average price level rose (inflation) due to the law of diminishing returns. As drawn in Figure 16.1, N_1 is still a less than full employment level, but the economy is experiencing rising prices with every increase in employment because of diminishing returns. If, moreover, workers insist on cost of living adjustments (COLAs) as prices rise, then the resulting money-wage inflation will exacerbate the inflationary problem induced by domestic demand expansion.

If the government were to wait for export-led growth (due to an initiating expansion in one's trading partner's economy), then the real wage-determining curve would shift upwards from b_1 to b_1' as the improved export–import relationship of the domestic economy leads to an appreciation of the exchange rate.[13] In Figure 16.1, the real wage remains at w_0/P_0 (by construction) as employment rises from N_0 to N_1.

Even though domestic output prices rise due to diminishing returns, the domestic consumer does not experience inflation in the price level of the market basket of goods purchased as the cost of living is modified by lower import prices. There would be less pressure for higher money wages for COLAs as the domestic economy expands. The appreciating exchange rate improves the competition of foreign firms with domestic producers while making less expensive foreign workers 'outsourcing' available to multinationals currently operating domestic factories. This weakens workers' bargaining power for higher money wages. Simultaneously it strengthens any anti-labour resolve of the government and consumers to resist giving into impenitent strikers' demands for higher money wages. Finally, previously employed workers (N_0) do not experience decline in real wages as additional workers are employed. Hence they are not likely to become restive.

Export-led growth can, therefore, lead to expansion without inducing any domestic inflationary pressures that might otherwise arise if a domestic component of demand is exogenously increased. Export-led growth weakens labour unions' ability (and the rank and file's desire) to raise money wages.[14] Internally stimulated growth in aggregate demand can result in expansion with inflation due initially to diminishing returns. The resulting lower real wages of the previously employed may then induce wage-price inflation as workers vainly attempt to reestablish the original real wage through COLAs.[15]

In a flexible exchange rate system, therefore export-led growth can permit policy makers in any one nation to achieve higher employment without inflation provided some trading partner is willing and able to take on the task of acting as an initial engine of economic growth. In a world of fixed exchange rates, on the other hand, there can be no exchange appreciation to offset any domestic inflationary tendencies. There would be no significant difference in the rate of inflation experienced in the nation whether growth was due to being export led or whether growth was driven by some increase in an internal component of domestic demand.[16] In Figure 16.1 under a fixed exchange rate regime, employment expands only by a movement down the b_1 curve.

If domestic industries operate under constant returns rather than diminishing returns, the result is not significantly different. If, in a flexible exchange rate system, the economy's *MPL* curve is horizontal as in Figure 16.2, then export-led growth that results in exchange rate appreciation leads to higher real wages and a falling price level for the consumer's market basket as long as money wages unchanged. For example, as the economy moves from N_0 to N_1 under export-led growth in Figure 16.2, the real wage would rise from w_0/P_0 to w_0/P_0'. In this constant returns case, export-led growth leads to simultaneous rising real wages, rising employment, and falling prices.[17] This situation may resemble West Germany's experience between 1985 and 1989.

Of course, this delightful situation of rising employment, real wages and little or no inflation that the export-led growth nation enjoys does not imply that global inflation and unemployment problems have been resolved. These problems are, as in the card game of Old Maid, merely being passed on to other players in the international economy. Inflationary tendencies (and unemployment if the authorities undertake orthodox policies to stop inflation) will appear in trading partners whose rising trade deficits lead to depreciating exchange rates. If the deficit nation tries to maintain employment while workers demand real wage protection either by cost-of-living adjustments, or catch-up negotiations in new labour contracts, then inflationary tendencies will be exacerbated.

From a global perspective, the existence of flexible exchange rates encourages nations to resolve problems of unemployment and inflation by pushing them off, in an uncivilized way, to their trading partners. If all nations act this way, then the result may be a global recession and stagnation (or even global stagflation). If one nation acts as the engine of growth, and continues to expand – even as it runs a balance of payment deficit – those trading partners who pursue export-led growth will experience an economic miracle that they may attribute to their virtuous ways and even to their superior Central Bank.

Under a fixed exchange rate system, on the other hand, there is no advantage to pursuing export-led expansion as a means of exporting inflation, while hoping for a trading partner to act as an engine of growth. A fixed exchange rate system focuses the public's eye and the minds of policy makers on ways to avoid painful global recessions and stagnation. No longer will the pursuit of constraining domestic components of demand to limit wage increases be seen as a virtue that gains the economic miracle of obtaining a noninflationary environment while awaiting others to act as an engine of growth. The trading partner that drives for higher real output without planned recessions will be seen as the virtuous member of the global community. Planned recessions and unemployment due to tight monetary and fiscal policies will be clearly revealed as an economic Emperor without clothes. Then, positive policies for expanding domestic demand and using an incomes policy to fight inflation can again be raised for discussion in public policy forums.

THE FACTS VS. THE THEORY OF FLEXIBLE EXCHANGE RATES

Since the breakdown of Bretton Woods, it has been popular to assume that freely fluctuating exchange rates in a *laissez-faire* market system are efficient. Every well-trained classical economist whose work is logically consistent with a Walrasian, Arrow–Debreu microfoundation 'knows' that the beneficial effects of a freely flexible exchange rate include:

1. the impossibility of any one country running a persistent balance of payments deficit;
2. permitting each nation to pursue monetary and fiscal policies for full employment without inflation independent of what is occurring in its trading partners;[18] and
3. encouraging the flow of capital from the rich creditor (i.e. developed) nations to the poor debtor (i.e. less-developed) nations. This theoretical capital flow is the result of a classical belief in the universality of the 'law of variable proportions' that determines the real return to the factors of production.[19] The effect of this classical international capital flow is to encourage more rapid development of the LDCs and, in the long run, a more equitable distribution of income and wealth. Moreover, it is often implied that investment projects financed by this free market capital flow from rich to poor nations will generate sufficient sales and foreign earnings for the LDCs to repay the capital loans, i.e. international capital flows are temporary[20] *and self-liquidating.*

The facts since the breakup of Bretton Woods are not consistent with these classical Panglossian promises. First, since the oil shock of 1973 and continuing through the 1980s, many Latin American nations have continued to run persistent deficits in their balance of payments. Second, since the late 1970s the major trading nations of the developed world have been under increasing pressure for international coordination of their monetary and fiscal policies. For example in September 1987 the United States and Germany publicly clashed over incompatible monetary policies. The great October 1987 crash of world financial markets followed. This experience has reinforced the idea among the Central Bankers of the developed nations that if they don't all hang together they will all hang separately. Third, flight capital has drained resources from the relatively poor nations towards the richer ones, resulting in a global inequitable redistribution of income and wealth, thereby increasing poverty in the LDCs.

REFORMING THE INTERNATIONAL PAYMENTS SYSTEM

The current international payments system does not serve the emerging global economy well. *The Financial Times* and *The Economist*, both previously strong advocates of the existing floating rate system, have acknowledged that the system is a failure and was sold to the public and the politicians under false advertising claims.[21] Can we do better?

Too often economic discussions on the requirements for a good international payments system have been limited to the question of the advantages and disadvantages of fixed versus flexible exchange rates. Although this issue is very important, the facts of experience plus Keynes's revolutionary analysis indicate that more is required than simply choosing between fixed and flexible exchange rates if a mechanism is to be adopted that resolves payments imbalances while simultaneously promoting full employment economic growth and a long-run stable international standard of value.

The post-war world has conducted several experiments with the international payments system. For a quarter of a century after the war, there was a fixed, but adjustable, exchange rate system (1947–72) set up under the Bretton Woods Agreement. Since 1973 we have operated under a flexible exchange rate system.

The period from 1947 to 1973 was 'an era of unprecedented sustained economic growth in both developed and developing countries'.[22] The growth in real Gross Domestic Product per capita in OECD nations escalated to 2.6 times that of the interwar period (4.9 per cent annually compared to 1.9 per cent). This real growth rate was almost double the previous *peak* growth rate exhibited by the industrializing nations during the period from 1820 to 1914, while the growth in productivity during the Bretton Woods era was more than triple that of 1820–1914.[23]

This unprecedented prosperity was transmitted to developing nations through world trade, aid, and foreign investment. The real per capita GNP growth rate for *all* developing nations rose to 3.3 per cent, more than triple the growth experienced by the early industrializing nations between 1820 and 1914. Real total GNP growth of developing nations was almost the same as in developed countries.[24]

Free economies experienced unprecedented real economic growth during the Bretton Woods epoch. Also there was 'a much better overall record of price level stability' *vis-à-vis* either the post-1973 period or the previous era of fixed exchange rates under the gold standard (1879–1914).[25]

The dismal post-1973 experience of recurrent unemployment and inflationary crises, slow growth in OECD countries, and debt-burdened growth and/or stagnation (and even falling real GNP per capita) in developing countries contrasts sharply with the experience during the Bretton Woods period.

The free world's economic performance in terms of both real growth *and* price level stability during the Bretton Woods period is unprecedented.

Even the economic record during the earlier gold standard rate period was better than the experience since the 1973 adoption of flexible rates.

What can be surmised from these facts? First, almost two hundred years of experience support the thesis that a fixed exchange rate system provides an international environment that is more compatible with greater real economic growth and price stability compared to what is experienced under a flexible exchange rate regime. Second, the significantly superior performance of the free world's economies during the Bretton Woods period compared to the earlier gold standard period suggests that there must have been an additional condition besides exchange rate fixity that contributed to the unprecedented growth during the 1947–73 period. That additional condition was discussed by Keynes in developing his proposals for an international payments scheme.

To reduce entrepreneurial uncertainties and the possibility of massive currency misalignments Keynes recommended the adoption of a fixed, but adjustable, exchange rate system. What is more important, Keynes argued that the 'main cause of failure' of any traditional payments system – whether based on fixed or flexible rates – was its inability to foster continuous global economic expansion when persistent current account imbalances among trading partners occurred. This failure, Keynes wrote,

> can be traced to a single characteristic. I ask close attention to this, because I shall argue that this provides a clue to the nature of any alternative which is to be successful.
>
> It is characteristic of a freely convertible international standard that it throws the main burden of adjustment on the country which is the *debtor* position on the international balance of payments – that is, on the country which is (in this context) by hypothesis the *weaker* and above all the *smaller* in comparison with the other side of the scales which (for this purpose) is the rest of the world.[26]

Keynes concluded that an essential improvement in designing an international payments system requires transferring 'the *onus* of adjustment from the debtor to the creditor position', and aiming 'at the substitution of an expansionist, in place of a contractionist, pressure on world trade'.[27] To achieve a golden era of economic development requires combining a fixed, but adjustable, rate system with a mechanism for requiring the surplus trading nation(s) to initiate most of the effort necessary to adjust a payments imbalance, without removing all discipline from the deficit trading partner.

During the first half of the Bretton Woods era, almost accidentally, the world's major creditor nation, the United States, accepted responsibility for curing deficits in the current account balance via the Marshall Plan and other forms of foreign and military aid. It was the failure of the Bretton

Woods system after the 1950s to perpetuate this creditor nation action that led to its ultimate abandonment and the end to the world's golden era of economic development.

After World War II, the economic recovery of the free capitalist world required the European nations to run huge import surpluses to feed their populations and rebuild their stock of capital. Under the rules of free market economies, this implied that the United States would have to provide enormous credits to finance the required export surplus to Europe. The resulting European indebtedness would be so burdensome that it was unlikely that, even in the long run, the European nations could ever service this debt. Moreover, United States policy makers were mindful that reparation payments after World War I were financed by United States private sector investors lending Germany foreign exchange. Germany never repaid these loans. Given this history and existing circumstances it was obvious that private lending facilities could not be expected to provide the credits necessary for European recovery.

Under the fixed exchange rate system of Bretton Woods, the only mechanism available for redressing this potentially lopsided global import–export trade flow was for the debtors to accept the main burden of adjustment by 'tightening their belt' and by reducing demand for imports to what they could earn from exports.[28] The result would have been to depress further the standard of living of Western Europeans. This could have induced political revolutions in most of Western Europe.

Instead the United States produced the Marshall Plan and other foreign grants and aid programmes. The Marshall Plan provided $5 billion in aid in 18 months and a total of $13 billion in four years. (In 1991 dollars this is equivalent to over $100 billion.)

Marshall Plan transfers represented approximately 2 per cent per annum of the GNP of the United States.[29] Yet no United States resident felt deprived of goods and services. Real GNP per capita in the United States during the first year of the Marshall Plan was still 25 per cent larger than in the last peacetime year of 1940. Per capita GNP continued to grow throughout the 1950s.[30] There was no real sacrifice associated with this generous gift of exports. These exports were produced by employing what otherwise would have been idle resources. For the first time in its history, the United States did not suffer from a severe recession immediately after the cessation of a major war. The world experienced an economic 'free lunch' as both the potential debtors and the creditor nation gained from this 'give away'.

By 1958, although the United States still had a goods and services export surplus of over $5 billion, United States governmental and military transfers exceeded $6 billion, while there was a net private capital outflow of $1.6 billion.[31] The post-war United States surplus position on current accounts was at an end. As the United States current account swung into deficit, other nations began to experience current account surpluses. These nations converted a portion of their dollar current account surpluses into gold. In 1958, the United States lost over $2 billion in gold reserves. These trends accelerated in the 1960s, partly as a result of increased United States military and financial aid responses to the construction of the Berlin Wall in 1961 and later because of the United States' increasing involvement in Vietnam. At the same time, a rebuilt Europe and Japan became important producers of exports so that the rest of the world became less dependent on the United States exports.

The United States maintained a positive merchandise trade balance until the first oil price shock in 1973. More than offsetting this trade surplus during most of the 1960s were foreign and military unilateral transfers plus net capital outflows. The Bretton Woods system had no way of automatically forcing the emerging current account surplus nations to step into the adjustment role that the United States had been playing since 1947. Instead they continued to convert some portion of their annual dollar surpluses into calls on United States gold reserves. The seeds of the destruction of the Bretton Woods system and the golden age of economic development were sown as surplus nations drained gold reserves from the United States.

When the United States closed the gold window and unilaterally withdrew from Bretton Woods, the last vestige of Keynes's enlightened international monetary approach was lost – apparently without regret or regard as to how well it served the global economy.

A NEW INTERNATIONAL PAYMENTS SYSTEM

The following proposal for an international payments system builds on Keynes's proposals that were the successful basis for producing the expansionist pressure on world trade and development during the 1947–73 period.

In an interdependent world economy, some degree of economic co-operation among trading partners is necessary. This Post Keynesian proposal does not require the establishment of a Supranational Central Bank to create a Unionized Monetary System (UMS) – even if this is believed desirable on other grounds. Keynes's original 'bancor' plan for the post-World War II environment was developed around the idea of a single Supranational Bank. At this stage in the evolution of world politics, a global UMS with a Supranational Central Bank is not feasible.[32] This Post

Keynesian suggestion is a more modest one aimed at obtaining an international agreement that does not require surrendering national control of local banking systems and fiscal policies.

Fifty years ago, Keynes provided a clear outline of what is needed when he wrote:

> We need an instrument of international currency having general acceptability between nations. . . . We need an orderly and agreed upon method of determining the relative exchange values of national currency units. . . . We need a quantum of international currency . . . [which] is governed by the actual current [liquidity] requirements of world commerce, and is capable of deliberate expansion. . . . We need a method by which the surplus credit balances arising from international trade, which the recipient does not wish to employ can be set to work . . . without detriment to the liquidity of these balances.[33]

What is required is a *closed*, double-entry bookkeeping clearing institution to keep the payments 'score' among the various trading regions plus some mutually agreed upon rules to create and reflux liquidity while maintaining the international purchasing power of the international currency. The eight provisions of the clearing system suggested in this section meet the criteria laid down by Keynes. The rules of this Post Keynesian proposed system are designed (1) to prevent a lack of global effective demand[34] due to any nation(s) either holding excessive idle reserves or draining reserves from the system, (2) to provide an automatic mechanism for placing a major burden of payments adjustments on the surplus nations, (3) to provide each nation with the ability to monitor and, if desired, to control movements of flight capital,[35] and finally (4) to expand the quantity of the liquid asset of ultimate international redemption as global capacity warrants.

Some elements of such a clearing system would include:

1. The unit of account and ultimate reserve asset for international liquidity is the International Money Clearing Unit (IMCU). All IMCUs are held *only* by Central Banks, not by the public.

2. Each nation's or UMS's Central Bank is committed to guarantee one way convertibility from IMCU deposits at the clearing union to its domestic money. Each Central Bank will set its own rules regarding making available foreign monies (through IMCU clearing transactions) to its own bankers and private sector residents.[36]

   Since Central Banks agree to sell their own liabilities (one-way convertibility) against the IMCU only to other Central Bankers and the International Clearing Agency while they simultaneously hold only IMCUs as liquid reserve assets for international financial transactions, there can be no draining of reserves from the system. Ultimately, all major private international transactions clear between Central Banks' accounts in the books of the international clearing institution.

3. The exchange rate between the domestic currency and the IMCU is set *initially* by each nation – just as it would be if one instituted an international gold standard. Since enterprises that are already engaged in trade have international contractual commitments that would span the change-over interval, then, as a practical matter, one would expect that the existing exchange rate structure (with perhaps minor modifications) would provide the basis for initial rate setting.

    Provisions Nos. 7 and 8 *infra* indicate when and how this nominal exchange rate between the national currency and the IMCU would be changed in the future.

4. Contracts between private individuals will continue to be denominated into whatever domestic currency is permitted by local laws and agreed upon by the contracting parties. Contracts to be settled in terms of a foreign currency will therefore require some announced commitment from the Central Bank (through private sector bankers) of the availability of foreign funds to meet such private contractual obligations.

5. An overdraft system to make available short-term unused creditor balances at the clearing house to finance the productive international transactions of others who need short-term credit. The terms will be determined by the *pro bono* clearing managers.

6. A trigger mechanism to encourage a creditor nation to spend what is deemed (in advance) by agreement of the international community to be *'excessive' credit balances accumulated by running current account surpluses.* These excessive credits can be spent in three ways: (1) on the products of any other member of the clearing union, (2) on new direct foreign investment projects, and/or (3) to provide unilateral transfers (foreign aid) to deficit members. Spending on imports forces the surplus nation to make the adjustment directly through the balance on goods and services. Spending by way of unilateral transfers permits adjustment directly by the current account balance, while that on direct foreign investment provides adjustment by the capital accounts (without setting up a contractual debt that will *require* reverse current account flows in the future).

    Proviso No. 6 provides the surplus country with considerable discretion in deciding how to accept the 'onus' of adjustment in the way it believes is in its residents' best interests. It does not permit the surplus nation to shift the burden to the deficit nation(s) through contractual requirements for debt service charges independent of what the deficit nation can afford.[37] The important thing is to make sure that continual oversaving[38] by surplus nations cannot unleash depressionary forces and/or a building up of international debts so encumbering as to impoverish the global economy of the twenty-first century.

In the unlikely event that the surplus nation does not spend or give away these credits within a specified time, then the clearing agency would confiscate (and redistribute to debtor members) the portion of credits deemed excessive.[39] This last resort confiscatory action by the managers of the clearing agency would make a payments adjustment through unilateral transfer payments in the current accounts.

Under either a fixed or a flexible rate system, nations may experience persistent trade deficits merely because trading partners are not living up to their means – that is because other nations are continually hoarding a portion of their foreign export earnings (plus net unilateral transfers). By so doing, these oversavers are creating a lack of global effective demand. Under provision No. 6, deficit countries would no longer have to deflate their real economy merely to adjust payment imbalances because others are oversaving. Instead, the system would seek to remedy the payment deficit by increasing opportunities for deficit nations to sell abroad.

7. A system to stabilize the long-term purchasing power of the IMCU (in terms of each member nation's domestically produced market basket of goods) can be developed. This requires a system of fixed exchange rates between the local currency and the IMCU that changes only to reflect permanent increases in efficiency wages.[40] This assures each Central Bank that its holdings of IMCUs as the nation's foreign reserves will never lose purchasing power in terms of foreign-produced goods, even if a foreign government permits wage-price inflation to occur within its borders. The rate between the local currency and the IMCU would change with inflation in the local money price of the domestic commodity basket.

If increases in productivity lead to declining nominal production costs, then the nation with this decline in efficiency wages (say of 5 per cent) would have the option of choosing either (a) to permit the IMCU to buy (up to 5 per cent) less units of domestic currency, thereby capturing all (or most of) the gains from productivity for its residents while maintaining the purchasing power of the IMCU, or (b) to keep the nominal exchange rate constant. In the latter case, the gain in productivity is shared with all trading partners. In exchange, the export industries in this productive nation will receive an increased relative share of the world market.

By altering the exchange rate between local monies and the IMCU to offset the rate of domestic inflation, the IMCU's purchasing power is stabilized. By restricting use of IMCUs to Central Banks, private speculation regarding IMCUs as a hedge against inflation is avoided. Each nation's rate of inflation of the goods and services it produces is determined solely by (a) the local government's policy towards the level of domestic money wages and profit margins *vis-à-vis* productivity gains, i.e., the nation's efficiency wage. Each nation is therefore free to experiment with policies for stabilizing its efficiency wage to prevent inflation. Whether the nation is successful or not, the IMCU will never lose its international purchasing power. Moreover, the IMCU has the promise of gaining in purchasing power over time, if productivity grows more rapidly than money wages and each nation is willing to share any reduction in real production costs with its trading partners.

Provision No. 7 produces a system designed to maintain the relative efficiency wage parities amongst nations. In such a system, the adjustability of nominal exchange rates will be primarily (but not always, see provision No. 8) to offset changes in efficiency wages among trading partners. A beneficial effect that follows from this proviso is that it eliminates the possibility of a specific industry in any nation being put at a competitive disadvantage (or securing a competitive advantage) against foreign producers solely because the nominal exchange rate was changed independently of changes in efficiency wages and the real costs of production in each nation.

Nominal exchange rate variability will no longer create the problem of a loss of competitiveness due solely to the overvaluing of a currency as, for example, experienced by the industries in the American 'rust belt' during the period 1982–85. Even if temporary, currency appreciation can have significant permanent real costs, e.g. industries may abandon markets and the resulting idle existing plant and equipment may be cast aside as too costly to maintain.

Proviso No. 7 also prevents any nation from engaging in a beggar-thy-neighbour, export-thy-unemployment policy by pursuing a real exchange rate devaluation that does not reflect changes in efficiency wages. Once the initial exchange rates are chosen and relative efficiency wages are locked in, reductions in real production costs that are associated with a relative decline in efficiency wages are the main factor (with the exception of provision No. 8) justifying an adjustment in the real exchange rate.

Although provision No. 6 prevents any country from piling up persistent excessive surpluses this does not mean that it is impossible for one or more nations to run persistent deficits. Proposal No. 8 *infra* provides a programme for addressing the problem of persistent export–import deficits in any one nation.

8. If a country is at *full employment* and still has a tendency towards persistent international deficits on its current account, then this is *prima facie* evidence that it does not possess the productive capacity to maintain its current standard of living. If the deficit nation is a poor one, then surely there is a case for the richer nations who are in surplus to transfer some of their excess credit balances to support the poor nation.[41] If it is a relatively rich country, then the deficit nation must alter its standard of living by reducing the relative terms of trade with major trading partners. Rules, agreed upon in advance, would require the trade deficit rich nation to devalue its exchange rate by stipulated increments per period until evidence becomes available to indicate that the export–import imbalance is eliminated without unleashing significant recessionary forces.[42]

    If, on the other hand, the payment deficit persists despite a continuous positive balance of trade in goods and services, then there is evidence that the deficit nation might be carrying too heavy an international debt service obligation. The *pro bono* officials of the clearing union should bring the debtor and creditors into negotiations to reduce annual debt service payments by (1) lengthening the payments period, (2) reducing the interest charges, and/or (3) debt forgiveness.[43]

    If any government objects to the idea that the IMCU provisions provide governments with the ability to limit the free movement of 'capital' funds, then this nation is free to join other nations of similar attitude in forming a regional currency union (UMS) and thereby assuring a free flow of funds among the residents of the currency union.

ALTERNATIVE PROPOSALS

Two other alternative proposals for an international payments system have appeared in the recent literature: Williamson's target zone fixed real rate system (with additional detail found in Williamson and Miller's paper) and McKinnon's fixed nominal PPP exchange rate system.[44]

Both Williamson and McKinnon accept the argument that the existing flexible rate system is fundamentally flawed. McKinnon notes the tremendous 'dissatisfaction with wildly fluctuating relative currency values, euphemistically called "floating" or "flexible" exchange rates'.[45] Williamson argues that the post-Bretton Woods flexible exchange rate system 'has proved unsatisfactory' for two major reasons. First, it has led to 'recurring, and at times massive, currency misalignments . . . [where a] misalignment is defined as a persistent deviation of the real exchange rate from the "fundamental equilibrium exchange rate" [or FEER], the level that can be expected in the medium term to reconcile internal and external balance'.[46] Second, according to Williamson, the flexible rate system fails to pressure nations 'to coordinate their economic policies'.[47]

Williamson recommends a 'target zone system' where 'a limited number of major countries negotiate a set of mutually consistent targets' for fixing real exchange rates and rates of growth in nominal domestic demand for each country. This will maintain internal and external balance in the 'medium term'. Internal balance is described as 'the lowest unemployment rate consistent with the control of inflation', without specifying, in his 1987 paper, what inflation rate and what unemployment rate is acceptable under this internal equilibrium concept. In Williamson and Miller, internal balance is associated with an unspecified 'acceptably low rate of inflation and with unemployment at the NAIRU' (nonaccelerating inflation rate of unemployment). If the economy is in internal balance, the target rate of growth of nominal income is the inflation rate 'plus the growth of potential output'.[48]

External balance is defined as 'a current account balance that is sustainable and appropriate in light of thrift and productivity'.[49] Exchange rates would be permitted to fluctuate within a broad zone of plus or minus 10 per cent around the target FEER. The zone is defined as a 'soft buffer' where 'a country would not have an absolute obligation to prevent rates from straying outside the zone under strong market pressures'.[50]

McKinnon recommends a system where the major Central Banks would announce targeted fixed nominal exchange rates (within a narrow band) 'set at approximately sustainable purchasing power parities'. Once set, McKinnon claims that all that would be necessary would be for the major central banks to 'adjust their domestic money supplies to maintain these nominal exchange rate parities and, concomitantly, maintain the same rates of domestic price inflation in internationally tradeable goods'.[51]

WILLIAMSON'S 'SOCIAL FUNCTIONS' AND A BUFFER ZONE

Despite the flaws in the current flexible rate system, Williamson claims that flexible exchange rates have four important 'social functions' that are not possessed by any fixed rate system. These alleged advantages are (a) a *facilitating payments adjustments function* whenever export–import imbalances occur; (b) *a speculative pressures absorbing function* which prevents 'every change in speculative sentiment to lead to a change in international reserves and/or interest rates' which might harm the economy; (c) *a liberating monetary policy function* which permits nations to pursue different interest rate targets and (d) *a reconciling function* which harmonizes inflation rates among nations. Williamson argues that the broad zones of flexibility around the fixed FEER are desirable to obtain the advantages of these social functions in the context of a fixed exchange rate system.[52]

Williamson fails to provide any empirical evidence to demonstrate that these claimed advantages of flexible rates have been achievable in the real world. On the other hand, the historical experience of both the gold standard era and the Bretton Woods period *vis-à-vis* the existing flexible system indicates that

1. a flexible rate system has not made payments adjustments easier as the division between the international debtors and creditors has worsened over the past two decades;
2. the flexible system 'reconciles' differential rates of inflation by leading to higher (correlated) rates of inflation in all nations compared to the experience under the fixed rates of either the gold standard or the Bretton Woods periods;
3. the flexible system has forced the major G7 nations to deliberately and explicitly coordinate monetary and interest rate policy rather than being able to run independent monetary policies, and
4. at times the existing system has been unable to absorb speculative pressures. Instead, massive, coordinated action by major nations' Central Banks to alleviate the speculative pressure on the exchange rate has often been required.

The evidence does not support Williamson's assertion that a large zone around FEER is justified on the basis of the operative usefulness of these alleged social functions. Moreover, by quietly introducing two exceptions, Williamson admits the possible non-operativeness of these social functions. Williamson argues that by altering relative prices, flexibility facilitates payments adjustment by changing 'incentives to export and import ... *except* where disequilibrium [between exports and imports] is due purely to excess or deficient demand'.[53] If the targets are chosen to permit sufficient unemployment to control inflation, then, in the absence of some deliberate incomes policy,[54] Williamson's proposed system will always require a long-run deficiency in effective demand so that the unemployment rate does not fall permanently below the magic NAIRU. In other words, in defining the target for internal equilibrium in terms of a NAIRU concept, Williamson introduces the exception that prevents the facilitating payments social function from being operative.

Williamson's second warning is that the alleged 'absorbing speculative pressures' function of a broad flexible rate zone is applicable provided speculative 'changes *do not lead to the prolonged and substantial movements away from equilibrium that constitute misalignments*'.[55] It is gratifying to know that if speculative pressures are not prolonged and do not lead to substantial misalignments, then large flexible zones can absorb the resulting relatively insignificant problems thrown up by speculation.

Williamson's proposal can generate significant disruptive speculative pressures since (i) targets are 'regularly updated in the light of new data on differential rates of inflation' and (ii) each nation 'need not accept an absolute obligation to keep its exchange rate within the target zone'.[56] Finally Williamson and Miller admit that the wide zones are justified in part by 'skepticism as to our ability to calculate sensible exchange rate targets with any degree of accuracy'[57] and that within the system there needs to be sufficient flexibility 'to allow for derogation from normal rules when circumstances warrant'.[58] These admissions suggest that any time enough speculators believe they can beat the authorities in recognizing 'the light of major changes' or circumstances that warrant 'a derogation from normal rules', excessive speculation will occur. As McKinnon states, Williamson's proposal 'which keeps open the option for occasional official adjustments in par values ... remain[s] vulnerable to speculative attacks'.[59] One should not expect Williamson's large zones to serve a speculative absorbing function at those times when such a facility is most needed.

THE NEUTRALITY OF MONEY ASSUMPTION

McKinnon claims that his proposal for setting nominal targets at approximate sustainable purchasing power parities would force Central Banks to gear their monetary policies to produce 'roughly the same rates of domestic price inflation in internationally tradable goods'.[60]

Underlying McKinnon's argument is the belief in the quantity theory of money. Milton Friedman has stated that 'the quantity theory presumption ... [is] that changes in the quantity of money as such *in the long run* have a negligible effect on real income, so that nonmonetary forces are "all that matter" for changes in real income over decades and money "does not matter". On the other hand, we have regarded the quantity of money ... as essentially "all that matter" for the long run determination of nominal income'.[61] Any analysis based on the quantity theory requires acceptance of the axiom of the *neutrality of money* so that the price level of producible goods is then a joint outcome of the monetary forces that solely determine nominal income and the real forces that are the only determinants of real income.

McKinnon's analysis and recommendations are conditional on the neutrality presumption that changes in the quantity of money have *no effect* on real output, employment, or economic growth for the 'indefinite future' for which McKinnon would fix nominal exchange rates. It is only because of this neutrality presumption that McKinnon can argue that once these PPP rates are fixed there is no need ever to change them as long as each nation follows his monetary rule – even if *real disturbances occur*. Monetary policy to maintain the PPP nominal rate, McKinnon assures us, will prevent any real shock from altering the full employment level of real output.[62]

If money is not neutral, as Keynes argued and most macroeconomists including Friedman admit (at least in the short run), then McKinnon's proposals would not provide the smooth adjusting mechanism that he describes except perhaps in the long run, when 'we are all dead'.

Williamson's analysis also assumes the neutrality of money when he indicates that his 'basic argument is that a nominal income rule [in a closed economy] fulfills the same function as a money supply rule'.[63] By targeting nominal growth in domestic income (in a closed system) or nominal domestic demand (in an open system) Williamson is presuming that the authorities can always control inflation without altering the long-run NAIRU.

Williamson's medium run is analytically equivalent to Friedman's long run. If money is not neutral, then Williamson's target nominal demand growth will not yield the same long-run results as Friedman's money supply rule. Because money is presumed neutral the only things that determine long-run real potential growth in output capacity (and the long-run NAIRU) in Williamson's system are the exogenous real forces.

A COMPARISON OF THE THREE PROPOSALS

The basis for fixing the exchange rate. All the proposals recommend fixed exchange rates, but the basis of the fix differs.

Williamson would have Central Bankers negotiate a set of *real* exchange rates based on an amorphous concept of maintaining simultaneous internal and external balance. Even Williamson admits such equilibrium notions 'involve an element of subjective judgment and will therefore permit obfuscation'.[64] Although the target exchange rate (FEER) is defined with apparent concreteness as that 'rate which is expected to generate a current account surplus or deficit equal to the underlying capital flow over the cycle'[65] this target is idiosyncratic. Ultimately, the calculated FEER depends upon what Williamson believes the authorities think will (should?) be the future current account surplus or deficit that financial free markets are willing to maintain over some nonspecific future calendar time labelled either the 'cycle' or the 'medium run'. Each year (and perhaps sooner) the target FEER could be updated upon the fancy of the authorities[66] considering unspecified 'major changes' in the current account balance.

McKinnon[67] would have the initial *nominal* rates 'set to approximate sustainable purchasing power parities' and announced to be 'fixed into the indefinite future'.

In contrast to both Williamson and McKinnon, our proposal would start neither by searching for a hypothetical FEER, nor for the correct PPP. Instead, our system would start with the existing nominal exchange rate parities in order not to disrupt existing trade relations (e.g. money contracts, ongoing real investments) merely to start up a new system. Since both the Williamson and McKinnon proposals envisage significant changes in the existing exchange rate at the date of conversion to the new system,[68] both proposals involve potentially large real start-up costs. Since our proposal accepts the existing rate structure, no additional start-up costs would be incurred.

Under what conditions should the fixed rate target be changed? Williamson indicates that the FEER rates would not change as long as the authorities used coordinated interest rate policy to 'manage the exchange rate'. The targets 'should be regularly updated in light of new data on differential inflation between countries ... [and] real shocks or new information'. Exchange rate changes are permitted whenever the governmental authorities (or their econometricians[69]) think conditions warrant a change. No discipline is imposed on the authorities to adopt policies either to control inflation differentials or otherwise to cushion the economy against real shocks that change the underlying conditions upon which the FEERs were estimated.

The assumption that one can know the correct targets to achieve internal and external balances presumes the existence of a steady state macro-equilibrium with values for normal capital flows, FEERs and NAIRUs for each country that are independent of the time path of the system over the medium run. Of course, if such an equilibrium state exists in terms of parameters and variables that are independent of the past behaviour of the system, then a free market system will always revert to this equilibrium. Williamson and Miller are dissatisfied with the 'speed of convergence' occurring under the 'automatic pilot' of a free market.[70] They prefer that intelligent authorities prod the economy to a greater convergence speed. It is not obvious why Williamson and Miller believe that their authorities will establish the correct FEER quicker than the free market can, especially given all the possibilities for change and/or obfuscation.

Williamson and Miller never raise the question whether there exists an ergodic steady-state equilibrium path for the economy to converge on. If the existence of a steady-state equilibrium position cannot be proven, then neither the free market nor Williamson and Miller's target setting authorities will achieve simultaneous internal and external equilibrium under the Williamson and Miller proposal.

Cross[71] has argued that a properly employed concept of hysteresis will not support the belief in the existence of an immutable long-run (or even medium-run) NAIRU towards which the economy can revert. Setterfield has argued that hysteresis implies treating the entire structure of macro-models as evolving endogenous systems where future values of short-, medium- and long-run parameters and variables are never independent of the path.[72]

If the actions of the authority to 'adjust' targets create, *inter alia*, continuing changes, then there need not exist any simultaneous internal or external equilibrium that the economy can converge towards. For example, suppose the authorities change the FEER and/or nominal demand targets and this change causes some domestic and/or international debtors to default. The resulting bankruptcies jeopardize, as Arrow and Hahn have clearly demonstrated, all existence proofs for general equilibrium, i.e. there need not exist any position of simultaneous internal and external equilibrium.[73]

McKinnon, because he believes in the neutrality of money, argues that there is never a need for the authority to change the initial PPP rate provided they follow the rules he suggests. In the McKinnon proposal, it is presumed that efficiency wages and real wealth transfers due to trade imbalances will adjust to the nominal anchor of fixed PPP rates. In essence, McKinnon's proposal requires a belief in a *laissez-faire* mechanism after the rules of the game are established once and for all.

Provision Nos. 7 and 8 of our proposal, on the other hand, provide specific criteria to indicate when, and if, there should be a change in exchange parities. These changes will primarily reflect the relative changes experienced in the real costs of production among trading partners and/or prevent domestic inflation in efficiency wages from spilling over to other countries. Under specific circumstances, exchange rate changes also will be made to alter the terms of trade against nations who are living beyond their full employment level of real income.

What about speculative pressures? Since a nation can exercise capital controls under our proposal, any speculative pressures can be shut down –

as long as there is cooperation among trading partners and law-abiding residents in the various nations. Williamson's scheme, on the other hand, is vulnerable to speculative excesses that can defeat the whole purpose of his proposal. McKinnon assumes away speculative pressures by asserting that as long as market traders *believe* the authorities will keep the rates unchanged, there can be no reason to speculate. McKinnon does not deal with the case where traders begin to doubt either the authorities' ability or their will!

What about persistent current account imbalances? In McKinnon's fixed exchange rate scheme, trade deficits or surpluses can persist if there are 'relative national imbalances between savings and investments'.[74] Those countries where *ex post* savings (including government deficits) exceed domestic investment must, by definition, generate trade surpluses. Those with investments exceeding savings must experience trade deficits.

McKinnon has argued that Williamson's claim that flexibility provides a facilitating payments adjustment function is 'a false economic doctrine' since trade imbalances are more a response to 'pervasive macroeconomic repercussions', i.e. the export–import balance depends primarily on income elasticities and income effects, and only secondarily on price elasticities and substitution effects.[75] McKinnon admits that a trade imbalance can persist because of different income elasticities for imports and exports.

The Post Keynesian version of this argument is Thirlwall's Law. This Law indicates that a sustainable current account balance can be achieved only if the income growth of a nation is equal to the ratio of income elasticities of demand for exports to imports multiplied by the rate of income growth of the nation's trading partners. Differentials in income elasticities can therefore, through a balance of payments constraint, force nations with trade deficits to reduce their growth rate to one that is compatible with the oversavings of their trading partners.

As Chapter 13 suggests there is good reason to suspect that income elasticity differentials can force those LDCs which specialize in the production of crops and/or minerals (except perhaps oil) to grow at a much slower pace than the more industrialized nations of the world. Since population growth is likely to be larger in these LDCs than in industrialized countries, such a scenario could, under the McKinnon proposal, easily lead to a decline in per capita GNP for the poorest of the LDCs. Would McKinnon continue to recommend his plan if the configuration of income elasticities for imports and exports is such as to condemn the poorest nations of the world to a continual lowering of the standard of living (either in absolute terms or relative to the developed world)?

Who should bear the onus of adjustment? According to McKinnon, there is no need for either trading partner to initiate an adjustment process to any persistent trade imbalance. All that is required is a net transfer of real capital from the deficit to the surplus trading partner. This transfer is accomplished by normal market processes where the deficit nation bears the entire costs of adjustment. The relative expansion of bank money in the deficit nation, because of the neutrality of money, results only in a price increase of nontradables (relative to tradables) in the trade deficit nation. The oversaving (surplus) nation experiences 'a slower rate of increase in . . . nontradables prices'.[76]

McKinnon claims, but does not prove, that '[a]lthough these relative price movements within both countries would be modest, gradual, and need not be permanent, they would be sufficient to support the transfer of savings from one highly open economy to another, as with past experiences of fixed exchange rate regimes'.[77] This wealth transfer could continue until either the deficit nation ran its stock of wealth down to zero, or the rising real wealth of the surplus nation increased its demand for imports while the declining real wealth of the deficit nation reduced its demand for imports sufficiently to bring about a trade balance. Although the surplus nation becomes richer and the deficit nation poorer because of this hypothesized wealth transfer, global economic growth is unaffected as long as one accepts the neutrality of money axiom.

In the absence of money neutrality one cannot demonstrate that the McKinnon proposal will resolve the problem of payments imbalances without imposing *real* deflationary consequences on all trading partners – at least in the short run in which we live.

Williamson's scheme would permit only those persistent current account imbalances that are consistent with the underlying normal capital flow over the cycle. Williamson and Miller admit the difficulty in estimating, or even defining 'normal' net capital flows. They believe that ratios such as external debt to GNP (or exports) among other criteria put 'a limit on the size of acceptable current account deficits in the medium term'.[78] Williamson and Miller conclude that 'admittedly there is no formula that permits translation of such criteria into an objective number for the flow of capital'. They encourage the authorities to make 'guesstimates' of normal medium-run capital flows apparently hoping wide zones compensate for the possibility of wild guesstimates.

Both the Williamson and McKinnon proposals recognize the possibility of persistent current account imbalances. Both believe that the imbalances will end through normal market processes with the debtor nation bearing the entire costs of adjustment without default. For example, if existing targets were to generate current account deficits that progressively increased the ratio of external debt to GNP, then Williamson and Miller would argue it was the responsibility of the debtor nation's authorities to reduce the target for growth in domestic demand, thereby increasing unemployment, and/or lower its FEER, thereby reducing its terms of trade.

Williamson's and McKinnon's proposals are devoid of that essential feature of any international payments system that Keynes identified as necessary for a golden age, namely shifting the onus of adjustment to the creditor nation. Our proposal, on the other hand, explicitly requires creditors to accept significant responsibility for resolving persistent current account deficits.

Should the success of any international payments system rely on the presumption of the existence of a steady-state equilibrium? If one presumes neutral money, then McKinnon's proposals logically assure that a free market system will find the prosperity that is just around the corner. If, on the other hand, one adopts the Williamson and Miller view that the required market adjustment process is too slow to turn that proverbial corner, then authorities making small adjustments in exchange rates and nominal demand targets are all that are necessary to get the system more quickly back on track.

If one adopts the Keynes view on 'the necessity of central controls to bring about an adjustment between the propensity to consume and the inducement to invest [which in an open system includes net foreign investment]'[79] in a decentralized market-oriented entrepreneurial economy, then one believes that the economic system requires some controls to avoid Great Depressions and Inflations that inflict lasting economic woes on great segments of the population. Post Keynesians do not believe that we should rely upon a *laissez-faire* system operating under rules alone to assure either the existence or the attainment of a full employment (or a natural NAIRU[80]) equilibrium. It is more prudent to design a system that controls and coordinates adjustments among consumption, domestic investment and the current account to offset the debilitating effects that might otherwise arise from national differences between savings, investment, and the income elasticities of demand for imports and exports.

What about a long-run stable international monetary standard? The Williamson plan assumes that each nation will have an acceptable but unspecified nonaccelerating rate of inflation. McKinnon argues that if foreign exchange traders believe that governments will fix nominal rates 'into the indefinite future, [then] commodity arbitrage and mutual monetary adjustments assure conversion to the same rate of commodity price inflation'.[81] Although this conversion inflation rate is 'preferably zero', there is nothing in McKinnon's system that assures that inflation will converge to a rate not significantly different from zero. Neither the

Williamson nor the McKinnon proposals provide for a long-run stable international standard of value.

Under provision No. 7 of our proposal, on the other hand, the IMCU would provide its holders with an invariant international monetary standard no matter whether the domestic rates of inflation in the various nations converged (or not) or accelerated (or not).

By implicitly invoking the theoretical 'law of one price', McKinnon argues that private sector free market arbitrage involving *standardized* tradable commodities assures that the derived demand for labour and therefore money wages 'would *eventually* reflect differentials in productivity growth'[82] so that relative efficiency wages would, in the long run, be fixed. My proposal, on the other hand, does not rely on the definitionally true, but pointless, 'law of one price'[83] to assure the long-run alignment of relative efficiency wages among trading partners. Instead our proposal builds such a requirement directly into its operation.

What happens when there is an increase in domestic core inflation? Increases in core inflation can be due to many different causes, e.g. the demands of militant unions or powerful cartels for higher relative incomes, or social demands for domestic limitations on industrial pollution, or unsafe workplaces. Williamson and Miller argue that an increase in 'core inflation' need not result in a change in the target FEER. Instead they claim 'the appropriate response might be a rise in the target unemployment rate'.[84] In essence, Williamson and Miller are suggesting that truculent demands by unions or cartels, as well as humane domestic demands for a socially responsible production environment (unmatched by similar demands in trading partner nations) can be squelched by reducing profit opportunities and laying off workers. McKinnon, on the other hand, would rely on a money supply rule either to limit the nominal growth in the domestic costs of production by depressing market demand and/or force an international convergence towards a common higher inflation rate under such circumstances.

If these domestic social and political demands are squeezed from the system by higher unemployment, the result can be a global negative sum game. The originating nation and its trading partners will lose real income if the response to an increase in core inflation from any cause is domestic slowdown in real demand for domestic goods *and* imports. Even if the solution involves solely a convergence to a higher international inflation rate, some portion of the costs of these domestic demands would be borne by foreigners.

In the Williamson and McKinnon proposals, there is no containment building limiting the fallout of a core inflation meltdown to a very localized community. Our proposed system, on the other hand, would require the increasing costs resulting from any domestic social and political demands that increase domestic core inflationary tendencies to be borne entirely by the domestic population causing the problem. The intermediation of the IMCU under provision No. 7 assures containment. This containment forces the domestic authorities to deal directly with the cause and/or effect of core inflationary increases. The authorities can permit rising product prices (to domestic buyers only), while the purchasing power of the IMCU remains unchanged. Alternatively, the authorities can institute an incomes policy (augmented by antitrust policy) to limit domestic product price increases by a social contract that constrains powerful unions and cartels.

If the increase in core inflation is due to social demands (e.g. environmental or workplace improvements), then an incomes policy can provide for the sharing of any additional costs among domestic workers and capitalists who benefit from these social improvements; betterments that the residents of the trading partners have, by hypothesis, not demanded. The authorities could use the domestic tax system to pay for the costs of these social advancements in production processes. Our proposal permits each national polis to determine how to handle these domestically caused changes in core inflation. What our system does not permit is a deliberate policy of fostering indiscriminate unemployment to resolve these issues. Not only is this tool unfair to many domestic workers and employers who did not necessarily initiate the demands that increased domestic inflation, but, through import elasticities, can spread unemployment to workers and entrepreneurs in other nations.

What about the arbitrary and inequitable international distribution of income and wealth? Neither the Williamson nor the McKinnon proposal addresses the plight of the LDCs in recent decades. Yet, trade driven by differing income elasticities may push poor-deficit LDCs into increasing poverty. Our system is designed to foster behaviour by the richer members of the global community to assure that poorer nations are (a) provided with sufficient effective international demand to employ fully their labour force and facilities and (b) to encourage grants and direct foreign investment from the creditor nations of the world to the impoverished debtors.

CONCLUSION

The suggested provisions for a new Post Keynesian international payments system are not unalterable either in principle or for practical reasons. Instead they should provide the basis for the beginning of a sound analytical discussion of how to prepare for a twenty-first century international monetary system.

The problems facing the international payments system are not easily resolved. If we start with the defeatist attitude that it is too difficult to change the awkward system we are enmeshed in, then no progress will be made. We must reject such defeatism at this exploratory stage and merely ask whether these particular proposals for improving the operations of the international payments system to promote global growth will create more difficulties than other proposed innovations. The health of the world economic system will not permit us to muddle through.

NOTES

1. M. Friedman, 'A Response to His Critics', in *Milton Friedman's Monetary Framework: A Debate With His Critics*, edited by R.J. Gordon, University of Chicago Press, Chicago, 1974, p. 151.
2. *The Collected Writings of John Maynard Keynes*, 25, p. 25.
3. Ibid., p. 87.
4. Nations with banking institutions which make it difficult for foreign authorities to obtain information regarding bank accounts held by depositors are likely to encourage the influx of funds trying to escape national tax collectors, criminal investigators, and the Central Banks of nations that try to limit capital outflows. Thus, it is not surprising that often exchange rates reflect speculative, and flight capital, flows rather than purchasing power parities.
5. To argue, from the outset, that international cooperation in sharing records and helping enforce capital flows cannot be achieved is unduly pessimistic. It paints a picture of the human condition where nations are willing to cooperate in military wars at a cost of the lives of a large portion of their youth, but unwilling to cooperate even if it costs the recipient nations a 'fast buck'.
6. The one practical exception to this generalization is when a small, unimportant, nation pursues export-led growth. If a nation is so insignificant, then its trade surpluses are unlikely to inflict significant deficits or inflationary tendencies on any of the other trading nations. Thus the importance of being unimportant for export-led growth.
7. See P. Davidson and E. Smolensky, *Aggregate Supply and Demand Analysis*, Harper & Row, New York, 1964, pp. 128–39.
8. See J. Brothwell, 'Wages and Employment', *Journal of Post Keynesian Economics*, 6, 1984, and P. Davidson, 'The Marginal Product Is Not The Demand Curve For Labor', *Journal of Post Keynesian Economics*, 6, 1984.
9. Nothing of substance would be lost if less than perfect competition was analysed; all that would be required is that the *MPL* curve be multiplied by a scalar whose magnitude was less than unity.
10. J.M. Keynes, *The General Theory of Employment, Interest and Money*, p. 17.
11. This is likely to be true as long as the economy is at less than full employment, so that any increase in output is associated with an expansion of production in both the consumer goods sector and the other sectors of the system. At full employment, however, if consumption is reduced to permit expansion of investment goods, then the productivity of labour in the various sectors, and hence sectoral price levels, may move in different directions or at significantly different rates.
12. This situation is consistent with Keynes's definition of involuntary unemployment on p. 128 of his *General Theory*.
13. If there is some substitutability of imports for exports, the higher exchange rate would

increase the openness of the domestic economy as the proportion of spending on foreign products increased *at each level of employment*. This would increase the magnitude of ϕ, thereby shifting the real wage-determining curve further upwards. For simplicity we will ignore this further factor increasing the real wage with export-led growth, since this would only increase the force of our argument as developed here.

14. As the domestic currency appreciates, the cheaper imports yield higher real wages without labour having to demand higher money wages at the bargaining table.

15. If some other nations are tied to this nation via a common market which maintains fixed exchange rates, then these common market partners can share in the benefits of an appreciating exchange rate that raises real wages in the common market *at the expense of the rest of the world*.

16. There might be some small *ceteris paribus* differences, if the rate of diminishing returns differs in the foreigners' export industry compared to the diminishing returns experienced in the domestic industries.

17. Or if money-wage rates are rising, less inflationary pressure.

18. In 1968, Professor Harry Johnson wrote [in *The Times* of London, 12/9] 'the basic argument for floating exchange rates is so simple that most people have considerable difficulty in understanding it ... a floating exchange rate would save a country from having to reverse its full employment policies because they lead to inflation and deficit'.

19. It assumes that the poor LDCs are capital short and labour rich, while the rich developed nations are capital rich and labour short. Accordingly, the 'real' marginal product of capital must be higher in the LDCs than in the developed nations, and therefore the real return on capital higher in the LDCs.

20. Apparently, classical economists do not conceive of 'flight capital' as an economic problem. Indeed naïve classicists claim that those with wealth have the right in any circumstance to choose when and where they move their reserves independent of the damage such moves may inflict on the national and international economy. But all the rights of the individual are always constrained by its potential impacts on society. For example, no one would defend someone shouting 'Fire' in a crowded auditorium as indisputably protected under an individual's right of free speech. In many circumstances, flight capital can cause more damage then yelling fire in an auditorium!

21. The *Economist* magazine (January 6, 1990) indicated that the decade of the 1980s will be noted as one in which 'the experiment with floating currencies failed'. Earlier (February 17, 1987), the *Financial Times* admitted that 'floating exchange rates, it is now clear, were sold on a false prospectus ... they held out a quite illusory promise of greater national autonomy ... [but] when macropolicies are inconsistent and when capital is globally mobile, floating rates cannot be relied upon to keep the current accounts roughly in balance'.

22. I. Adelman, 'Long Term Economic Development' (working paper No. 589), California Agricultural Experiment Station, Berkeley, California, March 1991, p. 15.

23. Adelman, op. cit., p. 15. Depressions disappeared, recessions were minor and exports grew more than 50 per cent faster than GDP.

24. Adelman, op. cit., p. 17.

25. R.I. McKinnon, 'Interest Rate Volatility and Exchange Rate Risk: New Rules For a Common Monetary Standard', *Contemporary Policy Studies*, **8**, 1990, p. 10.

26. J.M. Keynes, *The Collected Writings of J.M. Keynes*, 25, edited by D. Moggridge, 1980, p. 27.

27. Keynes, 1980, op. cit. p. 176.

28. The 'scarce currency' clause of the Bretton Woods Agreement would permit European nations to discriminate against American imports. But this would not resolve the problem since there was no other major source of the goods necessary to feed and rebuild Europe.

29. In 1991, Japan's export surplus is running at approximately 2 per cent of her GNP, while 2 per cent of America's GNP is equal to $111 billion.

30. Only in the small recessions of 1949 and 1957 did per capita GNP stop growing. But even during these brief periods, it never declined.

31. Figures obtained from *Statistical Abstract of the United States 1959*, US Bureau of Census, Washington, 1959, p. 870.
32. This does not deny that some groups of trading partners may wish to integrate their Central Banks and banking systems into a regional UMS common market. Implicit in much of 'Europe 1992' planning was the belief that 'ultimately' there will be a single currency among the European Community of Nations governed by a single Supranational Central Bank. If some nations were willing to develop an interregional UMS they would be free to develop their own UMS clearing mechanism which would operate as a single unit in the larger global clearing union proposed below.
33. Keynes, 1980, op. cit., p. 168.
34. Williamson recognizes that when balance of payments 'disequilibrium is due purely to excess or deficient demand', flexible exchange rates *per se* cannot facilitate international payments adjustments, J. Williamson, 'Exchange Rate Management: The Role of Target Zones' *American Economic Review Papers and Proceedings*, **77**, 1987, pp. 200–204.
35. This provides an added bonus by making tax-avoidance and profits from illegal trade more difficult to conceal.
36. Correspondent banking will have to operate through the International Clearing Agency, with each Central Bank regulating the international relations and operations of its domestic banking firms. Small-scale smuggling of currency across borders, etc., can never be completely eliminated. But such movements are merely a flea on a dog's back – a minor, but not debilitating, irritation. If, however, most of the residents of a nation hold and use (in violation of legal tender laws) a foreign currency for domestic transactions and as a store of value (e.g. it is estimated that Argentinians hold close to 5 billion US dollars), this is evidence of a lack of confidence in the government and its monetary authority. Unless confidence is restored, all attempts to restore economic prosperity will fail.
37. Some may fear that if a surplus nation is close to the trigger point it could short circuit the system by making loans to reduce its credit balance *prior* to setting off the trigger. Since preventing unreasonable debt-service obligations is an important objective of this proposal, a mechanism which monitors and can restrict such pretrigger lending activities may be required.

    One possible way of eliminating this trigger avoidance lending loophole is as follows: An initial agreement as to what constitutes sensible and flexible criteria for judging when debt-servicing burdens become unreasonable is established. Given these criteria, the clearing-union managers would have the responsibility for preventing additional loans which push debt burdens beyond reasonable servicing levels. In other words, loans that push debt burdens too far could not be cleared though the clearing union, i.e. the managers would refuse to release the IMCUs for loan purposes from the surplus country's account. (I am indebted to Robert Blecker for suggesting this point.)

    The managers would also be required to make periodic public reports on the level of credits being accumulated by surplus nations and to indicate how close these surpluses are to the trigger point. Such reports would provide an informational edge for debtor nations permitting them to bargain more successively regarding the terms of refinancing existing loans and/or new loans. All loans would still have to meet the clearing union's guidelines for reasonableness.

    I do not discount the difficulties involved in setting up and getting agreement on criteria for establishing unreasonable debt-service burdens. (For some suggestions, however, see the second paragraph of provision No. 8.) In the absence of cooperation and a spirit of goodwill that is necessary for the clearing union to provide a mechanism assuring the economic prosperity of all members, however, no progress can ever be made.

    Moreover, as the current international debt problem of African and Latin American nations clearly demonstrates, creditors ultimately have to forgive some debt when they previously encourage excessive debt burdens. Under the current system, however, debt forgiveness is a last resort solution acceptable only after both debtor and creditor nations suffer from faltering economic growth. Surely a more intelligent option is to develop an institutional arrangement which prevents excessive debt-servicing burdens from ever occurring.

38. Oversaving is defined as a nation persistently spending less on imports plus direct equity foreign investment than the nation's export and investment earnings plus net unilateral transfers.

39. Whatever 'excessive' credit balances are redistributed shall be apportioned among the debtor nations (perhaps on the basis of a formula which is inversely related to each debtor's per capita income and directly related to the size of its international debt) to be used to reduce debit balances at the clearing union.

40. The efficiency wage is related to the money wage divided by the average product of labour, it is the unit labour cost modified by the profit mark-up in domestic money terms of domestically produced GNP. At this preliminary stage of this proposal, it would serve no useful purpose to decide whether the domestic market basket should include both tradable and non-tradable goods and services. (With the growth of tourism more and more nontradable goods become potentially tradable.) I personally prefer the wider concept of the domestic market basket, but it is not obvious that any essential principle is lost if a tradable only concept is used, or if some nations use the wider concept while others use the narrower one.

41. This is equivalent to a negative income tax for poor fully employed families within a nation. (See P. Davidson, 'A Modest Set of Proposals for Resolving The International Debt Problem', *Journal of Post Keynesian Economics*, **10**, 1987–88, for further development of this argument.)

42. Although relative prices of imports and exports would be altered by the change in the terms of trade, the adjustment is due to the resulting real income effect, not a substitution effect. The deficit nation's real income will fall until its import surplus disappears.

43. The actual programme adopted for debt-service reduction will depend on many parameters including: the relative income and wealth of the debtor *vis-à-vis* the creditor, the ability of the debtor to increase its per capita real income, etc.

44. See Williamson, op. cit.; J. Williamson and M.H. Miller, *Targets and Indicators*, Institute for International Economics, Washington, 1987, and R.I. McKinnon, 'Monetary and Exchange Rate Policies for International Financial Stability: A Proposal', *Journal of Economic Perspectives*, **2**, 1988.

45. McKinnon, loc. cit, p. 87.

46. Williamson, 1987, p. 202.

47. Williamson, 1987, p. 200.

48. If initially the economy is not at this equilibrium position, then Williamson and Miller (op. cit., pp. 8–9) argue one either increases or decreases the target nominal growth until said internal balance is achieved. Consequently, the target growth in nominal demand is endogenized to secure a 'soft landing' onto the presumed exogenous NAIRU and acceptable inflation rate.

49. Williamson, 1987, p. 202.

50. Williamson and Miller, op. cit., p. 12.

51. McKinnon, 1988, p. 87.

52. Williamson, 1987, pp. 201–2.

53. Williamson, 1987, p. 201, italics added.

54. If inflation is initially at an unacceptable level, Williamson would set a nominal growth target that deliberately pushes unemployment up. Williamson [1987, p. 9] does recognize the possible use of an incomes policy *as a temporary measure* to reduce, but not eliminate, this unemployment cost of disinflation. Once the acceptable inflation level is achieved by this depressionary policy, however, Williamson would revise the target to achieve NAIRU. In the absence of a permanent incomes policy, most would agree that NAIRU (if such an immutable structural parameter actually exists) would involve significant unemployment.

55. Williamson, 1987, pp. 201–2, italics added.

56. Williamson, op. cit., p. 202.
57. Williamson and Miller, op. cit., p. 12.
58. Williamson and Miller, op. cit., p. 19.
59. McKinnon, 1988, p. 100.
60. McKinnon, 1988, p. 87.
61. M. Friedman, in *Milton Friedman's Monetary Framework: A Debate With His Critics*, edited by R.J. Gordon, University of Chicago Press, Chicago, 1974, p. 27.
62. McKinnon, 1988, pp. 87–8.
63. Williamson and Miller, op. cit., p. 7. Thus, Williamson and Miller turn Friedman's motto (quoted *supra*) on its head so that all that matters for the determination of the growth in the money supply is the growth in nominal income.
64. Williamson, 1987, p. 202.
65. Williamson and Miller, op. cit., p. 10.
66. In fact, the FEERs actually estimated by WM 'were based on calculations with current account targets for the years 1976–1977 and . . . then [subjectively] updated in the light of major changes in the world economy'. WM admit that 'no systematic effort' was made in their updating the calculated FEER for each nation. They promise a more systematic method of updating 'in subsequent work' (WM, 1987b, p. 73).
   Can one estimate a benchmark 'normal' capital flow from observations occurring during the current flexible rate regime which both Williamson and McKinnon argue are fundamentally flawed? If the initial target is in error, then significant adjustments will be required in future periods. If the public suspects that adjustments will be made, then the WM plan is subject to the possibility of excessive speculative movements.
67. McKinnon, 1988, p. 93.
68. If significant changes are not envisaged by either McKinnon or WM, this would imply that the existing system had already established the 'correct' exchange rate.
69. Williamson, 1987, p. 202. Williamson thinks it is merely a 'technical exercise' to determine the set of exchange rates which simultaneously produce internal and external equilibrium.
70. Williamson and Miller, op. cit., p. 50.
71. R. Cross, 'The NAIRU: Not an Uninteresting Rate of Unemployment?', mimeo, 1991.
72. M. Setterfield, 'Towards A Long Run Theory of Effective Demand', *Journal of Post Keynesian Economics*, **15**, 1993.
73. K.J. Arrow and F.H. Hahn, '*General Competitive Equilibrium*, Holden-Day, San Francisco, 1971.
74. McKinnon, 1988, p. 98.
75. McKinnon, 1988, p. 94.
76. McKinnon, 1988, pp. 98–9.
77. McKinnon, 1988, p. 99. McKinnon apparently does not recognize that during the early Bretton Woods period, Marshall Plan unilateral aid payments were an important vehicle for transferring savings.
78. Williamson and Miller, op. cit., p. 59.
79. Keynes, *The General Theory*, p. 370.
80. In the Williamson and Miller (op. cit., p. 57) 'paradigm, the output and inflation paths are pinned down by the requirement for internal balance'. This hypothetical path is secured by the assumption of a neutral money and the existence of a NAIRU which is a 'natural' variable whose value is independent of the path of any economy. Our analysis, on the other hand, presumes that any unemployment rate which requires those who are willing, and competent, to work at the going real wage to remain unemployed in order to control inflation is neither natural nor a desirable target for policy. How many economists would recommend a policy to target for NAIRU, if those who advocate such a target were required to exchange their paycheque for the compensation an unemployed worker receives?
81. McKinnon, 1988, p. 97.
82. McKinnon, 1988, p. 97, italics added.
83. This law lacks substance because, if any two units of a commodity are associated with

different prices, then, by definition, they are different commodities. Accordingly, relying on arbitrage to maintain purchasing power parity over time defines away the problem. If apples on Friday do not have the same price as they had on Monday, then, according to neoclassical economic theory, Friday's apples are a different commodity. There is no change in PPP when different commodities have different prices.

84. Williamson and Miller, op. cit., p. 50.

17. Epilogue: truth in labelling and economic textbooks

If John Maynard Keynes was alive today could he endorse anything that is labelled Keynesian in economic textbooks? Would Keynes, the master logician, accept the fundamental analytical building blocks of New Keynesians as the aspects of his analysis that distinguished his framework from the pre-Keynesian old classical system?

Under a truth in labelling law, a minimum quantity of beef is required in a patty before the United States Department of Agriculture permits anyone to sell it as a hamburger. Similarly the community of economists, if they believe in truth in labelling, should require some minimum quantity of Keynes's logical analysis as an essential ingredient in any theory being sold (especially in textbooks to as yet uneducated consumers) as Keynesian. Paraphrasing a famous slogan of the 1988 Democratic presidential primary, 'Where's the Keynesian beef in New Keynesian economics?'

WHAT IS NEW KEYNESIAN ECONOMICS?

In an article entitled 'What is New Keynesian Economics?', Gordon[1] attributes the invention of the New Keynesian label to Parkin. Before analysing the Gordon explanation, Parkin was contacted and asked for his definition of New Keynesianism. Parkin indicated to me[2] that his original definition of New Keynesian economics was 'A class of models of the labor market that assume rational expectations and fixed term multiperiod possibly but not necessarily overlapping wage contracts'. Parkin stated that this old definition contrasts with his old definition of New Classical economics, where the latter was 'A class of models of the labor market based on rational expectations and market clearing'.

Under his old definition, Parkin wrote that there were four 'key' assumptions of 'The New Keynesian Theory of Aggregate Supply':[3]

1. Money wages are set for an agreed period and do not continuously adjust.
2. The actual quantity of labor traded is determined by the quantity demanded.

3. Money wages are set so as to achieve equality between expected supply and demand for labor.
4. Money wage contracts last for a longer term than the frequency with which the economy is hit by shocks and overlap in time.

What differentiates Parkin's 'old' New Keynesian definition from his 'old' New Classical definition is the postulated existence of a constraint, a short-run fixity of nominal wages, on the New Classical aggregate supply function. It is ironic that Keynes, whose supreme contribution was developing an aggregate demand curve separate from aggregate supply, should have his named enshrined by Parkin in an analysis that requires an imperfection in the classical aggregate supply function.

Keynes specifically denied that the fixity of nominal wages and prices was a necessary condition for his argument. Keynes indicated that he initially:

> will assume that the money wage and other factor costs are constant per unit of labour employed. But this simplification, with which we will dispense later, is introduced solely to facilitate the exposition. The essential character of the argument is precisely the same whether or not money wages, etc. are liable to change. The essential character of the argument is precisely the same whether or not money-wages, etc., are liable to change'.[4]

Keynes's 'difference of analysis' was that he permitted flexible wages to feed back to components of aggregate demand.[5] This led to two major conclusions regarding the effect of instantaneously flexible money wages. 'There is, therefore, no ground for the belief that a flexible wage policy is capable of maintaining a state of continuous full employment . . . [and] to suppose that a flexible wage policy is a right and proper adjunct of a system which on the whole is one of *laissez-faire*, is the opposite of the truth'.[6] Complete wage (or price) flexibility is neither a necessary nor a sufficient condition for full employment equilibrium.

Anyone selling theoretical patties for student (or uneducated policy-makers') consumption in which the fixity of nominal wages or prices is an essential ingredient would not get a franchise from the originator of Keynesian economics to use his name.

Parkin indicated that he would now propose new and different definitions for both New Classical economics and New Keynesianism. He now defines New Classical economics as: 'a research program that seeks to explain aggregate fluctuations as the consequence of perfectly coordinated Pareto efficient intertemporal substitution'. Parkin's new definition of New Keynesianism is 'a research program that seeks to explain aggregate fluctuations as the consequence of impediments to the coordination of the choices of rational agents who are individually maximizing but who are collectively prevented from achieving a Pareto efficient allocation'.

Parkin's old and new definitions of New Keynesianism are designed to contrast with his benchmark old and new definitions of New Classical economics. This implies that New Classical economics is the general theory and New Keynesian economics is a special case. New Keynesians are a subset of Classical economists who accept the axioms of New Classical economics as the foundation for 'theory'. New Keynesians have added onto the classical system one or more *ad hoc* supply-side imperfections in terms of rigidities and/or coordination failures to explain short-term unemployment and aggregate output fluctuations. In the long run, free markets will find the classical solution. In the words of New Keynesian Mankiw 'Classical theory is right in the long run ... [and] the long run is not so far away'.[7] From Parkin's New Keynesian perspective a more honest title for Keynes's book would be *The Special Case Theory of Employment, Interest and Money (Why Market Failure Prevents Flexible Wages and Prices From Doing Their Job)*.

From Ricardo's time until Keynes's *General Theory*, most mainstream economists believed that the old classical economics of their day was *the* general theory. Full employment was the inevitable outcome of a free market economy with flexible wages and prices. Ricardo, who used this classical general theory to formulate policy prescriptions, 'offered us the supreme intellectual achievement, unattainable by weaker spirits, of adopting a hypothetical world remote from experience as though [as if?] it were the world of experience and then living in it consistently'.[8] Other economists accepted classical analysis as 'theory' yet their native good judgement told them that unemployed workers were not enjoying voluntary leisure. These 'reasonable' classical economists attempted to explain unemployment as short-run maladjustments due to rigidities, frictions, erroneous expectations, etc., that lengthen the time until free markets produce the long-run full employment equilibrium outcome. Keynes characterized those classical economists who relied on rigidities, etc. to explain unemployment as 'weaker spirits' whose 'common sense cannot help breaking in – with injury to their logical consistency'.[9]

WHAT ARE THE ESSENTIAL ASPECTS OF NEW KEYNESIANISM?

Survey articles by New Keynesians adopt the Parkin perspective.[10] For example, Gordon defines New Keynesianism as 'research *within the*

Keynesian tradition that attempts to build the microfoundations of wage and price stickiness'.[11] Gordon insists that

> price setting behavior is the essence of Keynesian economics. Any attempt to embed it in microfoundations must begin from monopolistic or imperfect competition.... The game is to tease a failure of macro markets to clear from a starting point of rational expectations and the maximization of profits and individual welfare at the micro level.... Any satisfactory explanation of business cycles that warrants the label Keynesian must incorporate not just price stickiness, but ... [must also recognize that] the necessary condition for non-market clearing is a barrier to the full adjustment of nominal prices'.[12]

The short-run stickiness of nominal values imperfection embedded in an aggregate supply function is the *sine qua non* for New Keynesian analysis.

Gordon's New Keynesianism concept does not permit contemplating the prospect that a perfectly flexible wage and price system is theoretically capable of experiencing a lack of effective demand. Gordon rationalizes this view by arguing that the complete research agenda for macroeconomics is circumscribed by 'Lucas' famous paper on the international output–inflation tradeoff'.[13] Gordon asserts that 'demand side topics can be omitted, simply because they are not at the heart of the conflict between New-Keynesian and new-classical macroeconomics'.[14]

Gordon's Keynesian blind spot is imposed by Lucas who rules out what Keynes thought was the essence of his general theory, namely that unemployment is primarily the result of an insufficiency in aggregate demand and not a constraint on aggregate supply. Unwilling to challenge Lucas's vision as to what macroeconomics is about, Gordon can only cast New Keynesians as developers of special cases invoking *ad hoc* constraints on what Keynes called 'our old friend' the classical supply function to short-circuit the power of supply to create its own demand. In the absence of such *ad hoc* constraints in a Lucas world – one which Lucas describes as 'a patently artificial world'[15] – full employment is an inevitable outcome.

Mankiw suggests that the New Keynesian research agenda is determined as a response to the Lucas critique where it is argued that it was not proper to assume exogenous and unchanging expectations in response to policy interventions.[16] Mankiw argues that there are many economists who accept classical axiomatic analysis as the basis of all 'theory', but find the logical explanations of employment fluctuations derived from this axiomatic foundation distasteful. New Classical explanations of employment fluctuations due to agents confusing changes in the price level with changes in relative prices or due to random fluctuations in the rate of technological change are at odds with the 'common presumptions ... [and] the strong prior beliefs of many economists ... [and are] unlikely to be plausibly reconciled with observed economic fluctuations'.[17] The common sense of these latter-day New Keynesian Saints rejects the inevitable logical conclusion of *the* classical general theory as inconsistent with their native good judgement (i.e., prior beliefs).

Gordon, for example, states that 'any satisfactory explanation of the business cycle that warrants the label *Keynesian* must incorporate not just price stickiness, but in addition some element that explains the evident unhappiness of the employed in recessions and depressions'.[18] Gordon's common sense tells him that during a recession even the remaining employed experience an uneasiness as they fear for their jobs. Unemployed workers do not prefer the enforced leisure of being laid off *vis-à-vis* receiving income currently.

It is the common sense of the New Keynesians that forces them to 'tease out' special cases within the microfoundations that Lucas has used to circumscribe the acceptable research agenda for macroeconomics. To step outside the Lucas-drawn boundary is to expose themselves to charges of non-scientific thinking by the Economics Establishment. New Keynesians envy the attribute of 'hard headedness' associated with the intellectually prestigious results forged in the axiomatic ovens of the New Classical analysis. New Keynesians seek to demonstrate that their heads are just as hard as the New Classicals. They attempt to forge different results from the same axiomatic ovens and thereby deflect attention from the nakedness of their soft hearts (or what Mankiw calls their 'strong prior beliefs') that recognize that the unemployed who lose their jobs during recession are not maximizing utility in their economic position in the market-place. *Ad hoc* limitations on the 'scientific' axiomatic microtheory tools of the New Classical analysis are developed to explain special cases where fluctuations in employment and output are not 'the Pareto-efficient response of the economy to changes in tastes and technology, but rather some sort of market failure on a grand scale'.[19] Thus, New Keynesians claim that their 'hard heads' have developed a 'tough minded economics for a just society'.[20]

The New Keynesian research agenda is to develop 'a cogent theoretical foundation of *hard-headed* microeconomic reasoning' to explain the failure of market wages and prices to adjust instantaneously 'to clear the market'.[21] New Keynesians equate the need for 'hard-headed' foundations with the acceptance of the fundamental axioms of the New Classical economics as the general case. The litmus test that separates New Keynesians from New Classicals is to develop a rationale for a special case where wages and prices are not instantaneously fully flexible – and therefore the classical neutrality of money axiom is temporarily (i.e., in the short run) inoperative.

By specifying that the New Keynesian research agenda must 'tease a market failure' out of the New Classical axiomatic microfoundation, both Gordon and Mankiw are in the position of a defendant trying to respond to the classic 'when did you stop beating your wife?' cross-examination. In limiting the New Keynesian research to finding 'barriers to the full adjustment of nominal prices',[22] New Keynesians accept the Classical presumption that, at least in the long run, a free market 'is for the best in the best of all possible worlds provided we will let well enough alone'.[23] As Mankiw boasts, 'Old classical economists, such as David Hume, asserted that money was neutral in the long run but not the short run. This is exactly the position held by new Keynesians'.[24]

If, as a matter of faith,[25] the axioms of classical economics are believed to be the basis for *all* theory, then the only fundamental difference between New Keynesians and New Classical economic analysis involves the time it takes for nominal values to be fully flexible so that the system achieves the Panglossian equilibrium where everyone stops beating their wives. After all, in the long run when we are all dead, no one can lift a hand to strike one's spouse!

Initially, New Keynesians looked for market failure in the labour market – and Parkin's original definition of New Keynesian reflected that search effort. Dissatisfaction with 'hard-headed' but weak explanations regarding agents setting wages to equal lifetime (long-run) marginal products ultimately led New Keynesians to abandon the search for a grand scale failure in the labour market. The search was shifted to the product market – and the existence of menu costs where 'literally these menu costs are the resources required to post new price lists'.[26] In the days before computers and bar codes, the real costs of changing labels, printing new menus, etc., might have been substantial, but given modern technology, one should be somewhat sceptical that menu costs are so large and pervasive as to be the *major* explanation of the large volume of unemployed workers observed during the many months when modern economies experience recessions.[27]

Keynes argued that as a general case long-period underemployment equilibrium can be a normal outcome of a market economy, even with freely flexible prices and perfect competition. This was not because Keynes thought that real world markets were necessarily perfectly competitive and possessed instantaneously and fully flexible prices. Keynes wanted to demonstrate that a general theory of employment did not require any unique specification for either the degree of competition or the magnitude of price flexibility to demonstrate the existence of an involuntary unemployment equilibrium, even in the long run.[28] The fundamental cause of unemployment in an entrepreneurial economy is not nested in imperfect competition and sticky money wages. Unemployment is a fundamental 'fault' of a money-using *laissez-faire* economy.

Keynes's underemployment equilibrium concept does not require, as a necessary condition, Mankiw's 'grand scale market failure'. Neither is the absence of what Mankiw calls a 'grand scale market failure' a sufficient condition to assure continuous full employment in Keynes's general theory. What Mankiw and Gordon claim is the essence of the New Keynesian research agenda is conceptually unnecessary. It diverts attention from Keynes's logical analysis of the necessary and sufficient condition for the existence of underemployment equilibrium *and the long-run policy decisions necessary for restoring and maintaining full employment to an economy in recession.*

TYING UP SOME LOOSE ENDS OF NEW KEYNESIANISM

There are two additional New Keynesian points that should be addressed. These points are sometimes wheeled out – when all else fails – as a New Keynesian explanation of short-run unemployment. They are the efficiency wage argument and the general coordination failure concept.

The efficiency wage model. Perhaps the only really new wrinkle to come out of New Keynesianism is the 'efficiency wage' argument that 'firms do not reduce wages in the face of persistent unemployment because to do so would reduce productivity'.[29] Of course, this argument violates the classical presumption that productivity is determined by exogenous technical progress; productivity is not endogenous to the decision of workers regarding effort per hour.

If real productivity is assumed to be endogenously determined by rewards paid per unit of labour effort, then logical symmetry implies that if firms were to increase workers' wages, workers' productivity (with the same technology) would increase and aggregate output and profits (and as long as the marginal profit share exceeded zero) would rise. Indeed a variant of this upside efficiency wage argument underlies the general discredited 'supply-side economics' policy of using tax cuts to increase tax revenues by stimulating people to work harder.

If one accepts the efficiency wage notion, then logic implies that it is not optimal for employers to offer employment compensation contracts in terms of a fixed nominal wage per unit of labour effort. If New Keynesians accept the efficiency wage argument as the 'hard-headed' explanation of why there is a grand scale market failure in the labour market, then they should explain why firms (and unemployed workers) have not picked up the $100 bills lying in the street by negotiating either piece-rate employment contracts or revenue-sharing employment contracts. Why do most firms and workers use a money wage per unit of labour time contract instead?

Moreover, if the efficiency wage concept has any logical symmetry in it, then why does the community, through the Monetary Authority, not make easier financing available for money-wage increases if these will stimulate productivity increases? Why do hard-headed conservative governments (who have accepted the supply-side arguments that lower marginal tax rates increase the productivity of the rich) not pass legislation encouraging the upward escalation of hourly wages to stimulate productivity increases by the working poor? The answer to these queries is obvious. Not many practically-minded people are willing to subscribe to the logical upside of the efficiency wage argument where each wage increase induces a more hard-working labour force.[30]

Phrased in terms of encouraging escalation of money wage per unit of labour effort to increase productivity per labour-hour, the efficiency wage argument sounds foolish – really, another 'when did you stop beating your wife?' argument. Nevertheless, Weitzman[31] has relied on a variant of the upside efficiency wage analysis to develop a policy suggestion that has been characterized as 'the best idea since Keynes' in the mass media.[32] Weitzman suggested that if workers were compensated with a fixed share of sales revenue there would be no grand scale labour market failure and full employment would prevail.

In the Weitzman analysis, substituting a form of 'sharecropping' employment contract for a money wage per unit of labour effort promotes full employment. But if a labour-sharing compensation contract is so desirable, then how can Weitzman explain the virtual disappearance of sharecropping contracts and the *pari passu* growth of money-wage employment hiring in American industries, and especially in agriculture despite its lack of unionization, over the last century? If sharecropping is an ideal solution compared to the traditional money wage per unit labour effort employment contract, why has the historical trend of market-oriented economic systems been away from 'sharing' to money-wage labour hiring? From a historical perspective, why has the productive efficiency of workers in US agriculture improved so dramatically with the decline in the importance of sharecropping as an employment contract and the use of money-wage payments instead?[33]

The sharecropping employment contract disappeared, not because of government regulation, but because this nineteenth century agricultural labour compensation arrangement could not compete in terms of the reduction in production costs (i.e., increases in labour productivity) that

accrued to large-scale agricultural firms who used money-wage employment contracts.

Revenue sharing-employment contracts reduce the incentive of entrepreneurs–capitalists to economize on the use of scarce labour resources by
adopting (and innovating) labour-saving technology. Sharing is a poor way
of organizing the labour market in a world of possible technological change
where research and development are focused on finding cost savings.
Unlike a share contract, fixed money-wage contracts can be a stimulus for
firms to search for new ways to save on labour effort per unit of output.[34]

Coordination failure. Gordon claims that 'coordination problems represent the core problem in economics'. Any market failure is ultimately due
to no single private agent having an incentive to respond fully 'unless it
believes that all other agents will do likewise'.[35]

Following this logic, Gordon must have supported President Reagan's
1982 proposal for solving the unemployment problem that then was
approaching 10.7 per cent of the labour force. At a Press Conference in the
Spring of 1982 the President stated that the unemployment problem could
be solved if each business firm immediately hired one more worker. The
solution was, of course, statistically accurate as there were more operating
firms than unemployed workers. Unless the employment by each of these
additional workers created a demand for additional output produced at a
profitable price (additional supply creating *pari passu* additional demand),
it would not be profitable for entrepreneurs to hire additional workers.
Gordon and other New Keynesians who attribute unemployment to a
coordination failure should have applauded Reagan's clarion call for the
coordinated increased hiring by enterprises. Keynes, on the other hand,
would never have endorsed Reagan's use of a Say's Law supply side
solution to the unemployment problem.[36]

WHAT ABOUT MONEY AND NEW KEYNESIAN ANALYSIS?

Neither Parkin, Mankiw, nor Gordon associated the existence of unemployment directly and explicitly with the use of a nominal quantity of
money *per se* in a money-using production economy. The rationale for this
textual omission can be understood by studying Oliver Blanchard's article
'Why Does Money Affect Output? A Survey'.[37]

Blanchard begins his essay by accepting a fundamental axiom of classical
economics as a basic constituent of *all* theory. Blanchard asserts that
'economic theory does not lead us to expect' that the existence of money
per se can cause fluctuations in output and employment; 'indeed it [theory]

holds that, with flexible prices, money should be approximately neutral'.[38] Blanchard insists that all New Keynesian models based on hard-headed microfoundations must 'impose long-run neutrality of money as a maintained presumption. This is a matter of faith, based on theoretical considerations rather than on empirical evidence'.[39] The only explanation for short-run non-neutral money involves studying 'why prices do not adjust fully and instantaneously to nominal money ... to focus on the reasons for and the implications of imperfect price adjustment'.

Keynes insisted there is a fundamental analytical distinction between a money-using production economy where even 'in the long period' money is not neutral and the real exchange economy of classical economics where money is presumed neutral as a matter of faith. There can be no necessary logical connection between the New Keynesian analysis that sees non-flexible prices as the essential characteristic explaining fluctuations and Keynes's analysis where non-neutral money and unemployment can co-exist even with perfect price flexibility in both the short and the long run.

SO WHAT IF THERE IS NO KEYNESIAN BEEF IN NEW KEYNESIANISM?

So what if New Keynesian analysis is logically different from Keynes's analysis? Mankiw states 'one might suppose that reading Keynes is an important part of Keynesian theorizing. In fact quite the opposite is the case ... [the goal is] not to clarify the views of one particular man. If new Keynesian economics is not a true representation of Keynes's views, then so much the worst for Keynes'.[40] The research of the New Keynesians would still exist in the literature even if they had taken a different name more in keeping with their belief in the long-run correctness of the classical system. What's in a name? Our response is: Although a rose by any other name is still a [sweet smelling] rose, it does not follow that calling the foul smelling fruit of the ginkgo tree a rose will make it smell any better.

Economists are not only selling truth to their students, but they are also selling policy advice to all who will listen. The New Keynesian and Keynes's *General Theory* approaches have significantly different – and often conflicting – domestic and international policy implications for important economic questions. Keynes's analysis demonstrates that creating a flexible wage and price system (including flexible exchange rates[41]) would not remove the ugly wart of unemployment from the face of capitalism.

The unemployment problem involves the 'public scandal of wasted [unemployed] resources'.[42] Keynes's 'theory is moderately conservative in its implications'[43] requiring government to exercise a long-run influence on aggregate spending decisions while preserving decentralized production decision making and the play of self-interest to secure full employment. Authoritarian State planning or forcing more flexibility into relative prices is not required and might only make things worse.

New Keynesian analysis, on the other hand, implicitly accepts the public scandal of unemployed resources as an inevitable short-run outcome due to the inherent rigidities and the lack of perfect coordination in an imperfectly competitive system. New Keynesian logic implies that prosperity is just around the long-run corner, as Mankiw claims, this 'long run is not so far away'.[44] Only short-run, unexpected shocks prevent the attainment of continuous full employment.

What are the policy implications of this New Keynesian logic? Securing continuous full employment is unlikely – except in the most stationary worlds that never experience any shocks. *Laissez-faire* is the best long-run policy. At best, the role for government should be to encourage more flexible wage and product prices through freeing up domestic markets and, in an open system, requiring exchange rate flexibility. There can be *no permanent* positive role for government deficits in creating and maintaining a long-run full employment environment.

The New Keynesian prescription contains medicines that Keynes would have labelled as dangerous to the health of the economic system in which we live. Keynes would have argued that the New Keynesian pillbox does not contain the necessary medicine to ensure a prosperous capital economy where unemployment is never a serious problem – in either the short run or the long run!

SPEED OF ADJUSTMENT DIFFERENCES AMONG OLD KEYNESIAN, NEW KEYNESIAN, AND NEW CLASSICAL THEORIES

The entire controversy amongst New Classical, New Keynesians and Old Keynesians is a tempest in a tea pot involving different assumptions about the length of time it takes prices as compared to output to adjust to an exogenous change in demand. The debate is solely about the relative speed of adjustment of prices versus output.

Classical economist 'Alfred Marshall's distinction among market equilibrium, short-period equilibrium, and long-period equilibrium was . . . [based on] the assumption that prices adjusted more rapidly than quantities, indeed so rapidly that the price adjustment can be regarded as instantaneous. . . . It takes time for output to adjust but no time for prices to do so'.[45] If the speed of adjustment of prices is more rapid than that of output, then money is neutral. The short-run neutrality of money in the New Classical system requires the presumption that prices can adjust instantaneously and output cannot.

Friedman is representative of all classically trained scholars when he asserts that Keynesian economics requires a reversal of the speed of adjustments that Marshall had assigned to prices and output.[46] Old and New Keynesians accept Friedman's interpretation of Keynesian economics when they insist that inflexibilities in prices are essential to the Keynesian explanation of why output and employment respond in the short run to a change in demand. This difference in the assumed relative speeds of reaction underlies Mankiw's claim that the difference between New Keynesian and New Classical economists is that the former believe that money is 'neutral in the long run but not the short run. . . . By contrast, new classical economists claim that money is neutral even in the short run'.[47]

Tobin accepts this difference in speeds of reaction as the distinguishing characteristic between classical and Keynesian analysis. Tobin proclaims that perfectly flexible market prices are necessary and sufficient to assure full employment.[48] He insists that 'the absence of instantaneous and complete market clearing' (and therefore an uncleared labour market[49]) is solely due to the 'failure of prices' to be perfectly flexible,[50] i.e. the output speed of reaction is more rapid than the price speed of reaction. The essence of Old Keynesian economics is the reversal of the Marshallian assumption of price and output speeds of reaction.

Tobin believes that the major difference between Old and New Keynesians hinges on the distinction between the Old Keynesian concept of nominal *stickiness* and the New Keynesian notion of nominal *rigidities*. According to Tobin, New Keynesians see *rigidities*, i.e. unchanging nominal values for long periods of calendar time, as an essential aspect of Keynesianism, while Old Keynesians are willing to make a 'much less restrictive assumption' regarding the time duration before prices move. Tobin claims that the less restrictive Old Keynesian stickiness assumption 'leaves plenty of room for flexibility in any common sense meaning of the word'.[51] In sum, the fundamental distinction between Old and New Keynesians can be seen as that the latter presume rigidities with a slower speed of price adjustment than Tobin's less than perfectly flexible price stickiness.

In 1968 Leijonhufvud was the first to attribute to Keynes this reversal of Marshall's speed of adjustment argument.[52] Six years later, Leijonhufvud recanted by stating: 'It is *not* correct to attribute to Keynes a general reversion of the Marshallian ranking of relative price and quantity adjustment velocities. In the "shortest run" for which the system behavior can be defined in Keynes' model, output-prices *must* be treated as perfectly flexible'.[53]

Leijonhufvud's recantation is a belated recognition that in numerous places in *The General Theory*, Keynes specifically accepted the notion that any change in expected future market demand will instantaneously alter all current (spot[54]) market prices. For example, Keynes wrote: 'There is no escape from the dilemma that if it [a change] is not foreseen there will be no effect on current affairs, while if it is foreseen, the [spot] price of existing goods will be forthwith so adjusted'.[55]

Old Keynesians have always seen Keynes as providing a 'theory of nominal wage *stickiness*',[56] while New Keynesians see wage and/or price *rigidities* as the essence of Keynes. Neither think it is important to consider what Keynes claimed are the essential properties of interest and money in describing what they think are the essential ingredients of Keynesian economics.

If economists would only take up the challenge of Keynes's revolutionary general theory and investigate the properties of a system of microeconomic demand and supply functions that has thrown out the axioms of ergodicity, ubiquitous gross substitutability, and non-neutral money, then a truly New Keynesianism – dare I call it Post Keynesian economics – could be developed which could again permit economists to provide useful and realistic guides to both micro and macroeconomic policies.[57] This would be a New Keynesianism that Keynes could readily endorse.

NOTES

1. R.J. Gordon, 'What Is New Keynesian Economics?', *Journal of Economic Literature*, **28**, 1990.
2. In a fax dated 6/6/91.
3. M. Parkin, *Macroeconomics*, Prentice-Hall, New Jersey, 1984, p. 74.
4. J.M. Keynes, *The General Theory*, p. 27.
5. See Chapter 11 *supra*.
6. J.M. Keynes, *The General Theory*, pp. 267–9.
7. N.G. Mankiw, 'The Reincarnation of Keynes', *European Economic Review*, **36**, 1992, p. 561.
8. J.M. Keynes, *The General Theory*, p. 192.
9. J.M. Keynes, *The General Theory*, p. 192.
10. R.J. Gordon, 'What is New Keynesian Economics?', *Journal of Economic Literature*, **28**, 1990. N.G. Mankiw, 'A Quick Refresher Course in Macroeconomics', *Journal of Economic Literature*, **28**, 1990. O.J. Blanchard, 'Why Does Money Affect Output? A Survey', in *Handbook of Monetary Economics*, II, edited by B.M. Friedman and F.H. Hahn, Elsevier, New York, 1990.
11. Gordon, op. cit., p. 1115, italics added.
12. Gordon, op. cit., pp. 1136–9.
13. Gordon, op. cit., p. 1118.
14. Gordon, op. cit., p. 1117.
15. R.E. Lucas, 'Tobin on Monetarism: A Review Article', *Journal of Economic Literature*,

19, 1981, p. 563.
16. G. Mankiw, 'A Quick Refresher Course in Macroeconomics', *Journal of Economic Literature*, **28**, 1990, p. 1647.
17. Mankiw, op. cit., pp. 1653–4.
18. Gordon, op. cit., p. 1138.
19. Mankiw, op. cit., p. 1654.
20. A.S. Blinder, *Hard Heads: Soft Hearts: Tough Minded Economics For A Just Society*, Addison-Wesley, Reading, 1987.
21. Mankiw, op. cit., pp. 1654–5, italics added.
22. Gordon, op. cit., p. 1139.
23. Keynes, *The General Theory*, p. 33.
24. N.G. Mankiw, 'The Reincarnation of Keynesian Economics', *European Economic Review*, **36**, 1992, p. 563.
25. As in the quote from Blanchard in Section IV *infra*, classical axioms are accepted by all 'theorists' as a matter of faith.
26. Mankiw, op. cit., p. 1657.
27. Even before the computer, during the great German inflation of 1923, price lists often changed many times in a single day. Those who collect postage stamps of this period can cite the overlay of zeros that the post office put on each stamp it sold to indicate the current costs of mailing a letter.
28. In 1939 Keynes admitted his task would have been easier had he simply assumed away perfect competition. He defended not making imperfect competition the basis of unemployment when he indicated the need 'for conceding a little' to the classical argument to demonstrate that it was in the aggregate demand determinants, and not supply, that the unemployment equilibrium could be explained. (See *The Collected Writings of John Maynard Keynes*, 13, edited by D. Moggridge, Macmillan, London, 1973, p. 400.)
29. Mankiw, op. cit., p. 1658.
30. Maybe I'll work harder if my employer pays me more, but other lazy louts who work for a living will not.
31. M. Weitzman, 'The Simple Macroeconomics of Profit Sharing', *American Economic Review*, **75**, 1985.
32. In a 1987 editorial, *The New York Times*. Many other serious mass media and professional journals, e.g. *The Economist, The American Economic Review*, have taken such proposals seriously.
33. True believers in the efficiency wage argument must explain why self-interested workers and entrepreneurs have evolved away from any form of a labour contract that specifies any form of piece-rate compensation.
34. During the twentieth century, sharing arrangements have been encouraged primarily in centrally planned economic systems. The collapse of communist regimes throughout Eastern Europe has convincingly demonstrated the inability of these systems to compete with the money-wage systems of the market economies of Western Europe, Japan, and the NICs. Although they provided full employment, they did not provide incentives to efficiently use the scarce labour resources to produce output and to stimulate technological innovation.
35. Gordon, op. cit., pp. 1138–9.
36. For a detailed analysis see Davidson 1984 and section V *infra*.
37. O.J. Blanchard, 'Why Does Money Affect Output? A Survey' in *Handbook of Monetary Economics*, II, edited by B.M. Friedman and F.H. Hahn, Elsevier, New York, 1990.
38. Blanchard, op. cit., p. 780.
39. Blanchard, op. cit., p. 828.
40. Mankiw, 'The Reincarnation of Keynesian Economics', p. 560.
41. Keynes's post-war proposals for an international payments system always involved some institutional arrangement to maintain fixed, but adjustable, exchange rates.
42. Keynes, *The General Theory*, pp. 380–81.
43. J.M. Keynes, *The General Theory*, p. 377.

44.	Mankiw, 'The Reincarnation of Keynesian Economics', *European Economic Review*, **36**, 1992, p. 561.

45.	M. Friedman, 'A Theoretical Framework For Monetary Analysis', *Milton Friedman's Monetary Framework: A Debate With his Critics*, edited by R.J. Gordon, University of Chicago Press, Chicago, 1974, pp. 16–17.

46.	For example, see Friedman, op. cit., p. 18. Friedman indicates that 'we are indebted to a brilliant book by Leijonhufvud for a full appreciation of the importance of this proposition in Keynes' system' and that Friedman's argument 'owes much to Leijonhufvud's penetrating analysis' (pp. 16–17, n. 7.). As noted *infra*, Leijonhufvud has since recanted on this point.

47.	Mankiw, 'The Reincarnation of Keynesian Economics', p. 563.

48.	J. Tobin ('Price Flexibility and Output Stability: An Old Keynesian View', *Journal of Economic Perspectives*, **7**, 1993, p. 53) justifies this belief by arguing that 'In standard Walrasian/Arrow–Debreu theory, perfect flexibility of all wages and prices ... would maintain full employment equilibrium'. But both Arrow and Hahn (*General Competitive Equilibrium*, Holden-Day, San Francisco, 1970) and Hahn ('Keynesian Economics and General Equilibrium Theory', in *The Microfoundations of Macroeconomics*, edited by G.C. Harcourt, Macmillan, London, 1977) have shown that in the absence of special assumptions (besides instantaneously flexible prices) in a Walrasian system, all existence proofs of full employment equilibrium are jeopardized, i.e. there need not exist a full employment equilibrium position even with the existence of a complete set of present and future markets and complete price flexibility.

49.	By definition involuntary unemployment implies the lack of clearing of the labour market. Walrasian economics conflates clearing with equilibrium. Marshall, however, used the concept of equilibrium (in the physical science sense) as a state of rest, i.e. where the forces bearing on the system were in balance. Under a Marshallian definition clearing is a sufficient but not a necessary condition for market equilibrium.

	Keynes used equilibrium in the Marshallian sense so that involuntary unemployment meant there were no market forces that would move the system away from this point of rest. In explaining Keynes's employment analysis, Leijonhufvud ('Keynes's Employment Function', *History of Political Economy*, **6**, 1974, pp. 164–5) states that theory has neglected 'the differences between Marshallian and Walrasian thought. ... But Keynes was, of course, a price-theoretical Marshallian, and in the present context, ignoring this fact will simply not do'.

50.	J. Tobin, 'Price Flexibility and Output Stability: An Old Keynesian View', *Journal of Economic Perspectives*, **7**, p. 47.

51.	Tobin, op. cit., p. 46.

52.	A. Leijonhufvud, *On Keynesian Economics and the Economics of Keynes*, Oxford University Press, Oxford, 1968.

53.	A. Leijonhufvud, 'Keynes's Employment Function', *History of Political Economy*, **6**, 1974, p. 169.

54.	Spot prices are, of course, the only market prices existing for goods available for delivery today!

55.	Keynes, *The General Theory*, p. 142. For additional statements regarding the possibility of perfectly flexible prices in his analysis, see pp. 227, 231–2.

56.	Tobin, op. cit., p. 48, italics added.

57.	Interestingly, none of the New Keynesian expositors ever questions whether classical microeconomics is a 'correct' foundation for macroeconomics. Is it necessarily the case that self-interested individuals will automatically attempt to achieve an intertemporal optimality via their expenditure patterns? In his Nobel Prize lecture entitled 'On Maximizing Principles in Economics' (*American Economic Review*, **62**, 1972, p. 235) Samuelson warns that the insistence that individuals can know how to maximize their utility can easily degenerate into 'a sterile tautology', as the Austrian economists 'when challenged ... found themselves replying circularly that however people behaved, they would presumably not have done so unless it maximized their satisfaction' (Samuelson, 1972, p. 235).

Index

M/